DATE DUE		

The New York Times

BOOK OF
BROADWAY

The New York Times

BOOK OF BROADWAY

On the Aisle for the
Unforgettable Plays of the Last Century

Edited and with an Introduction by

Ben Brantley

ST. MARTIN'S PRESS ❧ NEW YORK

www.stmartins.com

Book design by James Sinclair

Library of Congress Cataloging-in-Publication Data
The New York Times book of Broadway : on the aisle for the unforgettable plays of the last century / Ben Brantley, editor.—1st ed.
    p. cm.
  ISBN 0-312-28411-X
  1. Theater—New York (State)—New York—Reviews. 2. Musical theater—New York (State)—New York—Reviews. I. Brantley, Ben.
PN2277.N5 N45 2001
792.9'5'097471—dc21

2001041968

First Edition: November 2001

10 9 8 7 6 5 4 3 2 1

Contents

Introduction   vii

**Twenty-five Productions That
Defined the Century**

The Hairy Ape   2
Show Boat   4
Waiting for Lefty   6
Porgy and Bess   8
You Can't Take It with You   10
Our Town   12
Oklahoma!   14
A Streetcar Named Desire   16
Death of a Salesman   18
My Fair Lady   20
Waiting for Godot   22
Long Day's Journey into Night   24
West Side Story   26
A Raisin in the Sun   28
The Caretaker   30
Who's Afraid of Virginia Woolf?   32
Peter Brook's production of
A Midsummer Night's Dream   34
A Chorus Line   36
Sweeney Todd   38
Cats   40
Glengarry Glen Ross   42
Ma Rainey's Black Bottom   44
Angels in America (Part 1: Millennium
Approaches)   46
Rent   48
The Wooster Group's production of
The Emperor Jones   50

**The Unforgettable Productions
of the Century**

Peter Pan   54
Sarah Bernhardt's La Dame aux Camélias   56
The Little Millionaire   57

Heartbreak House   59
Ziegfeld Follies of 1921   61
The Hairy Ape   62
Abie's Irish Rose   64
Six Characters in Search of an Author   65
John Barrymore's Hamlet   66
The Adding Machine   68
The Green Hat   69
Sex   71
Funny Face   72
Show Boat   73
The Front Page   75
Animal Crackers   77
Girl Crazy   78
Private Lives   79
Mourning Becomes Electra   80
Design for Living   83
The 3-Penny Opera   84
Tobacco Road   85
Anything Goes   86
Waiting for Lefty   88
Porgy and Bess   89
Dead End   91
Idiot's Delight   92
John Gielgud's Hamlet   94
You Can't Take It with You   95
The Women   96
Our Town   98
The Boys from Syracuse   99
The Little Foxes   100
The Philadelphia Story   102
Life with Father   103
Pal Joey   105
Arsenic and Old Lace   106
Lady in the Dark   108
Oklahoma!   110
Paul Robeson's Othello   111

On the Town	112	Oh! Calcutta!	178
The Glass Menagerie	114	No, No, Nanette	180
Annie Get Your Gun	115	Peter Brook's A Midsummer Night's Dream	182
No Exit	116	Follies	183
A Streetcar Named Desire	117	The Basic Training of Pavlo Hummel	185
Kiss Me, Kate	119	Much Ado About Nothing	187
Death of a Salesman	120	Butley	188
South Pacific	122	The Hot L Baltimore	190
Gentlemen Prefer Blondes	124	A Moon for the Misbegotten	191
The Member of the Wedding	125	Short Eyes	193
Come Back, Little Sheba	127	Equus	194
Guys and Dolls	128	A Chorus Line	196
Laurence Olivier & Vivien Leigh's		For Colored Girls . . .	198
Antony and Cleopatra	130	The Cherry Orchard	199
The Crucible	131	Uncommon Women and Others	201
Damn Yankees	133	Ain't Misbehavin'	203
The Diary of Anne Frank	134	Buried Child	205
My Fair Lady	136	Sweeney Todd	206
Waiting for Godot	137	Sister Mary Ignatius Explains . . .	208
Long Day's Journey into Night	138	Dreamgirls	210
West Side Story	139	Cats	213
Look Back in Anger	141	Plenty	215
The Music Man	142	Moose Murders	218
A Raisin in the Sun	143	Glengarry Glen Ross	219
Gypsy	144	The Mystery of Irma Vep	221
The Fantasticks	146	Ma Rainey's Black Bottom	222
Rhinoceros	147	Les Misérables	224
The Blacks	148	Frankie and Johnny in the Clair de Lune	226
The Caretaker	150	Six Degrees of Separation	228
Who's Afraid of Virginia Woolf?	151	Angels in America (Part 1: Millennium	
Beyond the Fringe	152	Approaches)	231
Hello, Dolly!	154	Twilight: Los Angeles, 1992	233
The Blood Knot	156	Rent	235
Funny Girl	157	Bring in da Noise/Bring in da Funk	237
Richard Burton's Hamlet	158	Chicago	240
Fiddler on the Roof	160	A Doll's House	242
The Odd Couple	162	The Lion King	245
Marat/Sade	164	The Beauty Queen of Leenane	247
Cabaret	166	The Wooster Group's The Emperor Jones	250
Rosencrantz and Guildenstern Are Dead	168	Wit	252
The Boys in the Band	170	The Play About the Baby	254
Hair	172	The Producers	257
The Living Theater's Frankenstein	174	The Pulitzer Prizes in Drama	261
The Great White Hope	175	The Tony (Antoinette Perry) Awards for	
Promises, Promises	177	Best Play and Best Musical	263

Introduction

"An atmosphere of historical happening surrounded John Barrymore's appearance last night as the Prince of Denmark; it was unmistakable as it was undefinable."
  —John Corbin on *Hamlet,* 1922

"There has never been anything like this before in human society."
  —Brooks Atkinson on Carol Channing in *Gentlemen Prefer Blondes,* 1949

"There are some performances in the theater, just a few, that surge along as if they were holding the whole world on a tidal wave."
  —Clive Barnes on *A Moon for the Misbegotten,* 1973

"When Broadway history is being made, you can feel it. What you feel is a seismic emotional jolt that sends the audience, as one, right out of its wits. While such moments are uncommonly rare these days, I'm here to report that one popped up at the Imperial last night."
  —Frank Rich on *Dreamgirls,* 1981

Theater criticism in daily newspapers—or at least in *The New York Times*—tends to run a high temperature. Try reading the quotations above out loud in a flat, bored tone of voice. It's impossible. No other form of journalism, except possibly for sports coverage, is so consistently, well, theatrical, so prone to what the uninitiated might take for flaming hyperbole.

The urgency in the *Times* accounts of opening nights over the past century often brings to mind the adrenaline-coated voice of Edward R. Murrow, bearing breathless witness to battles and bombings in wartime, or perhaps Phil Rizzuto yelling "Holy cow!" as a baseball soars into oblivion.

History, it is said again and again, has been made; the world is somehow a little different this morning, and if you were lucky enough to have been at the theater last night, you will never, ever forget what you have seen.

You aren't wrong in pausing here to ask, "What's the big deal?" Sweat was most likely shed during the evenings described so passionately and maybe some tears, but certainly no blood to speak of. The principal things at stake were artistic pride, a limited number of jobs and money invested by people who could usually afford to lose it. After all, as the saying goes, it's only a play.

Still, it wouldn't have done much good to have pointed this out to the opening-night audiences for *A Streetcar Named Desire* or *My Fair Lady*. When the elements of a play or a musical cohere into surreally smooth symmetry or jangling novelty, an electricity starts flowing both between the audience and the performers on stage and within the audience itself. And that's what the *Times* reviews assembled in these pages are often trying to measure and reflect.

Listen, for example, to Alexander Woollcott on the first performance of *The Hairy Ape* in 1922: "The little theatre of the Provincetownsmen in Macdougal Street was packed to the doors with astonishment last evening as scene after scene unfolded in the new play by Eugene O'Neill." And here is Brooks Atkinson, speaking of Moss Hart's *Lady in the Dark* in 1941, describing scenes that soar "into a sphere of gorgeously bedizened make-believe that will create theatrical memories for everyone who sees them."

Notice how—whether describing the present-tense visceral kick of an opening night or the future pleasures of savored recollection—Woollcott and Atkinson take for granted the idea of a shared experience. This collective response is, in its way, as intense and as atavistic as that of the spectators at an Olympics meet in which records are broken.

To this day, no other narrative art generates quite the same reaction as theater does. Reading novels is a solitary experience for which the reader sets his own pace. Movies have no risk factor: they are as fixed in their forms as paintings, and they are never going to change.

Plays, on the other hand, happen in real time, with real actors unprotected by the safety nets of retakes and editing. They need an audience's attention to sustain them, and theatergoers can never be passive in the way moviegoers are.

Atkinson, writing of the cast members of *Death of a Salesman,* speaks of how "they all realize that for once in their lives they are participating in a rare event in the theatre." Implicitly, the audience shares that realization, and there is a heady spirit of self-congratulation in the air. Of course, there are also those nights described by the writer Jean Kerr, the wife of the critic Walter Kerr, when "you sit there in stunned disbelief, fearing for your sanity while on all sides people are beating their way to the exits."

But there can be an aura of momentousness about those performances, too. As

Frank Rich wrote of a comedy that ran for exactly one performance in 1983, "From now on, there will always be two groups of theatergoers in the world: those who have seen *Moose Murders* and those who have not."

The *Times* reviews capture both the positive and negative sides of this dynamic, the ecstasy and the outrage, the vicarious triumph and the schadenfreude of a century on the aisles of Manhattan theaters where history has been made and remade. They are generally less temperate than most works of criticism—more visceral and less analytical—which makes reading them more fun.

Even allowing for the homogenizing effects of the *Times* house style, which has been remarkably consistent over the past hundred years or so, there is still a great variety in the critical voices. And it's fun to observe the increasing self-consciousness among the reviewers about their status as individuals with subjective points of view. The often-anonymous critics from the early years of the twentieth century sound almost Jovian in their detachment, reflecting a Victorian confidence in the shared discernment of the moral and the educated.

The reviews of the early 1920s—when Woollcott was writing for *The Times* and George S. Kaufman was its drama editor—have an insider's cockiness, in which "New York" is treated as a pronoun of sorts, like the savvy "we" of the Talk of the Town stories in the old *New Yorker* magazine. (Example: "New York last night was treated to the best and fairest example of the newer expressionism in the theatre that it has yet experienced.")

This eventually gives way to more direct acknowledgments that judgment is being passed by a single person, usually referred to in the third person as "this column," which evolved into "this critic," for which could be substituted the omniscient, academic "one." Finally, by the mid-1960s the personal, fallible "I" has arrived, roughly a decade after *The Times* switches from "theatre" (in the King's English spelling) to "theater" reviews. It was only a matter of time before my personal favorite, the flattering, coercive "you" (as in "from the first strains of the overture, you sense that something has gone very wrong"), slips into the lexicon.

The conditions under which the reviews were written have also changed. Before the mid-1960s, New York critics followed the practice, widely and erroneously believed to exist to this day, of attending opening-night performances, for which curtains rose at 6:30 P.M., as opposed to the customary and civilized hour of 8:00 or 8:30.

As the final curtain came down, the reviewer would bolt from his seat (there is a reason that it was on the aisle) and rush back to his office to hammer out his judgment on what he had just seen. It's tempting to imagine all this taking place in a high-adrenaline frenzy, as in the newsrooms portrayed so savagely and entertainingly in the 1928 comedy *The Front Page*.

In truth, the descriptions of the work habits of Brooks Atkinson, who reviewed plays for *The Times* over an astonishing four decades, suggest a calmer approach. According to a former *Times* copy boy (named Joseph Lelyveld and now the executive editor of the paper), Atkinson would return from the theater, sit down, light his pipe (such things were permitted in those days), and reflect. Then he would write his review, calmly and methodically, in longhand on a yellow legal pad, tearing off pages as he finished to be sent to the composing room to be set in type.

By the mid-1960s (at the urging of critics like Kerr and Stanley Kauffmann), producers began letting reviewers into performances during the last nights of previews, in part because the out-of-town try-out was becoming obsolete. Though the tradition of an early opening-night curtain lives on, the reviews that are now read aloud at cast parties have usually been filed a day or two before, at relative leisure.

Perhaps I should admit that despite this expanded writing period, and despite my having been a *Times* theater critic since 1993, I—unlike Atkinson—tend to pace and mutter angrily to myself while mentally composing my reviews, rather like those jumped-up characters in *The Front Page*. Metabolism, it seems, plays as defining a role as deadlines in the way we write.

There have also, of course, been significant changes in the technology of journalism, with word processors taking the place of typewriters—manual and electric—and Atkinson's yellow legal pads. (I can—and do—file my stories without setting foot in the office.) Yet in combing through *Times* reviews of the past century, I was struck by a strong continuity of voice that transcended social context and the personality of the critic.

Whether the writer is the scalpel-tongued Woollcott or the whimsical Clive Barnes, the gentlemanly Atkinson or the two-fisted Frank Rich, there is a bracing immediacy about these reviews, which confirms both the daily and the news aspects of being part of a daily newspaper. Implicit is an understanding between writer and reader that what is described is a public event—just as much as it was in the age of Pericles and open-air amphitheaters—as well as a work of art. Or a bit of fluff or a piece of garbage.

The Broadway of *The New York Times Book of Broadway* is a shifting, even chimerical phenomenon. It may take its name from something as specific and substantial as the arterial avenue that runs diagonally through Manhattan. But Broadway the theatrical mecca—a name to be writ in flashing neon and pronounced with a drum roll—is too mythic to be confined by geography. It belongs on the same map that includes Camelot, Brigadoon and Shangri-la. The idealized, glamorous Broadway—in which the theater was the city's heart and a new play opened every night—existed, if ever, only briefly.

In *Broadway,* his history of the New York theater, Brooks Atkinson goes so far as to limit those glory years to between the wars. Even before World War II, he wrote, "Broadway began to lose its originality and drive." The statistics, at least, bear out this theory. The record season for Broadway openings was 1927–28, in which 270 productions were mounted. (These included Eugene O'Neill's *Strange Interlude* and the epochal musical *Show Boat.*) In the 1999–2000 season, 37 shows opened, which is pretty close to the average of new productions over the past fifteen years.

Actually, the forty-two-block neighborhood around Times Square, now identified as the city's central theater district, is only a part of the world that has fallen under its rubric. At the turn of the twentieth century, the theater district began at 13th Street, stretching northward to 45th. Today it embraces the Vivian Beaumont Theater at Lincoln Center in the West 60s. What technically qualifies a theater as a Broadway house is its size—a minimum of 499 seats—and its contractual relationship with theater unions.

Not all of the plays reviewed in this collection officially qualify as Broadway productions. Much of Eugene O'Neill's early work, for example, was seen in the tiny Provincetown Players theater in Greenwich Village. Atkinson, reviewing a double bill of Samuel Beckett's *Krapp's Last Tape* and Edward Albee's *The Zoo Story* in 1960, wrote, "After the banalities of Broadway it tones the muscles and freshens the system to examine the squalor of Off Broadway."

And from the 1960s onward, in particular, you'll find a greater emphasis on smaller theaters and institutional houses, because much of the most important work was originating there. And it wasn't all experimental arcana and naked bodies. It's worth noting that from 1969 on, a majority of the Pulitzer Prizes for drama—a barometer of mainstream tastes—go to Off Broadway plays. Reviewing Jason Miller's *That Championship Season* at the Public Theater (in East Greenwich Village) in 1972, Clive Barnes was moved to write: "Wow! Here at last is the perfect Broadway play, perfectly acted and perfectly staged. There is only one minor thing wrong with it. It happens not to be on Broadway."

What Broadway suggests to tourists these days, of course, is often a theme park of brand-names and celebrities, with Walt Disney productions like *The Lion King* and *Beauty and the Beast* ruling the box office. But while pundits may bewail a vanished urbanity of the Broadway that was, it should be pointed out that the Broadway of a hundred years ago was largely regarded as an emporium of flash and silliness: melodramas, extravaganzas, showcases for minimally talented people who were famous for being famous. Familiar sounding objections, indeed.

The mostly unsigned *Times* reviews from this period tend to look upon such spectacles from an amused Olympian height. The audience becomes as much a subject for review as the play itself. Here, from *The Times* of January 9, 1900, are a few observations on a "melodrama of the melodramas" called *The Gunner's Mate:*

> It is a play in which pictorial effect, deeds of daring, high-sounding speeches, and deep-dyed villainy are rivals for the attention of the spectator, and the gallery gods declared that it was good. Their declaration was unmistakable, too, for a more vigorous tribute of applause, laughter, and hisses, each paid at the time most gratifying to the actors, a drama of this sort seldom receives. A few catcalls did mar the harmony of the occasion, but they were only uttered at moments of great provocation.

And as a reminder that celebrity worship is a venerable American tradition, consider this priceless description from the same year of the beauteous Lillie Langtry, whose renown had little to do with her acting abilities:

> The first performances of *The Degenerates,* at the Garden Theatre, last evening, turned out, as might have been expected, to be largely a personal exhibition of Mrs. Langtry in gorgeous and daring attire—Mrs. Langtry in flesh-colored satin with sapphires, Mrs. Langtry in pale-blue satin with diamonds in dazzling array, Mrs. Langtry in white with pearls, Mrs. Langtry, after the trying first act, almost as handsome as ever; Mrs. Langtry amiable, rattling, purposeful, triumphant and astonishingly, alarmingly décolleté.

In other instances, however, *The Times* could be reduced to the status of any heavy-breathing fan, although without dropping the formality of diction. The fabled Sarah Bernhardt, visiting New York as Dumas's Camille in 1905, evoked the following response: "In the presence of such a work of art as Mme. Bernhardt provided last night the ordinary processes of analytical criticism seem hopelessly inadequate."

Or here, in a very similar vein indeed, is *The Times* on Maud Adams in James Barrie's *The Little Minister:* "The charm of Miss Adams's acting in this role is, indeed, irresistible. It also defies analysis."

The idea of being struck mute by a quality that eludes concrete description (commonly known as "stage presence") recurs throughout the early *Times* reviews, helping to further the mythic aura of certain performers and performances. By 1911, a certain era-defining song-and-dance man has already earned the following, only slightly flippant encomium: "George M. Cohan, like necessity, knows no law. Which is one of the reasons, perhaps, why a George M. Cohan show is like nothing else in the heavens above (presumably) or on the earth below."

That knowing air, the equivalent of a jaunty wink to theatergoers, becomes ever more pronounced in the 1920s. It is in this decade, and in the 1930s, that you start to get a whiff of the Broadway of legend, of the epicenter of culture both high (think Barrymore) and low (think Runyon).

In the reviews, in particular, of Woollcott and the fledgling critic J. Brooks Atkinson (he would later drop that first initial), there is an assumption of knowledge on the part of the reader that I can only envy today.

In their writing, it is a given that the theater is an essential part of the everyday experience of any New Yorker worthy of the name. The big stars—from Katherine Cornell and John Barrymore to Fannie Brice and Eddie Cantor—are invoked as casually as Madonna or Puff Daddy might be today. "Our Tallulah is taking a valiant fling at Cleopatra," begins Atkinson's review of Tallulah Bankhead's notorious foray into Shakespeare in 1937. Of course, you know who Tallulah is; she's family.

The same, more remarkably, is true of playwrights and songwriters, who are often referred to with a fond, familial proprietariness. Here, for instance, is Atkinson's opening for his review of Robert Sherwood's *Idiot's Delight* in 1936: "Mr. Sherwood's love of a good time and his anxiety about world affairs result in one of his most likable entertainments. . . ." This is a sentence that presumes intimate knowledge of not only the work but also the personality of Sherwood. It also suggests an abundance of plays by the same author from which one has sampled regularly over the years, with more to come. One can only sigh at that taken-for-granted richness.

An easygoing air of community pervades the *Times* reviews from that era, a sense of critics and artists occupying the same side of the street, jostling elbows and annoying and tickling one another. Of course, the social boundaries between journalists and their subjects were more fluid then.

One need only remember that George S. Kaufman was the theater editor of *The New York Times* and that the so-called Algonquin Round Table seated critics (Woollcott, Dorothy Parker, Robert Benchley) as well as theater folk (Edna Ferber, Tallulah Bankhead). You would be highly unlikely today to find, say, John Simon and Liza Minnelli sharing an antipasto at Elaine's. Not relishing martinis being flung in my face, I personally limit my social life to parties where I know beforehand there will be no one from the theater. (Such barriers remain much less rigid in London, for some reason; flay your best friend in print that morning, and meet for cozy drinks at the Ivy that night.)

With World War II, the breezy, animated and slightly complacent tone that had dominated *Times* theater criticism for two decades comes to an end. Atkinson leaves New York to become a war correspondent in China and a postwar correspondent in Moscow. He is replaced for several years by Lewis Nichols, who on his watch gets such plums as *Oklahoma!* and *The Glass Menagerie,* but is more detached sounding than Atkinson presumably would have been in describing them. It is hard, with hindsight filling in the blanks, to avoid a feeling that the party is, if not over, at least quieter.

The theater that Atkinson returns to in 1946 is indeed less hedonistic. The big, silly revues and skit-driven musicals are mostly gone. The songwriting team of the moment isn't jaunty, acerbic Rodgers and Hart but sentimental, sober Rodgers and Hammerstein. Instead of the sybaritic revels of *Babes in Arms* and *The Boys from Syracuse,* there is the brooding romanticism of *Carousel* and the social conscience of *South Pacific.*

The domestic drama is suddenly reaching for lyric tragedy in works like *Death of a Salesman* and *A Streetcar Named Desire.* Everyone is sounding more sobered up and grown-up, and that includes *The Times*'s reviewers. Atkinson's appraisals often have a new gravity. "A suburban epic that may not be intended as poetry but becomes poetry in spite of itself," he writes of *Salesman* in 1949. And with the opening of O'Neill's *Long Day's Journey into Night,* says Atkinson in 1956, "the American theater acquires size and stature."

If there is a single hero in this collection, it is certainly Brooks Atkinson, whose tenure at *The Times* runs from the Jazz Age to the Atomic Age and who never succumbed to either academic stiffness, dismissive flippancy or the jadedness of a long-running reviewer. As the theater became more restless and confrontational in the postwar years, dismantling its old structures and pieties, Atkinson rarely drew away from the unfamiliar, approaching it instead with a truly admirable open mind.

Here is a man who got to review the Ziegfeld *Follies* and the first New York production of Samuel Beckett and discovered particular virtues in both. *Waiting for Godot* baffled him, he admitted in 1956, but he acknowledged the play's unearthly power. "Theatergoers can rail at, but they cannot ignore it," he said. And while the violent subject matter of the 1957 musical *West Side Story* appalled him, he found it "a profoundly moving show that is as ugly as the city jungles and also pathetic, tender and forgiving." He retired as chief critic at *The Times* three years later. His successors, to borrow from *King Lear,* "shall never see so much nor live so long."

The early 1960s belong largely to Howard Taubman, who captured the new feelings of dissonance and disaffection in reviews of plays like *Who's Afraid of Virginia Woolf?* and *Marat/Sade.* In reading him, you also glean increasing suggestions of a theater in flux, searching for a solid identity that would set it apart in an age dominated by television.

Do plays matter as they once did? he seems to be asking, going so far as to note, in his review of *Fiddler on the Roof* in 1964, "It has been prophesied that the Broadway musical theater would take up the mantle of meaningfulness worn so carelessly by the American drama in recent years." (This was not, one is quick to add, a prophecy that would be fulfilled.) Clive Barnes, considering the avant-garde Living Theater's improvisation-shaped production *Frankenstein* in 1967 wonders whether "the playwright may be a disappearing species like the buffalo."

Such form-shattering theater pieces have become commonplace by this time, and *The Times* is now obliged to take note of another, still relatively foreign country in the landscape of drama: Off Off Broadway. Mel Gussow, who arrives in 1969, makes it his business to introduce *Times* readers to a whole new stable of taboo-baiting talents, found well south and east of Times Square and often in dank, claustrophobically small spaces.

Among the young turks are playwrights who are now elder statesmen of the American drama, including Sam Shepard and Lanford Wilson. Drag, psychedelic fragmentation and disconnectedness, nudity and direct confrontations with the audience become commonplace production tools. Like many respectable institutions of a certain age in the 1960s, Broadway begins to look anxiously and enviously to its younger, more energetic countercultural siblings.

Soon the rock musical *Hair*—which celebrates self-expression through psychedelic drug use, masturbation and frolicsome nudity, among other things—has settled onto the Great White Way for a four-year run. The more middle-class, but also more insistently naked, *Oh, Calcutta!* will run even longer, although its earlier, Off

Broadway incarnation prompted Barnes to remark, "It is curious how anti-erotic public nudity, as opposed to private nudity, is." Broadway is starting to give off the sweaty smell of desperation.

By the time Frank Rich appears on the scene, for a thirteen-year tenure as the *Times*'s chief drama critic, the theater is increasingly regarded as a cultural dinosaur in the United States. A note of special pleading has entered the *Times* reviews by now, a sense that the world regularly needs reminding of the singular and abiding power of live theater. Rich is well equipped to dispense such reminders, with a passionate, often fierce prose that demands that attention be paid.

Here he is in 1987 on the London import, *Les Misérables:* "If anyone doubts that the contemporary musical theater can flex its atrophied muscles and yank an audience right out of its seats, he need look no further than the Act I finale of *Les Misérables.*" Three years later, writing of Brian Friel's *Dancing at Lughnasa,* he points out, "Just as living is not a literary experience, neither is theater at its fullest." Once such observations were taken for granted.

The critic's mantle that I—and my immediate predecessors, David Richards and Vincent Canby—inherited inevitably includes that of the teacher and the cheerleader. What you hope, always, is to instill in your readers your own love of live drama and musicals, the pure visceral thrill they can provide.

Writing about the English actress Janet McTeer's performance in *A Doll's House,* I felt compelled to observe: "It just doesn't happen that often, and when it does, you sit there open-mouthed, grateful, admiring and shaken and think, 'This is why I love the theater.' . . . The pulse quickens, the eyes well. And there is somehow the sense that ordinary life has been heightened to the bursting point." All true. That was exactly the way I felt. But in the early days of Atkinson, the description might have seemed unnecessary and slightly hysterical.

One of the great pleasures of culling a century of *Times* reviews has been encountering mots justes that will forever sum up for me a star, a performance, a moment in the theater. Here, for example, are two wonderful (and, alas, unsigned) descriptions from 1928 that simply and definitively capture their subjects' enduring appeal.

First, there is this on Mae West's attitude about sex in her *Diamond Lil:* "Miss West has a fine and direct way of approaching that subject that is almost Elizabethan." And then this, on the stars of *Animal Crackers:* "They are nihilists—these Marx Boys."

We are also afforded early glimpses of Ethel Merman in *Girl Crazy* (1930), "whose peculiar song style was brought from the night clubs to the stage to the vast delight last evening of the people who go places and watch things being done." And of her costar in that musical, Ginger Rogers, "an oncoming young person of the type whom, at first appearance, half the audience immediately classifies as cute."

Moving on, here is Atkinson on Carol Channing in *Gentlemen Prefer Blondes* (1949), "husky enough to kick in the teeth of any gentlemen on the stage, but mincing coyly in high-heel shoes and looking out on a confused world through big, wide eyes." And Taubman on the Broadway debut of another star in the making in *I Can Get It for You Wholesale* in 1962: "The evening's find is Barbra Streisand, a girl with an oafish expression, a loud irascible voice and an arpeggiated laugh."

Walter Kerr freezes for eternity the image of Joel Grey as the Weimar M.C. in *Cabaret* (1966): "In a pink vest with sunburst eyes gleaming out of a cold-cream face, he is the silencer of bad dreams, the gleeful puppet of pretended joy, sin on a string."

Clive Barnes tells you exactly what you need to know about Angela Lansbury in the 1974 revival of *Gypsy:* "Miss Lansbury not only has a personality as big as the Statue of Liberty, but also a small core of nervousness that can make the outrageous real." And Frank Rich blissfully describes Maggie Smith's voice as "the only good argument yet advanced for the existence of sinus passages."

Playwrights are also encapsulated with Homeric resonance. Listen to Atkinson in 1937 on Clifford Odets's *Golden Boy:* "He takes pride in some of the most pretentiously low-life dialogue that has ever been poured out of an animated beer keg." Or Richard Eder, forty years later, on Wendy Wasserstein's *Uncommon Women:* "Unexpectedly, just when her hilarity threatens to become gag writing, she blunts it with compassion."

Annoying elements that we identify as peculiar to the contemporary theater turn out to have been with us for at least several decades. Writing about the musical *Mame* in 1966, Stanley Kauffmann complained of the score, "Like most others, it comes to our ears through an amplifying of which we are never unaware." (I am sad to report that things have not improved one whit in this respect.)

And Barnes, speaking of the revival of *No, No, Nanette!* (1971), could not have known how relevant his prescient definition of one decade would continue to be thirty years later: "Nostalgia may prove to be the overriding emotion of the seventies, with remembrance of things past far more comfortable than the realization of things present."

Posterity of course, has a way of blithely overruling the judgments of the critic.

Like the scandalized anonymous reviewer who observed in 1905 that Shaw's *Mrs. Warren's Profession* "bears about the same relation to the drama that the post-mortem bears to the science of which it is a part." Or the fellow who, on seeing Noel Coward's *Hay Fever* in 1925, noted, "Mr. Coward, it appears, does not scintillate in the use of words." And here is Atkinson on an Off Broadway musical that opened in 1960 and is still running today: "Perhaps *The Fantasticks* is by nature the sort of thing that loses magic the longer it endures."

There are 125 reviews reproduced in their entirety in *The New York Times Book of Broadway,* which would seem to be aplenty. But in making the final selection with my colleague Peter Marks—a former *Times* theater critic and eternal theater enthusiast whose work on this project has been invaluable—I soon discovered that there were destined to be many painful omissions. "You can't leave that out," Peter yelled at me about the Royal Shakespeare Company's production of *Nicholas Nickleby.* "That show changed my life."

In cold blood, however, we did leave out poor *Nicholas Nickleby,* though I too have exceedingly fond memories of it. I should point out immediately that the reviews gathered here by no means represent a "Top 125" list of a century's greatest performances or literary masterpieces. In narrowing down the roster, Peter and I focused not only on the intrinsic merits of the work reviewed but also on its historical context and the degree to which it engages the critic.

It was a definite plus when the reviewer seemed to feel that something new and perhaps transforming was occurring in the theater—as Atkinson did with *Look Back in Anger* and *Waiting for Godot,* or Barnes did with Peter Brook's production of *A Midsummer Night's Dream,* or Rich did with Tony Kushner's *Angels in America.* Sometimes, of course, we felt compelled to include reviews in which the critic gave little indication that the work under consideration might have long-reaching significance. (See *Show Boat, Oklahoma!* and *Six Characters in Search of an Author.*)

By and large, however, we were going for what made for the liveliest reading. Hence an outraged review of Mae West's *Sex* in 1926, rather than her better received *Diamond Lil* two years later. We also saw fit to include three different productions of *Hamlet* that represented the summit of Shakespearean performance in their respective eras, embodied by John Barrymore, John Gielgud and Richard Burton.

There will doubtless be many objections to the omissions and inclusions here, and I can't promise that Peter or I will be able to fully justify them after the fact.

But that is the nature of such lists; they are inevitably, to some degree, arbitrary, and half the fun is arguing about them once they have been made.

What I do regret is the exclusion of certain writers who added shading and richness to the collective critical voice of *The Times*. Because we limited ourselves to daily reviews, passing over the longer and more contemplative pieces that appeared in the Sunday paper, such wonderful essayists as Kerr, Richards, Margo Jefferson and the late Vincent Canby, an unflaggingly graceful and passionate critic of both film and theater, are only scantily represented, if at all.

I can only hope that those reviews we have chosen evoke for you, as they do for me, a very specific sense of 125 very particular nights at the theater. You are sure to find some wonderfully telling concrete details. But critics, being mere mortals, are sometimes reduced to paying bewildered homage to what is finally ineffable.

I'll leave you, if I may, more or less where we began, with John Corbin's description of the sense of "historical happening," as "unmistakable as it was undefinable," that pervaded John Barrymore's Hamlet on November 17 in 1922: "It sprang from the quality and intensity of the applause, from the hushed murmurs that swept the audience at the most unexpected moments, from the silent crowds that all evening long swarmed the theater entrance. It was nowhere—and everywhere."

—BEN BRANTLEY

Twenty-five Productions That Defined the Century

Alexander Woollcott ON

The Hairy Ape

BY Eugene O'Neill

March 9, 1922

Provincetown Theatre

108 Performances

Eugene O'Neill NICKOLAS MURAY

The little theatre of the Provincetowns-men in Macdougal Street was packed to the doors with astonishment last evening as scene after scene unfolded in the new play by Eugene O'Neill. This was *The Hairy Ape,* a bitter, brutal, wildly fantastic play of nightmare hue and nightmare distortion. It is a monstrously uneven piece, now flamingly eloquent, now choked and thwarted and inarticulate. . . . But it has a little greatness in it, and it seems rather absurd to fret overmuch about the undisciplined imagination of a young playwright towering so conspicuously above the milling, mumbling crowd of playwrights who have no imagination at all. . . .

It is true talk, all of it, and only those who have been so softly bred that they have never really heard the vulgate spoken in all its richness would venture to suggest that he has exaggerated it by so much as a syllable in order to agitate the refined. . . .

In Macdougal Street now and doubtless headed for Broadway, we have a turbulent and tremendous play, so full of blemishes that the merest fledgling among the critics could point out a dozen, yet so vital and interesting and teeming with life that those playgoers who let it escape them will be missing one of the real events of the year.

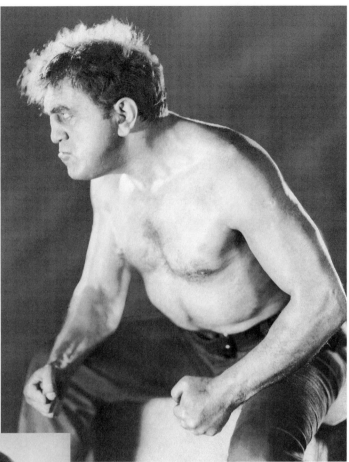

Louis Wolheim in the leading role of *The Hairy Ape,* presented by the Provincetown Players ABBE

Mary Blair   WIDE WORLD STUDIO

THE HAIRY APE, a play in eight scenes, by Eugene G. O'Neill.

Robert Smith ....Louis Wolheim
Paddy...Henry O'Neill
Long ....Harold West
Mildred Douglas ....Mary Blair
Her Aunt...Eleanor Hutchison
Second Engineer..Jack Gude
A Guard...Harry Gottlieb
A Secretary..Harold McGee

J. Brooks Atkinson ON

Show Boat

BOOK AND LYRICS BY

Oscar Hammerstein 2d

MUSIC BY

Jerome Kern

December 27, 1927

Ziegfeld Theatre

572 Performances

Oscar Hammerstein 2d *(left)* and composer Jerome Kern
J. E. PURDY

From such remote centres of theatrical omniscience as Pittsburgh, Washington and Philadelphia had come the advance word that it was better than good—some reports even extravagantly had it that here was Mr. Ziegfeld's superlative achievement. It would be difficult to quarrel with such tidings, for last night's performance came perilously close to realizing the most fulsome of them. . . .

The adaptation of the novel has been intelligently made, and such liberties as the demands of musical comedy necessitate do not twist the tale nor distort its values. For this, and for the far better than average lyrics with which it is endowed, credit Oscar Hammerstein 2d. . . .

Then, too, *Show Boat* has an exceptionally tuneful score—the most lilting and sat-isfactory that the wily Jerome Kern has contrived in several seasons. Potential song hits were as common last night as top hats. Such musical recordings of amorous reaction as "You Are in Love," "I Can't Help Lovin' That Man," "Why Do I Love You?" are sufficient for any show—to say nothing of the "Old Man River." . . .

If these three contributions—book, lyrics and score—call for a string of laudatory adjectives, the production compels that they be repeated again—and with a short tiger. . . .

The settings are all atmospherically perfect; the costumes are in the style of each of the periods and there is a finish and polish about the completed entity that caused even a first performance to move with unusual smoothness.

The cast of *Show Boat* WHITE STUDIO

SHOW BOAT, "An all-American musical comedy" in two acts, adapted from Edna Ferber's novel of the same name. Book and lyrics by Oscar Hammerstein 2d with music by Jerome Kern. Settings by Josef Urban; dances arranged by Sammy Lee; dialogue directed by Zeke Colvan; costumes designed by John Harkrider; produced by Florenz Ziegfeld.

Windy ....Allan Campbell
Queenie...Aunt Jemima
Steve..Charles Ellis
Pete...Bert Chapman
Parthy Ann Hawks.................................Edna May Oliver
Cap'n Andy ....Charles Winninger
Ellie ....Eva Puck
Frank..Sammy White
Rubber Face.......................................Francis X. Mahoney
Julie...Helen Morgan
Gaylord Ravenal.......................................Howard Marsh
Vallon ....Thomas Gunn
Magnolia...Norma Terris
Joe ....Jules Bledsoe
Dealer...Jack Wynn
Gambler ....Phil Sheridan
Backwoodsman...Jack Daley
Jeb ....Jack Wynn
La Belle Fatima ....Dorothy Denese
Old Sport..Bert Chapman
Landlady ....Annie Hart
Ethel ....Estelle Floyd
Sister ....Annette Harding
Mother Superior ....Mildred Schewenke
Kim (child) ....Eleanor Shaw

Norma Terris as Magnolia and Howard Marsh as Ravenal in the 1927 production. "This show is the opportunity of my life," said the producer Florenz Ziegfeld. CULVER PICTURES

Kim (as young woman)...............................Norma Terris
Jake ....Robert Farley
Max..Jack Daley
Man with Guitar...Ted Daniels
Charlie...J. Lewis Johnson
Lottie ....Tana Kamp
Dolly ....Dagmar Oakland
Old Lady on Levee......................................Laura Clairon

Brooks Atkinson ON

Waiting for Lefty

BY Clifford Odets

February 10, 1935

Civic Repertory Theatre

96 Performances

Clifford Odets in the thirties   ASSOCIATED PRESS

The dynamics of the program are the property of Mr. Odets's *Waiting for Lefty*. His saga, based on the New York taxi strike of last year, is clearly one of the most thoroughly trenchant jobs in the school of revolutionary drama. It argues the case for a strike against labor racketeering and the capitalist state by using the theatre auditorium as the hall where the taxi union is meeting. In four or five subordinate scenes, played with a few bare props in corners of the stage, the personal problems of several representative insurgents are drawn sharply. Mr. Odets is the author of *Awake and Sing!*

which the Group Theatre expects to produce next week. *Waiting for Lefty* is soundly constructed and fiercely dramatic in the theatre, and it is also a keen preface to his playwriting talents.

His associates have never played with more thrust, drive and conviction. *Waiting for Lefty* suits them down to the boards. Incidentally, the progress of the revolutionary drama in New York City during the last two seasons is the most obvious recent development in our theatre.... Now the Group Theatre gives its most slashing performance in a drama about the taxi strike.

Elia Kazan playing Clancy   THE NEW YORK TIMES
PHOTO ARCHIVES

Morris Carnovsky   BEN PINCHOT

WAITING FOR LEFTY, play in six scenes, by Clifford
    Odets. Directed by Sanford Meisner and Clifford
    Odets. At the Civic Repertory Theatre.
Fatt..Morris Carnovsky
Joe...Art Smith
Edna...Ruth Nelson
Miller...Gerrit Kraber
Fayette...Morris Carnovsky
Irv...Walter Coy
Florrie...Phoebe Brand
Sid..Jules Garfield
Clayton..Russell Collins
Clancy..Elia Kazan
Gunman..David Korchmar
Henchman..Alan Baxter
Secretary..Paula Miller
Actor...William Challee
Grady..Morris Carnovsky
Dr. Barnes..Roman Bohnen
Dr. Benjamin...Luther Adler
Agate Keller...J. E. Bromberg

A man...Bob Lewis
Voices in the audience ....Herbert Ratner, Clifford Odets,
                                                        Lewis Leverett

Brooks Atkinson ON

Porgy and Bess

BOOK BY Du Bose Heyward
LYRICS BY Du Bose Heyward AND
Ira Gershwin
MUSIC BY George Gershwin

October 8, 1935

Alvin Theatre

124 Performances

Before the opera's 1935 Boston tryout, Gershwin *(at piano)* exchanged autographed pictures with Du Bose Heyward *(center)* and Ira Gershwin. EDWARD JABLONSKI

After eight years of savory memories, *Porgy* has acquired a score, a band, a choir of singers and a new title, *Porgy and Bess,* which the Theatre Guild put on at the Alvin last evening. Du Bose and Dorothy Heyward wrote the original lithograph of Catfish Row, which Rouben Mamoulian translated into a memorable work of theatre dynamics. But *Porgy and Bess* represents George Gershwin's longing to compose an American folk opera on a suitable theme. Although Mr. Heyward is the author of the libretto and shares with Ira Gershwin the credit for the lyrics, and although Mr. Mamoulian has again mounted the director's box, the evening is unmistakably George Gershwin's personal holiday. . . .

Mr. Mamoulian is an excellent director for dramas of ample proportions. He is not subtle, which is a virtue in showmanship. His crowds are arranged in masses that look as solid as a victory at the polls; they move with simple unanimity. . . .

In the world of sound that Mr. Gershwin has created the tattered children of a Charleston byway are still racy and congenial. Promoting *Porgy* to opera involves considerable incidental drudgery for threatregoers who agree with Mark Twain that "classical music is better than it sounds." But Mr. Gershwin has found a personal voice that was inarticulate in the original play. The fear and the pain go deeper in *Porgy and Bess* than they did in penny-plain *Porgy.*

The cast of *Porgy and Bess* pray during the hurricane scene.
CULVER PICTURES

PORGY AND BESS, "An American folk-opera" in three acts and nine scenes, based on the play, *Porgy*, by Du Bose and Dorothy Heyward. Score by George Gershwin, libretto by Mr. Heyward, and lyrics by Mr. Heyward and Ira Gershwin. Staged by Rouben Mamoulian; scenery by Sergei Soudeikine; orchestra conducted by Alexander Smallens; produced by the Theatre Guild.

John Bubbles *(left)* as Sportin' Life, Anne Brown as Bess, and Todd Duncan as Porgy   CULVER PICTURES

Mingo	Ford L. Buck
Clara	Abbie Mitchell
Sportin' Life	John W. Bubbles
Jake	Edward Matthews
Maria	Georgette Harvey
Annie	Olive Ball
Lily	Helen Dowdy
Serena	Ruby Elzy
Robbins	Henry Davis
Jim	Jack Carr
Peter	Gus Simons
Porgy	Todd Duncan
Crown	Warren Coleman
Bess	Anne Wiggins Brown
Detective	Alexander Campbell
Two Policemen	Harold Woolf, Burton McEvilly
Undertaker	John Garth
Frazier	J. Rosamond Johnson
Mr. Archdale	George Lessey
Nelson	Ray Yeates
Strawberry Woman	Helen Dowdy
Crab Man	Ray Yeates
Coroner	George Carleton

Residents of Catfish Row, fishermen, children, stevedores, &c.................The Eva Jessye Choir: Catherine Jackson Ayres, Lillian Cowan, Sara Daigeau, Darlean Duval, Kate Hall, Altonell Hines, Louisa Howard, Harriet Jackson, Rosalie King, Assotta Marshall, Wilnette Mayers, Sadie McGill, Massie Patterson, Annabelle Ross, Louise Twyman, Helen R. White, Musa Williams, Reginald Beane, Caesar Bennett, G. Harry Bolden, Edward Broadnax, Carroll Clark, Joseph Crawford, John Diggs, Leonard Franklin, John Garth, Joseph James, Clarence Jacobs, Allen Lewis, Jimmie Lightfoot, Lycurgus Lockman, Henry May, Junius McDaniel, Arthur McLean, William O'Neil, Robert Raines, Andrew Taylor, Leon Threadgill, Jimmie Waters, Robert Williams, Ray Yeates.

Choral Conductor ....Eva Jessye.
Children ....Naida King, Regina Williams, Enid Wilkins, Allen Tinney, William Tinney, Herbert Young.
The Charleston Orphans' Band ....Sam Anderson, Eric Bell, Le Verria Bilton, Benjamine Browne, Claude Christian, Shedrack Dobson, David Ellis, Clarence Smith, John Strachan, George Tait, Allen Tinney, William Tinney, Charles Williams, Herbert Young.

Brooks Atkinson ON

You Can't Take It with You

BY Moss Hart AND
George S. Kaufman

December 14, 1936

Booth Theatre

837 Performances

The playwriting team of George Kaufman and Moss Hart.
Here they are on the job: Kaufman at the typewriter, Hart
"kibitzing." ASSOCIATED PRESS

Moss Hart and George S. Kaufman have written their most thoroughly ingratiating comedy, *You Can't Take It with You,* which was put on at the Booth last evening. It is a study in vertigo about a lovable family of hobby-horse riders, funny without being shrill, sensible without being earnest. In *Once in a Lifetime,* Mr. Hart and Mr. Kaufman mowed the audience down under a machine-gun barrage of low comedy satire, which was the neatest trick of the season. But you will find their current lark a much more spontaneous piece of hilarity; it is written with a dash of affection to season the humor and played with gayety and simple good spirit. To this column, which has a fondness for amiability in the theatre, *You Can't Take It with You* is the best comedy these authors have written. . . .

Mr. Hart and Mr. Kaufman are fantastic humorists with a knack for extravagances of word and episode and an eye for hilarious incongruities. Nothing this scrawny season has turned up is quite so madcap as a view of the entire Sycamore tribe working at their separate hobbies simultaneously. . . .

Mr. Hart and Mr. Kaufman have been more rigidly brilliant in the past, but they have never scooped up an evening of such tickling fun.

A scene from the 1936 production CULVER PICTURES

Josephine Hull THE NEW YORK TIMES PHOTO ARCHIVES

YOU CAN'T TAKE IT WITH YOU, a "farcical comedy" in three acts, by Moss Hart and George S. Kaufman. Staging by Mr. Kaufman; settings by Donald Oenslager; produced by Sam H. Harris.

Penelope Sycamore ....Josephine Hull
Essie ....Paula Trueman
Rheba..Ruth Attaway
Paul Sycamore...Frank Wilcox
Mr. De Pinna ....Frank Conlan
Ed ....George Heller
Donald ....Oscar Polk
Martin Vanderhof ....Henry Travers
Alice ....Margot Stevenson
Henderson...Hugh Rennie
Tony Kirby ....Jess Barker
Boris Kolenkhov...George Tobias
Gay Wellington ....Mitzi Hajos
Mr. Kirby ....William J. Kelly
Mrs. Kirby ....Virginia Hammond
Three Men ....George Leach, Ralph Holmes,
　　　　　　　　　　　　　　　　　　　　　Franklin Heller
Olga...Anna Lubowe

Brooks Atkinson ON

Our Town

BY Thornton Wilder

February 4, 1938

Henry Miller's Theatre

336 Performances

Thornton Wilder   ERIC SCHAAL, PIX PUBLISHING

Although Thornton Wilder is celebrated chiefly for his fiction, it will be necessary now to reckon with him as a dramatist. His *Our Town,* which opened at Henry Miller's last evening, is a beautifully evocative play. Taking as his material three periods in the history of a placid New Hampshire town, Mr. Wilder has transmuted the simple events of human life into a universal reverie. He has given familiar facts a deeply moving, philosophical perspective. Staged without scenery and with the curtain always up, *Our Town* has escaped from the formal barrier of the modern theatre into the quintessence of acting, thought and speculation. In the staging, Jed Harris has appreciated the rare quality of Mr. Wilder's handiwork and illuminated it with a shining performance. *Our Town* is, in this column's opinion, one of the finest achievements of the current stage. . . .

Out of respect for the detached tone of Mr. Wilder's script, the performance as a whole is subdued and understated. The scale is so large that the voices are never lifted. But under the leisurely monotone of the production there is a fragment of immortal truth. *Our Town* is a microcosm. It is also a beautifully haunting play.

Martha Scott, in the white dress, as Emily in the drama's touching funeral scene   CULVER PICTURES

Frank Craven in the role of the Stage Manager
VANDAMM STUDIO

OUR TOWN, a play by Thornton Wilder; directed and produced by Jed Harris.

Stage Manager ....Frank Craven
Dr. Gibbs..Jay Fassett
Joe Crowell ....Raymond Roe
Howie Newsome...Tom Fadden
Mrs. Gibbs...Evelyn Varden
Mrs. Webb ....Helen Carew
George Gibbs...John Craven
Rebecca Gibbs ....Marilyn Erskine
Wally Webb...Charles Wiley Jr.
Emily Webb ....Martha Scott
Professor Pepper...Arthur Allen
Mr. Webb ....Thomas W. Ross
Woman in the Balcony...............................Carrie Weller
Man in the Auditorium ....Walter O. Hill
Lady in the Box.....................................Aline McDermott
Simon Stimson..Philip Coolidge
Mrs. Soames ....Doro Merande
Constable Warren ....E. Irving Locke
Si Crowell...Billy Redfield
Baseball Players............Alfred Ryder, William Roehrick,
                                                                    Thomas Coley
Sam Craig...Francis G. Cleveland
Joe Stoddard.....................................William Wadsworth

Lewis Nichols ON

Oklahoma!

BOOK AND LYRICS BY
Oscar Hammerstein 2d
MUSIC BY Richard Rodgers

March 31, 1943

St. James Theatre

2,212 Performances

Broadway's foremost composer/lyricist team—Richard Rodgers, at the piano, and Oscar Hammerstein 2d, who also wrote their librettos   ZINN ARTHUR STUDIO

For years they have been saying the Theatre Guild is dead, words that will obviously have to be eaten with breakfast this morning. Forsaking the sometimes somber tenor of her ways, the little lady of Fifty-second Street last evening danced off into new paths and brought to the St. James a truly delightful musical play called *Oklahoma!* Wonderful is the nearest adjective, for this excursion of the Guild combines a fresh and infectious gayety, a charm of manner, beautiful acting, singing and dancing, and a score by Richard Rodgers, which doesn't do any harm either, since it is one of his best.

Oklahoma! is based on Lynn Riggs's saga of the Indian Territory at the turn of the century, *Green Grow the Lilacs,* and, like its predecessor, it is simple and warm. It relies not for a moment on Broadway gags to stimulate an appearance of comedy, but goes winningly on its way with Rouben Mamoulian's best direction to point up its sly humor, and with some of Agnes de Mille's most inspired dances to do so further. . . .

Mr. Rodgers's scores never lack grace, but seldom have they been so well integrated. . . . Possibly in addition to being a musical play, *Oklahoma!* could be called a folk operetta; whatever it is, it is very good.

OKLAHOMA! a musical play in two acts and five scenes, derived from *Green Grow the Lilacs*, by Lynn Riggs. Music by Richard Rodgers; book and lyrics by Oscar Hammerstein 2d. Staged by Rouben Mamoulian; choreography by Agnes de Mille; settings by Lemuel Ayers; costumes designed by Miles White; produced by the Theatre Guild.

Aunt Eller...Betty Garde
Curly ....Alfred Drake
Laurey ....Joan Roberts
Ike Skidmore..Barry Kelley
Fred ....Edwin Clay
Slim...Herbert Rissman
Will Parker ....Lee Dixon
Jud Fry...Howard da Silva
Ado Annie Carnes ....Celeste Holm
Ali Hakim ....Joseph Buloff
Gertie Cummings...Jane Lawrence
Ellen..Katharine Sergava
Kate ....Ellen Love
Sylvie ....Joan McCracken
Armina..Kate Friedlich
Aggie...Bambi Linn
Andrew Carnes...Ralph Riggs
Cord Elam ....Owen Martin
Jess...George Church
Chalmers...Marc Platt
Mike..Paul Schierz
Joe...George Irving
Sam ....Hayes Gordon

Joan McCracken leads the French postcards in the same ballet. VANDAMM STUDIO

Left to right: Joan Roberts (Laurey), Alfred Drake (Curly) and Celeste Holm (Ado Annie), as they appeared in the original cast. EILEEN DARBY, GRAPHIC HOUSE

Brooks Atkinson ON

A Streetcar Named Desire

BY Tennessee Williams

December 3, 1947

Barrymore Theatre

855 Performances

Tennessee Williams TIMES WIDE WORLD

Tennessee Williams has brought us a superb drama, *A Streetcar Named Desire,* which was acted at the Ethel Barrymore last evening. And Jessica Tandy gives a superb performance as a rueful heroine whose misery Mr. Williams is tenderly recording. This must be one of the most perfect marriages of acting and playwriting. For the acting and playwriting are perfectly blended in a limpid performance, and it is impossible to tell where Miss Tandy begins to give form and warmth to the mood Mr. Williams has created.

Like *The Glass Menagerie,* the new play is a quietly woven study of intangibles. But to this observer it shows deeper insight and represents a great step forward toward clarity. And it reveals Mr. Williams as a genuinely poetic playwright whose knowledge of people is honest and thorough and whose sympathy is profoundly human. . . .

By the usual Broadway standards, *A Streetcar Named Desire* is too long; not all those words are essential. But Mr. Williams is entitled to his own independence. For he has not forgotten that human beings are the basic subject of art. Out of poetic imagination and ordinary compassion he has spun a poignant and luminous story.

Marlon Brando *(left)* as Stanley Kowalski, Jessica Tandy *(middle)* as Blanche du Bois and Kim Hunter as Stella Kowalski
THE NEW YORK TIMES PHOTO ARCHIVES

Marlon Brando, Kim Hunter and Jessica Tandy in a scene
from *A Streetcar Named Desire*   THE NEW YORK TIMES
PHOTO ARCHIVES

A STREETCAR NAMED DESIRE, a play in three acts,
by Tennessee Williams. Staged by Elia Kazan;
scenery and lighting by Jo Mielziner; costumes by
Lucinda Ballard; produced by Irene M. Selznick.

Negro Woman...Gee Gee James
Eunice Hubbel ....Peg Hillias
Stanley Kowalski.......................................Marlon Brando
Harold Mitchell (Mitch) ....Karl Malden
Stella Kowalski ....Kim Hunter
Steve Hubbel...Rudy Bond
Blanche du Bois ....Jessica Tandy
Pablo Gonzales ....Nick Dennis
A Young Collector ....Vito Christi
Mexican Woman..Edna Thomas
A Strange Woman...Ann Dere
A Strange Man..Richard Garrick

Brooks Atkinson ON

Death of a Salesman

BY Arthur Miller

February 10, 1949

Morosco Theatre

742 Performances

Playwright Arthur Miller in his Brooklyn Heights home
THE NEW YORK TIMES

Arthur Miller has written a superb drama. From every point of view *Death of a Salesman,* which was acted at the Morosco last evening, is rich and memorable drama. It is so simple in style and so inevitable in theme that it scarcely seems like a thing that has been written and acted. For Mr. Miller has looked with compassion into the hearts of some ordinary Americans and quietly transferred their hope and anguish to the theatre. Under Elia Kazan's masterly direction, Lee J. Cobb gives a heroic performance, and every member of the cast plays like a person inspired. . . .

Mr. Cobb's tragic portrait of the de-feated salesman is acting of the first rank. Although it is familiar and folksy in the details, it has something of the grand manner in the big size and the deep tone. Mildred Dunnock gives the performance of her career as the wife and mother—plain of speech but indomitable in spirit. The parts of the thoughtless sons are extremely well played by Arthur Kennedy and Cameron Mitchell, who are all youth, brag and bewilderment. . . . If there were time, this report would gratefully include all the actors and fabricators of illusion. For they all realize that for once in their lives they are participating in a rare event in the theatre.

DEATH OF A SALESMAN, a play by Arthur Miller. Staged by Elia Kazan; scenery and lighting by Jo Mielziner; incidental music by Alex North; costumes by Julia Sze; produced by Kermit Bloomgarden and Walter Fried.

Willy Loman ....Lee J. Cobb
Linda ....Mildred Dunnock
Happy ....Cameron Mitchell
Biff..Arthur Kennedy
Bernard..Don Keefer
The Woman..Winnifred Cushing
Charley..Howard Smith
Uncle Ben..Thomas Chalmers
Howard Wagner..Alan Hewitt
Jenny..Ann Driscoll
Stanley..Tom Pedi
Miss Forsythe..Constance Ford
Letta..Hope Cameron

Lee J. Cobb and Mildred Dunnock

Lee J. Cobb *(seated)* with Arthur Kennedy *(right)* and Cameron Mitchell

Brooks Atkinson ON

My Fair Lady

BOOK AND LYRICS BY
Alan Jay Lerner
MUSIC BY Frederick Loewe

March 15, 1956

Mark Hellinger Theatre

2,717 Performances

Alan Jay Lerner (with cigarette) watches composer Frederick Loewe. THE NEW YORK TIMES PHOTO ARCHIVES

Bulletins from the road have not been misleading. *My Fair Lady,* which opened at the Mark Hellinger last evening, is a wonderful show. . . .

Shaw's crackling mind is still the genius of *My Fair Lady.* Mr. Lerner has retained the same ironic point of view in his crisp adaptation and his sardonic lyrics. As Professor Higgins and Eliza Doolittle, Rex Harrison and Julie Andrews play the leading parts with the light, dry touch of topflight Shavian acting.

My Fair Lady is staged dramatically on a civilized plane. Probably for the first time in history a typical musical comedy audience finds itself absorbed in the art of pronunciation and passionately involved in the proper speaking of "pain," "rain" and "Spain."

And yet it would not be fair to imply that *My Fair Lady* is only a new look at an old comedy. For the carnival version adds a new dimension; it gives a lift to the gayety and to the romance. In his robust score, Mr. Loewe has made the Covent Garden scenes more raffish and hilarious. . . . Not being afraid of melody, he has written some entrancing love music and a waltz. . . . All this is, no doubt, implicit in *Pygmalion.* But Mr. Loewe has given it a heartier exuberance. Although the Old Boy had a sense of humor, he never had so much abandon.

Julie Andrews as Eliza Doolittle
FRIEDMAN-ABELES

Rex Harrison *(right)* as Professor Higgins and Stanley Halloway as Alfred P. Doolittle THE NEW YORK TIMES PHOTO ARCHIVES

MY FAIR LADY, a musical comedy adapted from George Bernard Shaw's *Pygmalion*. Book and lyrics by Alan Jay Lerner, with music by Frederick Loewe. Production staged by Moss Hart; presented by Herman Levin; choreography by Hanya Holm; scenery by Oliver Smith; costumes by Cecil Beaton; musical arrangements by Robert Russell Bennett and Phil Lang; lighting by A. H. Feder; dance music arranged by Trude Rittman; musical director, Franz Allers; production stage manager, Samuel Liff.

Mrs. Eynsford-Hill	Viola Roache
Eliza Doolittle	Julie Andrews
Freddy Eynsford-Hill	John Michael King
Colonel Pickering	Robert Coote
Henry Higgins	Rex Harrison
Bartender	David Thomas
Jamie	Rod McLennan
Alfred P. Doolittle	Stanley Holloway
Mrs. Pearce	Philippa Bevans
Mrs. Hopkins	Olive Reeves-Smith
Mrs. Higgins	Cathleen Nesbitt
Lord Boxington	Gordon Dilworth
Zoltan Karpathy	Christopher Hewett

Brooks Atkinson ON

Waiting for Godot

BY Samuel Beckett

—

April 19, 1956

John Golden Theatre

59 Performances

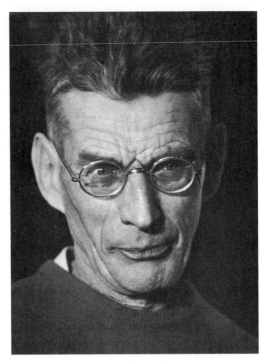

Samuel Beckett DOMINIC, CAMERA PRESS LONDON

Don't expect this column to explain Samuel Beckett's *Waiting for Godot,* which was acted at the John Golden last evening. It is a mystery wrapped in an enigma.

But you can expect witness to the strange power this drama has to convey the impression of some melancholy truths about the hopeless destiny of the human race. Mr. Beckett is an Irish writer who has lived in Paris for years, and once served as a secretary to James Joyce.

Since *Waiting for Godot* has no simple meaning, one seizes on Mr. Beckett's experience of two worlds to account for his style and point of view. The point of view suggests Sartre—bleak, dark, disgusted.

The style suggests Joyce—pungent and fabulous. Put the two together and you have some notion of Mr. Beckett's acrid cartoon of the story of mankind. . . . Mr. Beckett's drama adumbrates—rather than expresses—an attitude toward man's experience on earth; the pathos, cruelty, comradeship, hope, corruption, filthiness and wonder of human existence. . . .

Although the drama is puzzling, the director and the actors play it as though they understand every line of it. . . . And Bert Lahr has never given a performance as glorious as his tatterdemalion Gogo, who seems to stand for all the stumbling, bewildered people of the earth who go on living without knowing why.

E. G. Marshall *(left),* Kurt Kasznar *(center)* and Bert Lahr
IMPACT

WAITING FOR GODOT, a tragicomedy in two acts by Samuel Beckett; staged by Herbert Berghof; presented by Michael Myerberg, by arrangement with Independent Plays, Ltd.; scenery by Louis Kennel; costumes by Stanley Simmons; production supervisor, John Paul.

Estragon (Gogo)..Bert Lahr
Vladimir (Didi)..E. G. Marshall
Lucky..Alvin Epstein
Pozzo...Kurt Kasznar
A Boy...Luchino Solito de Solis

Bert Lahr *(left)* and E. G. Marshall IMPACT

Brooks Atkinson ON

Long Day's Journey into Night

BY Eugene O'Neill

November 7, 1956

Helen Hayes Theatre

390 Performances

Florence Eldridge and Fredric March GJON MILI

With the production of *Long Day's Journey into Night* at the Helen Hayes last evening, the American theatre acquires size and stature.

The size does not refer to the length of Eugene O'Neill's autobiographical drama, although a play three and three-quarter hours long is worth remarking. The size refers to his conception of theatre as a form of epic literature.

Long Day's Journey into Night is like a Dostoyevsky novel in which Strindberg had written the dialogue. For this saga of the damned is horrifying and devastating in a classical tradition, and the performance under José Quintero's direction is inspired. . . .

The characters are laid bare with pitiless candor. The scenes are big. The dialogue is blunt. Scene by scene the tragedy moves along with a remorseless beat that becomes hypnotic, as though this were life lived on the brink of oblivion. . . .

Although the text is interesting to read between covers, it does not begin to flame until the actors take hold of it. Mr. Quintero, who staged the memorable *The Iceman Cometh* in the Village, has directed *Long Day's Journey into Night* with insight and skill. He has caught the sense of a stricken family in which the members are at once fascinated and repelled by one another. . . . It restores the drama to literature and the theatre to art.

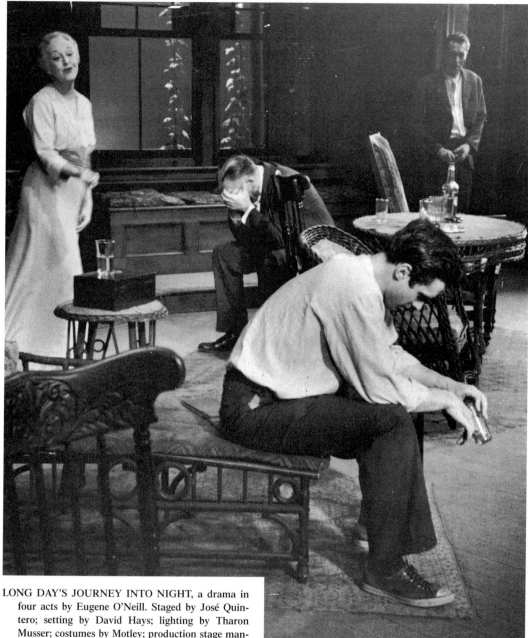

LONG DAY'S JOURNEY INTO NIGHT, a drama in
four acts by Eugene O'Neill. Staged by José Quintero; setting by David Hays; lighting by Tharon
Musser; costumes by Motley; production stage manager, Elliott Martin; presented by Leigh Connell,
Theodore Mann and Mr. Quintero.

James Tyrone ....Fredric March
Mary Cavan Tyrone ....Florence Eldridge
James Tyrone Jr.....................................Jason Robards Jr.
Edmund Tyrone ....Bradford Dillman
Cathleen ....Katherine Ross

A tense scene at the Tyrone family's home, with Florence
Eldridge, Bradford Dillman *(foreground)*, Fredric March
(with face in hands) and Jason Robards Jr.

Brooks Atkinson ON

West Side Story

BOOK BY Arthur Laurents
LYRICS BY Stephen Sondheim
MUSIC BY Leonard Bernstein

September 26, 1957

Winter Garden

732 Performances

Jerome Robbins, choreographer and director   THE NEW
YORK TIMES PHOTO ARCHIVES

Although the material is horrifying, the workmanship is admirable.

Gang warfare is the material of *West Side Story*, which opened at the Winter Garden last evening, and very little of the hideousness has been left out. But the author, composer and ballet designer are creative artists. Pooling imagination and virtuosity, they have written a profoundly moving show that is as ugly as the city jungles and also pathetic, tender and forgiving.

Arthur Laurents has written the story of two hostile teen-age gangs fighting for supremacy amid the tenement houses, corner stores and bridges of the West Side. . . . In the design of *West Side Story,* he has powerful allies. Leonard Bernstein has composed another one of his nervous, flaring scores that capture the shrill beat of life in the streets. And Jerome Robbins, who directed the production, is also its choreographer. . . .

Everything in *West Side Story* is of a piece. Everything contributes to the total impression of wildness, ecstasy and anguish. . . . For this is one of those occasions when theatre people, engrossed in an original project, are all in top form. The subject is not beautiful. But what *West Side Story* draws out of it is beautiful. For it has a searching point of view.

Leonard Bernstein instructing singers. At the piano is Stephen Sondheim, who wrote the lyrics. FRIEDMAN-ABELES

Jerome Robbins used ballet here more than any Broadway show ever had. VIVIENNE BYERLEY

WEST SIDE STORY, a musical comedy, based on a conception of Jerome Robbins, with book by Arthur Laurents, music by Leonard Bernstein and lyrics by Stephen Sondheim. Entire production directed and choreographed by Mr. Robbins; presented by Robert E. Griffith and Harold S. Prince, by arrangement with Roger L. Stevens; scenery by Oliver Smith; costumes by Irene Sharaff; lighting by Jean Rosenthal; co-choreographer, Peter Gennaro; production associate, Sylvia Drulle; musical direction, Max Goberman; orchestrations by Mr. Bernstein, Sid Ramin and Irwin Kostaf; production stage manager, Ruth Mitchell.

The Jets ....Riff, Mickey Calin; Gee-Tar, Tommy Abbott; Tony, Larry Kert; Mouth Piece, Frank Green; Action, Eddie Roll; Tiger, Lowell Harris; A-Rab, Tony Mordente; Graziella, Wilma Curley; Baby John, David Winters; Velma, Carole D'Andrea; Snowboy, Grover Dale; Minnie, Nanette Rosen; Clarice, Marilyn D'Honau; Big Deal, Martin Charnin; Pauline, Julie Oser; Diesel, Hank Brunjes; Anybodys, Lee Becker.

The Sharks ....Bernardo, Ken Le Roy; Juano, Jay Norman; Maria, Carol Lawrence; Toro, Erne Castaldo; Anita, Chita Rivera; Moose, Jack Murray; Chino, Jamie Sanchez; Rosalia, Marilyn Cooper; Pepe, George Marcy; Consuelo, Reri Grist; Indio, Noel Schwartz; Terestia, Carmen Guiterrez; Luis, Al De Sio; Francisca, Elizabeth Taylor; Anxious, Gene Gavin; Estella, Lynn Ross; Nibbles, Ronie Lee; Marguerita, Liane Plane.

The Adults.................................Doc, Art Smith; Krupke, William Bramley; Schrank, Arch Johnson; Gladhand, John Harkins.

Brooks Atkinson ON

A Raisin in the Sun

BY Lorraine Hansberry

March 11, 1959

Ethel Barrymore Theatre

530 Performances

Lorraine Hansberry FRIEDMAN-ABELES

In *A Raisin in the Sun,* which opened at the Ethel Barrymore last evening, Lorraine Hansberry touches on some serious problems. No doubt, her feelings about them are as strong as anyone's.

But she has not tipped her play to prove one thing or another. . . . She has told the inner as well as the outer truth about a Negro family in the southside of Chicago at the present time. Since the performance is also honest and since Sidney Poitier is a candid actor, *A Raisin in the Sun* has vigor as well as veracity and is likely to destroy the complacency of anyone who sees it. . . .

You might, in fact, regard *A Raisin in the Sun* as a Negro *The Cherry Orchard.* Although the social scale of the characters is different, the knowledge of how character is controlled by environment is much the same, and the alternation of humor and pathos is similar.

If there are occasional crudities in the craftsmanship, they are redeemed by the honesty of the writing. And also by the rousing honesty of the stage work. . . . That is Miss Hansberry's personal contribution in an explosive situation in which simple honesty is the most difficult thing in the world. And also the most illuminating.

Left to right: Sidney Poitier, Claudia McNeil, Ruby Dee, Glynn Turman and Diana Sands MAX EISEN

Lloyd Richards, director of *A Raisin in the Sun*   ALFREDO
VALENTE

A RAISIN IN THE SUN, a drama by Lorraine Hansberry. Staged by Lloyd Richards; presented by Philip
Rose and David J. Cogan; scenery and lighting by
Ralph Alswang; costumes by Virginia Volland; production stage manager, Leonard Auerbach.

Ruth Younger	Ruby Dee
Travis Younger	Glynn Turman
Walter Lee Younger	Sidney Poitier
Beneatha Younger	Diana Sands
Lena Younger	Claudia McNeil
Joseph Asagai	Ivan Dixon
George Murchison	Louis Gossett
Bobo	Lonne Elder 3d
Karl Lindner	John Fiedler
Moving Men	Ed Hall, Douglas Turner

Howard Taubman ON

The Caretaker

BY Harold Pinter

————

October 4, 1961

Lyceum Theatre

165 Performances

Harold Pinter, playwright   THE NEW YORK TIMES

O ut of a scabrous derelict and two mentally unbalanced brothers, Harold Pinter has woven a play of strangely compelling beauty and passion. *The Caretaker,* which opened last night at the Lyceum, proclaims its young English author as one of the most important playwrights of our day.

At first glance the materials of this play could hardly be less promising. Two of the characters are just this side of articulate, and the third spins a glib, wild line about real estate, leases, interior decoration and other common concerns. Yet Mr. Pinter finds comedy, tenderness and heartbreak in all three. He builds his spare elements into

powerful drama with a climax that tears at the heart. . . .

Mr. Pinter has been vehement in his assertions that his play is no more than the story it tells. But he cannot prevent his audiences from finding in it a modern parable of derisive scorn and bitter sorrow. . . .

Donald McWhinnie's staging in Brian Currah's imaginatively cluttered set has the strength of character to begin patiently and to build with cumulative force.

A work of rare originality, *The Caretaker* will tease and cling to the mind. No matter what happens in the months to come, it will lend luster to this Broadway season.

Left to right: Robert Shaw and Alan Bates as two brothers who try to help Donald Pleasence   WNET

Donald Pleasence *(left)* as the derelict threatens Robert Shaw.   SAM SIEGEL

THE CARETAKER, a comedy-drama by Harold Pinter. Staged by Donald McWhinnie; presented by Roger L. Stevens, Frederick Brisson and Gilbert Miller; scenery by Brian Currah; supervision and lighting by Paul Morrison; production stage manager, Fred Hebert.

Mick ....Alan Bates
Aston..Robert Shaw
Davies..Donald Pleasence

Howard Taubman ON

Who's Afraid of Virginia Woolf?

BY Edward Albee

October 13, 1962

Billy Rose Theatre

664 Performances

Playwright Edward Albee directed a revival of *Who's Afraid of Virginia Woolf?* in 1976. ASSOCIATED PRESS

Thanks to Edward Albee's furious skill as a writer, Alan Schneider's charged staging and a brilliant performance by a cast of four, *Who's Afraid of Virginia Woolf?* is a wry and electric evening in the theater. . . .

Moving onto from off Broadway, Mr. Albee carries along the burning intensity and icy wrath that informed *The Zoo Story* and *The American Dream.* He has written a full-length play that runs almost three and a half hours and that brims over with howling furies that do not drown out a fierce compassion. After the fumes stirred by his witches' cauldron are spent, he lets in, not sunlight and fresh air, but only an agonized prayer. . . .

Sympathize with them or not, you will find the characters in this new play vibrant with dramatic urgency. In their anger and terror they are pitiful as well as corrosive, but they are also wildly and humanly hilarious. . . . Like Strindberg, Mr. Albee treats his men remorselessly, but he is not much gentler with his women. If he grieves for the human predicament, he does not spare those lost in its psychological and emotional mazes.

His new work, flawed though it is, towers over the common run of contemporary plays. It marks a further gain for a young writer becoming a major figure of our stage.

WHO'S AFRAID OF VIRGINIA WOOLF?, a play by
Edward Albee. Staged by Alan Schneider; presented
by Richard Barr and Clinton Wilder; production designed by William Ritman; stage manager, Mark
Wright.

Martha ....Uta Hagen
George ....Arthur Hill
Honey...Melinda Dillon
Nick...George Grizzard

Left to right: Uta Hagen, Arthur Hill, Melinda Dillon and
George Grizzard in the original Broadway production
THE NEW YORK TIMES PHOTO ARCHIVES

Clive Barnes ON

Peter Brook's

A Midsummer Night's Dream

January 20, 1971

Billy Rose Theater

62 Performances

Peter Brook   JACK MITCHELL

It is a celebration of life and fancy, of man and his imagination, his fate, and the brevity of his brief candle in the light of the world. Shakespeare gave us "the lunatic, the lover and the poet," and Brook smilingly adds the acrobat.

This is without any equivocation whatsoever the greatest production of Shakespeare I have ever seen in my life—and for my joys and my sins I have seen literally hundreds. Its greatness lies partly in its insight into man, and best of all its remarkable insight into Shakespeare. But it also lies in its originality. It is the most genuinely and deeply original production of Shakespeare in decades. . . .

Brook takes the elements of the theater and mixes them as if he were a chef trying out a recipe. Circus tricks, Indian chants, flamenco guitar, children's streamers, paper plates, mock and mocked Mendelssohn, all are thrown into some eclectic broth. Only the text is sacred. . . .

If you have any interest in the theater, in life or in your fellow men, I think you will be transfixed by this *Dream*. And, if you haven't, well, even so you might appreciate still the fun and the juggling. As Shakespeare would surely be the first to admit, jugglers have their place.

Alan Howard *(left)* as Oberon and John Kane as Puck in *A Midsummer Night's Dream*   DOUGLAS H. JEFFERY

A MIDSUMMER NIGHT'S DREAM, the Royal Shakespeare Company production of Shakespeare's comedy. Directed by Peter Brook; settings and costumes by Sally Jacobs; music by Richard Peaslee; lighting by Lloyd Burlingame. Presented by the David Merrick Arts Foundation.

Theseus/Oberon	Alan Howard
Hippolyta/Titania	Sara Kestelman
Philostrate/Puck	John Kane
Egeus/Quince	Philip Locke
Bottom	David Waller
Flute	Glynne Lewis
Starveling	Phillip Manikum
Snout	Patrick Stewart
Snug	Barry Stanton
Hermia	Mary Rutherford
Lysander	Terence Taplin
Helena	Frances De La Tour
Demetrius	Ben Kingsley
Fairies:	
Cobweb	Hugh Keays Byrne
Moth	Ralph Cotterill
Peaseblossom	Cella Quické
Mustardseed	John York

Clive Barnes ON

A Chorus Line

BOOK BY James Kirkwood AND
Nicholas Dante
LYRICS BY Edward Kleban
MUSIC BY Marvin Hamlisch

May 21, 1975

Newman/Public Theater

6,137 Performances

Joseph Papp and Michael Bennett in front of the theater
DON HOGAN CHARLES/THE NEW YORK TIMES

The conservative word for *A Chorus Line* might be tremendous, or perhaps terrific. Michael Bennett's new-style musical opened at the Newman Theater of the New York Shakespeare Festival Public Theater on Lafayette Street last night, and the reception was so shattering that it is surprising if by the time you read this, the New York Shakespeare Festival has got a Newman Theater still standing in its Public Theater complex on Lafayette Street. It was that kind of reception, and it is that kind of a show.

We have for years been hearing about innovative musicals: now Mr. Bennett has really innovated one. *A Chorus Line* takes a close, hard squint at Broadway babies on parade—here and now. . . .

It is in a small theater and here, at last, is the intimate big musical. Everything is made to work. The groupings are always faultless, the dances have the right Broadway surge, and two numbers, the mirror-dance for Ms. McKechnie and the Busby Berkeley–inspired finale, deserve to become classics of musical staging. And talking of classics, while there will be some to find fault, perhaps with a certain reason, with the hard-edged glossiness of *A Chorus Line,* it is a show that must dance, jog and whirl its way into the history of the musical theater.

Michael Bennett at the Shubert Theater September 29, 1983, during the record-breaking 3,389th performance of *A Chorus Line*. He was joined onstage by 332 dancers from various casts of the musical. FRED R. CONRAD/THE NEW YORK TIMES

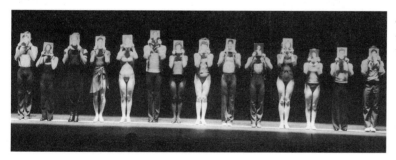

The cast of *A Chorus Line*
WILLIAM E. SAURO/THE NEW
YORK TIMES

A CHORUS LINE, conceived, choreographed and directed by Michael Bennett. Book by James Kirkwood and Nicholas Dante; music by Marvin Hamlisch; lyrics by Edward Kleban; co-choreographer, Bob Avian; setting by Robin Wagner; costumes by Theoni V. Aldredge; lighting by Tharon Musser; orchestrations by Bill Byers, Hershy Kay and Jonathan Tunick; music coordinator, Robert Thomas; music direction and vocal arrangements by Don Pippin; production stage manager, Jeff Hamlin. Presented by The New York Shakespeare Festival Public Theater, Joseph Papp, producer, Bernard Gersten, associate producer.

With Scott Allen, Renée Baughman, Carole Bishop, Pamela Blair, Wayne Cilento, Chuck Cissel, Clive Clerk, Kay Cole, Ronald Dennis, Donna Drake, Brandt Edwards, Patricia Garland, Carolyn Kirsch, Ron Kuhlman, Nancy Lane, Baayork Lee, Priscilla Lopez, Robert LuPone, Cameron Mason, Donna McKechnie, Don Percassi, Michael Serrecchia, Michel Stuart, Thomas J. Walsh, Sammy Williams and Crissy Wilzak.

Richard Eder ON

Sweeney Todd

BOOK BY Hugh Wheeler

MUSIC AND LYRICS BY

Stephen Sondheim

March 1, 1979

Uris Theater

557 Performances

Stephen Sondheim FRED R. CONRAD/THE NEW YORK TIMES

The musical and dramatic achievements of Stephen Sondheim's black and bloody *Sweeney Todd* are so numerous and clamorous that they trample and jam each other in that invisible but finite doorway that connects a stage and its audience, doing themselves some harm in the process.

That is a serious reservation, and I will get back to it. But it is necessary to give the dimensions of the event. There is more of artistic energy, creative personality and plain excitement in *Sweeney Todd,* which opened last night at the enormous Uris Theater and made it seem like a cottage, than in a dozen average musicals.

It is in many ways closer to opera than to most musicals; and in particular, and some-

times too much for its own good, to the Brecht-Weill *Threepenny Opera.* Mr. Sondheim has composed an endlessly inventive, highly expressive score that works indivisibly from his brilliant and abrasive lyrics.

It is a powerful, coruscating instrument, this muscular partnership of words and music. Mr. Sondheim has applied it to making a Grand Guignol opera with social undertones. . . . Mr. Sondheim and his director, Harold Prince, have taken this set of rattletrap fireworks and made it into a glittering, dangerous weapon. With the help of Hugh Wheeler, who adapted the book from Mr. Bond's play, they amplify every grotesque and exaggerated detail and step up its horsepower.

SWEENEY TODD, musical, with book by Hugh Wheeler; music and lyrics by Stephen Sondheim; based on *Sweeney Todd* by Christopher Bond; directed by Harold Prince; settings by Eugene Lee; costumes by Franne Lee; lighting by Ken Billington; orchestrations by Jonathan Tunick; musical direction by Paul Gemignani; production stage manager, Alan Hall. Presented by Richard Barr, Charles Woodward, Robert Fryer, Mary Lee Johnson and Martin Richards in association with Dean and Judy Manos; associate producer, Marc Howard.

Anthony Hope ....Victor Garber
Sweeney Todd ....Len Cariou
Beggar Woman ....Merle Louise
Mrs. Lovett ....Angela Lansbury
Judge Turpin ....Edmund Lyndeck
Beadle..Jack Eric Williams
Johanna ....Sarah Rice
Tobias Ragg ....Ken Jennings
Pirelli..Joaquin Rornaguera
Jonas Fogg ....Robert Ousley
The Company ....Duane Bodin, Walter Charles, Carole Doscher, Nancy Eaton, Mary-Pat Green, Cris Groenendaal, Skip Harris, Marthe Ihde, Betsy Joslyn, Nancy Killmer, Frank Kopyc, Spain Logue, Craig Lucas, Pamela McLernon, Duane Morris, Robert Ousley, Richard Warren Pugh, Maggie Task, Heather B. Withers and Robert Hendersen.

Mrs. Lovett (Angela Lansbury) makes the worst pies in London, with Sweeney Todd (Len Cariou). MARTHA SWOPE

Harold Prince *(foreground)* with Angela Lansbury and Len Cariou during a rehearsal of *Sweeney Todd*
PAUL HOSEFROS/THE NEW YORK TIMES

Frank Rich ON

Cats

MUSIC BY Andrew Lloyd Webber

October 7, 1982

Winter Garden

7, 485 Performances

Andrew Lloyd Webber   JOHN SWANNELL, CAMERA PRESS
LONDON

There's a reason why *Cats*, the British musical which opened at the Winter Garden last night, is likely to lurk around Broadway for a long time—and it may not be the one you expect.

It's not that this collection of anthropomorphic variety turns is a brilliant musical or that it powerfully stirs the emotions or that it has an idea in its head. Nor is the probable appeal of *Cats* a function of the publicity that has accompanied the show's every purr since it first stalked London seventeen months ago. No, the reason why people will hunger to see *Cats* is far more simple and primal than that: it's a musical that transports the audience into a complete fantasy world that could only exist in the theater and yet, these days, only rarely does. Whatever the other failings and excesses, even banalities of *Cats*, it believes in purely theatrical magic, and on that faith it unquestionably delivers. . . .

One wishes . . . that we weren't sporadically jolted from Eliot's otherworldly catland to the vulgar precincts of the video-game arcade. . . . But maybe it's asking too much that this ambitious show lift the audience—or for that matter, the modern musical—up to the sublime heaviside layer. What *Cats* does do is take us into a theater overflowing with wondrous spectacle—and that's an enchanting place to be.

Dance captain Rene Clemente *(left)* and production dance supervisor T. Michael Reed drill new *Cats* recruits. LOUIS GOLDMAN

Trevor Nunn *(foreground),* director of *Cats,* during a rehearsal break with members of the cast DON HOGAN CHARLES/THE NEW YORK TIMES

CATS, music by Andrew Lloyd Webber; based on *Old Possum's Book of Practical Cats* by T. S. Eliot; directed by Trevor Nunn; orchestrations by David Cullen and Mr. Lloyd Webber; production musical director, Stanley Lebowsky; musical director, René Wiegert; sound design by Martin Levan; lighting design by David Hersey; designed by John Napier; associate director and choreographer, Gillian Lynne; executive producers, R. Tyler Gatchell Jr. and Peter Neufeld. Presented by Cameron Mackintosh, The Really Useful Company Ltd., David Geffen and the Shubert Organization.

Alonzo..Hector Jaime Mercado
Bustopher Jones, Asparagus and
Growltiger..................................Stephen Hanan
Bornbalurina................................Donna King
Carbucketty ....Steven Geifer
Cassandra ....René Cebalios
Coricopat and Mungojerrie ....René Clemente

Demeter...Wendy Edmead
Etcetera and Rumpleteazer ....Christine Langer
Grizabella ....Betty Buckley
Jellylorum and Griddlebone ....Bonnie Simmons
Jennyanydots..Anna McNeely
Mistoffolees....................................Timothy Scott
Munkustrap ....Harry Groener
Old Deuteronomy..Ken Page
Plato, Macavity and Rumpus Cat ....Kenneth Ard
Pouncival ....Herman W. Sebek
Rum Tum Tugger ....Terrence V. Mann
Sillabub..Whitney Kershaw
Skimbleshanks...Reed Jones
Tantomile ....Janet L. Hubert
Tumblebrutus..Robert Hoshour
Victoria ....Cynthia Onrubia
Cat Chorus......................Walter Charles, Susan Powers,
Carol Richards and Joel Robertson.

Frank Rich ON

Glengarry Glen Ross

BY David Mamet

March 25, 1984

John Golden Theater

378 Performances

David Mamet   PAUL O. BOISVERT FOR THE NEW YORK TIMES

The only mellifluous words in David Mamet's new play are of those of its title—*Glengarry Glen Ross*. In this scalding comedy about small-time, cutthroat real-estate salesmen, most of the language is abrasive—even by the standards of the author's *American Buffalo*. . . .

Yet the strange—and wonderful—thing about the play at the Golden is Mr. Mamet's ability to turn almost every word inside out. The playwright makes all-American music—hot jazz and wounding blues—out of his salesmen's scatalogical native lingo. In the jagged riffs of coarse, monosyllabic words, we hear and feel both the exhilaration and the sweaty desperation of the huckster's calling. . . .

Mr. Mamet's talent for burying layers of meaning into simple, precisely distilled, idiomatic language—a talent that can only be compared to Harold Pinter's—is not the sum of *Glengarry Glen Ross*. This may well be the most accomplished play its author has yet given us. As Mr. Mamet's command of dialogue has now reached its dazzling pitch, so has his mastery of theatrical form. Beneath the raucous, seemingly inane surface of *Glengarry,* one finds not only feelings but a detective story with a surprise ending.

GLENGARRY GLEN ROSS, by David Mamet; directed by Gregory Mosher; lighting by Kevin Rigdon, costumes by Nan Cibula; sets by Michael Merritt. Presented by Elliot Martin, the Shubert Organization, Arnold Bernhard and the Goodman Theater.

Shelly Levene	Robert Prosky
John Williamson	J. T. Walsh
Dave Moss	James Tolkan
George Aaronow	Mike Nussbaum
Richard Roma	Joe Mantegna
James Lingk	Lane Smith
Baylen	Jack Wallace

Joe Mantegna *(left)* and James Tolkan BRIGITTE LACOMBE

Frank Rich ON

Ma Rainey's Black Bottom

BY August Wilson

———

October 11, 1984

Cort Theater

275 Performances

August Wilson CHESTER HIGGINS, JR./THE NEW YORK
TIMES

In *Ma Rainey's Black Bottom,* the writer August Wilson sends the entire history of black America crashing down upon our heads. This play is a searing inside account of what white racism does to its victims—and it floats on the same authentic artistry as the blues music it celebrates. Harrowing as *Ma Rainey's* can be, it is also funny, salty, carnal and lyrical. Like his real-life heroine, the legendary singer Gertrude (Ma) Rainey, Mr. Wilson articulates a legacy of unspeakable agony and rage in a spellbinding voice.

The play is Mr. Wilson's first to arrive in New York, and it reached here, via the Yale Repertory Theater, under the sensitive hand of the man who was born to direct it, Lloyd Richards. On Broadway, Mr. Richards has honed *Ma Rainey's* to its finest form. What's more, the director brings us an exciting young actor—Charles S. Dutton—along with his extraordinary dramatist. One wonders if the electricity at the Cort is the same audiences felt when Mr. Richards, Lorraine Hansberry and Sidney Poitier stormed into Broadway with *A Raisin in the Sun* a quarter-century ago.

Left to right: Charles S. Dutton, Leonard Jackson, Theresa Merritt, Robert Judd and Joe Seneca   BERT ANDREWS PHOTO

MA RAINEY'S BLACK BOTTOM, by August Wilson; directed by Lloyd Richards, costumes by Daphne Pascucci; setting by Charles Henry McClennahan; lighting by Peter Maradudin; music direction by Dwight Andrews; sound by Jan Nebozenko; production stage manager, Mortimer Halpern; associated producers, Bart Berman, Hart Productions and William P. Suter. The Yale Repertory Theater production presented by Ivan Bloch, Robert Cole and Frederick M. Zollo.

Sturdyvant.................................John Carpenter
Irvin ....Lou Criscuolo
Cutler ....Joe Seneca
Toldeo..Robert Judd
Slow Drag................................Leonard Jackson
Levee ....Charles S. Dutton
Ma Rainey ....Theresa Merritt
Dussie Mae...................................Aleta Mitchell
Sylvester...................Scott Davenport-Richards
Policeman...........................Christopher Loomis

Theresa Merritt as the jazz singer Ma Rainey   BERT ANDREWS STUDIO

Frank Rich ON

Angels in America (Part 1: Millennium Approaches)

BY Tony Kushner

May 4, 1993

Walter Kerr Theater

367 Performances

Tony Kushner EDWARD KEATING/THE NEW YORK TIMES

History is about to crack open," says Ethel Rosenberg, back from the dead, as she confronts a cadaverous Roy Cohn, soon to die of AIDS, in his East Side town house. "Something's going to give," says a Brooklyn housewife so addicted to Valium she thinks she is in the Antarctic. The year is 1985. It is fifteen years until the next millennium. And a young man drenched in death fevers in his Greenwich Village bedroom hears a persistent throbbing, a thunderous heartbeat, as if the heavens were about to give birth to a miracle so that he might be born again.

That is the astonishing theatrical landscape, intimate and epic, of Tony Kushner's *Angels in America,* which made its much-awaited Broadway debut at the Walter Kerr Theater last night. This play has already been talked about so much that you may feel you have already seen it, but believe me, you haven't, even if you actually have. The new New York production is the third I've seen of *Millennium Approaches. . . .* As directed with crystalline lucidity by George C. Wolfe and ignited by blood-churning performances by Ron Leibman and Stephen Spinella, this staging only adds to the impression that Mr. Kushner has written the most thrilling American play in years.

Ron Leibman as the political wheeler-dealer Roy Cohn, a cynical and self-hating closet case, in *Angels in America*.
JOAN MARCUS

ANGELS IN AMERICA: MILLENNIUM APPROACHES by Tony Kushner; directed by George C. Wolfe; sets by Robin Wagner; costumes by Toni-Leslie James; lighting by Jules Fisher; music by Anthony Davis; additional music by Michael Ward; sound by Scott Lehrer; production supervisors, Gene O'Donovan and Neil A. Mazzella; production stage manager, Perry Cline. Produced in association with the New York Shakespeare Festival. Associate producers, Dennis Grimaldi, Marilyn Hall, Ron Kastner, Hal Luftig/126 Second Avenue Corporation and Suki Sandler; executive producers, Benjamin Mordecai and Robert Cole. Presented by Jujamcyn Theaters and Mark Taper Forum/Gordon Davidson, with

Margo Lion, Susan Quint Gallin, Jon B. Platt, the Baruch-Frankel-Viertel Group and Frederick Zollo, in association with Herb Alpert.

Rabbi Chemelwitz, Henry, Hannah Pitt and Ethel Rosenberg ....Kathleen Chalfant
Roy Cohn and Prior 2 ....Ron Leibman
Joe Pitt, Prior 1 and the Eskimo ...David Marshall Grant
Harper Pitt and Martin Heller ....Marcia Gay Harden
Mr. Lies and Belize ....Jeffrey Wright
Louis Ironson ....Joe Mantello
Prior Walter and Man in the Park.........Stephen Spinella
Emily, Ella Chapter, the Woman in the South Bronx and the Angel ....Ellen McLaughlin

Ben Brantley ON

Rent

BOOK, MUSIC AND LYRICS BY
Jonathan Larson

February 13, 1996

New York Theater Workshop

2213+ Performances

Jonathan Larson AP PHOTO/COLUMBIA UNIVERSITY

The subject of the work is death at an early age. And in one of the dark dramatic coincidences theater occasionally springs on us, its thirty-five-year-old author died only weeks before its opening. Yet no one who attends Jonathan Larson's *Rent,* the exhilarating, landmark rock opera at the New York Theater Workshop, is likely to mistake it for a wake.

This vigorous tale of a marginal band of artists in Manhattan's East Village, a contemporary answer to *La Bohème,* rushes forward on an electric current of emotion that is anything but morbid. Sparked by a young, intensely vibrant cast directed by Michael Greif and sustained by a glittering, inventive score, the work finds a transfixing brightness in the shadow of AIDS. Puc-

cini's ravishingly melancholy work seemed . . . to romance death; Mr. Larson's spirited score and lyrics defy it.

Rent inevitably invites reflections on the incalculable loss of its composer, who died of an aortic aneurysm on January 25, but it also shimmers with hope for the future of the American musical. . . . While Mr. Larson plays wittily with references to Puccini's masterpiece, the excitement around *Rent* more directly recalls the impact made by a dark-horse musical Off Broadway in 1967: *Hair.* Like that meandering, genial portrait of draft-dodging hippies, this production gives a pulsing, unexpectedly catchy voice to one generation's confusion, angst and anarchic, pleasure-seeking vitality.

The cast of *Rent* SARA KRULWICH/THE NEW YORK TIMES

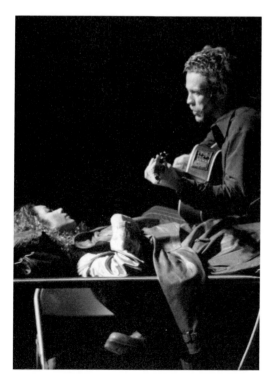

Adam Pascal as Roger Davis and Daphne Rubin-Vega as Mimi Marquez in *Rent* SARA KRULWICH/THE NEW YORK TIMES

RENT by Jonathan Larson; directed by Michael Greif; musical director, Tim Weil; choreography by Marlies Yearby; sets by Paul Clay; costumes by Angela Wendt; lighting by Blake Burba; sound by Darron L. West; dramaturge, Lynn M. Thomson; musical arranger, Steve Skinner; assistant director, Martha Banta; original concept and additional lyrics, Billy Aronson; film, Tony Gerber; production manager, Susan R. White; production stage manager, Crystal Huntington; assistant stage manager, Catherine J. Haley. New Director/New Directions Series. Presented by New York Theater Workshop, James C. Nicola, artistic director; Nancy Kassak Diekmann, managing director.

Mark Cohen...Anthony Rapp
Roger Davis ....Adam Pascal
Tom Collins...Jesse L. Martin
Benjamin Coffin 3d ....Taye Diggs
Joanne Jefferson ....Fredi Walker
Angel Schunard.......................Wilson Jermaine Heredia
Mimi Marquez..................................Daphne Rubin-Vega
Maureen Johnson...Idina Menzel
With Kristen Lee Kelly, Byron Utley, Gwen Stewart, Timothy Britten Parker, Gilles Chiasson, Rodney Hicks and Aiko Nakasone

Ben Brantley ON

The Emperor Jones

BY Eugene O'Neill

March 12, 1998

The Performing Garage

15 Performances

Kate Valk *(left)* in the title role and Willem Dafoe as
Smithers   MARY GEARHART, THE WOOSTER GROUP

"An uncommonly powerful and imaginative performance," wrote Alexander Woollcott in the fall of 1920 of a little-known actor named Charles S. Gilpin, who was appearing in a strange, bruising new play that had uptown cosmopolites swarming to a small theater in Greenwich Village.

After a series of marginal roles, Gilpin finally had a star part: the title character of the black railroad porter turned West Indies monarch in Eugene O'Neill's *Emperor Jones.* Woollcott rounded off his tribute with a coda you might have thought was unnecessary: "Mr. Gilpin is a Negro."

Seventy-eight years later, *The Emperor Jones* has been revived by the Wooster Group, some blocks south of where the work was first seen. The drama still seems strange and bruising, and it has again provided the occasion for an uncommonly powerful and imaginative performance in the title role. That part is played by Kate Valk. Ms. Valk is a Caucasian. . . .

The particular triumph of Elizabeth LeComte's interpretation, which also features Willem Dafoe, is its ability to relocate the play in a contemporary context while holding on to the shadowy, hypnotic qualities that first unsettled audiences of the 1920s. You should know that while doing so, the production uses such unlikely (but for this company, classic) devices as a set of television monitors, a wheelchair and Kabuki-flavored soft-shoe routines.

Kate Valk and Willem Dafoe   MARY GEARHART, THE WOOSTER GROUP

THE EMPEROR JONES by Eugene O'Neill; directed by Elizabeth LeCompte; music by David Linton; sound by James Johnson and John Collins; video by Christopher Kondek; designed by Jim Clayburgh; lighting by Georg Bugiel; lighting consultant, Jennifer Tipton; costumes and choreography by the Wooster Group; stage manager, Clay Hapaz. Presented by the Wooster Group.

Brutus Jones ....Kate Valk
Smithers ....Willem Dafoe
Stage Assistants ....Dave Shelley and Ari Fliakos

The Unforgettable Productions of the Century

Peter Pan

BY James Barrie

November 7, 1905

Empire Theatre

223 Performances

Maude Adams scored a critical and popular triumph as Peter Pan.   THE NEW YORK TIMES PHOTO ARCHIVES

Peter Pan	Miss Maude Adams
Mr. Darling	Ernest Lawford
Mrs. Darling	Grace Henderson
Wendy Moira Angela Darling	Mildred Morris
John Napoleon Darling	Walter Robinson
Michael Nicolas Darling	Martha McGraw
Nana	Charles H. Weston
Tinker Bell	Jane Wren
Tootles	Violet Rand
Nibs	Lula Peck
Slightly	Frances Sedgwick
Curly	Mabel Kipp
First Twin	Katherine Kappell
Second Twin	Ella Gilroy
James Hook	Ernest Lawford
Smee	Thomas McGrath
Starkey	Wallace Jackson
Cookson	William Henderson
Ceceo	Paul Tharp
Mullins	Thomas Valentine
Jukes	Harry Gynette
Noodler	Frederick Raymond
Great Big Little Panther	Lloyd Carleton
Tiger Lilly	Margaret Gordon
Liza	Anna Wheaton

Barrie, the fanciful; Barrie, the one-who-will-never-grow-up; Barrie, the talented father of so many sweet and delicate-mind children, has introduced to us another of his fledglings—Peter Pan by name. *Peter Pan* isn't a play. It is just a gentle jogging of the memory and a reminiscence of your childhood. It is what you remember thinking long ago, or, if you didn't think it, you should have thought it, and weren't a normal child, anyway, so it doesn't matter about you.

Peter comes at such an opportune time, just when there is to be heard in the farthest far distance the jingle of Santa's reindeer bells, and when each of us has a deep-rooted yearning—which none of us would be weak enough to confess—for the power so long gone of feeling the old Christmassy glow and expectation, and the perfectly mad enthusiasm and the pure unadulterated joy of little-boy-and-girldom. To each and every one who has the faintest stirring in his heart of such a yearning, let it be said, "You needn't confess it if you're ashamed, but just run over and listen to the message of little Peter Pan, and you can lay the most expensive shaving mug you expect to get at Christmas (or you, Madam, the box of Paris gloves) that you will not be drawn out of yourself into forgetting the latest scandals, and the existence of those strange places of strange amusements called theatres—and you'll lose.

In *The Little White Bird* Peter Pan was a joy to read about. And in the person of Maude Adams, so delicately suited to the child-lore of which the story is a part, Peter Pan is a joy to meet. Winsome, lonely little dreamer of dreams, Peter has lost his shadow. It all happened (don't let there be any dispute, if you please, about the certainty of that. Of course it happened!) because Peter was too fond of gazing in at the children in the nursery, and his shadow got caught in the window sash.

Poor little Peter, he wants that shadow, which has been found and kept carefully hidden away in a big drawer by Mrs. Darling, the mother of the three little Darlings, Wendy, John, and Michael, in whose nursery we first meet Peter. So he determines to recover what is his and when the children are asleep he steals in at the window, accompanied by a glancing flame of light and a musical tintinnabulation, ephemeral witnesses that Tinker Bell (of the ilk of the fairies) is his companion, and makes a search for his shadow.

But Wendy wakes, and with the maternal instinct which is sometimes very strong in tiny women of six or so she offers Peter her sympathy and a kiss. But Peter is ignorant of that most familiar observation of nursery life, and so Wendy withdraws her proffer and gives him a thimble instead. And ever after that to Peter a thimble and a kiss are identical. John and Michael are awakened now, and Peter regales the three with the story (oh, blessed be Barrie,) of how children, lost through nursemaidery carelessness, are given sanctuary in the far-off-Never-Never-Never-Land—his home. Their curiosity being aroused, Peter teaches them to fly, and they depart, under the self-assigned guardianship of Wendy, who is already full of the delightful assurance that she shall play mother to the whole party of motherless children in the about-to-be-visited lands.

When they arrive (in the next act) they find the ill-starred charges of careless nursemaids living together most cozily, making their homes in the trunks of trees, and Wendy, true to her instinct, mothers them, one and all. Wendy and John and Michael and the others (all save Peter) fall into the hands of the pirate horde at the head of which is the fearsome James Hook, so-called because of the fashion of his right arm, which ends in a hook instead of a hand, à la Captain Cuttle. (Question: How did the doughty James style himself before his hook came into requisition and christened him, and whence this custom of selecting surnames so late in life?) But to continue: Things look dark for the little hostages, and the audience should properly (if they are any audience at all) prepare to wipe fey beads of terror from their brows. But

pshaw! where is our faith? Have you never heard of Peter Pan? Know you not that "Peter the Avenger" is near? Fear not, he will save them. But how?

Like all men of cruel mould, the Terrible Hook has his vulnerable point, his pet bugbear as it were. This same bugbear (somewhat incongruous this) is in shape of a crocodile, who has feasted off James Hook's hand, when James's hand was where his hook is now. The crocodile, peculiar in tastes—very—and with a mind to finish the meal it had begun, consecrates its life to the mission of pursuing the rest of Hook. But it is unfortunate in its internal organism, for a clock swallowed long ago, and never properly digested, announces its approach in the most baffling way, to the mingled terror and delight of Hook.

Peter is wily. Peter provides himself with a clock and frightens the pirate into hiding. He loosens the bonds of his little friends, saves them from "walking the plank," and sends Hook and his crew splashing over the side. Home now for Wendy, John, and Michael Darlings, and happiness for everybody—everybody except little Peter Pan, who is left to gaze in at the window as of old, a pathetically lonely little lad, half child, half fairy.

Maude Adams is Peter—most ingratiatingly simple and sympathetic. True to the fairy idea, true to the child nature, lovely, sweet, and wholesome. She combines all the delicate sprightliness and the gentle, wistful pathos necessary to the role, and she is supremely in touch with the spirit of it all.

It was a night of triumph for Maude Adams. But though she is the centre of it all, there are several others in the cast who deserve more space for praise than can be spared just now. Especially Mildred Morris, whose task next to hers was perhaps the most difficult; Ernest Lawford, who in his dual role of Papa and Pirate developed the proper ferocity to suit the case, and his chief bloodthirsty assistant, Thomas McGrath, who was also most excellently ferocious. Violet Rand and Anna Wheaton contributed a share of the generally sympathetic acting, while the dog, the crocodile, and the rest of the live stock were—well, they were very much like life.

All New York may not believe in fairies, but there was no doubt last night, when Tinker Bell was dying, that the audience in the Empire, irrespective of age or condition, had gotten back very near to second childhood.

Sarah Bernhardt's
La Dame aux Camélias
BY Alexander Dumas *fils*

December 12, 1905

Lyric Theatre

Sarah Bernhardt's performance as Marguerite Gauthier ranged from girlish ingenuousness to heartbreaking pathos.
W & D DOWNEY PHOTOGRAPHERS

Marguerite Gauthier	Mme. Sarah Bernhardt
Armand Duval	M. Deneubourg
Saint Guadens	M. Chameroy
De Varville	M. Krauss
Georges Duval	M. Piron
Le Docteur	M. Cauroy
Compte de Giray	M. Guide
Gustave	M. Puylagarde
Gaston Rieux	M. Bary
Un Domestique	M. Habay
Un Commissionaire	M. Cartereau
Nichette	Mlle. Seylor
Nanine	Mme. Boulanger
Olympe	Mlle. Cerda
Prudence	Mme. Irma Perrot
Anais	Mlle. Alisson
Un Groom	Mlle. Duc
Esther	Mlle. MacLean
Une Dame	Mlle. Roger

The role of Marguerite Gauthier was played by Sarah Bernhardt at the Lyric Theatre last night, which is equivalent to the statement that, for the time, the unfortunate Lady of the Camellias became a living, breathing, humanized being, enforcing rapt attention, demanding admiration, compelling sympathy, no matter what one's previous views may have been upon the dubious ethics involved in the familiar Dumas play.

The ordinary superlatives of appreciation fall short when one seeks to describe the actress's achievement in this role. More years ago than one likes to remember she made it her own, and exercised the potent spell which was again manifest last night. Time has worked few changes in her methods, has had little effect upon the means she employs to gain her ends.

If there has been any change at all in her playing of the part it is perceptible only in an emphasized repression here and there, a suggestion now and again of an effort to produce her effects with the least possible expenditure of energy of voice and gesture and movement. Her Marguerite Gauthier stands revealed as a portrait, painted for the most part in pastel shades, its subdued tints only now and then relieved by a flare of brilliant coloring.

Of moments of excessive passion the characterization has few, but in the infrequent instances in which suffering and disappointment give the cue for an outburst of emotion, Mme. Bernhardt still succeeds in wringing the heart as few players, we may assume, have ever succeeded in doing. As a matter of fact, not to have seen her as Marguerite Gauthier is not to have seen her at her greatest.

In the varying passages of the five long acts her

magnificent accomplishments are in evidence with a steady progression from the lighter phases of a most natural comedy method to the equally natural but more infinitely moving power of heart-rending pathos. As in her performance the night before, the chief occasion for astonishment here is the realization of the fact that to all intents and purposes she is as young to-day as she was forty years ago.

Occasionally, to be sure, her face revealed in the full glare of light, shows some lines of time underneath its mask of chalk and rouge, but in the Bernhardt's case it is apparently a reversal of the old saying. Here one is justified in believing that the woman is only as old as she feels.

There are actresses on our stage to-day, capable, clever ingénues, who, with all the natural graces in their favor, could not begin to approximate in simulation her reflection of the spirit and abandon of youth. Still, even in the gayest passages of the first two acts one was made to feel the undercurrent of seriousness, the suggested note of impending sadness.

In the presence of such a work of art as Mme. Bernhardt provided last night the ordinary processes of analytical criticism seem hopelessly inadequate. One might indulge in all the verbal extravagances, utilize a broad vocabulary, and fall back upon a handy book of synonyms without feeling that justice had been done or the subject exhausted.

To the reviewer, hurried and hastening—for the performance lasted until well on to midnight and linotypes and forms wait for no man—there come memories of scene after scene of the most proficient employment of the means of dramatic expression and execution that can be imagined. Time is lacking for their description even were a description possible. But one may recall in a word the scene with the elder Duval, which, conceived and executed for a time in a spirit of almost girlish ingenuousness and charm, developed subsequently into an exhibition of hysteria and moving pathos.

Here, as elsewhere, there was never a suggestion of excess, not the slightest semblance of any-thing that resembled ranting or the tearing of a passion to tatters. And in its very restraint, suggestive of the weakened physical capacity of this creature whose powers were being slowly undermined by disease, there was a tremendously increased impressiveness.

In the fifth act, with her slowly sinking vitality, she conveys a touching, childish gleefulness during the exquisite reading of her precious letter—it is a never-to-be-forgotten accomplishment, a perfect fragment of a perfect whole. Her death scene and the scene with Armand and Nanine, just preceding, are so utterly heartbreaking that they leave one with a sensation of comfortless desolation which is the best possible proof of the wonder of her art.

The Armand Duval of M. Deneubourg is more than ordinarily competent for the most part, though it falls a little short of what one might desire in the occasional dynamic outbursts, such as that with which Armand greets his father after the reading of Marguerite's letter at the close of the third act. In the final scene, however, his exhibition of emotion is so simulative of sincerity that it adds no little to the general impressiveness. The Prudence of Mme. Irma Perrot and the Georges Duval of M. Piron were the other conspicuously competent contributions to the performance.

The Little Millionaire
BY George M. Cohan

September 25, 1911

Cohan's Theatre

192 Performances

THE LITTLE MILLIONAIRE, a musical farce in three acts, by George M. Cohan.

Henry Spooner...Jerry J. Cohan
Robert Spooner....................................George M. Cohan
George Russell..George Parsons
Bill Costigan...Tom Lewis

Roscoe Handover	Sydney Jarvis
Danny Wheeler	Earl Benham
Edward Plumber	Donald Crisp
Rudolph	Donald Crisp
Starter at the "Beaux Arts"	William Ford
Mrs. Prescott	Mrs. Helen F. Cohan
Goldie Gray	Lila Rhodes
Berdina Busby	Julia Ralph
Bertha Burnham	Josephine Whittell
Miss Primper	Maude Allen
Mary	Amy Mortimer
Policeman	Dore Rogers
Page Boy	Charles W. Well

George M. Cohan, like necessity, knows no law. Which is one of the reasons, perhaps, why a George M. Cohan show is like nothing else in the heavens above (presumably) or on the earth below. But that is not the principal reason. The success of such an entertainment as *The Little Millionaire*—and of its success there is no doubt—is due to the fact that Mr. Cohan knows his little book from the first page to the last and, as he might say, then some, maybe.

And so *The Little Millionaire*, written by him, acted by him, and produced by him after a more or less protracted absence from the stage, represents him at his very best, and a best which is considerably ahead of what he has done in his earlier shows. Of their kind, these shows had much the same go and zip which kept last night's audience keyed up to concert pitch. But there was often in them something of bad taste, something which made sensitive people just a little sorry to see them as popular as they were. Exception of this kind cannot be taken to this newest entertainment. The best proof of the fact is that the one single broad line in the piece, and a line which will probably come out, did not get a laugh. The audience had been put into an entirely different kind of mood.

The Little Millionaire is in three acts, the first and third being musical comedy, the second carrying on the story in farce form without any musical accompaniment, and for the most part carrying it on very briskly and satisfactorily. This story, involving a youth who is in love with a chorus girl, but must forfeit his fortune if he marries without his father's consent, is treated by Mr. Cohan seriously now and then, and, again, in a vein of bur-

lesque. Some big laughs come from the introduction of two characters, supposedly the villains of the piece, who repeatedly announce that what they are doing is "dirty work," eventually describing their presence on the stage in a duet, "We Do the Dirty Work," which, like almost every song in the piece, is remarkable for the cleverness of the lyrics, the adroitness of the word combinations, and the descriptive quality of the melody and accompanying orchestration.

Best of all, perhaps, Mr. Cohan makes his people get the lyrics over intelligently.

Again through the piece garnering laughs with every entrance comes another figure, big Tom Lewis, without whom no Cohan show would seem complete, and for whom the author has written a better part than his own. It is Lewis, who, as Bill Costigan, a wine agent, always "on edge," dogs the hero's heels, follows him into his home, selects his own room, changing from a blue to a pink, and ultimately to a red one, and always for the sake of persuading the youth not to marry—as he, Costigan, already knows what it means to pay $1,000 alimony monthly.

Again in a capital ensemble number the same charge to remain single is impressed upon the young man, this time by the friends of the chorus, who have been called in to "foil the villains" in an attempted blackmailing scheme. These friends must hear the joyfully sung announcement of the coming marriage, but come back in minor key to beg the hero not to do it. Finally the marriage ceremony itself is performed in a capital pantomimic dance, with the best man first dancing on, the maids of honor following, the bride and bridegroom toeing it to the altar, and even the minister with book and ring entering in the same festive song and dance style to make it all complete.

Before this happens, however, there have been developments. For the little millionaire's father, returning from abroad, is anxious to announce his own engagement. He fears what his son will say as much as the latter has feared him. And the farce situation in which mutual misunderstandings alternate with mutual rejoicings at glad tidings is so well handled that it seems almost like fresh material. Of course the woman for whom father "has fallen," is the very one to whom Costigan has been paying alimony, and at sight of the wine agent she drops her handbag and runs. Costigan, presently picking up the bag, opens it, extracts from it a large roll of bills, and says, "Welcome home." Then the curtain falls.

Another act is required to straighten out the complications, but it is more important in respect to the fact that it brings the best song numbers of the piece.

Previously, of course, there had been a rollicking one about the flag, with a military drill, and a delightfully swingy one, "Come with Me to My Bungalow," while Mr. Cohan himself has had opportunities for his characteristic dancing alone, and with his cousin, Lila Rhodes, a near-Cohan, who is piquant, graceful, and dances like a sunbeam. Then the Cohans—father and son—do a step or two together. And the keynote of the show has been struck in a sparkling lyric sung by a chorus of chauffeurs, while a group of very pretty, smaller dancers have flirted in and out, keeping up the general lively pace.

Now the stage is given over to the "big" song number, "The Musical Moon," satirizing very cleverly the most popular of numbers, and followed by a richly melodious song, "Oh, You Wonderful Girl," which might be a satire of all the lovers in the world. In another vein is "Barnum Had the Right Idea," sung by Mr. Cohan. It might be described as the hymn of all showmen, and should form a part of the ceremony at the dedication services of all new theatres. And then, "The Dancing Wedding," already referred to, which brings the final note of novelty to an entertainment in which novelties abound.

In addition to himself, his clever father and mother, his charming little cousin, and the ever-present Tom Lewis, each of whom contributes materially to the success of the entertainment, Mr. Cohan's company contains other very capable people. Of these Julia Ralph, George Parsons, Sydney Jarvis, Earl Benham, Josephine Whittell, Amy Mortimer, and Maude Allen are each entitled to a word of praise.

Alexander Woollcott ON
Heartbreak House
BY George Bernard Shaw

November 10, 1920

Garrick Theatre

125 Performances

HEARTBREAK HOUSE, a comedy in three acts by George Bernard Shaw.

Ellie Dunn	Elizabeth Risdon
Nurse Guinness	Helen Westley
Captain Shotover	Albert Perry
Lady Utterword	Lucille Watson
Hesione Hushabye	Effie Shannon
Mazzini Dunn	Erskine Sanford
Hector Hushabye	Fred Eric
Boss Mangan	Dudley Digges
Randall Utterword	Ralph Roeder
The Burglar	Henry Travers

With the first production on any stage of the new Shaw play called *Heartbreak House,* the Theatre Guild recorded last evening its most ambitious effort and, all things considered, its most creditable achievement. At the Garrick this brilliant comedy is superbly mounted and, with one fairly insignificant exception, wisely and richly cast. An admirable play has been added to the season's rather scanty list and overnight that list has quite doubled in cerebral values.

Heartbreak House, despite the doldrums of tedium into which its second act flounders toward the end, is quite the larkiest and most amusing one that Shaw has written in many a year, and in its graver moments the more familiar mood of Shavian exasperation gives way to accents akin to Cassandra's. Of course that second act seems the more wearing because of our habit and disposition to a lunch-counter tempo, even in the theatre, but inasmuch as the Theatre Guild is not permitted to tamper with the sacred text, it is too bad that its company should feel so oppressed by it.

A good many of last evening's blurred

impressions can be traced to players so uneasily conscious of the play's unwonted length that they rattled nervously through their pieces. It will all go better when the conclusion is forced upon them that a mumbled scene may save time, but is the last device in the world to ward off boredom.

Heartbreak House is Shaw's Bunyanesque name for cultured, leisured England (or Europe, for that matter) before the war—as distinguished from that part of leisure England called Horse-back Hall, wherein the stables are the real centre of the household, and wherein, if any visitor wants to play the piano, he must upset the whole room, there are so many things piled on it.

The play is his picture of the idly charming but viciously inert and detached people who dwell in Heartbreak House, using their hard-earned (by some one else) leisure to no purpose. They are loitering at the halfway station on the road to sophistication. They have been stripped of their illusions and pretense, but instead of using this freedom to some end they sit around naked and doing nothing, except, perhaps, catching mortal colds.

The moral of the piece is spoken by Captain Shotover. It is always possible to find the clear, honest eyes of Bernard Shaw peering out from behind the thin disguise of one of his characters, and it is tempting in this comedy to identify him at times with this disconcerting and slightly mad old mariner whom the natives suspect of an ability to explode dynamite by looking at it. Captain Shotover is sick of a languid reliance on an overruling Providence. One of the casual ways of Providence with drunken skippers is to run them on the rocks. Not that anything happens, he hastily explains. Nothing but the smash of the drunken skipper's ship on the rocks, the splintering of her rotten timbers, the tearing of her rusty plates, the drowning of the crew like rats in a trap.

"And this ship that we are all in?" asks the heroic Hector. "This soul's prison we call England?"

"The Captain is in his bunk," retorts Captain Shotover, "drinking bottled ditch-water, and the crew is gambling in the forecastle. She will strike and sink and split. Do you think the laws of God

will be suspended in favor of England because you were born in it?"

No wonder the agitated Hector asks what he should do about it.

"Learn your business as an Englishman," replies the Captain, tartly.

"And what may my business as an Englishman be, pray?"

"Navigation—Learn it and live, or leave it and be damned."

But just then the war visits Heartbreak House in the guise of an air raid that sounds from a distance like Beethoven. It enraptures some, alarms others, exhilarates everybody, kills a burglar and a business man who had hidden too near the Captain's store of dynamite, destroys the rectory and passes on, leaving Heartbreak House not greatly changed, and with no firmer foundations than it had had before.

First honors in the cast must go to Henry Travers as the very Shavian burglar who serves so admirably the indisposition of Heartbreak House toward community service; to Effie Shannon as Mrs. Hushabye; to Elizabeth Risdon as Ellie Dunn; to Dudley Digges (who also directed the production) as Boss Mangan, and to Erskine Sanford as the gentle Mazzini Dunn.

Albert Perry as Captain Shotover, one of the most delightful characters Shaw ever invented, and Fred Eric as Hector Hushabye seem to have the right quality and understanding, but last night they forfeited a good deal of what is in their scenes by missing their right rhythm with almost painful regularity. Here was a defect you felt would pass.

It seems probable, too, that Lucille Watson will be very useful around the premises as soon as she has been persuaded to speak distinctly enough for you to catch at least the drift of her remarks. After all, Shaw never yet wrote a scene that could be expounded in dumb-show. About Ralph Roeder in the role of Randall, however, it seems unlikely that anything can be done.

The air raid which jounces *Heartbreak House* out of its purely conversational vein is capitally managed at the Garrick and both the settings, by

Lee Simonson, are rich and beautiful. Indeed, they are almost too handsome. Somehow, a lovely investiture of a Shaw play seems a little incongruous—like perfuming the board room in a bank. The austerity of his text seems to chafe against the Simonson opulence as Shaw himself might rebel disgustedly at any *étalage de luxe.*

Ziegfeld Follies of 1921

June 21, 1921

Globe Theatre

119 Performances

Florenz Ziegfeld was the era's foremost producer of spectacular musical revues. WIDE WORLD PHOTOS

ZIEGFELD FOLLIES OF 1921, a revue in two acts and twenty-nine scenes. Dialogue by Channing Pollock, Willard Mack and Ralph Spence; lyrics by Gene Buck and Bud De Silva; music by Victor Herbert, Rudolf Friml and Dave Stamper.
Principals.............Raymond Hitchcock, Vera Michelena, Ray Dooley, Mary Eaton, Mary Milburn, Florence O'Denishawn, Mary Lewis, Marie Astrova, Van and Schenck, W. C. Fields, John Clarke, O'Donnell and Blair, Frank and Albert Innis, Herbert Hoey, Janet

Stone, Mandal Brothers, the Keene Twins, Edna Wheaton, the Darling Twins, Phil Dwyer, Jessie Reed, Fanny Brice, Germaine Mitty and M. Tillio.

Mr. Ziegfeld's pre-eminence as a producer of lavish revue was evidenced anew at the Globe Theatre last night with the presentation before a first-night gathering such as only Mr. Ziegfeld's annual institution can attract, of *The Follies of 1921*. It may be reported, practically without reservation, that it is a good *Follies* this year—about the best of them all, as a matter of fact. Into the three or more hours of his newest harlequinade Mr. Ziegfeld has managed to crowd nearly everything that makes for popular revue—riots of color in settings and costumes, luxurious silks and satins, the best-looking chorus of this or any other year, some remarkable dancing, a dash of fair-to-middling singing, considerable comedy and an undefinable something that must simply be set down as tone. It is, let it be repeated, a good show.

Many hands have contributed to the fashioning of this new *Follies*—the program credits more than a score in various capacities. From this multitude it is difficult to single any one who contributed in greatest degree, but the youthful James Reynolds must certainly be mentioned high up in the list. Mr. Reynolds designed the scenery and costumes for two of the most gorgeous of last night's scenes—one a Persian episode of the twelfth century, the other a scene in the royal gardens at Versailles. Mr. Reynolds is fantastic, exotic, acutely imaginative. Ben Ali Haggin, to whom *Follies* audiences are better accustomed, is another contributor of beauty—his two tableaux are marvels of blending colors and flashing lights. And, of course, there is also Joseph Urban, now—so swift the tide in these days—almost a staid old conservative in the fashioning of stage settings.

Among the performers also there are divers successes to be recorded. There is, for example, a newcomer from Paris who is certain to be a sensation in these parts. Her name is Germaine Mitty, and with one Tillio as her partner, she appears in two dances. She is a leaping, lithesome person, performing difficult athletic feats with an easy grace that brings them all into the dance. Florence O'Denishawn, with her nearly bare body flashing in the light, is at her best in the Persian number, and appears later in more modest attire to prove that she can even sing in a small way.

There is, too, Fannie Brice in divers guises, but always seeming a little funnier than on the preceding occasion. This time, however, she has also a serious song, for Mr. Ziegfeld is still at his trick of making actors out of jugglers, tragedians out of comedians, and singers out of dancers—all for the glory of the *Follies*. Miss Brice has the best song of the evening—an elaborately staged number entitled "My Man," in French Apache vein. Earlier in the evening Miss Brice had been deliriously funny as an Ethel Barrymore Camille, with Raymond Hitchcock and W. C. Fields assisting as Lionel and Jack.

Mr. Fields juggles nary a jug on this occasion—Mr. Ziegfeld's rounding-off process, continued through the years, has finally brought him forth merely as an actor. As for Mr. Hitchcock, he has several moments of hilarity, but he has not been equipped with the best material in the world, and he is a bit outshone. He is, for example, more dependent upon the written word than is the diminutive Ray Dooley, who was vastly amusing last night in various juvenile characterizations. Incidentally, Miss Dooley gave a remarkably lifelike impersonation of Jack Dempsey, incredible as that feat may sound for one of her appearance and dimensions.

The pleasant-faced Mary Milburn, ever so reminiscent of Christie MacDonald, sings several numbers appealingly, but John Clarke, remembered as the baritone of *Monsieur Beaucaire*, is given no number that shows his voice at his best. Van and Schenck are present and singing as of yore, and are even given individual numbers to carry. There were those who, when the piping treble of Mr. Schenck floated on the air, found solace in the fact that he was not required to fill the larger auditorium of the New Amsterdam, where the *Follies* is customarily quartered.

In comedy way the *Follies* has a hilarious subway scene, a prize fight between Miss Brice and

Miss Dooley, a bit of magic by Mr. Hitchcock and a slam-bang episode contributed by Charles O'Donnell. Mr. O'Donnell—from vaudeville, patently—encounters various ill fortune while attempting no more strenuous feat than tuning a piano. Perhaps it is permissible while on the subject of comedy to lament the fact that a revue calling itself *The Follies of 1921* finds so scant inspiration in topical matters. But, of course, one cannot have everything. The *Follies* has nearly everything, and that is enough.

Alexander Woollcott ON
The Hairy Ape
BY Eugene O'Neill

March 9, 1922
Provincetown Theatre
108 Performances

THE HAIRY APE, a play in eight scenes, by Eugene G. O'Neill.

Robert Smith ....Louis Wolheim
Paddy..Henry O'Neill
Long ....Harold West
Mildred Douglas ....Mary Blair
Her Aunt...Eleanor Hutchison
Second Engineer...Jack Gude
A Guard...Harry Gottlieb
A Secretary..Harold McGee

The little theatre of the Provincetownsmen in Macdougal Street was packed to the doors with astonishment last evening as scene after scene unfolded in the new play by Eugene O'Neill. This was *The Hairy Ape,* a bitter, brutal, wildly fantastic play of nightmare hue and nightmare distortion. It is a monstrously uneven piece, now flamingly eloquent, now choked and thwarted and inarticulate. Like most of his writing for the theatre, it is the worse here and there for the lack of a fierce, unintimidated blue pencil. But it has a little greatness in it, and it seems rather absurd to fret overmuch about the undisciplined imagination of a young playwright towering so conspicuously above the milling, mumbling crowd of playwrights who have no imagination at all.

The Hairy Ape has been superbly produced. There is a rumor abroad that Arthur Hopkins, with a proprietary interest in the piece, has been lurking around its rehearsals and the program confesses that Robert Edmond Jones went down to Macdougal Street and took a hand with Cleon Throckmorton in designing the eight pictures which the play calls for. That preposterous little theatre has one of the most cramped stages New York has ever known, and yet on it the artists have created the illusion of vast spaces and endless perspectives. They drive one to the conclusion that when a stage seems pinched and little, it is the mind of the producer that is pinched and little. This time O'Neill, unbridled, set them a merry pace in the eccentric gait of his imaginings. They kept up with him.

O'Neill begins his fable by posing before you the greatest visible contrast in social and physical circumstances. He leads you up the gangplank of a luxurious liner bound for Europe. He plunges you first into the stokers' pit, thrusting you down among the men as they stumble in from the furnaces, hot, sweaty, choked with coal dust, brutish. Squirm as you may, he holds you while you listen to the rumble of their discontent, and while you listen, also, to speech more squalid than even an American audience heard before in an American theatre. It is true talk, all of it, and only those who have been so softly bred that they have never really heard the vulgate spoken in all its richness would venture to suggest that he has exaggerated it by so much as a syllable in order to agitate the refined. On the contrary.

Then, in a twinkling, he drags you (as the ghosts dragged Scrooge) up out of all this murk and thudding of engines and brawling of speech, to a cool, sweet, sunlit stretch of the hurricane deck, where, at lazy ease, lies the daughter of the President of the line's board of directors, a nonchalant dilettante who has found settlement work frightfully interesting and is simply crazy to go down among the stokers and see how the other half lives aboard ship.

Then follows the confrontation—the fool fop of a girl and the huge animal of a stoker who had taken a sort of dizzy romantic pride in himself and his work as something that was real in an unreal world, as something that actually counted, as something that was and had force. Her horrified recoil from him as from some loathsome, hairy ape is the first notice served on him by the world that he doesn't belong. The remaining five scenes are the successive blows by which this is driven in on him, each scene, as written, as acted and as intensified by the artists, taking on more and more of the nightmare quality with which O'Neill seemed possessed to endow his fable.

The scene on Fifth Avenue when the hairy ape comes face to face with a little parade of wooden-faced churchgoers who walk like automata and prattle of giving a "Hundred Per Cent. American Bazaar" as a contribution to the solution of discontent among the lower classes: the scene on Blackwell's Island with the endless rows of cells and the argot of the prisoners floating out of darkness; the care with which each scene ends in a retributive and terrifying closing in upon the bewildered fellow—all these preparations induce you at last, to accept as natural and inevitable, and right that the hairy ape should, by the final curtain, be found dead inside the cage of the gorilla in the Bronx Zoo.

Except for the role of the girl, which is pretty badly played by Mary Blair, the cast captured for *The Hairy Ape* is an exceptionally good one. Louis Wolheim, though now and then rather painfully off the beat in his co-operation with the others, gives a capital impersonation of the stoker, and lesser parts are well managed by Harry O'Neill as an Irish fireman dreaming of the old days of sailing vessels, and Harold West as a cockney agitator who is fearfully annoyed because of the hairy ape's concentrating his anger against this one little plutocrat instead of maintaining an abstract animosity against plutocrats in general.

In Macdougal Street now and doubtless headed for Broadway, we have a turbulent and tremendous play, so full of blemishes that the merest fledgling among the critics could point out a dozen, yet so vital and interesting and teeming with life that those playgoers who let it escape them will be missing one of the real events of the year.

Abie's Irish Rose
BY Anne Nichols

May 23, 1922

Fulton Theatre

2,327 Performances

ABIE'S IRISH ROSE. A Comedy in Three Acts. By Anne Nichols.

Mrs. Isaac Cohen	Mathilde Cottrelly
Isaac Cohen	Bernard Gorcey
Dr. Jacob Samuels	Howard Lang
Solomon Levy	Alfred Weisman
Abraham Levy	Robert B. Williams
Rosemary Murphy	Marie Carroll
Patrick Murphy	John Cope
Father Whalen	Harry Bradley
Flower Girl	Dorothy Grau

*A*bie's Irish Rose vindicated her middle name, at least, by coming to the Fulton last night after a merry war and temporary truce between the play's author, Anne Nichols, and its first producer elsewhere, Oliver Morosco. Judge Julian Mack in the Federal Court yesterday, at the request of Mr. Morosco as plaintiff, adjourned hearing on an injunction application until June 1.

Miss Nichols, whose play is still running with two companies in San Francisco and Los Angeles— ten weeks in the latter city alone—organized the New York production on her own account, contending that Mr. Morosco's option had been too long delayed. She feared, in effect, that *Abie's Irish Rose,* might be mistaken for a mere California poppy if it were much longer withheld from Broadway.

An "all-star" cast was billed in the piece under Miss Nichols's own direction. The veteran Mathilde Cottrelly was among the players last night, as were also Marie Carroll, John Cope, Alfred Weisman, Bernard Gorcey, Howard Lang, Harry Bradley, and as Abie himself, Robert Williams.

Why the play must sooner or later have been meant for New York was fairly easy to see when the curtain rose on old Solomon Levy's big apartment in the Bronx. It was far more clear when the last curtain fell on a Christmas Eve in the thrice-married Abie's and Rosemary's tiny flat "one year later." Fell, for instance, on Mme. Cottrelly as the kindly Jewish neighbor, cooking, against her will, a ham; on John Cope as the Irish grandfather and Alfred Weisman as the Jew who also "wanted grandchildren"—as Mr. Gorcey had said, he "always talked wholesale"—and finally on Harry Bradley and Howard Lang as the priest and the rabbi, and on "the family."

Abie was a Romeo, heir to riches in New York, but with the ghetto in his blood; Rose, a Juliet, with the blarney, an heiress in California. This Abie and Rose had met "over there" in France in the war; had been "married good and tight by a nice little Methodist minister," and when cast off as "unwelcome strangers," just lived and loved, "not wisely, but well." Perhaps this Irish Rose is a hybrid, but handsome Abie, too, was a bit of a Virginia rambler.

A highly sophisticated Summer audience took the little comedy very heartily, laughing uproariously at its juggling with some fundamental things in human life and at some others, not so fundamental, but deeply cherished, as lifelong feelings are wont to be. The New York scenes sagged on the lines in the play's first act as did the Brooklyn Bridge when the cables were being strung. The Irish, in the person of big John Cope, got the laughs going at the interrupted wedding at old Levy's.

Miss Marie Carroll's Rosemary Murphy-Levy, with a "Peg o' My Heart" brogue, was girlish and charming as she walked with her bridesmaids and flower girl, a picture from her forgotten days in

Oh Boy or *Oh Lady, Lady* down at the Princess. Robert Williams, too, who told everybody "You'll like her; she's a great girl," was himself a fine, likable lad as Abie Levy, who "wasn't marrying a religion." It wasn't orange-blossom time, so the knot was tied under "real California navy oranges." Small wonder when Mr. Cope exclaimed, "Good God, is she marrying an A.P.A.?"

The play has its little sermon that earned one of the heartiest bits of applause last night. Priest and rabbi, it appeared, also had met "over there." "I gave the last rites to many Jewish boys," said the fighting chaplain. "And I to many of your Catholic lads," the Jewish chaplain replied. "We're all on the same road, I guess, even though we do travel by different trains."

It takes two to make a quarrel, family or otherwise, fathers or sons. And to make that quarrel up, it takes two—but that would be telling. Rosebuds and ramblers never grow singly. And as the good priest said at last, "Sure, Abie's a great boy." Personally, we hope to be present at little Rebecca Rachel and Patrick Joseph Levy's second birthday, if not their Hudson-Fulton centennial.

Six Characters in Search of an Author

BY Luigi Pirandello

October 30, 1922

Princess Theatre

136 Performances

SIX CHARACTERS IN SEARCH OF AN AUTHOR, a play in three acts from the Italian of Luigi Pirandello, translation by Edward Storer.

The Father	Moffat Johnston
The Mother	Margaret Wycherly
The Stepdaughter	Florence Eldridge
The Son	Dwight Frye
The Boy	Ashley Buck
The Little Girl	Constance Lusby
Mme. Pace	Ida Fitzhugh
The Manager	Ernest Cossart
The Leading Man	Fred House
The Leading Lady	Eleanor Woodruff
The Juvenile	Elliott Cabot
The Ingenue	Kathaleen Graham
The Character Woman	Maud Sinclair
The Third Actor	Jack Amory
The Fourth Actor	William T. Hays
The Third Actress	Leona Keefer
The Fourth Actress	Blanche Gervals
The Fifth Actress	Catherine Atkinson
The Stage Manager	Russell Morrison
The Property Man	John Saunders

Philosophical fooling and shrewd criticism on the art of the theatre mingle in the Italian play which Brock Pemberton is presenting in translation at the Princess. Imagine a playwright whose creative mind is haunted by six characters, the persons of a harrowing family drama, all urging insistently that they be given full and subtly shaded representation in the theatre. That is the normal condition of authentic creation; but as art consists in rigid elimination as well as in delicate emphasis, many of the aspirations of the six for self-expression have to be denied. Imagine next that the subject of their suffering is not sympathetic to the public, and that the only true and significant outcome is undramatic—not moving and inspiring, but static. That very often happens when a dramatist takes his real inspiration from life as it is actually lived, and in the supreme court of the manager's office he is non-suited. There is no play.

But there are characters more live and vital than most of those that see the footlights. Imagine, finally, that these characters, still longing to live out their lives on the scene, go out in search of a more obliging author—and find a stage manager who has a company but no new play, only the stock stuff of a world somewhat deficient in new inspiration. Recognizing raw materials of interest and power, the enterprising business man undertakes to supply the place of author. It seems to him a positive windfall to be relieved of that insistent and obnoxious incident of production. He will allow the six characters to live out their own lives while a secretary takes down the dialogue and his company stands by preparing to assume the parts. Magnificent!

Those who look upon ordinary rehearsals as a madhouse will receive illumination. Instead of a single author, long subdued in misery, the manager has his six orphans to contend with. The actors of his company, accustomed to have parts ruthlessly adapted to their personalities, are confronted each with a fury of unreason, demanding the absolute. For these characters, though the shadows of a dream, are "real" in the sense of being raw vitality unshaped to the necessities of art and the practical ends of the theatre. In the turmoil that ensues there is much satire on the foibles of player folk and managers and no little philosophy of dramatic art and dramatic criticism.

Margaret Wycherly is Mother in the roving dramatis personae and lends to the character genuine imagination and emotional power. Moffat Johnston is the garrulous father, eagerly philosophic and disquisitional. Florence Eldridge is the stepdaughter, overflowing with eager youth and charm. Throughout, the production is able and highly competent. The audience last night, largely composed of folk of the theatre, rose to the novelty and humor of the idea, and lingered long in applause after the brief three acts were over.

What the public will say to this rather slender and technical satire remains to be seen, but already it may be said that the season is indebted to Mr. Pemberton for one more exploration of strange fields and pastures new.

John Corbin ON
John Barrymore's *Hamlet*

November 16, 1922

Sam H. Harris Theatre

101 Performances

John Barrymore as Hamlet in 1922   MUSEUM OF THE CITY OF NEW YORK

Francisco	John Clark
Bernardo	Lark Taylor
Horatio	Frederick Lewis
Marcellus	E. J. Ballantine
Ghost of Hamlet's Father	Reginald Pole
Hamlet	John Barrymore
Claudius	Tyrone Power
Gertrude	Blanche Yurka
Polonius	John S. O'Brien
Laertes	Sidney Mather
Ophelia	Rosalind Fuller
Rosencrantz	Paul Huber
Guildenstern	Lawrence Cecil
First Player	Lark Taylor
Player King	Burnel Lundee
Second Player	Norman Hearn
Player Queen	Richard Skinner
Lucianus	Vadini Uraneff
A Gentlewoman	Stephanie D'Este
King's Messenger	Frank Boyd
First Grave Digger	Whitford Kane
Second Grave Digger	Cecil Clovelly
A Priest	Reginald Pole
Osric	Edgar Stehli
Fortinbras	Lowden Adams

The atmosphere of historic happening surrounded John Barrymore's appearance last night as the Prince of Denmark; it was unmistakable as it was indefinable. It sprang from the quality and intensity of the applause, from the hushed murmurs that swept the audience at the most unexpected moments, from the silent crowds that all evening long swarmed about the theatre entrance. It was nowhere—and everywhere. In all likelihood we have a new and lasting Hamlet.

It was an achievement against obstacles. The setting provided by Robert Edmund Jones, though beautiful as his setting for Lionel Barrymore's *Macbeth* was trivial and grotesque, encroached upon the playing space and introduced incongruities of locale quite unnecessary. Scenically, there was really no atmosphere. Many fine dramatic values went by the board and the incomparably stirring and dramatic narrative limped. But the all-important spark of genius was there.

Mr. Barrymore disclosed a new personality and a fitting one. The luminous, decadent profile of his recent Italian and Russian impersonations had vanished, and with it the exotic beauty that etched itself so unforgettably upon the memory, bringing a thrill of admiration that was half pain. The youth was wan and haggard, but right manly and forthright—dark and true and tender as befits the North. The slender figure, with its clean limbs, broad shoulders and massive head "made statues all over the stage," as was once said of Edwin Booth.

Vocally, the performance was keyed low. Deep tones prevailed, tones of a brooding, half-conscious melancholy. The "reading" of the lines was flawless—an art that is said to have been lost. The manner, for the most part, was that of conversation, almost colloquial, but the beauty of rhythm was never lost, the varied, flexible harmonies of Shakespeare's crowning period in metric mastery. Very rarely did speech quicken or the voice rise to the pitch of drama, but when this happened the effect was electric, thrilling.

It is the bad custom to look for "originality" in every successive Hamlet. In a brief and felicitous curtain speech Mr. Barrymore remarked that every one knows just how the part should be acted and he expressed pleasure that, as it seemed, he agreed with them all. The originality of his conception is that of all great Hamlets. Abandoning fine-spun theories and tortured "interpretations" he played the part for its prima facie dramatic values—sympathetically and intelligently always, but always simply. When thus rendered, no doubt has ever arisen as to the character, which is as popularly intelligible in the theatre as it has proved mysterious on the critical dissecting table.

Here is a youth of the finest intelligence, the tenderest susceptibility, with a natural vein of gayety and shrewd native wit, who is caught up in the toils of moral horror and barbaric crime. Even as his will struggles impotently to master his external environment, perform the duty enjoined on him by supernatural authority, so his spirit struggles against the overbrooding cloud of melancholy.

If the performance had any major fault it was monotony, and the effect was abetted by the incubus of the scenic investiture. There was simply no room to play in. It may be noted as characteristic that the Ghost was not visible; the majesty of buried Denmark spoke off-stage while a vague light wavered fitfully in the centre of the backdrop. In one way or another the play within the play, the scene of the King at prayer and that of Ophelia's burial, all more or less failed to register dramatically.

The production came precious near to qualifying as a platform recitation. But even at that Mr. Barrymore might have vitalized more fully many moments. With repetition he will doubtless do so. The important point is that he revealed last night all the requisite potentialities of personality, of intelligence and of histrionic art.

The supporting company was adequate, but nothing more. The outstanding figures were the King of Tyrone Power and the Queen of Blanche Yurka. Neither Polonius nor the Grave Digger registered the comedy values of their parts, a fact which contributed largely to the effect of monotony. But, strange to relate, the speaking of lines was uniformly good.

The Adding Machine

BY Elmer L. Rice

March 19, 1923

Garrick Theatre

72 Performances

THE ADDING MACHINE, a play in seven scenes, by Elmer L. Rice.

Mr. Zero	Dudley Digges
Mrs. Zero	Helen Westley
Daisy Diana Dorothea Devore	Margaret Wycherly
The Boss	Irving Dillon
Mr. One	Harry McKenna
Mrs. One	Marcia Harris
Mr. Two	Paul Hayes
Mrs. Two	Therese Stewart
Mr. Three	Gerald Lundegard
Mrs. Three	Georgiana Wilson
Mr. Four	George Stehli
Mrs. Four	Edyth Burnett
Mr. Five	William M. Griffith
Mrs. Five	Ruby Craven
Mr. Six	Daniel Hamilton
Mrs. Six	Louise Sydmeth
Policemen	Irving Dillon, Lewis Barrington
Judy O'Grady	Elsie Bartlett
Young Man	Gerald Lundegard
Shrdlu	Edward G. Robinson
A Head	Daniel Hamilton
Lieutenant Charles	Louis Calvert
Joe	William M. Griffith

New York last night was treated to the best and fairest example of the newer expressionism in the theatre that it has yet experienced. The verdict, of course, depends upon the personal reaction on the sensibilities of the observer.

He will see and hear, this observer, in *The Adding Machine,* a Theatre Guild production at the Garrick—what starts out to be the short and simple annal of one of the great and glorious unsung of life; not too far above the submerged tenth, of a person, at times symbolical and at other times intensely personal, known simply as Mr. Zero.

For twenty-five years, day in and day out, excepting only national holidays and a week in the Summer, this Zero has added figures. Figures to right of him figures to left of him, volleyed and thundered from 9 to 5, six days a week, half Saturdays in July and August.

He married, this Zero, what must have been a sweet, moist-eyed, trusting bit of a girl, with infinite faith and pride in his tale of what lay just beyond this necessary beginning as a bookkeeper. But the days became weeks, the weeks became years, and the years decades—and still Zero is no further than his task of adding figures, and the little slip of a bride has become an ill-tempered, nagging, slovenly woman, bitter in her disillusionments and sharp with her tongue at him who is the cause of them.

Comes then, in the language of a great art, the twenty-fifth anniversary of Zero's career with the firm, of Zero still adding figures as he did a quarter of a century before. And at the close of the day's work his employer appears, notifies him that adding machines are to be installed, machines so simple that they can be operated by high school girls and informs him gently but firmly that his services are no longer required.

For one mad moment all the figures he has ever added whirl madly in the Zero brain—and when he is again aware of the world, he has stabbed his employer through the heart with a bill-file.

At his trial he becomes partly articulate—he tries to convey something of what the years of drudgery, endless, aimless drudgery, have done to him. He is sentenced to death and executed.

So far the larger part of his audience will go hand in hand with Mr. Rice, Mr. Moeller and Mr. Simonson, author, director and designer of last night's offering, and pronounce their work excellent. Mr. Rice, they will say, has written true dialogue, and Mr. Moeller has labored well to bring out the monotony and dullness and stupidity that are the life of the Zeros of the world, and Mr. Simonson, be his methods ever so unorthodox, has created what not even the most orthodox of all can fail to understand.

The part of the fable just outlined runs through two of the play's three acts and four of its seven scenes. One of these early scenes, in particular, displayed a novelty and power that will long keep it in the memory of the beholder. It is simple enough—Zero and a female Zero are reading and checking figures to each other, in a dreary and monotonous sing-song, and as they work they think aloud and show their inmost, sacred selves, but theatrical as the device sounds in cold print, it was weirdly effective and gripping on the stage.

At the beginning of the play's third act and fifth scene at least some part of the audiences will not feel able to carry through. For one thing, this fifth scene, whatever its author's intent may have been, is coldly and gratuitously vulgar.

Some day a doctor's thesis will probably be written on that inward motive that drives the young expressionists to scenes in graveyards. (The father of them all, of course, had such a scene in *Frühlings Erwachen.* Despite the lack, at present, of an explanation, the fact of the inevitability of such scenes will have to be accepted. Mr. Rice's graveyard last night served as the locale for a scene almost literally from Mr. Schnitzler's *Reigen*—with, it seemed, no reason for the enactment of the scene save that the author willed it so. Certainly there was nothing in the behavior or thoughts of any of the characters that brought it on.

Past the inevitable expressionistic graveyard, the action moves to a pleasant spot in the Elysian Fields. Here Zero is given ample opportunity to catch up with some of the repressions and suppressed desires of his former life, but he turns his back on them at the last moment for fear of being considered not thoroughly respectable. What this scene, and the next and last, are meant to convey is vague, perhaps purposely. Certainly they were not offered as things of beauty by themselves.

At this writing, with the final curtain not yet decently cold upon an expressionist heaven dominated by a gigantic adding machine, the last act remains curious, a vague blur, not, however, without excellent moments of satirical observation. It is, nevertheless, by far the weakest part of the play.

Expressionism, of course, is the modern definition for the method of production that covers all conceivable dramatic sins, and no one has a right to say to his brother what is and is not expressionism. To Messrs. Rice, Moeller and Simonson, obviously , it is the form of dramatic expression best conveying the illusion of reality in the presence of the obviously unreal.

The acting was excellent throughout. Helen Westley, without whom a Theatre Guild production is inconceivable, portrayed grandly the monster of a wife created by Zero and later destined to help push him to his earthly destruction. Dudley Digges as Zero lived the dumb, groping, plodding nature of the fellow. Margaret Wycherly played a female Zero with great restraint. Louis Calvert did nicely with an unobtrusive bit in the last scene.

Mr. Simonson's scenery is even more expressionistic than Mr. Rice's third act. In a courtroom scene, while Zero is tried, there is some excellent work by him. He shows us the Zero conception of justice, cold, inanimate, relentless, and the contrast between reality and unreality is heightened by the crooked bars and railings and walls. Mr. Simonson's, too, one suspects, is the effect of the whirling figures and the dashes of red that appear to Zero as his employer hands him his discharge for his faithful quarter century of labor.

Mr. Rice, it should be noted, is the author of *On Trial,* an equally revolutionary play, so far as technique is concerned, of a few seasons ago.

The Green Hat
BY Michael Arlen

September 15, 1925

Broadhurst Theatre

231 Performances

THE GREEN HAT, a play in four acts, by Michael Arlen. Staged by Guthrie McClintic; produced by A. H. Woods.
A Lady's Maid ....Antoinette Parr
An English Reporter....................................John Buckler
Manager of the Hotel Vendome.............Gustave Rolland
Dr. Conrad Masters ....A. P. Kaye

Gerald Havele March	Paul Guilfoyle
Napier Harpenden	Leslie Howard
Major General Sir Maurice Harpenden	Eugene Powers
Hilary Townshend	Gordon Ash
Iris Fenwick, née March	Katharine Cornell
Venice Pollen	Margalo Gillmore
Lord De Travest	John Redmond
A Lady	Jane Saville
Turner	Harry Lilford
Sister Virginia	Gwyneth Gordon
Sister Clothilde	Anne Tonetti
Madelaine	Florence Foster
Truble	Harry Barfoot

From the pages of a novel that has enjoyed vast popularity, Iris March and Napier Harpenden, chief characters of *The Green Hat,* passed last evening at the Broadhurst to a play that has enjoyed no less popularity in the several cities where it has been seen. The frustrated young woman who flitted uncannily through the feverish pages of Mr. Arlen's book came to the stage, in the flesh, with a speaking voice, in the person of Katharine Cornell. And her performance was a vibrant one, teeming with emotion that was always just suppressed and expressed in a voice of strange, haunting timbre. Miss Cornell is perfectly cast in this part. The sympathy that Iris March summoned from the audience was a tribute chiefly to her acting. She is well supported by a cast of excellent actors. Indeed, Mr. Arlen's play as been equipped auspiciously. The humming personality of the fable, which is never quite revealed, passes across the footlights.

Although novels do not always walk on to the stage without leaving a vast deal of baggage in the wings, *The Green Hat* seems to have become a play without losing much of the original romance. Iris March and her neurotic brother, Gerald, are both here, represented in the essential incidents. And, as one of the lines puts it, "the Marches are let off from nothing." Napier Harpenden, who always loved Iris, is here also, ably played by Leslie Howard; and his father, too, facing Iris more than once. Hilary Townshend, played by Gordon Ash, runs through the drama as a sort of moral standard against which the various incidents are measured. He, it appears, is rather more to the play than to the novel. And, finally, the wistful Venice Pollen is here, bewildered and generous, acted appealingly by Margalo Gillmore. Thus, none of the chief characters of the novel is missing; save the "first person singular," who originally told the story. That purely technical part could scarcely be represented on the stage.

If Mr. Arlen has managed quite adroitly to fit his novel to the theatre, he has not done it perfectly. The drama is singularly wordy, the story moves on sometimes clumsily, and the third act, in particular, made up largely of long conversations between various sets of two characters, serves its dramatic purpose without heightening the effect on the audience. If the drama were less intelligently acted, the piece-meal structure would destroy the illusion. And, as in the novel, one finds that the individual must yield a great deal to the playwright in order to come under the spell of the drama. For it is a curiously unhappy story, crowded with bitter, futile people who fly out at one another in frequent bad temper and often are most enigmatic in what they say. They suffer. The fates pursue Iris unrelentingly. But why? Whose fault is it—theirs or the gods? Mr. Arlen seems to blame the gods. The blame may be nearer at home, in the characters themselves, in their want of a sense of humor, in their want of ordinary willpower. Must we believe them the victims of circumstances? To enjoy the play, it is necessary to believe that, to blame the gods and to answer with a gesture of despair the questions "What is love?" or "What is happiness?" that Iris now and then propounds.

If we grant this initial impulse, we may catch strange beauties in the four acts of *The Green Hat.* The first act reveals the sitting-room of a hotel suite in Deauville, the morning after Boy Fenwick's unexpected death by falling from a window. It had been his wedding night with Iris March. And he died, Iris explains, "for purity." This is an exceptionally quarrelsome act, Gerald March, Napier, Hilary and Sir Maurice all shouting angrily at one another. Even Iris cannot keep them at peace. The second act, set ten years later in Napier's London flat, carries the story one peg further. Napier has just given a dinner to Venice, whom he is to marry shortly, and to relatives and intimate friends. After they have gone Iris appears unexpectedly. Napier finds that their childhood love is not dead. The third act in a Paris convent nursing home recounts the episode of Iris's illness there, and Napier's coming at the doctor's request. The last act in Sir Maurice's country home follows closely the last chapter in Mr. Arlen's novel. Here Iris and Napier defy the family and propose to run off together. Then Napier discovers that his wife, Venice, is with child, and he returns. Iris leaves madly in her motor. A crash and a flash of light indicate the rest.

This bare summary of the story makes no account of the beauty of the play. For that beauty is more properly a spell, a series of shades, or a light shadow. Beyond the movements of the characters and the abnormal glow of the dialogue is a subdued tone-quality that serves as unity. Much of this comes from the personality of Katharine Cornell. As she plays the part Iris March just misses the happiness, the release, that she is seeking. And the Venice Pollen whom Margalo Gillmore portrays shares in that blind groping for reality. Leslie Howard's acting in the part of Napier Harpenden serves as the wall beyond which this futile questioning and hunting cannot go. His playing is an able background to the mood of the drama. Mr. Arlen's story is sombre, brave and frequently touching. The acting preserves these qualities.

Sex

BY Jane Mast (Mae West)

April 26, 1926
Daly's Sixty-third Street Theatre
375 Performances

Mae West as Margie LaMont playing the piano for Barry O'Neill in *Sex*, her 1926 Broadway debut.
CULVER PHOTOS

SEX, a play in three acts, by Jane Mast. Staged by Edward Elsner; produced by C. William Morganstern.

Margie LaMont	Mae West
Lieutenant Gregg	Barry O'Neill
Rocky Waldron	Warren Sterling
Agnes Scott	Ann Reader
Clara Smith	Edda Von Buelow
Jimmy Stanton	Lyons Wickland
Robert Stanton	Pacie Ripple
Dawson	Gordon Burby
Jones	D. J. Hamilton
Curley	Al Re Alia
Marie	Constance Morganstern
Jenkins	Frank Howard
Captain Carter	George Rogers
Waiter	Gordon Earle
Red	Mary Morrisey
Condez	Conde Brewer
Spanish Dancer	Michael Markham
The Fleet Band	The Syncopators

A crude, inept play, cheaply produced and poorly acted—that, in substance, is *Sex*, which came last night to Daly's Sixty-third Street

Theatre as a late Spring entrant in the Broadway field. For at least one act it lived up to the promise of its name and was spicy enough to evoke "ohs," "ahs" and partially restrained titters from its audience and to send several couples out into the night, but after that act—the first—it seemed to reconsider, and except for a torrid love scene toward the end it contented itself with just being pretty feeble and disjointed.

Sex, lobby gossip had it, is the work of its leading woman, Mae West, who has written under the pseudonym of Jane Mast. Miss West, it was further rumored, is a singer out of the two-a-day. She acted a part she had especially written for herself. The cast assisting her was composed for the most part of unknowns, and there was no one of sufficient promise to warrant being lifted from that category.

The scenes of *Sex* are laid in Montreal, Trinidad and Westchester County. The authorities of all those places have ample cause for protest.

J. Brooks Atkinson ON

Funny Face

BOOK BY Fred Thompson AND
Paul Gerard Smith
LYRICS BY Ira Gershwin
MUSIC BY George Gershwin

November 22, 1927
Alvin Theatre
244 Performances

FUNNY FACE, a musical comedy in two acts and seven scenes. Book by Fred Thompson and Paul Gerard Smith; music by George Gershwin, lyrics by Ira Gershwin. Dances and ensembles arranged by Bobby Connolly; settings by John Wenger; produced by Alex A. Aarons and Vinton Freedley.

Dora	Betty Compton
June	Gertrude McDonald
Frankie	Adele Astaire
Jimmy Reeve	Fred Astaire
Dugsie Gibbs	William Kent
Chester	Earl Hampton
Herbert	Victor Moore
Peter Thurston	Allen Kearns
Sergeant of Police	Ted MacLean
Hotel Clerk	Edwin Hodge
Porter	Walter Munroe
Bell Hop	Dorothy Jordon

If there were not two or three good musical plays already in town, one might be reckless enough to dub *Funny Face*, at the Alvin last evening, as the best of them all. With Fred and Adele Astaire, Victor Moore and William Kent in the cast, with music by George Gershwin and lyrics by his brother, Ira, and with excellent dancing throughout, *Funny Face* makes for uncommonly rollicking entertainment. It opens the new Alvin Theatre auspiciously.

By this time it is no secret that Fred and Adele Astaire have a niche in musical comedy quite to themselves. They have not only humor but intelligence; not only spirit but good taste; not only poise but modesty; and they are not only expert eccentric dancers but they never make an ungraceful movement. Twice last evening Fred Astaire took the audience's breath away with his rapid footing and his intelligibility in a brand of clog-dance pantomime. In a particularly refreshing male chorus number, to the tune of "High Hat," he gave every indication of proceeding in two directions at once. As a gauche and prevaricating young lady, his sister also dances beautifully, meanwhile making the faces celebrated in the title of the comedy. Within their very individual field the Astaires appear to have things very much their own way.

Fred Thompson and Paul Gerard Smith, collaborating bookmakers for this racy diversion, propose Fred Astaire as the likable guardian of three young ladies and Adele as a harum-scarum ward. For some reason, which need not upset us in our critical orisons, two friendly gentlemen crack the family safe just before two professional safe experts appear on the scene. Now, as good fortune would have it in the modern theatrical world, the diminutive, wobbly William Kent and the comically thick-witted Victor Moore find themselves involved in this unlawful proceeding.

Forget all that. All that matters here is that Kent and Moore, as friendly enemies, put on one of the funniest shooting numbers seen during any Republican Administration. Those who remember Victor Moore from past musical shows know how full of sobs his voice can be. "Was you going any-wheres in particular?" he pleads, trying to find a convenient time for shooting Kent. In spite of Kent's blue eyes, which remind him compassion-ately of three kittens he drowned in his youth, Moore deferentially squares off to murder Kent when the question of a shooting license comes up. Well, after all, it is not the business of the act that matters: it is Moore's slow, ponderous motions, that absurd shape of his bulging head and his sob-bing voice. "Did it hit you?" he inquires hopefully after the first shot. No, one must not attempt to de-scribe it.

Mr. Kent with his fluttering comedy makes a good deal more than he ought of "symptoms I'm happy; symptoms I'm sad," and other devastating comic rot. Who is it, by the way, who says he has "turned in his Chivalry for a Cadillac"? One can-not remember all the jokes.

Mr. Gershwin, maker of tunes, has composed several good songs for *Funny Face,* the best of which naturally bears the same title as the play. "'S Wonderful, 's Marvelous," "Let's Kiss and Make Up," and "The Babbitt and the Bromide" manage successfully to avoid the old song banali-ties. The cast includes Betty Compton and Gertrude McDonald, and Allen Kearns, who makes a musical comedy vocalist less trying than usual. In directing the chorus Bobby Connolly has contrived to keep dancing vivacity from seeming ugly. In all its grimaces, *Funny Face* gives full en-tertainment measure.

The new Alvin Theatre, set defiantly across the street from the scholarly Theatre Guild, seems to have all the best features of the modern play-house—even an old English lounge where re-freshments may be had. The auditorium is decorated in pastel shades of blue and gray, with ivory and old gold decorations. The Alvin can serve 1,400 drama gluttons at one sitting. If *Funny Face* had been less engrossing the audience might have had more time to appreciate the new theatre.

J. Brooks Atkinson ON
Show Boat
BOOK AND LYRICS BY
Oscar Hammerstein 2d
MUSIC BY Jerome Kern

December 27, 1927
Ziegfeld Theatre
572 Performances

SHOW BOAT, "An all-American musical comedy" in two acts, adapted from Edna Ferber's novel of the same name. Book and lyrics by Oscar Hammerstein 2d, with music by Jerome Kern. Settings by Josef Ur-ban; dances arranged by Sammy Lee; dialogue di-rected by Zeke Colvan; costumes designed by John Harkrider; produced by Florenz Ziegfeld.

Windy	Alan Campbell
Queenie	Aunt Jemima
Steve	Charles Ellis
Pete	Bert Chapman
Parthy Ann Hawks	Edna May Oliver
Cap'n Andy	Charles Winninger
Ellie	Eva Puck
Frank	Sammy White
Rubber Face	Francis X. Mahoney
Julie	Helen Morgan
Gaylord Ravenal	Howard Marsh
Vallon	Thomas Gunn
Magnolia	Norma Terris
Joe	Jules Bledsoe
Dealer	Jack Wynn
Gambler	Phil Sheridan
Backwoodsman	Jack Daley
Jeb	Jack Wynn
La Belle Fatima	Dorothy Denese
Old Sport	Bert Chapman
Landlady	Annie Hart
Ethel	Estelle Floyd
Sister	Annette Harding
Mother Superior	Mildred Schewenke
Kim (child)	Eleanor Shaw

Kim (as young woman)	Norma Terris
Jake	Robert Farley
Max	Jack Daley
Man with Guitar	Ted Daniels
Charlie	J. Lewis Johnson
Lottie	Tana Kamp
Dolly	Dagmar Oakland
Old Lady on Levee	Laura Clairon

The worlds of Broadway and Park Avenue and their respective wives put on their best bibs and tuckers last night and converged at Mr. Ziegfeld's handsome new playhouse on Sixth Avenue. There they milled about elegantly in the lobby, were pictured by flashlight photographers and finally got to their seats and to the business in hand. That was the inspection of the newest offering from the workshops of the maestro, the much-heralded musical adaptation of Edna Ferber's novel, *Show Boat*.

From such remote centres of theatrical omniscience as Pittsburgh, Washington and Philadelphia had come the advance word that it was better than good—some reports even extravagantly had it that here was Mr. Ziegfeld's superlative achievement. It would be difficult to quarrel with such tidings, for last night's performance came perilously near to realizing the most fulsome of them.

All right, there you have it: *Show Boat* is, with a few reservations in favor of some of the earlier *Follies* and possibly *Sally,* just about the best musical piece ever to arrive under Mr. Ziegfeld's silken gonfalon. It has, barring perhaps a slight lack of one kind of comedy, and an overabundance of another, and a little slowness in getting under way—this last due to the fact that it is crammed with plot which simply must be explained—about every ingredient that the perfect song-and-dance concoction should have.

In its adherence to its story it is positively slavish. The adaptation of the novel has been intelligently made, and such liberties as the demands of musical comedy necessitate do not twist the tale nor distort its values. For this, and for the far better than the average lyrics with which it is endowed, credit Oscar Hammerstein 2d, who is rapidly monopolizing the function of author for the town's musical entertainments.

Then, too, *Show Boat* has an exceptionally tuneful score—the most lilting and satisfactory that the wily Jerome Kern has contrived in several seasons. Potential song hits were as common last night as top hats. Such musical recordings of amorous reaction as "You Are in Love," "I Can't Help Lovin' That Man," "Why Do I Love You?" are sufficient for any show—to say nothing of "Old Man River," which Jules Bledsoe and a Negro chorus make remarkably effective.

If these three contributions—book, lyrics and score—call for a string of laudatory adjectives, the production compels that they be repeated again—and with a short tiger. The colorful scenes on and around the showboat, plying its course along the Mississippi, that comprise the first act lend themselves well to a variety of effects and have been achieved with Mr. Ziegfeld's unimpeachable skill and taste.

In the second act the nine interludes carry the spectator from the gaudy Midway Plaisance of the World's Fair to the sombre quiet of St. Agatha's Convent and then back to the new and modernized floating theatre, 1927 variety. The settings are all atmospherically perfect; the costumes are in the style of each of the periods and there is a finish and polish about the completed entity that caused even a first performance to move with unusual smoothness.

To recount in any detail the plot of a musical comedy usually is a silly and banal business; to tell Miss Ferber's large and clamorous public what happens to Magnolia and Gaylord Ravenal is unnecessary. But to tell them of the manner in which these characters and the many others of the best seller have been brought to life is something else again.

As Magnolia, Norma Terris appeared to be a revelation, even to the first nighters who had watched her work in previous dance-and-tune saturnalias. Her realization of Captain Andy's daughter seemed complete, even when she got around to imitating Ted Lewis and Ethel Barrymore in the final, or 11:45 P.M., scene. Howard Marsh, one of the more facial tenors, made a handsome and satisfactory Ravenal. Helen Morgan, who is among the town's most adept song saleswomen, was Julie, and purveyed two numbers in her distinctive style. As the dour and formidable New England mother, Parthy Ann Hawks, Edna May Oliver played with requisite austerity, although she did forget herself long enough to engage in a dance.

But the outstanding hit of the evening seemed to be reserved for Charles Winninger, who cut capers to his heart's content as Captain Andy.

He is in top form, and when Mr. Winninger is in top form he is an extremely waggish fellow. And in a moment during the *Show Boat*'s performance when through the defection of an affrighted villain he is compelled to seize the stage and act out the remainder of the play himself, he is extraordinarily persuasive and convincing. Then there are the reliable Puck and White, presenting the low comedy specialties, and others too numerous to mention.

Show Boat, as it should not be too difficult for the reader to ascertain by now, is an excellent musical comedy; one that comes perilously close to being the best the town has seen in several seasons. It must have afforded its producer, who has poured dollars into it by the thousands, a certain ironic satisfaction to hear the play's Chicago cabaret manager say with an air of finality, "No, I can't afford to take chances with amateurs with a $2,000 production on my hands." Mr. Ziegfeld can't afford to, either.

The Front Page

BY Ben Hecht AND Charles MacArthur

August 14, 1928

Times Square Theatre

276 Performances

THE FRONT PAGE, a play in three acts, by Ben Hecht and Charles MacArthur. Staged by George S. Kaufman; settings by Raymond Sovey; produced by Jed Harris.

Wilson	Vincent York
Endicott	Allen Jenkins
Murphy	Willard Robertson
McCue	William Foran
Schwartz	Tammany Young
Kruger	Joseph Spurin-Calleia
Bensinger	Walter Baldwin
Mrs. Schlosser	Violet Barney
Woodenshoes Eichorn	Jay Wilson
Diamond Louis	Eduardo Ciannelli
Hildy Johnson	Lee Tracy
Jennie	Carrie Weller
Molly Molloy	Dorothy Stickney
Sheriff Hartman	Claude Cooper
Peggy Grant	Frances Fuller
Mrs. Grant	Jessie Crommette
The Mayor	George Barbier
Mr. Pincus	Frank Conlan
Earl Williams	George Leach
Walter Burns	Osgood Perkins
Carl	Matthew Crowley
Frank	Gene West

By superimposing a breathless melodrama upon a good newspaper play the authors and directors of *The Front Page,* shown at the Times Square last night, have packed an evening with loud, rapid, coarse and unfailing entertainment. Set in the press room of the Criminal Courts Building in Chicago, it stirs up reporters, criminals, politicians, wives and sweethearts into a steaming broth of excitement and comedy; and last evening an audience, obviously prepared to be delighted, hung on every line and episode until the end. Ben Hecht, novelist and dramatist and Chicago arbiter of taste, and Charles MacArthur, co-author of *Lulu Belle,* have told a racy story with all the tang of front-page journalism, and George S. Kaufman has poured it on the stage resourcefully. Acted in the vernacular and in a lurid key by Lee Tracy, Willard Robertson, Osgood Perkins, Claude Cooper, Dorothy Stickney, George Barbier and many others—all welded into a seamless performance—*The Front Page* begins a new season noisily.

In the escape of a prisoner just on the eve of a political execution, and in the draggle-tailed characters involved, the authors have such a picturesque yarn to spin that their insistence upon thrusting bespattered conversation down the throats of the audience is as superfluous as it is unpleasant. No one who has ground his heels in the grime of a police headquarters pressroom will complain that this argot misrepresents the gentlemen of the press. And the Chicago scribes of *The Front Page*, waiting impatiently for the hanging of Earl Williams while experimental sandbags are thumping on the gallows outside, are no cleaner of mouth than of linen. Wrangling at poker, leering over the political expediency of the execution, abusing the Sheriff and the Mayor insolently, they utter some of the baldest profanity and most slattern jesting that has ever been heard on the public stage. Graphic as it may be in tone and authenticity, it diverts attention from a vastly entertaining play.

The plot of *The Front Page* concerns Earl Williams's escape from jail on the eve of his hanging. For nearly an act he appears to be gone. In the fury of the excitement, when the pressroom is empty of all save Hildy Johnson of *The Herald-Examiner*, Williams feebly climbs in at the window and surrenders. But Hildy Johnson thinks fast. Instead of delivering Williams over to the police, who are searching for him far uptown, Johnson slams him into a roll-top desk and preserves him as a physical scoop for his newspaper. But even Walter Burns, the esoteric managing editor, cannot complete the kidnapping. Presently the police ferret out the mystery and only an eleventh-hour reprieve saves the neck of Earl Williams and saves Johnson and Burns from jail sentences.

After producing *Broadway* and *Spread Eagle*,

Jed Harris could not let such a plot cross the stage unembellished. And no stripped summary of *The Front Page* can convey the rowdy comedy of the pressroom, the whirr of the excitement, of nerves on edge, the apprehensive stupidity of the Sheriff, the flatulence of the Mayor, the impatience of Johnson's fiancée who is ready to be married, the bewilderment of her mother caught up defenseless in the hurly-burly of a big newspaper yarn, the attempted bribery of the Governor's messenger and the ridiculousness of the inconsequential items telephoned to the desk while the man-hunt still prowls on. It is all here, down to the popular scrub woman and the policeman dispatched for sandwiches. Author and directors have accounted for every moment, tossed their story rapidly back and forth, and pulled down their curtains on the tensest episodes of all.

Such plays have little leisure for character development. Yet *The Front Page* denies the audience none of Hildy Johnson as he abandons newspaper work forever, blackens the character of his chief decisively, and finally juggles his impending marriage and a newspaper sensation through the rest of the play. Lee Tracy, one-time hoofer in *Broadway*, acts the part vividly and impulsively. Willard Robertson, as the jaded sleuth for the *Journal*, plays admirably; and Osgood Perkins does as well by the managing editor. As Molly Malloy, a sinning sister of Clark Street, Dorothy Stickney gives one of her best performances. All the parts have been admirably cast. Equipped with a good script and directed with a sense of time and color, *The Front Page* keeps melodrama still the most able variety of current stage entertainment.

Animal Crackers

BOOK BY George S. Kaufman AND

Morrie Ryskind

MUSIC AND LYRICS BY Bert Kalmar AND

Harry Ruby

———

October 23, 1928

Forty-fourth Street Theatre

191 Performances

ANIMAL CRACKERS, a musical comedy in two acts and six scenes. Book by George S. Kaufman and Morrie Ryskind; lyrics and music by Bert Kalmar and Harry Ruby. Staged by Oscar Eagle; settings by Raymond Sovey; dances by Russell Market; produced by Sam H. Harris.

Hives	Robert Greig
Mrs. Rittenhouse	Margaret Dumont
M. Doucet	Arthur Lipson
Arabella Rittenhouse	Alice Wood
Mrs. Whitehead	Margaret Irving
Grace Carpenter	Bobby Perkins
Wally Winston	Bert Mathews
John Parker	Milton Watson
Roscoe W. Chandler	Louis Sorin
Mary Stewart	Bernice Ackerman
Jamison	Zeppo Marx
Captain Spalding	Groucho Marx
Emanuel Ravelli	Chico Marx
The Professor	Harpo Marx

Here come the Marx brothers again with their uproarious, slapstick comedy in a new fury of puns and gibes by George S. Kaufman and Morrie Ryskind, entitled *Animal Crackers* and displayed at the Forty-fourth Street Theatre last evening. And here come their merry audiences who chuckle and roar at Groucho's sad, glib, shrapnel waggery, at Harpo's mummery, which is as broad as it is long, and at Chico's barefaced jocosity. For if anything is more remarkable than the outrageous buffoonery of this team of cut-ups, it is their fabulous popularity.

Speculators swore they could get as much as $100 for two tickets to the opening performance. And most of those who had squeezed into the bulging theatre last evening were obviously in the flattering mood of expecting the Marx brothers to redeem in one evening all the dullness of the current theatrical season. That would be a large order. However, those who remembered that the Marx brothers are not supermen but merely the maddest troupe of comedians of the day, limited in their vein, and compelled to appear in a routine musical comedy—those who were sane were not disappointed.

Their previous appearances have worn some of the freshness off their fun. Especially in the first act, when the musical comedy fiddle-faddle is cluttering the stage, their vandalism leaves a good deal to be desired. Once or twice it is merely nasty. But the second act settles down hilariously to their robust Harlequin du Barry number and one astonishing nonsense sequence that somehow progresses from talk of a robbery to the erection and furnishing of a house. Even Groucho, the intellectual of the troupe, looks bewildered and apprehensive when he realizes where this convincingly rhymeless conversation has led.

To set off their particular brand of humor the authors have turned them loose in a fashionable Long Island house party where Groucho can hurdle over his puns, Harpo can break all the rules of good society and Chico scuttle the estate. The event of the evening is the robbery of a valuable picture.

But the Marx cabal accepts all this hodgepodge as so much dead weight, valuable theatrically only for its contrast. The Marx boys do the rest. Delivering his mad-cap chronicle of an African exploration, Groucho touches on nearly every topic of the day and makes some of the most insane verbal transitions heard since his last appearance. "I used to know a fellar by the name of Emanuel Ravelli who looked like you," he says to Chico. "I am Ravelli," says Chico. "No wonder you look like him," Groucho runs on. "I still insist there's a resemblance." Those who heard him last evening turn the title of a popular song into "You Took a Bandage Off Me"; advise a South American traveler "You go Uruguay and I'll go mine"; dictate a formal note to his attorney in full, "Dear

Madame: Regards—that's all"; and reply to a woman who charged him with bigamy, "Of course, it's big of me"—those who heard an evening of such things were shamelessly satisfied.

They are nihilists—these Marx boys. And the virtue of their vulgar mountebankery is its bewildering, passing, stinging thrusts at everything in general, including themselves. Burlesquing their own comedy, the show occasionally resolves itself into a vicious circle that is less amusing than it deserves to be. But their stock in trade has other ruffian advantages. They make a good deal of their ludicrous costumes—Groucho in the sun helmet of an African explorer and the morning coat of a floor walker; Harpo in evening dress that slides off and leaves him hideous in trunks and a tall hat; Chico in the ungainly attire of an immigrant.

And they have managed to refurbish some of the ridiculous routines that made their first show a memorable event. There is another rude card game full of chicanery, and a loud, thumping robbery scene in which they steal a portrait in the darkness during a thunderstorm. But their funniest scene is the du Barry costume assignation just before the close of the performance—the true offspring of their immortal Josephine and Napoleon number. Those who remember Groucho as the Little Corporal will know how comic he can be as the King.

Perhaps it is sentiment, or perhaps it is a fact that neither *The Cocoanuts* nor *Animal Crackers* packs the fun as freshly and rowdily as the original *I'll Say She Is*. Or perhaps we are too well acquainted with the Marxian style and range of humor. For all its topical foolery about the avid "Wally Winston" of the *Evening Traffic, Animal Crackers* is uncommonly perfunctory in its construction as a musical entertainment.

With the music and lyrics, Bert Kalmar and Harry Ruby have done a workmanlike if not a distinguished job. "The Long Island Low-Down" and "Cool Off" are agreeably written and sung. Although the dance designs are seldom original, some of them display the costumes well, and two or three of them are danced with spirit. The task of fitting the Marx boys into such a carnival is thankless at best.

Whatever the plot of the background may be these scurrilous mimes remain very much themselves.

Girl Crazy

BOOK BY Guy Bolton AND John McGowan
LYRICS BY Ira Gershwin
MUSIC BY George Gershwin

October 14, 1930
Alvin Theatre
272 Performances

GIRL CRAZY, a musical comedy in two acts and eight scenes. Book by Guy Bolton and John McGowan, music by George Gershwin and lyrics by Ira Gershwin. Settings by Donald Oenslager; staged by Alexander Leftwich; dances and ensembles arranged by George Hale; produced by Alex A. Aarons & Vinton Freedley.

Danny Churchill	Allen Kearns
Molly Gray	Ginger Rogers
Pete	Clyde Veaux
Lank Sanders	John Daley
Gieber Goldfarb	Willie Howard
Flora James	Eunice Healy
Patsy West	Peggy O'Connor
Kate Fothergill	Ethel Merman
Slick Fothergill	William Kent
Sam Mason	Donald Foster
Tess Parker	Olive Brady
Jake Howell	Lew Parker
Eagle Rock	Chief Rivers
Hotel Proprietor	Jack Classon
Lariat Joe	Starr Jones
The Foursome	Marshall Smith, Ray Johnson, Dee Porter, Dwight Snyder.

Antonio and Renée Demarco.
"Red" Nichols and His Orchestra.
Al Siegal at the Piano.

When the first curtain arose on last night's antics at the Alvin, a large sign on the stage informed the audience that it was looking at Custerville, Ariz., a happy community which feminine wiles had not penetrated for more than fifty years. But since this was a musical comedy, that manless state obviously could not long endure. Before ten minutes had elapsed the personable Ginger Rogers had made her entrance, and from then on the young women principals and jazz coryphées came in droves. And, what with one thing and another, it all helped to make *Girl Crazy* what Broadway would call a lively and expert show. There is, then, fairly consoling news from Fifty-second Street this morning.

Not the least important item in these tidings is the part played by the brothers Gershwin. George has written some good tunes, while Ira has provided tricky and ingratiating lyrics that should stimulate any ear surfeited with the usual rhyming insipidities of musical comedy. In one number, "Bidin' My Time," he has poked fun at the theme song school in verse; in all he has been fresh and amusing. And his brother has provided melody in "Embraceable You" and "But Not for Me," travestied the imperishable "Frankie and Johnnie" in "Sam and Delilah," and turned out several excellent rhythmic numbers, one of which, "I Got Rhythm," induces a veritable frenzy of dancing.

The book is serviceable, rather than distinguished. It gets its characters in and out of the proper entanglements and tears its hero and heroine apart at the end of the first act as every orthodox musical show libretto should. Set in the Southwest, *Girl Crazy* concentrates on affairs in a dude ranch. The ranch is run by a New York playboy who falls in love with an Arizona girl. Around the premises lurk a hardbitten pair of villains, who are alternately after somebody's $6,000 and the scalp of Willie Howard, who impersonates Gieber Goldfarb, a Broadway taxicab driver forced by the exigencies of the story to become a sheriff addicted to impersonations of Maurice Chevalier, Eddie Cantor and George Jessel. That is not all, but you get the idea. What is important is that, with the music, dancing and some of the comedy, it does not matter more than it should.

The dancing combines intricacy and speed in the manner of the day, and is definitely one of the assets. Another is Ethel Merman, whose peculiar song style was brought from the night clubs to the stage to the vast delight last evening of the people who go

places and watch things being done. Willie Howard is, as usual, Willie Howard; in several instances, particularly at the start of the show, he is funnier than he has been lately. He is, it may be recalled, in the role first intended for Bert Lahr, who was kept from joining the show by a previous contract. Assisting him in the comicalities of the evening is that gadfly merry-andrew, William Kent, who is permitted to be only moderately successful. The ingénue, Miss Rogers, is an oncoming young person of the type whom, at her first appearance, half of the audience immediately classified as "cute."

The premiere performance was conducted by George Gershwin, and he got as much applause as anyone on the stage. Under his baton were a pit full of experts in syncopation, who contributed their share to making *Girl Crazy* an agreeable diversion which seems destined to find a profitable place among the luxuries of Times Square, if not the necessities.

J. Brooks Atkinson ON
Private Lives
BY Noel Coward

January 27, 1931
Times Square Theatre
256 Performances

PRIVATE LIVES, a comedy in three acts, by Noel Coward. Staged by the author; settings by G. E. Calthrop; produced by Charles B. Cochran.

Sybil Chase	Jill Esmond
Elyot Chase	Noel Coward
Victor Prynne	Laurence Olivier
Amanda Prynne	Gertrude Lawrence
Louise	Therese Quadri

Noel Coward's talent for little things remains unimpaired. In *Private Lives,* in which he appeared at the Times Square last evening, he has nothing to say, and manages to say it with competent agility for three acts. Sometimes the nothingness of this comedy begins to show through the dialogue. Particularly in the long second act, which is as thin as a patent partition, Mr. Coward's talent for little things threatens to run dry. But when the time comes to drop the second act curtain his old facility for theatrical climax comes bubbling out of the tap again. There is a sudden brawl. Mr. Coward, in person, and Gertrude Lawrence, likewise in person, start tumbling over the furniture and rolling on the floor, and the audience roars with delight. For Mr. Coward, who dotes on pranks, has an impish wit, a genius for phrase-making, a subtlety of inflection, and an engaging manner on the stage. Paired with Miss Lawrence in a mild five-part escapade, he carries *Private Lives* through by the skin of his teeth.

Take two married couples on their respective honeymoons, divide them instantly, and there—if the two leading players are glamorous comedians—you have the situation. As a matter of fact, it has a little more finesse than that. For Elyot Chase, who feels rather grumpy about his second honeymoon, and Amanda Prynne, who feels rather grumpy about hers, were divorced from each other five years ago. When they see each other at the same honeymoon hotel in France they suddenly realize they should never have been divorced. Their new marriages are horrible blunders. Their impulse is to fly away together at once. They fly. How rapturously they love and quarrel in a Paris flat, and how frightfully embarrassed they are when their deserted bride and bridegroom finally catch up with them, is what keeps Mr. Coward just this side of his wits' end for the remaining two acts.

For the most part it is a duologue between Mr. Coward and Miss Lawrence. Jill Esmond, as the deserted bride, and Laurence Olivier, as the deserted bridegroom, are permitted to chatter foolishly once or twice in the first act, and to help keep the ball rolling at the end. After the furniture has been upset, Thérèse Quadri, as a French maid, is invited to come in, raise the curtains and jabber her Gallic distress over unseemly confusion. But these are utilitarian parts in the major tour de force of Mr. Coward and Miss Lawrence cooing and spatting at home.

Be it known that their passion is a troubled one. They coo with languid pleasure. But they are also touchy, and fly on the instant into feline rages. Mr. Coward's wit is not ostentatious. He tucks it away neatly in pat phrases and subtle word combinations and smartly bizarre allusions. Occasionally he comes out boldly with a flat statement of facts. "Certain women should be struck regularly like gongs," he declares. Acting just as he writes, he is crisp, swift and accurate. And Miss Lawrence, whose subtlety has not always been conspicuous, plays this time with rapidity and humor. Her ruddy beauty, her supple grace and the russet drawl in her voice keep you interested in the slightly wind-blown affairs of a scanty comedy. If Mr. Coward's talent were the least bit clumsy, there would be no comedy at all.

J. Brooks Atkinson ON
Mourning Becomes Electra
BY Eugene O'Neill

October 26, 1931
Guild Theatre
150 Performances

MOURNING BECOMES ELECTRA, a trilogy by Eugene O'Neill, consisting of HOMECOMING, a play in four scenes: THE HUNTED, a play in five scenes, and THE HAUNTED, a play in five scenes. Staged by Philip Moeller; settings and costumes designed by Robert Edmond Jones; produced by the Theatre Guild under the supervision of Theresa Helburn and Maurice Wertheim.

HOMECOMING

Seth Beckwith	Arthur Hughes
Amos Ames	Jack Byrne
Louisa	Bernice Elliott
Minnie	Emily Lorraine
Christine	Alla Nazimova
Lavinia Mannon	Alice Brady
Captain Peter Niles	Philip Foster
Hazel Niles	Mary Arbenz
Captain Adam Brant	Thomas Chalmers
Brig. Gen. Ezra Mannon	Lee Baker

THE HUNTED

Mrs. Josiah Borden ....Augusta Durgeon
Mrs. Everett Hills ....Janet Young
Dr. Joseph Blake ....Erskine Sanford
Josiah Borden ....James Bosnell
Everett Hills ....Oliver Putnam
Christine Mannon ....Alla Nazimova
Hazel Niles...Mary Arbenz
Peter Niles...Philip Foster
Lavinia Mannon ....Alice Brady
Orin Mannon...Earle Larimore
A Chantyman ....John Hendricks
Captain Adam Brant ....Thomas Chalmers

THE HAUNTED

Abner Small..Erskine Sanford
Ira Mackel...Oliver Putnam
Joe Silva...Grant Gordon
Amos Ames...Jack Byrne
Seth Beckwith ....Arthur Hughes
Peter Niles...Philip Foster
Hazel Niles...Mary Arbenz
Lavinia Mannon ....Alice Brady
Orin Mannon...Earle Larimore

Mr. O'Neill gives not only size but weight in *Mourning Becomes Electra,* which the Theatre Guild mounted at its own theatre for the greater part of yesterday afternoon and evening. The size is a trilogy that consumes six hours in the playing. The weight is the formidable earnestness of Mr. O'Neill's cheerless dramatic style. To him the curse that the fates have set against the New England house of Mannon is no trifling topic for a casual dramatic discussion, but a battering into the livid mysteries of life. Using a Greek legend as his model, he has reared up a universal tragedy of tremendous stature—deep, dark, solid, uncompromising and grim. It is heroically thought out and magnificently wrought in style and structure, and it is played by Alice Brady and Mme. Nazimova with consummate artistry and passion. Mr. O'Neill has written overwhelming dramas in the past. In *Strange Interlude* he wrote one almost as long as this trilogy. But he has never before fulfilled himself so completely; he has never commanded his theme in all its variety and adumbrations with such superb strength, coolness and coherence. To this department, which ordinarily reserves its praise for the dead, *Mourning Becomes Electra* is Mr. O'Neill's masterpiece.

As the title acknowledges, *Mourning Becomes Electra* follows the scheme of the Orestes-Electra legend which Aeschylus, Sophocles and Euripides translated into drama in the days of Greek classicism. Like the doomed house of Atreus, this New England family of Civil War time is dripping with foul and unnatural murder. The mother murders the father. The son murders his mother's lover. The mother mercifully commits suicide. The daughter's malefic importunities drive the son to suicide. It is a family that simmers with hatred, suspicion, jealousy and greed, and that is twisted by unnatural loves. Although Mr. O'Neill uses the Orestes legend as the scheme of his trilogy, it is his ambition to abandon the gods, whom the Greeks humbly invoked at the crises of drama, and to interpret the whole legend in terms of modern psychology. From royalty this story of vengeance comes down to the level of solid New England burghers. From divinity it comes into the sphere of truths that are known. There are no mysteries about the inverted relationships that set all these gaunt-minded people against one another, aside from the primary mystery of the ferocity of life. Students of the new psychology will find convenient labels to explain why the mother betrays her husband, why the daughter instinctively takes the father's side, why the son fears his father and clings to his mother, why the daughter gradually inherits the characteristics of her mother after the deaths of the parents, and why the son transfers his passion to his sister. As for Mr. O'Neill, he has been chiefly concerned with the prodigious task of writing these modern plays.

And through three plays and fifteen scenes he has kept the rhythm of his story sculptural in its stark outline. The Mannon curse is inherited. For this fine New England mansion was built in hatred when the Mannons cast off the brother who had sinned with a French-Canadian servant. Her son, Captain Brant, comes back into their lives to avenge his mother's dishonor and he becomes the lover of Ezra Mannon's wife. From that point on *Mourning Becomes Electra* stretches out as a strong chain of murders and revenge and the house of Mannon is a little island walled round with the dead.

There are big scenes all the way through. Before the first play is fairly started the dance of death begins with Lavinia upbraiding Christine, her mother, with secret adultery. Christine plotting with Captain Brant to poison her husband on the night when he returns from the Civil War; Christine poisoning her husband and being discovered with the tablets by Lavinia as the climax to the first play; Lavinia proving her mother's guilt to Orin, her brother, by planting the box of poison tablets on the breast of her dead father and admitting her terrified mother to the chamber of death; Lavinia and Orin following their mother to a rendezvous with the captain on his ship and murdering him in his cabin; Lavinia forcing her brother to suicide and waiting panic-stricken for the report of his pistol; Lavinia in the last scene of the last play sealing herself up with this haunted house to live with the spectres of her dead—all these are scenes of foreboding and horror.

Yet *Mourning Becomes Electra* is no parade of bravura scenes. For this is an organic play in which story rises out of character and character rises out of story, and each episode is foreshadowed by what precedes it. Although Mr. O'Neill has been no slave to the classic origins of his tragedy, he has transmuted the same impersonal forces into the modern idiom, and the production, which has been brilliantly directed by Philip Moeller, gives you some of the stately spectacle of Greek classicism. Lavinia in a flowing black dress sitting majestically on the steps of Robert Edmond Jones's set of a New England mansion is an unforgettable and portentous picture. Captain Brant pacing the deck of his ship in the ringing silence of the night, the murdered Mannon lying on his bier in the deep shadows of his study, the entrances and exits of Christine and Lavinia through doors that open and close on death are scenes full of dramatic beauty. To give you perspective on this tragedy Mr. O'Neill has a sort of Greek chorus in Seth, the hired man, and the frightened townsfolk who gather outside the house, laughing and muttering. Mr. O'Neill has viewed his tragedy from every side, thought it through to the last detail and composed it in a straightforward dialogue that tells its story without hysteria.

As Mr. O'Neill has mastered his play, so the actors have mastered their parts and so Mr. Moeller has molded the parts into a measured, fluent performance. Miss Brady, as Lavinia, has one of the longest parts ever written. None of her neurotic dramatics in the past has prepared us for the demoniac splendor of her Lavinia. She speaks in an ominous, full voice that only once or twice breaks into the splintery diffusion of artificial climaxes. Lavinia has recreated Miss Brady into a majestic actress. As Christine, Mme. Nazimova gives a performance of haunting beauty, rich in variety, plastic, eloquent and imaginatively transcendent. Lee Baker, as the Mannon father conveys little of the towering indomitability of that part and lets his death scene crumple into mediocrity. Earle Larimore plays Orin from the inside with great resource, elasticity and understanding. As Captain Brant, Thomas Chalmers has a solid body to his playing. There are excellently designed bits by Arthur Hughes and Erskine Sanford as townspeople. Philip Foster, and especially Mary Arbenz, give able performances as a brother and sister.

For Mr. O'Neill, for the Guild and for lovers of drama, *Mourning Becomes Electra*, is, accordingly, an occasion for great rejoicing. Mr. O'Neill has set his hand to a tremendous story, and told it with coolness and clarity. In sustained thought and workmanship it is his finest tragedy. All that he fretted over in the past has trained him for this masterpiece.

Brooks Atkinson ON
Design for Living
BY Noel Coward

January 24, 1933

Ethel Barrymore Theatre

135 Performances

DESIGN FOR LIVING, a play in three acts, by Noel
Coward. Staged by the author; settings by G. E.
Calthrop; produced by Max Gordon.

Gilda	Lynn Fontanne
Ernest Friedman	Campbell Gullan
Otto	Alfred Lunt
Leo	Noel Coward
Miss Hodge	Gladys Henson
Mr. Birbeck	Philip Tonge
Photographer	Ward Bishop
Grace Torrence	Ethel Borden
Helen Carver	Phyllis Connard
Henry Carver	Alan Campbell
Matthew	Macleary Stinnett

Mr. Coward, who has a way of his own with
musical romance and historical pageantry,
has a way of his own with the familiar triangle.
Design for Living, which came to the Ethel Barrymore Theatre last evening, is the proof. It is a
decadent way, if you feel obliged to pull a long
moral face over his breezy fandango. It is an audacious and hilarious way if you relish the attack
and retreat of artificial comedy that bristles with
wit. Occasionally Mr. Coward appears to be asking you to look upon the volatile emotions of his
characters as real, and that—if it is true—would
be a pity. For he is the master of impudence and
tart whimsy, of plain words that leap out of the dialogue like shafts of laughter. At least they do on
the lips of his three chief actors. As Leo, he is the
sharpest corner of his own triangle. As Otto and
Gilda, Alfred Lunt and Lynn Fontanne complete
this design for frivolous living. They are an incomparable trio of high comedians. And they give
Design for Living the sententious acting that
transmutes artificial comedy into delight.

What, with friends, acquaintances and servants, there are more than three characters in this
triangle. Mr. Coward needs a few dull persons to
victimize. But what he really enjoys is the bizarre
nonsense of his three characters. One is a playwright. One is an artist. The third is a woman who
is also an artist. Otto and Leo, who are close
friends of very long standing both love her very
much, and she loves them. To save herself from
the complications of this singular situation she escapes from both and marries a sober art merchant
who takes her to New York. But after a voyage
around the world on a freighter the two wild oats
turn up like Tweedledum and Tweedledee at her
penthouse apartment. Their impudent gayety dis-
arms her. After a stormy session with her husband,
who knows the code of a gentleman, she returns to
the exuberant disorder of her kind.

Unfortunately for the uses of artificial comedy,
establishing this triangular situation involves considerable sobriety. All through the first act Mr.
Coward writes as earnestly as a psychologist.
Through a long stretch of the third act he surrenders to the patter of ordinary folk and, incidentally, to ordinary actors who can make little of the
wrangling impertinence of their lines. When *Design for Living* sounds serious you wish impatiently that Mr. Coward would cut the cackle and
come to the main business, which is his brand of
satyr comedy. He touches that off with remarkable
dexterity. Otto and Leo drinking themselves into
silly merriment after Gilda has left them, Otto and
Leo striding pompously around Gilda's penthouse
in the last act, the fluff of worldly success and the
vaudeville of telephone conversations suit Mr.
Coward's skimming pen exactly. When he is in an
impish mood, which is most of the time, he is
enormously funny.

But the acting supplies the final brilliance. *Design for Living* is written for actors—in fact, for
the three actors who are now most conspicuous in
it. They are extraordinarily well balanced. Miss
Fontanne, with her slow, languorous deliberation;
Mr. Lunt, with his boyish enthusiasm; Mr. Coward, with his nervous, biting charity, create more
variety in the acting than Mr. Coward has got into
the parts. They enjoy this comedy as much as the

audience does. Being under no solemn delusions about it, they make *Design for Living* an actors' lark.

It is one of the paradoxes of the theatre that the most trifling things are often the most priceless. Skill, art, clairvoyance about the stage, even erudition of a sort, have gone into this gay bit of drollery. It is highly diverting for the evening thereof.

Lewis Nichols ON

The 3-Penny Opera

ORIGINAL GERMAN TEXT BY Bertolt Brecht

ENGLISH VERSION BY Gifford Cochran and

Jerrold Krimsky

MUSIC BY Kurt Weill

April 13, 1933

Empire Theatre

12 Performances

THE 3-PENNY OPERA, a musical show in a prologue, three acts and six scenes, derived from *The Beggar's Opera,* by John Gay. Book by Bert Brecht and adapted from the German by Gifford Cochran and Jerrold Krimsky. Music by Kurt Weill. Staged by Francesco von Mendelssohn and Zeke Colvan. Settings duplicated by Cleon Throckmorton from the designs of Caspar Neher. Produced by John Krimsky and Gifford Cochran.

Legend singer	George Heller
Jonathan Peachum	Rex Weber
Mrs. Peachum	Evelyn Beresford
Polly Peachum	Steffi Duna
Capt. Macheath (alias Mackie Messer)	Robert Chisholm
Jenny Diver	Marjorie Dille
Filch	Herbert Rudley
Matthew	Anthony Blair
Crooked Finger Jack	Burgess Meredith
Walter	Harry Bellaver
Robert	George Heller
Jimmy	Francis Kennelly
Wing	H. L. Donsu
Reverend Kimball	John Connolly
Sheriff Brown	Rex Evans
Beggar	Harry Hornick
Vixen	Mary Heberden
Trull	Eugenie Reed
Madame	Lotta Burnell
Tawd	Hilda Kosta
Dolly	Ruth Thomas
Betty	Lillian Okun
Molly Brazen	Jean de Koven
Smith	Gerald Hamer
Constable	Arthur Brady
Lucy Brown	Josephine Huston

There bounded over the ancient and honorable stage of the Empire Theatre last evening as nice a collection of rascals as it could ever boast. They appeared for and in *The 3-Penny Opera,* and on behalf of the restoration to a beer-complacent city of—the restoration drama. For the work which was put forward by Messrs. Krimsky and Cochran is founded on John Gay's *The Beggar's Opera,* which would be the *Of Thee I Sing* of 1728.

Such should do for historical identification, but unfortunately there must be a little more. For, while Gay was denouncing conditions, in his somber fashion, the creators of the German version of the Empire's present child were joking a bit with the past. When the most recent sponsors of Polly Peachum and Captain Macheath came along they incorporated the later whimsies. As a result *The 3-Penny Opera* is about three-dimensional satire, or humor, or whatever such an aggregation of things would be.

It does form, however, a gently mad evening in the theatre for those who like their spades in the usual nomenclature of the earnest. *The 3-Penny Opera* has a splendid score, one that is interesting, pleasant and quite in the air of the early day sinners of London. Its tunes run with the song of François Villon and of John Gay—which is to say they are at the same time merry and devilishly in earnest. The music is by Kurt Weill, carried over from the Teutonic *Die Dreigroschenoper,* which was step two in the history.

Bert Brecht has been responsible for the book. He has chosen from *The Beggar's Opera* all the necessary material, and has built thereupon. He has allowed the characters to remain about as they were—which, in the case of the Peachums, was a worthy thing, indeed. The beggars, the constables, the gang of cut-throats and pick-pockets still act with their old charming lack of principle.

The cast for the opera has been chosen excellently, and Francesco von Mendelssohn has directed them gayly. Rex Weber has the part of Jonathan Peachum. He can be Peachum, when necessary, and Brecht when necessary, all without the flickering of an eye. Mrs. Peachum is played by Evelyn Beresford, and Captain Macheath by Robert Chisholm. This last appears, perhaps, just a shade well-bred for *The Beggar's Opera*. Rex Evans has the part of Sheriff Brown, that friend of the Captain's, that scourge of London. And, finally, there is Steffi Duna, imported for the occasion from the Continent, via London. She is excellent as Polly Peachum, taking as noble a bow as you could wish.

On the whole, *The 3-Penny Opera* is worth the seeing. There are moments now and then that seem pretty much like other moments. But for entertainment of an unusual variety, it is there with its scoundrels, its chants, its ragamuffins and its thieves, all of them nicely held together for the occasion.

Brooks Atkinson ON
Tobacco Road
BY Jack Kirkland

December 4, 1933
Masque Theatre
3,182 Performances

TOBACCO ROAD, a play in three acts, by Jack Kirkland, adapted from the novel of the same name by Erskine Caldwell. Setting by Robert Redington Sharpe; staged and produced by Anthony Brown.

Jeeter Lester	Henry Hull
Dude Lester	Sam Byrd
Ada Lester	Margaret Wycherly
Ellie May	Ruth Hunter
Grandma Lester	Patricia Quinn
Lov Bensey	Dean Jagger
Henry Peabody	Ashley Cooper
Sister Bessie Rice	Maude Odell
Pearl	Reneice Rehan
Captain Tim	Lamar King
George Payne	Edwin Walter

Since it is based on a novel, *Tobacco Road,* which was acted at the Masque last evening, is not an organic play. Although Jack Kirkland has turned it into three acts, it is still Erskine Caldwell's novel at heart, which is to say that it is more like a soliloquy with variations than a dramatic character sketch. Under Mr. Caldwell's influence it is also one of the grossest episodes ever put on the stage. Once the theatre used to be sinful. But now it is the novel that ferrets out the abominations of life and exposes them for sale in the marketplace. The men of letters have stolen the dramatists' crimson badge; and the theatre has never sheltered a fouler or more degenerate parcel of folks than the hardscrabble family of Lester that lives along the *Tobacco Road.*

But that is not a full and disinterested report of the Masque Theatre's current tenant. For Mr. Caldwell is a demoniac genius—brutal, grimly comic and clairvoyant. No one has chronicled the complete degeneracy of the Georgia cracker with such inhuman detachment. He writes with the fiery sword. Although *Tobacco Road* reels around the stage like a drunken stranger to the theatre, it has spasmodic moments of merciless power when truth is flung into your face with all the slime that truth contains. That is why Mr. Caldwell's grossness cannot be dismissed as morbidity and gratuitous indecency. It is the blunt truth of the characters he is describing, and it leaves a malevolent glow of poetry above the rudeness of his statement.

Tobacco Road is the saga of Jeeter Lester, a good-for-nothing farmer who still lives on the land his father and grandfather farmed. But it is no longer his. Being lazy and dissolute, he has lost everything and now exists with his tatterdemalion family in the dirt and filth of a rickety shack. The Lesters are ragged, foul, starving and lazy. But still Jeeter preserves that fluency of talk and fecundity of crack-brained ideas and that animal sensuality which live in the lowest darkness. Everything exists on the same plane of inhumanity. Even death leaves no impression upon life that is dead in everything save the body.

As Jeeter Lester, Henry Hull gives the performance of his career. For years Mr. Hull has been charming and trivial about many things and singularly obtuse about some others. But here is a character portrait as mordant and brilliant as you can imagine. Dressed in loathsome rags, untidily bearded and heavily wrinkled, Mr. Hull's Georgia cracker staggers through a whole gamut of emotions and passions—pungent, pathetic, horrible and gargantuanly comic.

The performance is shabbily directed. But it includes an excellent portrait of a headlong boy by Sam Byrd and a picturesque setting by Robert Redington Sharpe. Plays as clumsy and rudderless as *Tobacco Road* seldom include so many scattered items that leave such a vivid impression.

Brooks Atkinson ON
Anything Goes
BOOK BY Guy Bolton AND P. G. Wodehouse
AND BY Howard Lindsay AND Russel Crouse
MUSIC AND LYRICS BY Cole Porter

November 21, 1934
Alvin Theatre
420 Performances

ANYTHING GOES, a musical comedy in two acts and nine scenes. Music and lyrics by Cole Porter. Book by Guy Bolton and P. G. Wodehouse and revised by Howard Lindsay and Russel Crouse. Staged by Mr. Lindsay; dances and ensembles arranged by Robert Alton; settings by Donald Oenslager; costumes designed by Jenkins; produced by Vinton Freedley.

Bartender	George E. Mack
Elisha J. Whitney	Paul Everton
Billy Crocker	William Gaxton
Bellboy	Irvin Pincus
Reno Sweeney	Ethel Merman
Reporter	Edward Delbridge
First camera man	Chet Bree
Second camera man	Neal Evans
Sir Evelyn Oakleigh	Leslie Barrie
Hope Harcourt	Bettina Hall
Mrs. Wadsworth T. Harcourt	Helen Raymond
Bishop Dodson	Pacie Ripple
Ching	Richard Wang
Ling	Charlie Fang
Snooks	Drucilla Strain
Steward	William Stamm
Assistant purser	Val Vestoff
First Federal man	Harry Wilson
Second Federal man	Arthur Imperato
Mrs. Wentworth	May Abbey
Mrs. Frick	Florence Earle
Reverend Dr. Moon	Victor Moore
Bonnie Letour	Vera Dunn
Chief officer	Houston Richards
Ship's drunk	William Barry
Mr. Swift	Maurice Elliot
Little boy	Billy Curtis
Captain	John C. King
Babe	Vivian Vance
The Foursome	Marshall Smith, Ray Johnson, Dwight Snyder, Dee Porter

The Ritz Quartette..Chet Bree,
          Bill Stamm, Neal Evans, Edward Delbridge
The Alvin Quartette ....Arthur Imperato, David
              Glidden, Richard Nealy, Stuart Fraser
Ship's Orchestra..The Stylists

By keeping their sense of humor uppermost, they have made a thundering good musical show out of *Anything Goes,* which was put on at the Alvin last evening. They are Guy Bolton and P. G. Wodehouse, whose humor is completely un-hackneyed; Cole Porter, who has written a dashing score with impish lyrics, and Howard Lindsay and Russel Crouse, who have been revising the jokes in person. After all, these supermen must have had a good deal to do with the skylarking that makes *Anything Goes* such hilarious and dynamic entertainment. But when a show is off the top shelf of the pantry cupboard it is hard to remember that the comics have not written all those jokes and the singers have not composed all those exultant tunes. If Ethel Merman did not write "I Get a Kick Out of You" and also the title song of the show she has made them hers now by the swinging gusto of her platform style.

Do you remember a pathetic, unsteady little man who answers to the name of Alexander Throttlebottom? Masquerading in the program as Victor Moore, he is the first clown of this festival, and he is tremendously funny. For it has occurred to the wastrels who wrote the book to represent him as a gangster disguised as a parson and to place him on a liner bound for Europe. Among the other passengers are a night-club enchantress, who sings with the swaggering authority of Ethel Merman, and a roistering man about town who enjoys the infectious exuberance of William Gaxton. There is also a lady of considerable breeding who can sing the soprano of Bettina Hall.

What a voyage! Last year Howard Lindsay staged a memorable comedy entitled *She Loves Me Not.* What he learned there in the vein of theatre versatility he has generously applied to *Anything Goes,* and the product is a rag, tag and bobtail of comic situations and of music sung in the spots when it is most exhilarating. Throttlebot-

tom looks mighty absurd in those prelate's vestments. When his gangster blood comes through his disguise and his bewildered personality, comedy is the most satisfying invention of the human race. He calls his portable machine gun "My little pal putt-putt-putt" with a dying inflection. He muses on the advisability of bumping off an annoying passenger as if he were composing a wistful sonnet. Whatever he does, Mr. Throttlebottom, who is just as sweet under any other name, is the quintessence of musical comedy humor, and the authors of *Anything Goes* have given him the sort of thing he can do best.

As far as that goes, it suits William Gaxton, too. Following the lead of a madcap book, he is in and out of all sorts of disguises—a sailor, a Spanish nobleman with false whiskers just clipped off a Pomeranian, a fabulous public enemy. Through the show he fairly dances with enjoyment and high spirits, making every song sound good on his old Gaxiolaphone. When he sings with Miss Merman the composer ought to be very grateful for a pair of performers who can make every note burst with vitality and every line sound like a masterpiece of wit. "You're the Top" is one of the most congenial songs Mr. Porter has written. Mr. Gaxton and Miss Merman put their toes as well as their voices into it.

Although Miss Hall has a nicer talent, she plays the part of a girl of exalted station with winning good humor and she sings "All Through the Night" with the thrilling beauty of a trained artist. For minor diversion there is a foursome of dry-humored sailors for whom Mr. Porter has written a droll chanty. Count as items worth sober consideration a platoon of chorus girls whose dancing is also well-planned; a suite of Oenslager settings; a wardrobe of gowns by Jenkins—and a general good time. Guy Bolton and P. G. Wodehouse were always funny fellows. It does them no harm to be associated with Cole Porter, Howard Lindsay, Russel Crouse and a thundering good song-and-dance show.

Brooks Atkinson ON
Waiting for Lefty
BY Clifford Odets

February 10, 1935
Civic Repertory Theatre
96 Performances

GROUP THEATRE SKETCHES, by Sanford Meisner, Florence Cooper, Bob Lewis, Clifford Odets, J. E. Bromberg, Walter Coy, Elia Kazan, Tony Kraber, Morris Carnovsky.

WAITING FOR LEFTY, play in six scenes, by Clifford Odets. Directed by Sanford Meisner and Clifford Odets. At the Civic Repertory Theatre.

Fatt	Morris Carnovsky
Joe	Art Smith
Edna	Ruth Nelson
Miller	Gerrit Kraber
Fayette	Morris Carnovsky
Irv	Walter Coy
Florrie	Phoebe Brand
Sid	Jules Garfield
Clayton	Russell Collins
Clancy	Elia Kazan
Gunman	David Korchmar
Henchman	Alan Baxter
Secretary	Paula Miller
Actor	William Challee
Grady	Morris Carnovsky
Dr. Barnes	Roman Bohnen
Dr. Benjamin	Luther Adler
Agate Keller	J. E. Bromberg
A man	Bob Lewis
Voices in the audience	Herbert Ratner
	Clifford Odets, Lewis Leverett

As actors in plays of conscious intellectual significance, the young people of the Group Theatre have been fumbling around without much success ever since they mounted *Men in White*. But their afternoon program, consisting of random sketches and Clifford Odets's *Waiting for Lefty,* which was repeated yesterday at the Civic Repertory Theatre, is an invigorating revelation of their skill and force as an acting company. For the first time in a good many months it is possible to write about them without fussy reservations. Like many other individuals and organizations, the Group Theatre is most stimulating when it is not competing with the entertainment business on Broadway, which is not interested in the studio craft of acting nor in the drama of social revolution.

Uptown the Group Theatre communicants are suspected of having no sense of humor. Nothing said between these column rules this morning is intended to suggest that they are native wits or mountebanks. But the fact remains that their bill of turns and improvisations is winningly good-humored. Their classroom presentation of the grave-digger scene from *Hamlet* is an amusing proof of the fact that words are less significant in the drama than acting styles and ideas of direction. In a nonsensical improvisation, labeled *Two Bums on a Bench,* Mr. Bromberg and Mr. Carnovsky suggest that the written word is virtually superfluous, for they clown their way through an unintelligible comic sketch speaking nothing but gibberish. The most overpowering number in the preliminary program is entirely in pantomime to the off-stage music of the allegretto of Beethoven's Seventh symphony. What psychological effect the music has in the theatre this reporter is unable to explain on the spur of the moment. But without props, scenery or costumes Mr. Bromberg and two assistants translate their pantomimic surgical operation into a vivid silent drama. Among the other items there are parodies, slap-stick bits and unblushing cowboy songs.

The dynamics of the program are the property of Mr. Odets's *Waiting for Lefty*. His saga, based on the New York taxi strike of last year, is clearly one of the most thorough, trenchant jobs in the school of revolutionary drama. It argues the case for a strike against labor racketeering and the capitalist state by using the theatre auditorium as the hall where the taxi union is meeting. In four or five subordinate scenes, played with a few bare props in corners of the stage, the personal problems of several representative insurgents are drawn sharply. Mr. Odets is the author of *Awake and Sing!* which the Group Theatre expects to produce next week. *Waiting for Lefty* is soundly constructed and fiercely dramatic in the theatre, and it is also a keen preface to his playwriting talents.

His associates in the Group Theatre have never played with more thrust, drive and conviction. *Waiting for Lefty* suits them down to the boards. Incidentally, the progress of the revolutionary drama in New York City during the last two seasons is the most obvious recent development in our theatre. In addition to the Theatre Union, with its productions of *Stevedore* and *Sailors of Cattaro,* there is the Artef band, which is playing *Recruits* in Yiddish as beautifully as the Habima troupe played *The Dybbuk.* Now the Group Theatre gives its most slashing performance in a drama about the taxi strike. This program will be repeated at intervals this Winter.

Brooks Atkinson ON
Porgy and Bess
BOOK BY Du Bose Heyward
LYRICS BY Du Bose Heyward AND
Ira Gershwin
MUSIC BY Ira Gershwin

October 8, 1935

Alvin Theatre

124 Performances

PORGY AND BESS, "An American folk-opera" in three acts and nine scenes, based on the play, *Porgy,* by Du Bose and Dorothy Heyward. Score by George Gershwin, libretto by Mr. Heyward, and lyrics by Mr. Heyward and Ira Gershwin. Staged by Rouben Mamoulian; scenery by Sergei Soudeikine; orchestra conducted by Alexander Smallens; produced by the Theatre Guild.

Mingo	Ford L. Buck
Clara	Abbie Mitchell
Sportin' Life	John W. Bubbles
Jake	Edward Matthews
Maria	Georgette Harvey
Annie	Olive Ball
Lily	Helen Dowdy
Serena	Ruby Elzy
Robbins	Henry Davis

Jim	Jack Carr
Peter	Gus Simons
Porgy	Todd Duncan
Crown	Warren Coleman
Bess	Anne Wiggins Brown
Detective	Alexander Campbell
Two Policemen	Harold Woolf, Burton McEvilly
Undertaker	John Garth
Frazier	J. Rosamond Johnson
Mr. Archdale	George Lessey
Nelson	Ray Yeates
Strawberry Woman	Helen Dowdy
Crab Man	Ray Yeates
Coroner	George Carleton

Residents of Catfish Row, fishermen, children, stevedores, &c. ....The Eva Jessye Choir: Catherine Jackson Ayres, Lillian Cowan, Sara Daigeau, Darlean Duval, Kate Hall, Altonell Hines, Louisa Howard, Harriet Jackson, Rosalie King, Assotta Marshall, Wilnette Mayers, Sadie McGill, Massie Patterson, Annabelle Ross, Louise Twyman, Helen R. White, Musa Williams, Reginald Beane, Caesar Bennett, G. Harry Bolden, Edward Broadnax, Carroll Clark, Joseph Crawford, John Diggs, Leonard Franklin, John Garth, Joseph James, Clarence Jacobs, Allen Lewis, Jimmie Lightfoot, Lycurgus Lockman, Henry May, Junius McDaniel, Arthur McLean, William O'Neil, Robert Raines, Andrew Taylor, Leon Threadgill, Jimmie Waters, Robert Williams, Ray Yeates.

Choral Conductor ....Eva Jessye.

Children....Naida King, Regina Williams, Enid Wilkins, Allen Tinney, William Tinney, Herbert Young.

The Charleston Orphans' Band ....Sam Anderson, Eric Bell, Le Verria Bilton, Benjamine Browne, Claude Christian, Shedrack Dobson, David Ellis, Clarence Smith, John Strachan, George Tait, Allen Tinney, William Tinney, Charles Williams, Herbert Young.

After eight years of savory memories, *Porgy* has acquired a score, a band, a choir of singers and a new title, *Porgy and Bess,* which the Theatre Guild put on at the Alvin last evening. Du Bose and Dorothy Heyward wrote the original lithograph of Catfish Row, which Rouben Mamoulian translated into a memorable work of theatre dynamics. But *Porgy and Bess* represents George Gershwin's longing to compose an American folk opera on a suitable theme. Although Mr. Heyward is the author of the libretto and shares with Ira Gershwin the credit for the lyrics, and although Mr. Mamoulian has again mounted the director's box, the evening is unmistakably George

Gershwin's personal holiday. In fact, the volume of music he has written during the last two years on the ebony fable of a Charleston rookery has called out a whole brigade of Times Square music critics, who are quite properly the masters of this occasion. Mr. Downes, soothsayer of the diatonic scale, is now beetling his brow in the adjoining cubicle. There is an authoritative ring to his typewriter clatter tonight.

In these circumstances, the province of a drama critic is to report on the transmutation of *Porgy* out of drama into music theatre. Let it be said at once that Mr. Gershwin has contributed something glorious to the spirit of the Heywards' community legend. If memory serves, it always lacked the glow of personal feeling. Being a fairly objective narrative of a neighborhood of Negroes who lived a private racial life in the midst of a white civilization, *Porgy* was a natural subject for theatre showmanship. The groupings, the mad fantasy of leaping shadows, the panic-stricken singing over a corpse, the evil bulk of the buzzard's flight, the screaming hurricane—these large audible and visible items of showmanship took precedence over the episode of Porgy's romance with Crown's high-steppin' gal.

Whether or not Mr. Gershwin's score measures up to its intentions as American folk opera lies in Mr. Downes's bailiwick. But to the ears of a theatre critic Mr. Gershwin's music gives a personal voice to Porgy's loneliness when, in a crowd of pitying neighbors, he learns that Bess has vanished into the capacious and remote North. The pathetic apprehension of the "Where's My Bess" trio and the manly conviction of "I'm on My Way" add something vital to the story that was missing before.

These comments are written by a reviewer so inured to the theatre that he regards operatic form as cumbersome. Why commonplace remarks that carry no emotion have to be made in a chanting monotone is a problem in art he cannot fathom. Even the hermit thrush drops into conversational tones when he is not singing from the topmost spray in a tree. Turning *Porgy* into opera has resulted in a deluge of casual remarks that have to

be thoughtfully intoned and that amazingly impede the action. Why do composers vex it so? "Sister, you goin' to the picnic?" "No, I guess not." Now why in heaven's name must two characters in an opera clear their throats before they can exchange that sort of information? What a theatre critic probably wants is a musical show with songs that evoke the emotion of situations and make no further pretensions. Part of the emotion of a drama comes from the pace of the performance.

And what of the amusing little device of sounds and rhythms, of sweeping, sawing, hammering and dusting, that opens the last scene early one morning? In the program it is solemnly described as "Occupational Humoresque." But any music hall would be glad to have it without its tuppence colored label. Mr. Mamoulian is an excellent director for dramas of ample proportions. He is not subtle, which is a virtue in showmanship. His crowds are arranged in masses that look as solid as a victory at the polls; they move with simple unanimity, and the rhythm is comfortably obvious.

Mr. Gershwin knows that. He has written the scores for innumerable musical shows. After one of them he was presented with the robes of Arthur Sullivan, who also was consumed with a desire to write grand. To the ears of a theatre critic there are intimations in *Porgy and Bess* that Mr. Gershwin is still easiest in mind when he is writing songs with choruses. He, and his present reviewer, are on familiar ground when he is writing a droll tune like "A Woman Is a Sometime Thing," or a lazy darky solo like "I Got Plenty o' Nuttin'," or made-to-order spirituals like "Oh, de Lawd Shake de Heaven," or Sportin' Life's hot-time number entitled "There's a Boat That's Leavin' Soon for New York." If Mr. Gershwin does not enjoy his task most in moments like this, his audience does. In sheer quality of character they are worth an hour of formal music transitions.

For the current folk opera Sergei Soudeikine has prepared Catfish Row settings that follow the general design of the originals, but have more grace, humor and color. In the world of sound that

Mr. Gershwin has created the tattered children of a Charleston byway are still racy and congenial. Promoting *Porgy* to opera involves considerable incidental drudgery for theatregoers who agree with Mark Twain that "classical music is better than it sounds." But Mr. Gershwin has found a personal voice that was inarticulate in the original play. The fear and the pain go deeper in *Porgy and Bess* than they did in penny plain *Porgy.*

Brooks Atkinson ON
Dead End
BY Sidney Kingsley

October 28, 1935

Belasco Theatre

687 Performances

DEAD END, a play in three acts, by Sidney Kingsley. Staged by the author; setting by Norman Bel Geddes; produced by Mr. Geddes.

Gimpty	Theodore Newton
T B	Gabriel Dell
Tommy	Billy Halop
Dippy	Huntz Hall
Angel	Bobby Jordan
Spit	Charles R. Duncan
Doorman	George Cotton
Old Lady	Marie R. Burke
Old Gentleman	George N. Price
First Chauffeur	Charles Benjamin
"Babyface" Martin	Joseph Downing
Hunk	Martin Gabel
Philip Griswald	Charles Bellin
Governess	Sidonie Espero
Milty	Bernard Punsly
Drina	Elspeth Eric
Mr. Griswald	Carroll Ashburn
Mr. Jones	Louis Lord
Kay	Margaret Muller
Jack Hilton	Cyril Gordon Weld
Lady with Dog	Margaret Linden
Three Small Boys	Billy Winston, Joseph Taibi, Sidney Lumet

Second Chauffeur	Richard Clark
Second Avenue Boys	David Gorcey, Leo Gorcey
Mrs. Martin	Marjorie Main
Patrolman Mulligan	Robert J. Mulligan
Francey	Sheila Trent
G.-Men	Francis de Sales, Edward P. Goodnow, Dan Duryea
Policemen	Francis G. Cleveland, William Toubin
Plainclothesman	Harry Selby
Interne	Philip Bourneuf
Medical Examiner	Lewis L. Russel
Sailor	Bernard Zaneville

Inhabitants of East River Terrace, Ambulance Men, &c. . . . Elizabeth Wragge, Drina Hill, Blossom MacDonald, Ethel Dell, Marc Daniels, Elizabeth Perlowin, Edith Jordan, Marie Dell, Bea Punsley, Bess Winston, Anne Miller, Elizabeth Zabelin, George Bond, Matthew Purcell, Herman Osmond, Rose Taibi, George Buzante, Betty Rheingold, Lizzie Leonard, Catherine Kemp, Mag Davis, Nellie Ransom, Betsy Ross, Charles Larue, Paul Meacham, Tom McIntyre, George Anspecke, Jack Kellert, Elizabeth Lowe, Gene Lowe, Charlotte Salkow, Morris Chertov, Charlotte Julien, Willis Duncan.

By adding a little thought and art to considerable accurate observation, Sidney Kingsley has compiled an enormously stirring drama about life in New York City, *Dead End*, which was produced at the Belasco last evening. Somewhere along the East River a raffish deadend street meets the rear entrance to a fashionable apartment house where private yachts have a slip of their own. It is one of those dramatic corners on which Manhattan advertises the distance that divides poverty from riches, and it is a brilliant place to study the case history of the metropolitan gangster. Norman Bel Geddes has filled the stage of the Belasco with one of those super-realistic settings that David Belasco liked to contrive, solid down to the ring of shoes on the asphalt pavement. When the curtain goes up on a scene torn out of the daily life of Manhattan you are prepared for a show. When the curtain falls you know that you have also listened to a drama.

What Mr. Kingsley has in the bottom of his mind is the social condition that breeds gangsters. One of his characters is a notorious gangster who came out of just such an environment and has slunk back to see his mother again and to meet the first girl he ever loved. Swarming around his feet is a shrill, dirty, nervous and shrewd mob of boys who are gangsters in the making.

Before *Dead End* is over Mr. Kingsley shows how a celebrated gangster can come to his end in a dirty gutter, when the Federal agents find him, and how a street urchin can develop into a gangster. Once "Babyface" Martin was only a tough kid like Tommy. When Tommy serves his apprenticeship at reform school, it is Mr. Kingsley's contention that he will be like "Babyface" Martin—a cheap killer, despised by his family and feared by every one who crosses his path.

Not that Mr. Kingsley has turned *Dead End* into a public social document. In its objective photograph of one section of New York it draws inevitable comparison with *Street Scene*. It is full of characters who move casually in and out of a loosely-woven story; it is strident with gutter argot. What you have seen and heard in New York, wondering and apprehensive as you trudge along our begrimed seacoast, has found lodgment in this flaring anecdote of an average day.

The boys' parts are played with such authenticity that there was a foul sidewalk canard last evening that a mob of East Side street arabs had been carted west in their street clothes. Certainly the pitch of their voices has the piercing note of the tenement streets, and their water-skater running across the stage has the rhythm of half-naked pierhead swimmers. According to the office encyclopedia, however, Billy Halop, as the leader of the mob, is Bobby Benson of the radio, famous these many years, and the others are members of the Professional Children's School or the Madison Square Boys Club, or come from stage families.

Although they are at war with the world, they have made their peace with the professional actors who play the mature parts. Joseph Downing as the head gunman, Elspeth Eric as the sister of one of the boys, Marjorie Main as the contemptuous mother of the gangster, Sheila Trent as a cheap prostitute, Theodore Newton as the brooding artist whose constant presence binds all the bizarre elements of the drama, give excellent realistic performances.

Sometimes Mr. Geddes breaks his dramas on the wheel of stage designing. But this time he has reared up a setting that pushes the thought of the author's drama ruthlessly into the audience's face. Not only in its accuracy of detail but in its perspective and its power his setting is a practical masterpiece. Mr. Kingsley is fortunate in his association, for *Dead End* is worth the best our theatre affords. As thought it is a contribution to public knowledge. As drama it is vivid and bold. When the Pulitzer judges gave Mr. Kingsley a prize for *Men in White,* they picked a first-rate man.

Brooks Atkinson ON
Idiot's Delight
BY Robert E. Sherwood

March 24, 1936
Shubert Theatre
300 Performances

IDIOT'S DELIGHT, a play in three acts, by Robert E. Sherwood, with incidental music. Staged by Bretaigne Windust; production conceived and supervised by Alfred Lunt and Lynn Fontanne; setting by Lee Simonson; dances arranged by Morgan Lewis; presented by the Theatre Guild as the sixth and last offering of its eighteenth subscription season.

Dumpsty	George Meader
Signor Palota	Stephen Sandes
Donald Navadel	Barry Thomson
Pittaluga	S. Thomas Gomez
Auguste	Edgar Barrier
Captain Locicero	Edward Raquello
Dr. Waldersee	Sydney Greenstreet
Mr. Cherry	Bretaigne Windust
Mrs. Cherry	Jean Macintyre
Harry Van	Alfred Lunt
Shirley	Jacqueline Paige
Beulah	Connie Crowell
Edna	Frances Foley
Francine	Etna Ross
Elaine	Marjorie Baglin
Bebe	Ruth Timmons
First Officer	Alan Hewitt
Second Officer	Winston Ross

Third Officer	Gilmore Bush
Fourth Officer	Tommaso Tittoni
Quillery	Richard Whorf
Signor Rossi	Le Roi Operti
Signora Rossi	Ernestine De Becker
Major	Giorgio Monteverde
Anna	Una Val
Irene	Lynn Fontanne
Achille Weber	Francis Compton
Musicians	Gerald Kunz, Max Rich, Joseph Knopf.

Mr. Sherwood's love of a good time and his anxiety about world affairs result in one of his most likable entertainments, *Idiot's Delight,* which the Theatre Guild put on at the Shubert last evening. Already it is widely known as the show in which Alfred Lunt plays the part of a third-rate hoofer and Lynn Fontanne wears an exotic blonde wig. That is true, and it represents Mr. Sherwood's taste for exuberance and jovial skullduggery. Having fought in the last war and having a good mind and memory, he is also acutely aware of the dangers of a relapse into bloodshed throughout the world today. His leg-show and frivolity in *Idiot's Delight* are played against a background of cannon calamity, and it concludes with a detonation of airplane bombs. At the final curtain, Mr. Sherwood shoots the works.

If this column observes that the discussion of war is inconclusive and that the mood of the play is somewhat too trivial for such a macabre subject, it is probably taking *Idiot's Delight* much too seriously. For Mr. Sherwood's new play is a robust theatre charade, not quite so heroic and ebullient as *The Petrified Forest,* but well inside the same tradition.

In the cocktail lounge of a hotel in the Italian Alps, near the frontiers of Switzerland and Austria, Mr. Sherwood has gathered a few representative citizens. Among them take notice of a German scientist, a high-strung leader of the labor movement, a munitions manufacturer, an English honeymoon couple, any quantity of Italian soldiers and an American song-and-dance troupe led by a gaudy American hoofer. International relations are so incendiary that they are all being detained by the Italian Government, pending further developments. While they are unhappily waiting

Mr. Sherwood has time to deliver a number of hard-fisted statements about war in general and international politics in particular and to indulge in some very pungent mountebankery, including an impromptu chorus-girl act.

As it happens, the munitions manufacturer is traveling with a fabulous blonde of many false airs whom the hoofer suspects of being a showgirl he entertained many years ago at the Governor Bryan Hotel in Omaha. This is the thread that binds the rambling piece together and permits Alfred Lunt and Lynn Fontanne to become friends once more at the final curtain.

Mr. Sherwood's talk is not conclusive, but it is interesting. In the course of the play he does manage to show that all but one of his characters are helpless victims of internationalism, drawn unwillingly into contests between fear and inferiority, jingoism and bravado. *Idiot's Delight* draws that grotesque distinction between the personal, casual lives people want to live and the roar and thunder that crack-brained governments foment. As the hoofer says, the people are all right as individuals. They are bowled down by a headlong, angry force that is generated apart from themselves.

All this Mr. Sherwood's play suggests, though not so forcefully as perhaps he intends, for the rag, tag and bobtail mood is misleading. What you will probably enjoy more than his argument is the genial humor of his dialogue, his romantic flair for character and his relish of the incongruous and the ridiculous.

The Theatre Guild has met him more than half way. Against an amusingly ostentatious setting by Lee Simonson, Bretaigne Windust has directed a busy and versatile performance. Mr. Lunt has declared another holiday for his cheap-mannered, jaunty hoofer and metallic-voiced balladier, and his musical comedy style is recognizable honky-tonk. Mr. Lunt likes a turkey as much as Mr. Sherwood does. As the spurious Russian, Miss Fontanne also puts on the flamboyant mantle, enjoying the bombast of her accent. If it is not unmannerly to say so, perhaps she enjoys it too much, for the space she takes makes the character a little irritating and also delays the show.

In other parts Richard Whorf, Sydney Greenstreet, Edward Raquello, Francis Compton and George Meader give excellent performances. As for the chorus girls, their culture is pleasantly professional. At the close of one of the best seasons the Theatre Guild has had, Mr. Sherwood has spoken passionately about a grave subject and settled down to writing a gusty show. He and Mr. Lunt have set their hearts on a larkish time.

Brooks Atkinson ON

John Gielgud's *Hamlet*

October 8, 1936

Empire Theatre

132 Performances

John Gielgud as Hamlet in 1936   WIDE WORLD PHOTOS

HAMLET in two acts and nineteen scenes. Settings and costumes by Jo Mielziner; staged and revived by Guthrie McClintic.

Francisco	Murvyn Vye
Bernardo	Reed Herring
Horatio	Harry Andrews
Marcellus	Barry Kelly
Ghost, Claudius	Malcolm Keen
Cornelius	Whitner Bissell
Voltimand	James Dinan
Laertes	John Emery
Polonius	Arthur Byron
Hamlet	John Gielgud
Gertrude	Judith Anderson
Ophelia	Lillian Gish
Reynaldo	Murvyn Vye
Rosencrantz	John Cromwell
Guildenstern	William Roehrick
The Player King	Harry Mestayer
Prologue	Ivan Triesault
The Player Queen	Ruth March
Lucianus	Whitner Bissell
Fortinbras	Reed Herring
A Captain	George Vincent
A Sailor	William Stanley
First Grave-Digger	George Nash
Second Grave-Digger	Barry Kelly
Priest	Ivan Triesault
Osric	Morgan Farley

Lords, ladies, soldiers, messengers and attendants.......... Evelyn Abbott, Neal Berry, James Dinan, John Galland, Stanley Gould, Peter Gray, Henry Hull Jr., Mary Lee Logan, Donaldson Murphy, Sydna Scott, Kurt Steinbart, Francis Wayne.

They have seen *Hamlet* well bestowed at the Empire, where he was produced last evening. They have brought to America John Gielgud, whose Hamlet has a prodigious reputation in London, and surrounded him with a cast that includes Judith Anderson, Lillian Gish, Arthur Byron, Malcolm Keen and John Emery. Under Guthrie McClintic's direction, Jo Mielziner has been poking ominous battlements into the night air and stretching royal brocades across the king's apartments. And so the magnificoes of the modern theater, who latterly were creating a masterly *Romeo and Juliet,* have come to a greater panel in the Shakespearean screen and performed honorably before it.

Although Mr. Gielgud once acted here in *The Patriot,* he comes now on the clouds of glory that in the last few years have been rising around him in London. He is young, slender and handsome, with a sensitive, mobile face and blond hair, and he plays his part with extraordinary grace and winged intelligence. For this is no roaring, robustious Hamlet, lost in melancholy, but an appealing young man brimming over with grief. His suffering is that of a cultivated youth whose affections are warm and whose honor is bright. Far from being a traditional Hamlet, beating the bass notes of some mighty lines, Mr. Gielgud speaks the lines with the quick spontaneity of a modern man. His emotions are keen. He looks on tragedy with the clarity of the mind's eye.

As the results prove in the theatre, this is one mettlesome way of playing the English stage's most familiar classic—one way of modernizing the character. But it is accomplished somewhat at the expense of the full-blooded verse of Shakespeare. What Mr. Gielgud's Hamlet lacks is a solid body of overpowering emotion, the command, power and storm of Elizabethan tragedy. For it is the paradox of Hamlet that vigorous actors who know a good deal less about the character than Mr. Gielgud does can make the horror more harrowing and the tragedy more deeply felt.

Like Mr. Gielgud, Mr. McClintic and his actors have studied the play with fresh eyes. Arthur Byron's Polonius, for example, is no doddering fool but a credible old man with the grooved mind of a trained statesman. Malcolm Keen's King is physically and mentally alive. As the Queen, Judith Anderson has abandoned the matronly stuffiness that usually plagues that part and given us a woman of strong and bewildered feeling. What any actress can do for Ophelia Lillian Gish has done with innocence of perception, but that disordered part contains some of the sorriest interludes that ever blotted paper. Inscribe on the credit side the Laertes of John Emery, the first grave-digger of George Nash and the honest Horatio of Harry Andrews.

Mr. McClintic and Mr. Mielziner have done better, especially in *Romeo and Juliet*. There is a studied balance to some of Mr. Mielziner's designs that gives them an unpleasant rigidity, although his costumes are vivid with beauty. And the performance of *Hamlet* does not proceed with the single impetuosity of a perfectly orchestrated work of art, as most of Mr. McClintic's do. This is an admirable *Hamlet* that requires comparison with the best. For intellectual beauty, in fact, it ranks with the best. But there is a coarser ferocity to Shakespeare's tragedy that is sound theatre and that is wanting in Mr. Gielgud's art.

Brooks Atkinson ON
You Can't Take It with You
BY Moss Hart AND George S. Kaufman

December 14, 1936
Booth Theatre
837 Performances

YOU CAN'T TAKE IT WITH YOU, a "farcical comedy" in three acts, by Moss Hart and George S. Kaufman. Staging by Mr. Kaufman; settings by Donald Oenslager; produced by Sam H. Harris.

Penelope Sycamore	Josephine Hull
Essie	Paula Trueman
Rheba	Ruth Attaway
Paul Sycamore	Frank Wilcox
Mr. De Pinna	Frank Conlan
Ed	George Heller
Donald	Oscar Polk
Martin Vanderhof	Henry Travers
Alice	Margot Stevenson
Henderson	Hugh Rennie
Tony Kirby	Jess Barker
Boris Kolenkhov	George Tobias
Gay Wellington	Mitzi Hajos
Mr. Kirby	William J. Kelly
Mrs. Kirby	Virginia Hammond
Three Men	George Leach, Ralph Holmes, Franklin Heller
Olga	Anna Lubowe

Moss Hart and George S. Kaufman have written their most thoroughly ingratiating comedy, *You Can't Take It with You*, which was put on at the Booth last evening. It is a study in vertigo about a lovable family of hobby-horse riders, funny without being shrill, sensible without being earnest. In *Once in a Lifetime*, Mr. Hart and Mr. Kaufman mowed the audience down under a machine-gun barrage of low comedy satire, which was the neatest trick of the season. But you will find their current lark a much more spontaneous piece of hilarity; it is written with a dash of affection to season the humor and played with gayety and simple good spirit. To this column, which has a fondness for amiability in the theatre, *You Can't*

Take It with You is the best comedy these authors have written.

To people from the punctilious world outside, the Vanderhof and Sycamore tribes appear to be lunatics. For thirty-five years, grandfather has done nothing but hunt snakes, practice dart throwing, attend commencement exercises and avoid income tax payments. His son-in-law makes fireworks for a hobby in the cellar; various members of the family write plays, study dancing, play the xylophone and operate amateur printing presses. Being mutually loyal they live together in a state of pleasant comity in spite of their separate hobbies. If Alice Sycamore had not fallen in love with the son of a Wall Street banker there would be no reason for this comedy. The contrast between his austerely correct world and their rhymeless existence in a cluttered room supplies the heartburn and the humor. By the time of the final curtain even the banker is convinced that there is something to be said for riding hobbies and living according to impulse in the bosom of a friendly family.

Not that *You Can't Take It with You* is a moral harangue. For Mr. Hart and Mr. Kaufman are fantastic humorists with a knack for extravagances of word and episode and an eye for hilarious incongruities. Nothing this scrawny season has turned up is quite so madcap as a view of the entire Sycamore tribe working at their separate hobbies simultaneously. When Mr. Kirby of Wall Street and the Racquet Club walks into their living-room asylum his orderly head reels with anguish. The amenities look like bedlam to him. What distinguishes *You Can't Take It with You* among the Hart-Kaufman enterprises is the buoyancy of the humor. They do not bear down on it with wisecracks. Although they plan it like good comedy craftsmen, they do not exploit it like gag-men.

And they have assembled a cast of actors who are agreeable folks to sit before during a gusty evening. As grandfather, Henry Travers, the salty and reflective one, is full of improvised enjoyment. Josephine Hull totters and wheedles through the part of a demented homebody. As a ferocious-minded Moscovite, George Tobias roars through the room. Under Mr. Kaufman's direction, which can be admirably relaxed as well as guffawingly taut, every one gives a jovial performance—Paula Trueman, Frank Wilcox, George Heller, Mitzi Hajos, Margot Stevenson, Oscar Polk. Well, just read the cast. The setting is by Donald Oenslager, as usual.

When a problem of conduct raises its head for a fleeting instant in the Sycamore family, grandfather solves it with a casual nod of philosophy, "So long as she's having fun." Mr. Hart and Mr. Kaufman have been more rigidly brilliant in the past, but they have never scooped up an evening of such tickling fun.

Brooks Atkinson ON
The Women
BY Clare Boothe

December 26, 1936
Ethel Barrymore Theatre
657 Performances

THE WOMEN, a play in three acts, by Clare Boothe. Staged by Robert B. Sinclair; settings by Jo Mielziner; produced by Max Gordon.

Jane	Anne Teeman
Sylvia (Mrs. Howard Fowler)	Ilka Chase
Nancy Blake	Jane Seymour
Peggy (Mrs. John Day)	Adrienne Marden
Edith (Mrs. Phelps Potter)	Phyllis Povah
Mary (Mrs. Stephen Haines)	Margalo Gillmore
Mrs. Wagstaff	Ethel Jackson
Olga	Ruth Hammond
First Hairdresser	Mary Stuart
Second Hairdresser	Jane Moore
Pedicurist	Ann Watson
Euphie	Eloise Bennett
Miss Fordyce	Eileen Burns
Little Mary	Charita Bauer
Mrs. Morehead	Jessie Busley
First Saleswoman	Doris Day
Second Saleswoman	Jean Rodney
Head Saleswoman	Lucille Fenton
First Model	Beryl Wallace
Third Saleswoman	Martina Thomas
Crystal Allen	Betty Lawford

A Fitter...Joy Hathaway
Second Model..Beatrice Cole
Princess Tamara ....Arlene Francis
Exercise Instructress....................................Anne Hunter
Maggie ....Mary Cecil
Miss Watts ....Virgilia Chew
Miss Trimmerback......................................Mary Murray
A Nurse..Lucille Fenton
Lucy...Marjorie Main
Countess de Lage ....Margaret Douglass
Miriam Aarons ....Audrey Christie
Helene...Arlene Francis
Sadie ....Marjorie Wood
Cigarette Girl..Lillian Norton

Not the ladies, but *The Women* are the brew in Clare Boothe's kettle of venom which the actors set to bubbling at the Ethel Barrymore Theatre on Saturday evening. With a good deal of feline wit and without benefit of either a single or a wedded male actor, she has told the divorce story of the smart women of New York against a cyclorama of bridge clubs, permanent-wave chambers of horror, fitting-rooms, maternity wards, night-club powder rooms and one elegant bathroom where a blond trollop languishes handsomely in the suds and talks with her lover over a gilded telephone handset. Max Gordon has produced it with lustrous scenery by Jo Mielziner and brilliant costuming supervised by John Hambleton; and the acting, especially Margalo Gillmore's, is altogether first-rate. "O, 'tis a wicked, censorious world," as Mrs. Fidget says in Wycherley's companion-piece now visible elsewhere in Times Square. Perhaps theatregoers of frail constitution may be pardoned for disliking it.

Miss Boothe has her back hair down. Left to their own devices, while their men-folk are either working at the office or deceiving their wives in the evening, Miss Boothe's alley-cats scratch and spit with considerable virtuosity. For the sake of practical playmaking, she introduces as her chief character Mrs. Stephen Haines, who loves her husband and is devoted to her home and children. But Mrs. Haines discovers through a prattling manicurist that her husband has succumbed to the blandishments of an ambitious salesgirl, and she goes to Reno to divorce him. For two years she lives in heartbroken retirement with her mother and children while her former husband does his best to tolerate her successor. In the last act the first Mrs. Haines learns that the second has fallen back into the old ways of infidelity, which is the chance she has been waiting for. Virtue outwits depravity at a conclave of all the hell-hags in the powder room of a night club; and the implication of the final curtain is that the first Mrs. Haines will have her old husband back as soon as the courts have freed him again.

Mrs. Haines's tribulations and her personal character bless the play with two or three poignant scenes, which are adorned by the most graceful acting in Miss Gillmore's career and by Charita Bauer's brave and moving performance as the unhappy daughter of divorced parents. But *The Women* is chiefly a multi-scened portrait of the modern New York wife on the loose, spraying poison over the immediate landscape. Miss Boothe has chosen amusing places for the background of her school for scandal, although the bathroom is not so illuminating as had been hoped for. She has also scribbled out some cleverly spiteful dialogue, arranged a scene of hair-pulling fisticuffs between two contenders for general ignobility, and gone extensively into the physiology of the female of the species.

Under Robert B. Sinclair's able direction, some excellent actresses give stingingly detailed pictures of some of the most odious harpies ever collected in one play. As the most malignant of the lot, Ilka Chase presides over the proceedings like the mother of all vultures; playing the part as it was written, she leaves no bone unpicked. With calculated industry, Miss Boothe has thus compiled a workable play out of the withering malice of New York's unregenerate worldlings. This reviewer disliked it.

Brooks Atkinson ON
Our Town
BY Thornton Wilder

February 4, 1938

Henry Miller's Theatre

336 Performances

OUR TOWN, a play by Thornton Wilder; directed and produced by Jed Harris.

Stage Manager ....Frank Craven
Dr. Gibbs..Jay Fassett
Joe Crowell ....Raymond Roe
Howie Newsome..Tom Fadden
Mrs. Gibbs..Evelyn Varden
Mrs. Webb ....Helen Carew
George Gibbs..John Craven
Rebecca Gibbs..Marilyn Erskine
Wally Webb...Charles Wiley Jr.
Emily Webb ....Martha Scott
Professor Pepper..Arthur Allen
Mr. Webb..Thomas W. Ross
Woman in the Balcony................................Carrie Weller
Man in the Auditorium ....Walter O. Hill
Lady in the Box.......................................Aline McDermott
Simon Stimson..Philip Coolidge
Mrs. Soames ....Doro Merande
Constable Warren ....E. Irving Locke
Si Crowell..Billy Redfield
Baseball Players..........Alfred Ryder, William Roehrick,
Thomas Coley
Sam Craig..Francis G. Cleveland
Joe Stoddard....................................William Wadsworth

Although Thornton Wilder is celebrated chiefly for his fiction, it will be necessary now to reckon with him as a dramatist. His *Our Town,* which opened at Henry Miller's last evening, is a beautifully evocative play. Taking as his material three periods in the history of a placid New Hampshire town, Mr. Wilder has transmuted the simple events of human life into universal reverie. He has given familiar facts a deeply moving, philosophical perspective. Staged without scenery and with the curtain always up, *Our Town* has escaped from the formal barrier of the modern theatre into the quintessence of acting, thought and

speculation. In the staging, Jed Harris has appreciated the rare quality of Mr. Wilder's handiwork and illuminated it with a shining performance. *Our Town* is, in this column's opinion, one of the finest achievements of the current stage.

Since the form is strange, this review must attempt to explain the purpose of the play. It is as though Mr. Wilder were saying: "Now for evidence as to the way Americans were living in the early part of the century, take Grover Corners, N.H., as an average town. Mark it 'Exhibit A' in American folkways." His spokesman in New Hampshire cosmology is Frank Craven, the best pipe and pants-pocket actor in the business, who experimentally sets the stage with tables and chairs before the house lights go down and then prefaces the performance with a few general remarks about Grover Corners. Under his benign guidance we see three periods in career of one generation of Grover Corners folks—"Life," "Love" and "Death."

Literally, they are not important. On one side of an imaginary street Dr. Gibbs and his family are attending to their humdrum affairs with relish and probity. On the opposite side Mr. Webb, the local editor, and his family are fulfilling their quiet destiny. Dr. Gibbs's boy falls in love with Mr. Webb's girl—neighbors since birth. They marry after graduating from high school; she dies several years later in childbirth and she is buried on Cemetery Hill. Nothing happens in the play that is not normal and natural and ordinary.

But by stripping the play of everything that is not essential, Mr. Wilder has given it a profound, strange, unworldly significance. This is less the portrait of a town than the sublimation of the commonplace; and in contrast with the universe that silently swims around it, it is brimming over with compassion. Most of it is a tender idyll in the kindly economy of Mr. Wilder's literary style; some of it is heartbreaking in the mute simplicity of human tragedy. For in the last act, which is entitled "Death," Mr. Wilder shows the dead of Grover Corners sitting peacefully in their graves and receiving into their quiet company a neighbor's girl whom they love. So Mr. Wilder's pathetically humble evidence of human living passes into the wise beyond. Grover Corners is a green corner of the universe.

With about the best script of his career in his hands, Mr. Harris has risen nobly to the occasion. He has reduced theatre to its lowest common denominator without resort to perverse showmanship. As chorus, preacher, drug store proprietor and finally as shepherd of the flock, Frank Craven plays with great sincerity and understanding, keeping the sublime well inside his homespun style. As the boy and girl, John Craven, who is Frank Craven's son, and Martha Scott turn youth into tremulous idealization, some of their scenes are lovely past all enduring. Jay Fassett as Dr. Gibbs, Evelyn Varden as his wife, Thomas W. Ross and Helen Carew as the Webbs play with an honesty that is enriching. There are many other good bits of acting.

Out of respect for the detached tone of Mr. Wilder's script the performance as a whole is subdued and understated. The scale is so large that the voices are never lifted. But under the leisurely monotone of the production there is a fragment of the immortal truth. *Our Town* is a microcosm. It is also a hauntingly beautiful play.

Brooks Atkinson ON
The Boys from Syracuse
BOOK BY George Abbott
LYRICS BY Lorenz Hart
MUSIC BY Richard Rodgers

November 23, 1938

Alvin Theatre

235 Performances

THE BOYS FROM SYRACUSE, a musical comedy in two acts and nine scenes, based on Shakespeare's *The Comedy of Errors.* Book by George Abbott, music by Richard Rodgers and lyrics by Lorenz Hart. Scenery and lighting by Jo Mielziner; choreography by George Balanchine; costumes designed by Irene Sharaff; staged and produced by Mr. Abbott.

Singing Policeman	Bob Lawrence
Another Policeman	James Wilkinson
Antipholus of Ephesus	Ronald Graham
Dromio of Ephesus	Teddy Hart
Dancing Policeman	George Church
Tailor	Clifford Dunstan
Tailor's Apprentice	Burl Ives
Antipholus of Syracuse	Eddie Albert
Dromio of Syracuse	Jimmy Savo
Merchant of Syracuse	Byron Shores
Duke of Ephesus	Carroll Ashburn
Aegeon	John O'Shaughnessy
Luce	Wynn Murray
Adriana	Muriel Angelus
Luciana	Marcy Wescott
Sorcerer	Owen Martin
Courtezan	Betty Bruce
Secretary to Courtezan	Heidi Vosseler
Assistant Courtezan	Dolores Anderson
Angelo	John Clarke
First Maid	Florine Callahan
Second Maid	Claire Wolf
Third Maid	Alice Craig
Merchant of Ephesus	Clifford Dunstan
Seeress	Florence Fair

Taking a swift glance at Shakespeare's *The Comedy of Errors,* George Abbott, who is the jack-of-all-trades in the theatre, has written and staged an exuberant musical comedy, *The Boys from Syracuse,* which was put on at the Alvin last evening. Nothing so gusty as this has come along for a week. Nothing so original has come along for a much longer period than that. For Mr. Abbott has a knack of giving everything he touches freshness, spontaneity and spinning pace. Rodgers and Hart have written him a versatile score. Jimmy Savo, who is usually lost when he strays away from his own routines, gives an immensely comic performance. And for the other parts, Mr. Abbott has again found attractive and bustling young people whose styles are never hackneyed. Add to this some volatile dancing under George Balanchine's direction, some of the most light-footed settings Jo Mielziner has recently designed and some gorgeous costumes by Irene Sharaff, and the local theatre wakes up to a beautiful feast of rollicking mummery this morning.

As things have turned out, it was a good notion to pilfer Shakespeare's idea and leave his text alone. Against a pseudo-classical setting, which is valuable for costumes and settings, Mr. Abbott has told a knavish tale of twin brothers and twin servants who have been separated for years and are now in the same town unbeknownst to each other. Since one pair of Antipholuses and Dromios is married and the other single, the mistaken identity results in ribald complications that suffuse this column in rosy blushes of shame. Some one will have to call out the fire department to dampen down the classical ardors of this hilarious tale.

Before rushing to the alarm box, however, consider the droll people Mr. Abbott has put to temptation. First of all, there is Savo, the pantomime genius, whose humorous gleams and fairy-tale capers have never been so delighted and disarming. As his master, Eddie Albert, whose boyishness and sparkle of comedy are altogether winning; as Luce, Wynn Murray, the fat Sapolio girl, who beams a song as much as she sings it; as the distressed wife, Muriel Angelus, who is beautiful in figure and voice; as her sister, the lovely Marcy Wescott, who has an enchanting way with a sentimental tune; as the incontinent Antipholus, Ronald Graham, who can master a song without cheapening it, and as the second Dromio, Teddy Hart, brother of the lyricist and an old hand with knockabout comedy—these are the principal people of the plot and they are all genial company.

Giving Shakespeare a commendable assist in the modern vernacular, Mr. Abbott has found plenty for them to do. Richard Rodgers, seated at his composing spinet, and Lorenz Hart, thumbing the rhyming dictionary, have distributed some of their gayest songs. Let us pass over their bawdries with decorous reserve, pausing only to remark that they are vastly enjoyable, and let us praise them extravagantly, for such a romantic song as "This Can't Be Love" and such gracious mischief as the "Sing for Your Supper" trio. Not that Mr. Rodgers and Mr. Hart are averse to the down beat and the thumping of good music hall balladry. To their way of thinking, Ephesus is the home of carnival.

Nor is the dancing a clever afterthought. George Balanchine has designed and staged it. In Betty Bruce and Heidi Vosseler he has a pair of dancers who are extraordinarily skillful and who can translate the revelry of a musical rumpus into dainty beauty. Particularly at the close of the first act Mr. Balanchine has found a way of turning the dancing into the theme of the comedy and orchestrating it in the composition of the scene. Not to put too solemn a face on it, the dancing is wholly captivating.

As the lady to the left remarked, kiss *The Boys from Syracuse* hello.

Brooks Atkinson ON
The Little Foxes
BY Lillian Hellman

———

February 15, 1939
National Theater
410 Performances

Tallulah Bankhead as the malevolent Regina Giddens in *The Little Foxes*   VANDAMM STUDIO

THE LITTLE FOXES, a play in three acts, by Lillian Hellman. Setting by Howard Bay; costumes designed by Aline Bernstein; staged and produced by Herman Shumlin.

Addie...Abbie Mitchell
Cal..John Marriott
Birdie Hubbard ....Patricia Collinge
Oscar Hubbard.....................................Carl Benton Reid
Leo Hubbard ....Dan Duryea
Regina Giddens.................................Tallulah Bankhead
William Marshall ....Lee Baker
Benjamin Hubbard ....Charles Dingle
Alexandra Giddens...............................Florence Williams
Horace Giddens...Frank Conroy

As a theatrical story-teller Lillian Hellman is biting and expert. In *The Little Foxes,* which was acted at the National last evening, she thrusts a bitter story straight to the bottom of a bitter play. As compared with *The Children's Hour,* which was her first notable play, *The Little Foxes* will have to take second rank. For it is a deliberate exercise in malice—melodramatic rather than tragic, none too fastidious in its manipulation of the stage and presided over by a Pinero frown of fustian morality. But out of greed in a malignant Southern family of 1900 she has put together a vibrant play that works and that bestows viable parts on all the members of the cast. None of the new plays in which Tallulah Bankhead has acted here has given her such sturdy support and such inflammable material. Under Herman Shumlin's taut direction Miss Bankhead plays with great directness and force, and Patricial Collinge also distinguishes herself with a remarkable performance. *The Little Foxes* can act and is acted.

It would be difficult to find a more malignant gang of petty robber barons than Miss Hellman's chief characters. Two brothers and a sister in a small Southern town are consumed with a passion to exploit the earth. Forming a partnership with a Chicago capitalist, they propose to build a cotton factory in the South, where costs are cheap and profits high. The Chicago end of the deal is sound. But Miss Hellman is telling a sordid story of how the brothers and the sister destroy each other with their avarice and cold hatred. They crush the opposition set up by a brother-in-law of higher principles; they rob him and hasten his death. But they also outwit each other in sharp dealing and they bargain their mean souls away.

It is an inhuman tale. Miss Hellman takes a dextrous playwright's advantage of the abominations it contains. Her first act is a masterpiece of skillful exposition. Under the gentility of a social occasion she suggests with admirable reticence the evil of her conspirators. When she lets loose in the other two acts she writes with melodramatic abandon, plotting torture, death and thievery like the author of an old-time thriller. She has made her drama air-tight; it is a knowing job of construction, deliberate and self-contained. In the end she tosses in a speech of social significance, which is no doubt sincere. But *The Little Foxes* is so cleverly contrived that it lacks spontaneity. It is easier to accept as an adroitly designed theatre piece than as a document in the study of humanity.

One practical advantage of a theatre piece is the opportunities it supplies to the actors. In a perfectly cast performance, none of them fumbles his part. Sometimes our Tallulah walks buoyantly through a part without much feeling for the whole design. But as the malevolent lady of *The Little Foxes* she plays with superb command of the entire character—sparing of the showy side, constantly aware of the poisonous spirit within. As a neurotic victim of circumstances, Miss Collinge also drags the whole truth out of a character, and acts it with extraordinary lightness and grace. Frank Conroy plays the part of a tired man of the house with patient strength of character. Florence Williams is singularly touching in the part of a bewildered, apprehensive daughter of the family. There are also vivid characterizations in the other parts by Charles Dingle, Abbie Mitchell, Carl Benton Reid, Dan Duryea, Lee Baker and John Marriott.

Howard Bay has provided a setting that conveys the dark stealthiness of the story, and Aline Bernstein has designed suitable costumes for a period narrative. As for the title, it comes from the Bible: "Take us the foxes, the little foxes, that spoil the vines; for our vines have tender grapes." Out of rapacity, Miss Hellman has made an adult horror-play. Her little foxes are wolves that eat their own kind.

The Philadelphia Story

by Philip Barry

March 28, 1939

Shubert Theatre

417 Performances

THE PHILADELPHIA STORY, a comedy in three acts, by Philip Barry. Staged by Robert B. Sinclair; scenery and lighting by Robert Edmond Jones; production committee, Theresa Helburn and Lawrence Langner; produced by the Theatre Guild.

Dinah Lords	Lenore Lonergan
Margaret Lord	Vera Allen
Tracy Lord	Katharine Hepburn
Alexander Lord	Dan Tobin
Thomas	Owen Coll
William Tracy	Forrest Orb
Elizabeth Imbrie	Shirley Booth
Macauley Connor	Van Heflin
George Kittredge	Frank Fenton
C. K. Dexter Haven	Joseph Cotten
Edward	Philip Foster
Seth Lord	Nicholas Joy
May	Myrtle Tannahill
Elsie	Lorraine Bate
Mac	Hayden Rorke

Considerable sustained purring ought to be audible around town this morning. For the Theatre Guild, Katharine Hepburn and Philip Barry have all come together in a gay and sagacious comedy entitled *The Philadelphia Story,* put on at the Shubert last evening. None of them has been rich in luck these past few seasons. But Mr. Barry is writing now in the light vein that becomes him and about the people most congenial to his talent. Miss Hepburn plays up to him with the flexibility of a professional stage actress. As for the Theatre Guild, which has been afflicted with disaster longer than one cares to think about, it has staged *The Philadelphia Story* with the taste and the sheen of better years—direction by Robert

Sinclair, settings by Robert Edmond Jones. Every one should be feeling fine this morning.

Although Mr. Barry always keeps within safe distance of the drawing room, he has a moral that saves his comedy from pure frivolity. He is looking for the human being beneath the cool, arrogant virtue of a daughter of the upper classes. She ruthlessly holds every one up to the austere standards she has set for herself. Having made one bad marriage to a man unworthy of her pride, she is now on the point of trying again with a self-made man of commerce who is getting on in the world. But a number of things intervene just before the ceremony—some brutal truth-telling by her first husband and her father and a wild affair with a tough-minded magazine writer who knows the facts of life. In the end the girl with the good mind and the disciplined body also acquires the understanding heart of a woman, and the marriage hastily turns into a reunion with the husband of her first choice.

Probably it is misleading to describe *The Philadelphia Story* as a study in the moral codes of human beings. For Mr. Barry's style is buoyant; his dialogue is silken and comic and his characters are witty, worldly folks with a reticent feeling about solemn topics. By an ingenious turn of story-telling, Mr. Barry has made his narrative a full one. To give it a little contemporary scope, he introduces two magazine investigators who might be representing *Fortune* if Mr. Barry did not specifically call it *Destiny*. It is the genius of the comedy of manners to spin through the lives of recognizable characters with complete plausibility. It must be confessed that *The Philadelphia Story* is a little too convenient in its conclusion, and just a trifle arch as well. But at best that is a matter of personal opinion, and at worst it is only the ghost of a flaw in a spirited and gossamer dance of comedy with just enough idea to season it pleasantly.

Certainly Mr. Barry has written Miss Hepburn's ideal part. It has whisked away the monotony and reserve that have kept her acting in the past within a very small compass. As the daughter of the rich she plays with grace, jauntiness and warmth—moving across the stage like one who is liberated from self-consciousness and taking a pleasure in acting that the audience can share. Mr. Sinclair has for several years been one of our wisest directors. He is very much up to the mark this time, and all the actors give beguiling performances. It would be hard to improve upon Van Heflin's honest and solid description of a tough-minded writer, and of Joseph Cotten's uphill fight with a part that looks forbidding in the early scenes. As the brat of the family, Lenore Lonergan, of a famous theatrical tribe, acts with a stout sort of humor that suits her groaning little figure. Let us also say something appreciative of Frank Fenton, Vera Allen, Shirley Booth, Forrest Orb and Nicholas Joy, who help to round out a joyful evening.

For this is an occasion that deserves appreciation. When the Theatre Guild, Miss Hepburn and Mr. Barry are in top form at the same time, all is for the best in the best of all possible Broadways. Although the comedy of manners has almost been lost in the dark whirl of world affairs, it is still a source of unholy delight when experts write, act and produce it.

Brooks Atkinson ON
Life with Father
BY Howard Lindsay AND Russel Crouse

November 8, 1939
Empire Theatre
3,224 Performances

Howard Lindsay in *Life with Father*   VANDAMM STUDIO

LIFE WITH FATHER, a play in three acts by Howard Lindsay and Russel Crouse, based on the writings of the late Clarence Day. Staged by Bretaigne Windust; settings and costumes by Stewart Chaney; produced by Oscar Serlin.

Vinnie ....Dorothy Stickney
Annie...Katherine Bard
Clarence ....John Drew Devereaux
John ....Richard Simon
Whitney..Raymond Roe
Harlan...Larry Robinson
Father...Howard Lindsay
Margaret...Dorothy Bernard
Cora ....Ruth Hammond
Mary ....Teresa Wright
Rev. Dr. Lloyd ....Richard Sterling

Delia	Portia Morrow
Nora	Nellie Burt
Dr. Humphreys	A. H. Van Buren
Dr. Sommers	John C. King
Maggie	Timothy Kearse

Sooner or later every one will have to see *Life with Father*, which opened at the Empire last evening. For the late Clarence Day's vastly amusing sketches of his despotic parent have now been translated into a perfect comedy by Howard Lindsay and Russel Crouse, and must be reckoned an authentic part of our American folklore. They were as genuine as that when they first appeared in *The New Yorker*, and later between covers in book form. In the form of a narrative drama of family life Mr. Lindsay and Mr. Crouse have now pulled that immortal saga together, wonderfully preserving the humanity as well as the fantastic humor. Mr. Lindsay plays the part of the choleric parent with rare taste and solid heartiness, and Dorothy Stickney plays the part of the wife with enormous skill and spirit. Last evening every one was falling jubilantly in love with a minor classic in the library of American humor.

Written and acted with infinite dexterity, *Life with Father* is no cartoon out of the funny papers. Under all his rage, Father is a representative parent with a warm regard for his sons and real affection for his wife, and his portrait might come out of any family album. What makes him so hilariously amusing to us today is the violence of his temper. He is rugged individualism in full flower—passionately logical, humorless, possessive and masterful. He is the civilized male in awful grandeur. If Mr. Lindsay and Mr. Crouse were less discerning as playwrights, Father might have emerged as a cheap-jack bully to be played only for the laughs. But they treat him with relish and respect against the manners of the late nineteenth century as one of the leading stalwarts of a materialistic civilization. His shouting and swearing are assertions of his importance as a responsible citizen in a hustling period in native history.

The story of *Life with Father* gives a rounded portrait of the Days' old man. At breakfast you hear him roaring at the new maid and frightening her out of her wits, stamping on the floor three times to summon the cook from the kitchen, and delivering a long, irate speech about taxes and politics that would scare the daylights out of any one who took the trouble to listen. That is the fierce part of Father. But the human side turns up in the course of the evening when his wife falls unaccountably ill and for a moment or two shatters his grand self-confidence. A good egg at heart, Father can rise to any domestic occasion.

The play is strewn with family crises natural to a house full of growing boys and tiresome relatives, and Father punctuates the episodes with bellows of righteous anger. When he lets himself go, the other members of the family shiver a little, but their regard for the old codger never weakens. For he is the head of the house by virtue of his innate ability. No one questions his right to wear all the pants in the family.

In Mr. Lindsay's acting Father is completely defined. Although he is stiff, he is not pompous; although he is overbearing, he is not insensitive. He is the high-spirited male of middle years who expresses his vitality in business-like procedure and runs the whole gamut of passion from sulkiness to ferocity. Miss Stickney's portrait of the wife is also brilliant acting, both sweet and witty, with a supple response to the storminess of her domestic economy. Under Bretaigne Windust's knowing direction, the performance is a thorough delight. John Drew Devereaux of the House of Drew gives an excellent performance as the oldest son. As the gawky second son, Richard Simon is also completely enjoyable; and the same things should be said for the other members of a splendid cast. Stewart Chaney has dressed them in costumes touched with humor and housed them in a gay nineteenth-century living room.

Clarence Day would have been proud of this stage version of his tribute to his father. The dialogue is sparkling, the story is shrewdly told, and the acting is a treasury of appreciative humor. Life with father may have been trying at black moments on Madison Avenue, but it is overpoweringly funny in the theatre. It is also enchanting, for *Life with Father* is a darlin' play.

Pal Joey

BOOK BY John O'Hara

LYRICS BY Lorenz Hart

MUSIC BY Richard Rodgers

———

December 25, 1940

Ethel Barrymore Theatre

198 Performances

Gene Kelly played Joey Evans, master of ceremonies in a Chicago nightclub, in *Pal Joey.* TALBOT

PAL JOEY, a "new" musical comedy in two acts taken from John O'Hara's series of letters of the same name. Book by Mr. O'Hara. Music by Richard Rodgers. Lyrics by Lorenz Hart. Dances arranged by Robert Alton; scenery and lighting by Jo Mielziner; costumes designed by John Koenig; staged and produced by George Abbott.

Joey Evans ....Gene Kelly
Mike Spears..........................Robert J. Mulligan
The Kid ....Sondra Barrett
Gladys ....June Havoc
Agnes....................................Diane Sinclair
Linda English.............................Leila Ernst
Valerie ....Amarilla Morris
Albert Doane...............................Stanley Donen
Vera Simpson...............................Vivienne Segal
Escort ....Edison Rice
Terry ....Jane Fraser
Victor ....Van Johnson
Ernest ....John Clarke
Stagehand ....Jerry Whyte
Max ....Averell Harris
The Tenor ....Nelson Rae
Melba Snyder ....Jean Casto
Waiter ....Dummy Spevlin
Ludlow Lowell..............................Jack Durant
Commissioner O'Brien....................James Lane
Assistant Hotel Manager ....Cliff Dunstan
Specialty dancer ....Shirley Paige
Dancing girls ....Claire Anderson, Sondra Barrett, Alice Craig, Louise de Forrest, Enez Early, Tilda Getze, Charlene Harkins, Frances Krell, Janet Lavis, June Leroy, Amarilla Morris, Olive Nicolson, Mildred Patterson, Dorothy Poplar, Diane Sinclair, Mildred Solly, Jeanne C. Trybom, Marie Vanneman.
Dancing boys ....Adrian Anthony, John Benton, Milton Chisholm, Stanley Donen, Henning Irgens, Van Johnson, Howard Ledig, Michael Moore, Albert Ruiz.

If it is possible to make an entertaining musical comedy out of an odious story, *Pal Joey* is it. The situation is put tentatively here because the ugly topic that is up for discussion stands between this theatregoer and real enjoyment of a well-staged show. Taking as his hero the frowsy night club punk familiar to readers of a series of sketches in *The New Yorker,* John O'Hara has written a joyless book about a sulky assignation. Under George Abbott's direction some of the best workmen on Broadway have fitted it out with smart embellishments.

Rodgers and Hart have written the score with wit and skill. Robert Alton has directed the dances inventively. Scenery out of Jo Mielziner's sketchbook and costumes off the racks of John Koenig—all very high class. Some talented performers also act a book that is considerably more dramatic than most. *Pal Joey,* which was put on at the Ethel Barrymore last evening, offers everything but a good time.

Whether Joey is a punk or a heel is something worth more careful thinking than time permits. Perhaps he is only a rat infested with termites. A night club dancer and singer, promoted to master of ceremonies in a Chicago dive, he lies himself into an affair with a rich married woman and opens a gilt-edged club of his own with her money. Mr. O'Hara has drawn a pitiless portrait of his small-time braggart and also of the company he keeps; and Gene Kelly, who distinguished himself as the melancholy hoofer of *The Time of Your Life,* plays the part with remarkable accuracy. His cheap and flamboyant unction, his nervous cunning, his trickiness are qualities that Mr. Kelly catches without forgetting the fright and gaudiness of a petty fakir. Mr. Kelly is also a brilliant tap dancer—"makes with the feet," as it goes in his vernacular—and his performance on both scores is triumphant. If Joey must be acted, Mr. Kelly can do it.

Count among your restricted blessings Vivienne Segal who can act with personal dignity and can sing with breeding. In a singularly sweet voice she sings some scabrous lyrics by Lorenz Hart to one of Richard Rodgers's most haunting tunes—"Bewitched, Bothered and Bewildered." June Havoc applies a broad, rangy style to some funny burlesques of night-club routines and manners. Jean Casto satirizes the strip-tease with humorous condescension. As a particularly rank racketeer Jack Durant, who is a sizable brute, contributes a few amazing and dizzy acrobatics. This department's paternal heart goes out especially to Leila Ernst who is the only uncontaminated baggage in the cast.

Occasionally *Pal Joey* absents itself a little from depravity and pokes fun at the dreariness of night-club frolics, and at the close of the first act it presents an admirable dream ballet and pantomime. Joey's hopeful look into a purple future is lyrically danced by Mr. Kelly. There is a kind of wry and wistful beauty to the spinning figures of Mr. Alton's dance design. But the story of *Pal Joey* keeps harking back to the drab and mirthless world of punk's progress. Although *Pal Joey* is expertly done, can you draw sweet water from a foul well?

Brooks Atkinson ON
Arsenic and Old Lace
BY Joseph O. Kesselring

January 10, 1941
Fulton Theatre
1,444 Performances

Josephine Hull played a hilariously genteel poisoner in *Arsenic and Old Lace.* VANDAMM STUDIO

ARSENIC AND OLD LACE, a "new comedy" in three acts, by Joseph O. Kesselring. Staged by Bretaigne Windust; production assistant, Carmen Lewis; setting by Raymond Sovey; produced by Howard Lindsay and Russel M. Crouse.

Abby Brewster	Josephine Hull
Rev. Dr. Harper	Wyrley Birch
Teddy Brewster	John Alexander
Officer Brophy	John Quigg
Officer Klein	Bruce Gordon
Martha Brewster	Jean Adair
Elaine Harper	Helen Brooks

Mortimer Brewster ....Allyn Joslyn
Mr. Gibbs ....Henry Herbert
Jonathan Brewster ....Boris Karloff
Dr. Einstein ....Edgar Stehli
Officer O'Hara ....Anthony Ross
Lieutenant Rooney...............................Victor Sutherland
Mr. Witherspoon ....William Parks

Let's not exaggerate. At some time there may have been a funnier murder charade than *Arsenic and Old Lace,* which was acted at the Fulton last evening. But the supposition is purely academic. For Joseph Kesselring has written one so funny that none of us will ever forget it and Bretaigne Windust has directed it like a man inspired.

It may not seem hilarious to report that thirteen men succumb to one of the blandest murder games ever played in Brooklyn. But Mr. Kesselring has a light style, an original approach to an old subject, and he manages to dispense with all the hocus-pocus of the crime trade. Swift, dry, satirical and exciting, *Arsenic and Old Lace* kept the first-night audience roaring with laughter. Although there have been some other good plays recently, this is the freshest invention. It is full of chuckles even when the scene is gruesome by nature.

As a matter of fact, the Brewsters of Brooklyn are homicidal maniacs. But Aunt Abby and Aunt Martha are, on the surface, two of the nicest maiden ladies who ever baked biscuits, rushed hot soup to ailing neighbors and invited the minister to tea. Part of their charitable work consists in poisoning homeless old men who have no families to look after them. Their lunatic brother, who, for no apparent reason, imagines that he is Theodore Roosevelt, buries the bodies in the cellar with military and presidential flourishes.

If their brightest nephew who, of course, is a drama critic, had not discovered a body under the window seat, the murder game might have continued indefinitely. But he is normal, although naturally more brilliant than ordinary people and he is so upset that he can only stay one act at the play he is supposed to review that evening. The riotous amusement of *Arsenic and Old Lace* consists in his attempt to keep the murders a secret and, at the same time, to commit his dear aunts to an institution where their foible will be stopped.

Nothing in Mr. Kesselring's record has prepared us for the humor and ingenuity of *Arsenic and Old Lace.* He wrote *There's Wisdom in Women* in 1935 and *Cross Town* in 1937. But his murder drama is compact with plot and comic situation. In addition to the homey aunts it includes a sinister maniac who looks enough like Boris Karloff to be Boris Karloff, which as a matter of fact he is. The lines are bright. The story is mad and unhackneyed. Although the scene is always on the verge of the macabre and the atmosphere is horribly ominous, Mr. Kesselring does not have to stoop to clutching hands, pistol shots or lethal screams to get his effects. He has written a murder play as legitimate as farce-comedy.

Give Mr. Windust's direction ample credit. In the casting and in the tone of the performance it preserves the casual point of view that is so robustly entertaining. There could hardly be sweeter ladies than the two played by Josephine Hull and Jean Adair. Allyn Joslyn gives an amazingly humorous and resourceful performance as the frightened drama critic. As the evil one, Mr. Karloff moves quietly through plot and poison without resorting to trickeries, and Edgar Stehli is light footed in the part of a satellite. As the cop who wants to write a play and tell the plot to a drama critic, Anthony Ross is also amusing. Helen Brooks plays the drama critic's baffled fiancée with patience and spirit.

All the comic rag-tag and bob-tail occurs inside Raymond Sovey's setting of a decaying Brooklyn mansion. *Arsenic and Old Lace* has been produced by Howard Lindsay and Russel Crouse, who wrote the stage version of *Life with Father.* Perhaps that gives you the idea.

Brooks Atkinson ON
Lady in the Dark
BOOK BY Moss Hart

LYRICS BY Ira Gershwin

MUSIC BY Kurt Weill

January 23, 1941

Alvin Theatre

162 Performances

Gertrude Lawrence played a troubled magazine editor in *Lady in the Dark.* VANDAMM STUDIO

LADY IN THE DARK, a play with music in two acts and seven scenes, by Moss Hart. Music by Kurt Weill. Lyrics by Ira Gershwin. Play staged by Mr. Hart. Production supervised and lighted by Hassard Short. Scenery by Harry Horner. Costumes designed by Irene Sharaff and Hattie Carnegie. Choreography by Albertina Rasch. Produced by Sam H. Harris.

Dr. Brooks	Donald Randolph
Miss Bowers	Jeanne Shelby
Lisa Elliott	Gertrude Lawrence
Miss Foster	Evelyn Wyckoff
Miss Stevens	Ann Lee
Maggie Grant	Margaret Dale
Alison Du Bois	Natalie Schafer
Russell Paxton	Danny Kaye
Charley Johnson	Macdonald Carey
Randy Curtis	Victor Mature
Joe, an office boy	Ward Tallmon
Tom, an office boy	Nelson Barclift
Kendall Nesbitt	Bert Lytell
Helen, a model	Virginia Peine
Ruthie, a model	Gedda Petry
Carol, a model	Patricia Deering
Marcia, a model	Margaret Westberg
Ben Butler	Dan Harden
Barbara	Eleanor Eberle
Jack	Davis Cunningham

The Albertina Rasch Group Dancers........Dorothy Byrd, Audrey Costello, Patricia Deering, June MacLaren, Beth Nichols, Wana Wenerholm, Margaret Westberg, Jerome Andrews, Nelson Barclift, George Bockman, André Charise, Fred Hearn, Yaroslav Kirov, Parker Wilson.

The Singers............Catherine Conrad, Jean Cumming, Carol Deis, Hazel Edwards, Gedda Petry, June Rutherford, Florence Wyman, Davis Cunningham, Max Edwards, Len Frank, Gordon Gifford, Manfred Hecht, William Marel, Larry Siegle, Harold Simmons.

The Children....................Ann Bracken, Sally Ferguson, Ellie Lawes, Joan Lawes, Jacqueline Macmillan, Lois Volkman, Kenneth Casey, Warren Mills, Robert Mills, Robert Lee, George Ward, William Welch.

All things considered, the American stage may as well take a bow this morning. For Moss Hart's musical play, *Lady in the Dark,* which was put on at the Alvin last evening, uses the resources of the theatre magnificently and tells a compassionate story triumphantly. Note the distinction between "musical play" and "musical comedy." What that means to Mr. Hart's mind is a drama in which the music and the splendors of the production rise spontaneously out of the heart of the drama, evoking rather than embellishing the main theme.

Although the idea is not new, since *Cabin in the Sky* and *Pal Joey* have been moving in that direction this year, Mr. Hart and his talented associates have carried it as close to perfection as any one except an academician can require. Eschewing for the moment his blistering style of comedy, Mr. Hart has written a dramatic story about the anguish of a human being. Kurt Weill has matched it with the finest score written for the theatre in years. Ira Gershwin's lyrics are brilliant. Harry Horner's whirling scenery gives the narrative a transcendent loveliness. As for Gertrude Lawrence, she is a goddess: that's all.

What brings this about is the emotional confusion of the woman editor of a smart women's magazine. Up to now she has been contented, living happily with a married man whose wife would not divorce him, and absorbed in work at which she is conspicuously successful. But suddenly everything has gone awry. Frightened by the jangle of her nerves, she goes to a psychoanalyst. *Lady in the Dark* is the drama of the strange images he draws out of her memories. In the end the analyst resolves her confusion into an intelligible pattern—proving, incidentally, that you never know whom you love, which is a terrifying prospect, but that is neither here nor there.

If that sounds like a macabre theme, you can rely upon Mr. Hart's lightness of touch and his knack for tossing in a wise-crack to keep the narrative scenes bouyant. And the long, fantastic interludes when the editor is exploring her memories carry *Lady in the Dark* into a sphere of gorgeously bedizened make-believe that will create theatrical memories for every one who sees them. Mr. Weill's score is a homogenous piece of work, breaking out into song numbers over a mood of dark evocation—nostalgic at times, bursting also into humor and swing. And Mr. Gershwin, in turn, has written his lyrics like a thoroughbred. Uproariously witty when the time is right, he also writes in impeccable taste for the meditative sequences.

To carry the burden of such a huge production, Mr. Horner has set his scenery on four revolving stages that weave naturalism and fantasy into a flowing fabric; and Hassard Short, as usual, has lighted it regally. The production is a rhapsody in blue and gold, giving reality an unreal size, shape and color, and Irene Sharaff's costumes are boldly imaginative. As the mistress of the choreography, Albertina Rasch has designed vivid lines of dance movement, and the staging is full of grace and resourcefulness.

No one but Miss Lawrence could play a virtuoso part of such length and variety. She is on stage almost at curtain-rise, and she is never off it long—leaping from melancholy to revelry with a swiftness that would be bewildering if she could not manage caprices so well. She sings, she dances. After playing a scene as a mature woman, she steps across the stage to play a scene as a schoolgirl without loss of enchantment. Sometimes Miss Lawrence has been accused of overacting, which is a venial sin at most. But no one will accuse her of being anything but superb in *Lady in the Dark*. She plays with anxious sincerity in the narrative scenes and with fullness and richness in the fantasy. For good measure, she sings "The Saga of Jenny" like an inspired showgirl.

The cast, under Mr. Hart's direction, is excellent throughout. As a comic fashion photographer, Danny Kaye, who was cutting up in *The Straw Hat Revue* last year, is infectiously exuberant. Macdonald Carey, who played in the Globe Shakespeare at the World's Fair, acts the part of an aggressive magazine man with a kind of casual forthrightness. As a glamorous movie hero, Victor Mature is unobjectionably handsome and affable. Margaret Dale has an amusing part as a fashion editor and plays it with dry humor, and Natalie Schafer has some fun with a super-modish gadabout. In the unwelcome part of the sympathetic lover, Bert Lytell gives a good performance, and Donald Randolph, as the analyst, also behaves like a gentleman.

All these actors and variegated items of a show have been pulled into place by a theatre that has been put on its mettle by an occasion. *Lady in the Dark* is a feast of plenty. Since it also has a theme to explore and express, let's call it a work of theatre art.

Lewis Nichols ON

Oklahoma!

BOOK AND LYRICS BY

Oscar Hammerstein 2d

MUSIC BY Richard Rodgers

March 31, 1943

St. James Theatre

2,212 Performances

OKLAHOMA! a musical play in two acts and five scenes, derived from *Green Grow the Lilacs,* by Lynn Riggs. Music by Richard Rodgers; book and lyrics by Oscar Hammerstein 2d. Staged by Rouben Mamoulian; choreography by Agnes de Mille; settings by Lemuel Ayers; costumes designed by Miles White; produced by the Theatre Guild.

Aunt Eller	Betty Garde
Curly	Alfred Drake
Laurey	Joan Roberts
Ike Skidmore	Barry Kelley
Fred	Edwin Clay
Slim	Herbert Rissman
Will Parker	Lee Dixon
Jud Fry	Howard da Silva
Ado Annie Carnes	Celeste Holm
Ali Hakim	Joseph Buloff
Gertie Cummings	Jane Lawrence
Ellen	Katharine Sergava
Kate	Ellen Love
Sylvie	Joan McCracken
Armina	Kate Friedlich
Aggie	Bambi Linn
Andrew Carnes	Ralph Riggs
Cord Elam	Owen Martin
Jess	George Church
Chalmers	Marc Platt
Mike	Paul Schierz
Joe	George Irving
Sam	Hayes Gordon

For years they have been saying the Theatre Guild is dead, words that obviously will have to be eaten with breakfast this morning. Forsaking the sometimes somber tenor of her ways, the little lady of Fifty-second Street last evening danced off into new paths and brought to the St. James a truly delightful musical play called *Oklahoma!* Wonderful is the nearest adjective, for this excursion of the Guild combines a fresh and infectious gayety, a charm of manner, beautiful acting, singing and dancing, and a score by Richard Rodgers which doesn't do any harm either, since it is one of his best.

Oklahoma! is based on Lynn Riggs's saga of the Indian Territory at the turn of the century, *Green Grow the Lilacs,* and, like its predecessor, it is simple and warm. It relies not for a moment on Broadway gags to stimulate an appearance of comedy, but goes winningly on its way with Rouben Mamoulian's best direction to point up its sly humor, and with some of Agnes de Mille's most inspired dances to do so further. There is more comedy in one of Miss de Mille's gay little passages than in many of the other Broadway tom-tom beats together. The Guild has known what it is about in pursuing talent for its new departure.

Mr. Rodgers's scores never lack grace, but seldom have they been so well integrated as this for *Oklahoma!* He has turned out waltzes, love songs, comic songs and a title number which the State in question would do well to seize as an anthem forthwith. "Oh, What a Beautiful Morning," and "People Will Say" are headed for countless jukeboxes across the land, and a dirge called "Pore Jud"—in which the hero of the fable tries to persuade his rival to hang himself—is amazingly comic. "The Farmer and the Cowman" and "The Surry with the Fringe on the Top" also deserve mention only because they quite clearly approach perfection; no number of the score is out of place or badly handled. The orchestrations are by Russell Bennett, who knows his humor and has on this occasion let himself go with all the laughter he can command.

To speak and sing the words—Oscar Hammerstein 2d contributed the book and lyrics—the play has an excellent collection of players, none of whom yet is world-famous. Alfred Drake and Joan Roberts as the two leading singers are fresh and engaging; they have clear voices and the thought that the audience might also like to hear

Mr. Hammerstein's poetry. Joseph Buloff is marvelous as the peddler who ambles through the evening selling wares from French cards to Asiatic perfume—and avoiding matrimony. Howard da Silva, Lee Dixon, Celeste Holm and Ralph Riggs are some of the others, and Katharine Sergava and Marc Platt are two of the important dancers. Possibly in addition to being a musical play, *Oklahoma!* could be called a folk operetta; whatever it is, it is very good.

Lewis Nichols ON
Paul Robeson's *Othello*

October 19, 1943
Shubert Theatre
280 Performances

José Ferrer *(right)* and Paul Robeson in *Othello*
EILEEN DARBY, GRAPHIC HOUSE

OTHELLO, Shakespearean play in two acts and eight scenes. Staged by Margaret Webster; production designed and lighted by Robert Edmond Jones; music composed by Tom Bennett; associate producer, John Haggott; revived by the Theatre Guild.

Roderigo	Jack Manning
Iago	José Ferrer
Brabantio	Averell Harris
Othello	Paul Robeson
Cassio	James Monks
Duke	Robert E. Perry
Lodovico	Philip Huston
A Messenger	Henry Barnard
First Senator	Jack de Shay
Second Senator	Graham Velsey
Third Senator	John Ireys
Desdemona	Uta Hagen
Montano	William Woodson
First Soldier at Cyprus	Sam Banham
Second Soldier at Cyprus	Eugene Stuckmann
Third Soldier at Cyprus	Bruce Brighton
Emilia	Margaret Webster
Bianca	Edith King
Gratiano	Robert E. Perry

Senators, Soldiers, Servants, and Citizens............Martha Falconer, Timothy Lynn Kearse, David Koser, John Gerstad, Jeff Brown, Albert Hachmeister, Ronald Bishop.

Picking up where it left off in the spring with *Oklahoma!* the Theatre Guild has given the local theatre another distinguished production. This time it is *Othello,* which opened last evening at the Shubert, finally bringing to New York a Moor in the person of Paul Robeson, and in addition giving Broadway another of Margaret Webster's careful transcriptions of Shakespeare. Excellently done both in the production and in the acting, it is the best interpretation of *Othello* to be seen here in a good many years, and one that should remain on hand for a long time to come.

A production of *Othello* is not casual child's play for the drama courses, for a fair share of it in these days seems tedious, and the motivations of Iago and the unreal change of thought on the part of the Moor have been the subjects of long and bitter professorial debate. True, some of the present revival appears slow and ambling, and there is no definite attempt to stress what factors made Iago what he was, but on the whole the acting is such as to make these things unimportant. Which is what they are when Mr. Robeson is on hand, with José Ferrer as Iago.

The news, of course, is Mr. Robeson's arrival back home in a part he played a few seasons ago in London and tentatively experimented with in the rural playhouses the summer before last. He looks like the part. He is a huge man, taller by inches than anyone on the stage, his height and breadth accentuated by the costumes he wears. His voice, when he is the general giving orders to stop the street brawl, reverberates through the house; when he is the lover of Desdemona, he is soft. His final speech about being a man "who loved not wisely but too well" is magnificent. He passes easily along the various stages of Othello's growing jealousy. He can be alike a commanding figure, accustomed to lead, a lover willing to be led and the insane victim of his own ill judgment.

Mr. Ferrer also is excellent as Iago, his interpretation taking no sides in the long quarrel as to whether the Moor's "ancient" had been inspired by thoughts of Cassio's gaining a position he wished, or his wife's having yielded to the Moor. By taking no sides, Mr. Ferrer follows the track that Iago is unexplained evil, and he holds that throughout. The actor has a light walk and a light touch, and his Iago is a sort of half dancing, half strutting Mephistopheles, who does what he does probably in good part because there is pleasure in it. He and Mr. Robeson are excellent foils for one another.

Uta Hagen, who in private life is Mrs. Ferrer, is Desdemona, a very pretty, soft-spoken heroine and victim, whose death scene is the most moving of the play. Miss Webster, in addition to directing in her accustomed way, is playing Emilia with good humor and force. The Cassio is James Monks, who now and then does not seem to be the warrior Othello would trust as his lieutenant, and Jack Manning is Roderigo. Robert Edmond Jones has done excellent settings and has excellently lighted them.

Lewis Nichols ON
On the Town
BOOK BY Betty Comden
AND Adolph Green
LYRICS BY Betty Comden, Adolph Green
AND Leonard Bernstein
MUSIC BY Leonard Bernstein

December 28, 1944
Adelphi Theatre
463 Performances

ON THE TOWN, a musical comedy in two acts and seventeen scenes. Book by Betty Comden and Adolph Green, based on an idea by Jerome Robbins. Music by Leonard Bernstein. Lyrics by Miss Comden, Mr. Green and Mr. Bernstein. Musical numbers and choreography staged by Mr. Robbins; scenery designed by Oliver Smith and costumes by Alvin Colt; entire production directed by George Abbott; musical director, Max Goberman; presented by Mr. Smith and Paul Feigay.

Workman	Marten Sameth
2d Workman	Frank Milton
3d Workman	Herbert Greene
Ozzie	Adolph Green
Chip	Chris Alexander
Sailor	Lyle Clark
Gabey	John Battles
Andy	Frank Westbrook
Tom	Richard D'Arcy
Flossie	Florence MacMichael
Flossie's Friend	Marion Kohler
Bill Poster	Larry Bolton
Little Old Lady	Maxine Arnold
Policeman	Lonny Jackson
S. Uperman	Milton Taubman
Hildy	Nancy Walker
Policeman	Roger Treat
Figment	Remo Bufano
Claire	Betty Comden
High School Girl	Nellie Fisher
Sailor in Blue	Richard D'Arcy
Maude P. Dilly	Susan Steell
Ivy	Sono Osato
Lucy Schmeeler	Alice Pearce
Pitkin	Robert Chisholm
Master of Ceremonies	Frank Milton

Singer	Frances Cassard
Waiter	Herbert Greene
Spanish Singer	Jeanne Gordon
The Great Lover	Ray Harrison
Conductor	Herbert Greene
Bimmy	Robert Lorenz

There can be no mistake about it: *On the Town* is the freshest and most engaging musical show to come this way since the golden day of *Oklahoma!* Everything about it is right. It is fast and it is gay, it takes neither itself nor the world too seriously, it has wit. Its dances are well paced, its players are a pleasure to see, and its music and backgrounds are both fitting and excellent. *On the Town* even has a literate book, which for once instead of stopping the action dead speeds it merrily on its way. The Adelphi Theatre on West Fifty-fourth Street is the new Utopia.

On the Town is a perfect example of what a well-knit fusion of the respectable arts can provide for the theatre. Taking a book by Betty Comden and Adolph Green as a base, Leonard Bernstein has composed all manner of songs—some in Tin Pan Alley's popular style, some a bit removed. Jerome Robbins, whose idea was the basis for the show—it came from his ballet *Fancy Free*—has supplied perfect dances and found Sono Osato and others to do them. Oliver Smith's simple settings are in keeping with the spirit of the book and tunes. And finally, since the other participants were not experienced theatre people, George Abbott was invited to put the whole thing together. Mr. Abbott has done one of his perfect jobs.

On the Town is the story of three sailors on a twenty-four-hour pass from the Brooklyn Navy Yard. In the subway they see a picture of Miss Turnstiles, and in the effort to find her in person they give Miss Comden and Mr. Green a chance to roam through New York. As half of the Revuers, those two know their city. The book they have fashioned makes cheerful fun of Miss Turnstiles, the museums, night clubs and the upper floors of Carnegie Hall, where culture learns to cult. They are serious about nothing, and oftentimes they offer only suggestions of ideas, allowing the audience to fill in the thought. It has been a long time since a musical comedy audience has been allowed to enjoy a musical comedy book.

Only last spring Mr. Bernstein was earning the Music Critics' annual prize for the best new composition of the year; this morning he will start up the ladder of ASCAP. He has written ballet music and songs, background music and raucously tinny versions of the blues. It is possible that none of the individual numbers may spend a year on the Hit Parade, but "Lonely Town" is strict Broadway, "Lucky to Be Me" is strict torch. For a scene in Times Square he has provided the roar of that crossroads of the world. The music has humor and is unpedantic; Mr. Bernstein quite understands the spirit of *On the Town.*

So does the cast, of course. Miss Osato brought down the highest rafters when she appeared a year ago in *One Touch of Venus,* and there is no reason to replace any of those rafters now. Her dancing is easy and her face expressive. Any day now her picture will be in the trains as Miss Subway. Nancy Walker also is wonderful as a tough, firm, taxi driver who collects one of the sailors. She can shrill out a ballad like "Come Up to My Place" with all the harshness of a Coney Island barker and all the verve of—well, Nancy Walker. Miss Comden, in the role of another girl who likes the Navy, also is good at it; Adolph Green, Chris Alexander and John Battles are the sailors.

But the charm of *On the Town* is not so much in the individual performances as in the whole. The chorus and ballet numbers, many of them done with an edge of satire, are easy and graceful. Mr. Abbott permits no lags in his evening, and down in the pit and up on the stage everything always is in order. It is an adult musical show and a remarkably good one.

Lewis Nichols ON

The Glass Menagerie

BY Tennessee Williams

March 31, 1945

The Playhouse

561 Performances

Laurette Taylor, Anthony Ross *(left)* and Eddie Dowling in *The Glass Menagerie* M. A. ATWELL STUDIO

THE GLASS MENAGERIE, a play in two acts, by Tennessee Williams. Scenery by Jo Mielziner; original music composed by Paul Bowles, staged by Eddie Dowling and Margo Jones; produced by Mr. Dowling and Louis J. Singer.

The Mother ....Laurette Taylor
Her Son ....Eddie Dowling
Her Daughter ....Julie Haydon
The Gentleman Caller................................Anthony Ross

The theatre opened its Easter basket the night before and found it a particularly rich one. Preceded by warm and tender reports from Chicago, *The Glass Menagerie* opened at the Playhouse on Saturday, and immediately it was clear that for once the advance notes were not in error. Tennessee Williams' simple play forms the framework for some of the finest acting to be seen in many a day. "Memorable" is an overworked word, but that is the only one to describe Laurette Taylor's performance. March left the theatre like a lioness.

Miss Taylor's picture of a blowsy, impoverished woman who is living on memories of a flower-scented Southern past is completely perfect. It combines qualities of humor and human understanding. The Mother of the play is an amusing figure and a pathetic one. Aged, with two children, living in an apartment off an alley in St. Louis, she recalls her past glories, her seventeen suitors, the old and better life. She is a bit of a scold, a bit of a snob; her finery has worn threadbare, but she has kept it for occasions of state. Miss Taylor makes her a person known by any other name to everyone in her audience. That is art.

In the story the Mother is trying to do the best she can for her children. The son works in a warehouse, although he wants to go to far places. The daughter, a cripple, never has been able to finish school. She is shy, she spends her time collecting glass animals—the title comes from this—and playing old phonograph records. The Mother thinks it is time she is getting married, but there has never been a Gentleman Caller at the house. Finally the son brings home another man from the warehouse and out comes the finery and the heavy if bent candlestick. Even the Gentleman Caller fails. He is engaged to another girl.

Mr. Williams' play is not all of the same caliber. A strict perfectionist could easily find a good many flaws. There are some unconnected odds and ends which have little to do with the story: Snatches of talk about the war, bits of psychology, occasional moments of rather flowery writing. But Mr. Williams has a real ear for faintly sardonic dialogue, unexpected phrases and an affection for his characters. Miss Taylor takes these many good passages and makes them sing. She plays softly and part of the time seems to be mumbling—a mumble that can be heard at the top of the gallery. Her accents, like the author's phrases, are unexpected; her gestures are vague and fluttery. There is no doubt she was a Southern belle; there is no doubt she is a great actress.

Eddie Dowling, who is co-producer, and, with

Margo Jones, co-director, has the double job of narrator and the player of The Son. The narration is like that of *Our Town* and *I Remember Mama* and it probably is not essential to *The Glass Menagerie.* In the play itself Mr. Dowling gives his quiet, easy performance. Julie Haydon, very ethereal and slight, is good as the daughter, as is Anthony Ross as the Gentleman Caller. The Caller had been the hero in high school, but he, too, had been unsuccessful. Jo Mielziner's setting fits the play, as does Paul Bowles' music. In fact, everything fits. *The Glass Menagerie,* like spring, is a pleasure to have in the neighborhood.

Lewis Nichols ON
Annie Get Your Gun
BOOK BY Herbert AND Dorothy Fields
MUSIC AND LYRICS BY Irving Berlin

May 16, 1946

Imperial Theatre

1,147 Performances

Ethel Merman as Annie Oakley finally gets her man, Frank Butler (Ray Middleton), in *Annie Get Your Gun.*
VANDAMM STUDIO

ANNIE GET YOUR GUN, a musical comedy in two acts and nine scenes. Music and lyrics by Irving Berlin. Book by Herbert and Dorothy Fields. Staged by Joshua Logan; scenery and lighting by Jo Mielziner; dances by Helen Tamiris; costumes by Lucinda Ballard; orchestra directed by Jay S. Blackton; produced by Richard Rodgers and Oscar Hammerstein 2d.

Charlie Davenport	Marty May
Yellow Foot	Walter John
Mac	Cliff Dunstan
Foster Wilson	Art Barnett
Coolie	Beau Tilden
Dolly Tate	Lea Penman
Winnie Tate	Betty Anne Nyman
Tommy Keeler	Kenny Bowers
Frank Butler	Ray Middleton
Annie Oakley	Ethel Merman
Minnie (Annie's Sister)	Nancy Jean Raab
Jessie (Another Sister)	Camilla de Witt
Nellie (Another Sister)	Marlene Cameron
Little Jake (Her Brother)	Clifford Sales
Col. Wm. F. Cody (Buffalo Bill)	William O'Neal
Mrs. Little Horse	Alma Ross
Mrs. Black Tooth	Elizabeth Malone
Mrs. Yellow Foot	Nellie Ranson
Trainman	John Garth 3d
Waiter	Leon Ribb
Porter	Clyde Turner
Riding Mistress	Lubov Roudenko
Maj. Gordon Lillie (Pawnee Bill)	George Lipton
Chief Sitting Bull	Harry Bellaver
The White Horse	Daniel Nagrin
Sylvia Potter-Porter	Marjorie Crossland

The inadvertently postponed *Annie Get Your Gun* finally arrived at the Imperial last evening, and turned out to be a good professional Broadway musical. It has a pleasant score by Irving Berlin—his first since *This Is the Army*—and it has Ethel Merman to roll her eyes and to shout down the rafters. The colors are pretty, the dancing is amiable and unaffected, and Broadway by this time is well used to a book which doesn't get anywhere in particular. *Annie,* in short, is an agreeable evening on the town, and it takes little gift for prophecy to add that it, and she, will chant their saga of the sharpshooting lady for many months to come.

By now, Miss Merman is regarded as heaven's gift to the musical show, and there is nothing about the new one to detract from that reputation.

They have given her the part of Annie Oakley, who shot with Buffalo Bill's show, and Miss Merman is deadly with a rifle over her shoulder. She can scream out the air of a song so that the building trembles; and she can be initiated into an Indian tribe in such a way the event is singularly funny. Herbert and Dorothy Fields, as librettists, quite often have left her working in something of a void, but she has worked there before and can handle the situation adequately. Her inflections give a leering note to even sedate lyrics, and the toss of her head would be a credit to Bill's show, as it is to that of Rodgers and Hammerstein.

Mr. Berlin's return to home ground is news of high and important order. For that homecoming, he has written a good, steady score, with numbers which fit the events and the story. There is nothing like "White Christmas" or "Easter Parade" among them, but several which have a place a bracket or so below. "They Say It's Wonderful" is the love song, and that will be heard around; and "Moonshine Lullaby," "I'm an Indian Too," "Show Business" and "Sun in the Morning" all are good. Abandoning the piano for the accompanying pencil of the lyricist, Mr. Berlin has fitted gay, brisk words to his tunes, and he is blessed by singers who can enunciate them.

Although the shooting of *Annie Get Your Gun* is done most affably by Miss Merman and Mr. Berlin, there are others involved to a more or less important extent. Jo Mielziner's settings are in the style of lavish musical shows, colorful and complete. The costumes by Lucinda Ballard are summery, bright, Indian, wild West and when the time is ripe, sardonic. Helen Tamiris has designed dances which probably will not be studied at formal ballet schools but fit agreeably into the proceedings. The contributors all are professionals.

In any Merman show the other members of the acting company habitually take on the harassed air of the losing horses in a steeplechase. Ray Middleton is the Frank Butler of *Annie,* Frank being the lady's rival and sweetheart, and Mr. Middleton offering a voice to Mr. Berlin and no great acting ability otherwise. William O'Neal is a dignified

Buffalo Bill; Marty May is energetic as his manager; Harry Bellaver is fine as Chief Sitting Bull. The young people are played by Betty Anne Nyman and Kenny Bowers. The chorus is pleasant to look upon, the orchestrations are good, and if there are abrupt pauses with some frequency— well, Miss Merman must change costumes and Mr. Berlin is not writing continuous opera.

Brooks Atkinson ON
No Exit
BY Jean-Paul Sartre

November 26, 1946

Biltmore Theatre

31 Performances

NO EXIT, a play in two acts by Jean-Paul Sartre, adapted from the French by Paul Bowles. Staged by John Huston; setting and lighting by Frederick Kiesler; produced by Herman Levin and Oliver Smith.

Cradeau	Claude Dauphin
Bellboy	Peter Kass
Inez	Annabella
Estelle	Ruth Ford

Being a person of agile mind, Jean-Paul Sartre has written a fascinating and macabre play about three lost souls in hell. *No Exit,* they call it in Paul Bowles' excellent English adaptation, and it was played with horrible logic and pitiless skill by four actors at the Biltmore last evening. Since it lasts scarcely more than an hour and a half, it is a brief sensation. Short as it is, it still may be ten or fifteen minutes too long for its own good in the theatre.

But in this one hurried essay about the damned, M. Sartre has sharply dramatized the loneliness and despair of souls that are lost, imprisoned and condemned to eternal torture in each other's company. If you wish, you may accept it as a bitter and resentful comment on life by a man of intellect whose hopes have been shattered by the colossal disasters of recent experience.

On its own terms, *No Exit* is ingenious, ugly and scornful. Two women and one man are locked up together in one hideous room in hell. Their first impressions are distasteful, but not too bad. For they imagine that they can dwell at least in the privacy of their thoughts—retaining at least some private dignity in their personal "pipe dreams" about themselves. But that illusion soon passes. They wring out of each other the black secret of their squalid crimes on earth.

Each one of them fondly imagines that one of the others can save him. Each flings himself hopefully at one of the others. But in the end it turns out that none of them can escape from the acts they have committed, and must be damned by them forever. Probably this is what M. Sartre wishes to say in his flaring play about dead souls: Man is alone in this world; he is responsible to his own will and decisions; no one can save him from himself.

The picture he draws is as gruesome as the characters, who are in varying degrees unspeakable. The man has been a coward—probably a collaborator, certainly a sadistic tormentor of his wife. One of the women has been a cruel betrayer of her husband and her lover. The other is a loathsome homosexual who has poisoned and destroyed the life of a married woman of whom she had become enamored.

With such characters, *No Exit* is a grim experience to undergo in the theatre. What redeems it is the skill of M. Sartre's craftsmanship and the knife-edge dexterity of the writing, which must owe something to Mr. Bowles' idiomatic English translation. And beyond the trapped agony of the three doomed characters lies the intellectual climate in which M. Sartre is living. That has some bearing on this withered play. For M. Sartre is one of the prophets of the current vogue of a Parisian philosophy in which the individual dissociates himself from society (which has betrayed him) and acts for himself alone. Your drama courier does not understand it very clearly, and merely observes that *No Exit* proceeds out of such premises.

Under John Huston's evocative direction, the play is brilliantly acted. Frederick Kiesler, has designed a monumentally ugly room where this game of penance is played. As Cradeau, Claude Dauphin, recently from Paris, is giving a lively, pictorial performance of despair, rage and cowardice. Ruth Ford is playing the sensualist with nervous desperation; and as the homosexual, Annabella is giving a bold and calculated performance that packs one corner of hell with horror.

Not a care-free evening in the theatre, but one that gives you the creeps and also a furtive glance into the post-war state of mind of a Parisian intellectual.

Brooks Atkinson ON

A Streetcar Named Desire

BY Tennessee Williams

December 3, 1947

Barrymore Theatre

855 Performances

A STREETCAR NAMED DESIRE, a play in three acts, by Tennessee Williams. Staged by Elia Kazan; scenery and lighting by Jo Mielziner; costumes by Lucinda Ballard; produced by Irene M. Selznick.

Negro Woman	Gee Gee James
Eunice Hubbel	Peg Hillias
Stanley Kowalski	Marlon Brando
Harold Mitchell (Mitch)	Karl Malden
Stella Kowalski	Kim Hunter
Steve Hubbel	Rudy Bond
Blanche du Bois	Jessica Tandy
Pablo Gonzales	Nick Dennis
A Young Collector	Vito Christi
Mexican Woman	Edna Thomas
A Strange Woman	Ann Dere
A Strange Man	Richard Garrick

Tennessee Williams has brought us a superb drama, *A Streetcar Named Desire,* which was acted at the Ethel Barrymore last evening. And

Jessica Tandy gives a superb performance as rueful heroine whose misery Mr. Williams is tenderly recording. This must be one of the most perfect marriages of acting and playwriting. For the acting and playwriting are perfectly blended in a limpid performance, and it is impossible to tell where Miss Tandy begins to give form and warmth to the mood Mr. Williams has created.

Like *The Glass Menagerie,* the new play is a quietly woven study of intangibles. But to this observer it shows deeper insight and represents a great step forward toward clarity. And it reveals Mr. Williams as a genuinely poetic playwright whose knowledge of people is honest and thorough and whose sympathy is profoundly human

A Streetcar Named Desire is the history of a gently reared Mississippi young woman who invents an artificial world to mask the hideousness of the world she has to inhabit. She comes to live with her sister, who is married to a rough-and-ready mechanic and inhabits two dreary rooms in a squalid neighborhood. Blanche—for that is her name—has delusions of grandeur, talks like an intellectual snob, buoys herself up with gaudy dreams, spends most of her time primping, covers things that are dingy with things that are bright and flees reality.

To her brother-in-law she is an unforgiveable liar. But it is soon apparent to the theatregoer that in Mr. Williams' eyes she is one of the dispossessed whose experience has unfitted her for reality; and although his attitude toward her is merciful, he does not spare her or the playgoer. For the events of *Streetcar* lead to a painful conclusion which he does not try to avoid. Although Blanche cannot face the truth, Mr. Williams does in the most imaginative and perceptive play he has written.

Since he is no literal dramatist and writes in none of the conventional forms, he presents the theatre with many problems. Under Elia Kazan's sensitive but concrete direction, the theatre has solved them admirably. Jo Mielziner has provided a beautifully lighted single setting that lightly sketches the house and the neighborhood. In this shadowy environment the performance is a work of great beauty.

Miss Tandy has a remarkably long part to play. She is hardly ever off the stage, and when she is on stage she is almost constantly talking—chattering, dreaming aloud, wondering, building enchantments out of words. Miss Tandy is a trim, agile actress with a lovely voice and quick intelligence. Her performance is almost incredibly true. For it does seem almost incredible that she could understand such an elusive part so thoroughly and that she can convey it with so many shades and impulses that are accurate, revealing and true.

The rest of the acting is also of very high quality indeed. Marlon Brando as the quick-tempered, scornful, violent mechanic; Karl Malden as a stupid but wondering suitor, Kim Hunter as the patient though troubled sister—all act not only with color and style but with insight.

By the usual Broadway standards, *A Streetcar Named Desire* is too long; not all those words are essential. But Mr. Williams is entitled to his own independence. For he has not forgotten that human beings are the basic subject of art. Out of poetic imagination and ordinary compassion he has spun a poignant and luminous story.

Brooks Atkinson ON
Kiss Me, Kate
BOOK BY Bella AND Samuel Spewack

MUSIC AND LYRICS BY Cole Porter

—————

December 30, 1948

New Century Theatre

1,070 Performances

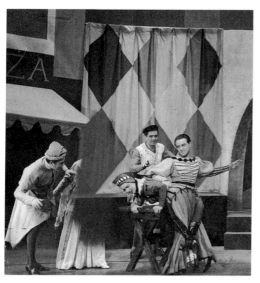

Alfred Drake in the double role of Fred Graham and *The Taming of the Shrew*'s Petruchio administers a spanking to Patricia Morison, the temperamental Lilli Vanessi, in a scene from *Kiss Me, Kate*. EILEEN DARBY, GRAPHIC HOUSE

KISS ME, KATE, a musical comedy. Music and lyrics by Cole Porter; book by Bella and Samuel Spewack; choreography by Hanya Holm; scenery and costumes by Lemuel Ayers; musical director, Pembroke Davenport; orchestrations by Robert Russell Bennett; incidental ballet music arranged by Genevieve Pitot; production staged by John C. Wilson; produced by Saint Subber and Mr. Ayers.

Fred Graham	Alfred Drake
Harry Trevor	Thomas Hoier
Lois Lane	Lisa Kirk
Ralph (Stage Manager)	Don Mayo
Lilli Vanessi	Patricia Morison
Hattie	Annabelle Hill
Paul	Lorenzo Fuller
Bill Calhoun	Harold Lang
First Man	Harry Clark
Second Man	Jack Diamond
Stage Doorman	Bill Lilling
Harrison Howell	Denis Green
Specialty Dancers	Fred Davis, Eddie Sledge
Gremio (First Suitor)	Edwin Clay
Hortensio (Second Suitor)	Charles Wood
Haberdasher	John Castello
Tailor	Marc Breaux

Taking an obliging hint from Shakespeare, the makers of *Kiss Me, Kate* have put together a thoroughly enjoyable musical comedy, acted at the New Century last evening. Shakespeare has supplied a few bedraggled scenes from *The Taming of the Shrew*. Using these as a springboard into festivity, Bella and Samuel Spewack have contrived an authentic book which is funny without the interpolation of gags.

Cole Porter has written his best score in years, together with witty lyrics. Under Hanya Holm's direction, the dancing is joyous. And Lemuel Ayers has provided carnival costumes and some interesting scenery.

Occasionally by some baffling miracle, everything seems to drop gracefully into its appointed place, in the composition of a song show, and that is the case here. No one has had to break his neck to dazzle the audience with his brilliance, and no one has had to run at frantic speed to get across the rough spots. As far as the Spewacks are concerned, *Kiss Me, Kate* is the story of a vainglorious actor and his temperamental ex-wife who are starring in a revival of *The Taming of the Shrew* in Baltimore. Although the Shakespeare circus has had some bad performances, none has been worse than the burlesque Alfred Drake and Patricia Morison have inflicted on it here.

The Italian setting has another practical advantage. It gives Mr. Porter an opportunity to poke beyond Tin Pan Alley into a romantic mood. Without losing his sense of humor, he has written a remarkable melodious score with an occasional suggestion of Puccini, who was a good composer, too. Mr. Porter has always enjoyed the luxury of rowdy tunes, and he has scribbled a few for the current festival—"Another O'p'nin', Another Show," "We Open in Venice," "Too Darn Hot" and "Brush Up Your Shakespeare," which is fresh out of the honky-tonks. All his lyrics are literate, and as usual some of them would shock the editorial staff of *The Police Gazette.*

But the interesting thing about the new score is the enthusiasm Mr. Porter has for romantic melodies indigenous to the soft climate of the Mediterranean. Although "Wunderbar" is probably a little north of the Mediterranean Sea, the warm breezes flow through it; and "So in Love Am I" has a very florid temperature, indeed.

The plot device concentrates the acting and singing in four people, and fortunately they are all uncommonly talented. As a greasepaint hussy, Miss Morison is an agile and humorous actress who is not afraid of slapstick and who can sing enchantingly. She has captured perfectly the improvised tone of the comedy, and she plays it with spirit and drollery. Lisa Kirk plays a subordinate part in a style that might be described as well-bred impudence. Given a sardonic song like "Always True to You (In My Fashion)," she can translate it into pert and gleaming buffoonery.

We have all been long acquainted with Mr. Drake as headman in musical shows. In the part of the egotistical actor who plays Petruchio on stage, Mr. Drake's pleasant style of acting and his unaffected singing are the heart of the show. By hard work and through personal sincerity, Mr. Drake has become about the most valuable man in his field. In the secondary male role, Harold Lang, who is principally a dancer, also gives a versatile and attractive performance.

Under the supervision of John C. Wilson there are other treasures in this humorous phantasmagoria of song—the torrid pavement dancing of Fred Davis and Eddie Sledge, the bland gunman fooling of Harry Clark and Jack Diamond, the antic dancing masquerade that serves as first scene to *The Taming of the Shrew* sequence.

All these items have been gathered up neatly into the flowing pattern of a pleasant musical comedy. To filch a good notion from *The New Yorker,* all you can say for *Kiss Me, Kate* is that it is terribly enjoyable.

Brooks Atkinson ON

Death of a Salesman

BY Arthur Miller

February 10, 1949

Morosco Theatre

742 Performances

DEATH OF A SALESMAN, a play by Arthur Miller. Staged by Elia Kazan; scenery and lighting by Jo Mielziner; incidental music by Alex North; costumes by Julia Sze; produced by Kermit Bloomgarden and Walter Fried.

Willy Loman	Lee J. Cobb
Linda	Mildred Dunnock
Happy	Cameron Mitchell
Biff	Arthur Kennedy
Bernard	Don Keefer
The Woman	Winnifred Cushing
Charley	Howard Smith
Uncle Ben	Thomas Chalmers
Howard Wagner	Alan Hewitt
Jenny	Ann Driscoll
Stanley	Tom Pedi
Miss Forsythe	Constance Ford
Letta	Hope Cameron

Arthur Miller has written a superb drama. From every point of view *Death of a Salesman,* which was acted at the Morosco last evening, is rich and memorable drama. It is so simple in style and so inevitable in theme that it scarcely seems like a thing that has been written and acted. For Mr. Miller has looked with compassion into the hearts of some ordinary Americans and quietly transferred their hope and anguish to the theatre. Under Elia Kazan's masterly direction, Lee J. Cobb gives a heroic performance, and every member of the cast plays like a person inspired.

Two seasons ago Mr. Miller's *All My Sons* looked like the work of an honest and able playwright. In comparison with the new drama, that seems like a contrived play now. For *Death of a Salesman* has the flow and spontaneity of a suburban epic that may not be intended as poetry but becomes poetry in spite of itself because Mr. Miller has drawn it out of so many intangible sources.

It is the story of an aging salesman who has reached the end of his usefulness on the road. There has always been something unsubstantial about his work. But suddenly the unsubstantial aspects of it overwhelm him completely. When he was young, he looked dashing; he enjoyed the comradeship of other people—the humor, the kidding, the business.

In his early sixties he knows his business as well as he ever did. But the unsubstantial things have become decisive; the spring has gone from his step, the smile from his face and the heartiness from his personality. He is through. The phantom of his life has caught up with him. As literally as Mr. Miller can say it, dust returns to dust. Suddenly there is nothing.

This is only a little of what Mr. Miller is saying. For he conveys this elusive tragedy in terms of simple things—the loyalty and understanding of his wife, the careless selfishness of his two sons, the sympathetic devotion of a neighbor, the coldness of his former boss' son—the bills, the car, the tinkering around the house. And most of all: the illusions by which he has lived—opportunities missed, wrong formulas for success, fatal misconceptions about his place in the scheme of things.

Writing like a man who understands people, Mr. Miller has no moral precepts to offer and no solutions of the salesman's problems. He is full of pity, but he brings no piety to it. Chronicler of one frowsy corner of the American scene, he evokes a wraith-like tragedy out of it that spins through the many scenes of his play and gradually envelops the audience.

As theatre *Death of a Salesman* is no less original than it is as literature. Jo Mielziner, always equal to an occasion, has designed a skeletonized set that captures the mood of the play and serves the actors brilliantly. Although Mr. Miller's text may be diffuse in form, Mr. Kazan has pulled it together into a deeply moving performance.

Mr. Cobb's tragic portrait of the defeated salesman is acting of the first rank. Although it is familiar and folksy in the details, it has something of the grand manner in the big size and the deep tone. Mildred Dunnock gives the performance of her career as the wife and mother—plain of speech but indomitable in spirit. The parts of the thoughtless sons are extremely well played by Arthur Kennedy and Cameron Mitchell, who are all youth, brag and bewilderment.

Other parts are well played by Howard Smith, Thomas Chalmers, Don Keefer, Alan Hewitt and Tom Pedi. If there were time, this report would gratefully include all the actors and fabricators of illusion. For they all realize that for once in their lives they are participating in a rare event in the theatre. Mr. Miller's elegy in a Brooklyn sidestreet is superb.

Brooks Atkinson ON
South Pacific

BOOK BY Oscar Hammerstein 2d
AND Joshua Logan

LYRICS BY Oscar Hammerstein 2d

MUSIC BY Richard Rodgers

April 7, 1949

Majestic Theatre

1,925 Performances

Mary Martin as the navy nurse Nellie Forbush and Ezio Pinza as a French planter have an enchanted evening in *South Pacific.* JOHN SWOPE

SOUTH PACIFIC, a musical play. Music by Richard Rodgers; lyrics by Oscar Hammerstein 2d; book by Mr. Hammerstein and Joshua Logan, adapted from James A. Michener's Pulitzer Prize–winning novel, *Tales of the South Pacific.* Book and musical numbers staged by Mr. Logan; scenery and lighting by Jo Mielziner; costumes by Motley; musical director, Salvatore Dell'Isola; orchestrations by Robert Russell Bennett; produced by the Messrs. Rodgers and Hammerstein in association with Leland Hayward and Mr. Logan.

Ensign Nellie Forbush	Mary Martin
Emile de Becque	Ezio Pinza
Bloody Mary	Juanita Hall
Abner	Archie Savage
Stewpot	Henry Slate
Luther Billis	Myron McCormick
Professor	Fred Sadoff
Lieut. Joseph Cable, U.S.M.C.	William Tabbert
Capt. George Brackett, U.S.N.	Martin Wolfson
Cmdr. Wm. Harbison, U.S.N.	Harvey Stephens
Radio Oper. Bob McCaffrey	Biff McGuire
Ensign Dinah Murphy	Roslyn Lowe
Ensign Janet MacGregor	Sandra Deel
Liat	Betta St. John
Lieut. Buzz Adams	Don Fellows

No one will be surprised this morning to read that Richard Rodgers, Oscar Hammerstein 2d and Joshua Logan have written a magnificent musical drama. Even before they set pencil to paper and chose "South Pacific" for the title, alert theatre-goers very sensibly started to buy tickets for it. With Mary Martin and Ezio Pinza in the leading parts, the opening performance at the Majestic last evening amply confirmed preliminary expectations and brought the town a wonderfully talented show.

Although Mr. Rodgers and Mr. Hammerstein are extraordinarily gifted men, they have not forgotten how to apply the seat of the pants to the seat of the chair. One thing that makes *South Pacific* so rhapsodically enjoyable is the hard work and organization that have gone into it under Mr. Logan's spontaneous direction. They have culled the story from James Michener's *Tales of the South Pacific,* which in some incredible fashion managed to retain sensitive perceptions toward the Pacific Islands and human beings in the midst of the callous misery, boredom and slaughter of war.

The perception has been preserved in this sombre romance about a French planter and an American nurse from Arkansas. Writing for Broadway, Mr. Rodgers and Mr. Hammerstein have not forgotten to entertain the customers with some exuberant antics by humorously sullen American Seabees who resent every thing they have to endure. But essentially this is a tenderly beautiful idyll of genuine people inexplicably tossed together in a strange corner of the world; and the music, the lyrics, the singing and the acting contribute to this mood.

If the country still has the taste to appreciate a masterly love song, "Some Enchanted Evening" ought to become reasonably immortal. For Mr. Rodgers' music is a romantic incantation; and, as usual, Mr. Hammerstein's verses are both fervent and simple. Mr. Pinza's bass voice is the most beautiful that has been heard on a Broadway stage for an eon or two. He sings this song with infinite delicacy of feeling and loveliness of tone. As a matter of fact, Mr. Pinza is also a fine actor; and his first appearance on the one and only legitimate stage is an occasion worth celebrating.

Since we have all been more or less in love with Miss Martin for several years, it is no surprise to find her full of quicksilver, pertness and delight as the Navy nurse. She sings some good knockabout melodies with skill and good nature, making something particularly enjoyable out of the stomping jubilee of "I'm Gonna Wash That Man Right Outa My Hair" and blowing out the walls of the theatre with the rapture of "I'm in Love with a Wonderful Guy." In the opinion of one inquiring theatregoer, there seems to be a little of Annie Oakley, the gun-girl, left in Miss Martin's attack on a song, and perhaps this should be exorcised by slow degrees. For the Navy nurse is a few cuts above Annie socially. Miss Martin is the girl who can make her captivating without deluging her in charm.

Since *South Pacific* is not an assembled show, but a thoroughly composed musical drama, you will find high standards of characterization and acting throughout. Take Juanita Hall, for example. She plays a brassy, greedy, ugly Tonkonese woman with harsh, vigorous, authentic accuracy; and she sings one of Mr. Rodgers' finest songs, "Bali Ha'i" with rousing artistry.

After wasting his talents on stereotyped parts for several years, Myron McCormick has a good one as a braggart, scheming Seabee, and plays it with great comic gusto. *South Pacific* naturally does well by the ruffians who saved democracy amid groans of despair in the Eastern ocean, and

"There Is Nothing Like a Dame" ought to go down as their theme song.

As evidence of the care that has gone into this drama take note of the part of Capt. George Brackett, U.S.N. The part is written with real invention on the model of a human being, and Martin Wolfson plays him admirably.

Jo Mielziner has provided entrancing settings that presumably have a Polynesian accent. Russell Bennett has written orchestrations, especially for the overtures, that are rich and colorful in instrumental sound. For the authors and producers have a high regard for professional skill, and everything they have put their hands to is perfectly wrought. Fortunately, Mr. Rodgers and Mr. Hammerstein are also the most gifted men in the business. And *South Pacific* is as lively, warm, fresh and beautiful as we had all hoped that it would be.

Brooks Atkinson ON
Gentlemen Prefer Blondes
BOOK BY Joseph Fields AND Anita Loos

LYRICS BY Leo Robin

MUSIC BY Jule Styne

December 8, 1949

Ziegfeld Theatre

740 Performances

Carol Channing *(left)* expounds her philosophy that diamonds are a girl's best friend to Yvonne Adair in *Gentlemen Prefer Blondes.* EILEEN DARBY, GRAPHIC HOUSE

GENTLEMEN PREFER BLONDES, a new musical comedy. Book by Joseph Fields and Anita Loos, based on the latter's novel. Music by Jule Styne; lyrics by Leo Robin; dances and ensembles by Agnes de Mille; production designed by Oliver Smith; costumes designed by Miles White; musical direction by Milton Rosenstock; musical arrangements by Don Walker; vocal direction and arrangements by Hugh Martin; lighting by Peggy Clark; entire production staged by John C. Wilson; produced by Herman Levin and Mr. Smith.

Dorothy Shaw	Yvonne Adair
A Steward	Jerry Craig
Lorelei Lee	Carol Channing
Gus Esmond	Jack McCauley
Frank	Robert Cooper
George	Eddie Weston
Lady Phyllis Beekman	Reta Shaw
Sir Francis Beekman	Rex Evans
Mrs. Ella Spofford	Alice Pearce
Deck Stewards	Bob Burkhardt, Shelton Lewis
Henry Spofford	Eric Brotherson
An Olympic	Curt Stafford
Josephus Gage	George S. Irving
Pierre	Bob Neukum
Bill	Peter Birch
Gloria Stark	Anita Alvarez
Taxi Driver	Kazimir Kokic
Leon	Peter Holmes
Robert Lemanteur	Mort Marshall
Louis Lemanteur	Howard Morris
A Flower Girl	Nicole France
Maitre d'Hotel	Crandall Diehl
Zizi	Judy Sinclair
Fifi	Hope Zee
Coles and Atkins	Themselves
The Tenor	William Krach
Policeman	William Diehl
Headwaiter	Kazimir Kokic
Mr. Esmond Sr.	Irving Mitchell

Happy days are here again. The musical version of *Gentlemen Prefer Blondes,* which lighted the Ziegfeld last evening, is a vastly enjoyable song-and-dance antic put on with humorous perfection. Millions of people doted on Anita Loos' comic fable when it appeared as a play in 1926 with a memorable cast and the laughs pitched fairly low in the diaphragm.

Fortunately they are going to have an opportunity to enjoy it again in a thoroughly fresh treatment. For Miss Loos and Joseph Fields have now fitted it to the formula of an old-fashioned row-de-dow with Tin Pan Alley tunes by Jule Styne and some brassy and amusing lyrics by Leo Robin.

Staged expertly in a festive manner by John C. Wilson, it brings back a good many familiar delights to a street that has been adding art to the musical stage for quite a long time. But thanks to the clowning of Carol Channing, it also brings us something new and refreshing. Let's call her portrait of the aureate Lee the most fabulous comic creation of this dreary period in history.

You will recall Lorelei Lee as the flapper gold-digger who made her way through masculine society with a good deal of success in the Twenties. In Miss Channing's somewhat sturdier image, Lorelei's rapacious innocence is uproariously amusing. Made up to resemble a John Held creature, she goes through the play like a dazed automaton—husky enough to kick in the teeth of any gentleman on the stage, but mincing coyly in high-heel shoes and looking out on a confused world through big, wide, starry eyes. There has never been anything like this before in human society.

Miss Channing can also act a part with skill and relish. They have given her a funny autobiographical ballad, "A Little Girl from Little Rock," which she translates into a roaringly entertaining number. She has something original and grotesque to contribute to every number. She can also speak the cockeyed dialogue with droll inflections. Her Lorelei is a mixture of cynicism and stupidity that will keep New York in good spirits all winter.

Having good taste in general, the producers of *Gentlemen Prefer Blondes* have hired Yvonne Adair to appear with Miss Channing as Dorothy, the more cautious brunette, and Jack McCauley to play the part of Lorelei's protector. Since they are both expert performers with a sense of humor, this turns out to be very happy casting. A pleasure-mad, teetering old lady by Alice Pearce; a handsome, genteel young man from Philadelphia by Eric Brotherson; a philandering Britisher by Rex Evans, and an indecently healthy zipper manufacturer by George S. Irving—round out the principal performers of a singularly affable cast.

Although the tone of *Gentlemen Prefer Blondes* is old-fashioned, the spirit is modern and the pace is swift. Oliver Smith has provided a suite of good travelogue settings, combining the best features of New York and Paris. And Miles White has designed stunning costumes with a humorous accent.

Agnes de Mille has done the ballets with a light touch—managing somehow to combine precision dancing with gay improvisations in her pleasant folk style. Anita Alvarez sweeps in and out of the show with a whole series of impish dances, performing one of the best with Kazimir

Kokic. As a matter of fact, there is a lot of entertaining and expert dancing through the many scenes of this plausible burlesque of one of the most ancient rackets of the world.

Every part of it is alive and abundantly entertaining. And above it all towers the blond thatch of Miss Channing, who is batting her big eyes, murdering the English language and carrying the whole golden world along with her by sheer audacity. *Gentlemen Prefer Blondes* was always funny. It is even funnier now that the lustrous Miss Channing has taken such a stranglehold on the part.

Brooks Atkinson ON
The Member of the Wedding
BY Carson McCullers

January 5, 1950
Empire Theatre
501 Performances

Ethel Waters with Julie Harris and Brandon De Wilde in the stage version of her novel
BOB GOLBY

THE MEMBER OF THE WEDDING, a play by Carson McCullers. Staged by Harold Clurman; scenery, costumes and lighting by Lester Polakov; produced by Robert Whitehead, Oliver Rea and Stanley Martineau.

Jarvis	James Holder
Frankie Addams	Julie Harris
Janice	Janet De Gore
Berenice Sadie Brown	Ethel Waters
Royal Addams	William Hansen
John Henry West	Brandon De Wilde
Mrs. West	Margaret Barker
Helen Fletcher	Mitzie Blake
Doris	Joan Shepard
Sis Laura	Phyllis Walker
T. T. Williams	Harry Bolden
Honey Camden Brown	Henry Scott
Barney McKean	Jimmy Dutton

If the drama were nothing but character sketches and acting, *The Member of the Wedding,* which opened at The Empire last evening, would be a masterpiece. For Carson McCullers' portrait of a harum-scarum adolescent girl in Georgia is wonderfully—almost painfully—perceptive; and her associated sketches of a Negro mammy and a busy little boy are masterly pieces of writing also.

Fortunately, they have fallen into the hands of Harold Clurman, who appreciates them. He has staged a performance by Ethel Waters, Julie Harris and young Brandon De Wilde that has incomparable insight, grace and beauty. Anyone who loves art ought to be humbly grateful for such acting and direction. Like Miss McCullers' character portraiture, they are masterly pieces of work.

Originally, *The Member of the Wedding* was a novel. That probably has some bearing on the fact that the play has no beginning, middle or end and never acquires dramatic momentum. Although Miss McCullers has taken the material out of the novel she has not quite got it into the form of a play.

What she has got is an infinitely poignant sketch of an unprepossessing adolescent girl who is looking around hungrily for human companionship and for something that she can join. The incident of the play concerns her brother's wedding. Fantasy-ridden like an overwrought adolescent, the girl plans to join it by going away with her brother and his bride and casting her lot with theirs permanently. Almost psychopathically imaginative, she foresees a very gaudy future of travel, excitement and friends.

That is about all there is to the narrative or plot of *The Member of the Wedding.* The rest is character analysis—the wild, whirling impulses of a girl on tip-toe with eagerness for a world she does not know how to take part in; the lumbering, elemental compassion of the Negro cook who knows all about life; the counterpoint activities of the little boy who is busy about his own affairs and runs in and out of the play like a sprite. Miss McCullers' insight is deep and sympathetic. Her literary style is deft and spinning. Her characterizations of the chief people and her sketches of them together in a ramshackle kitchen are superb pieces of work.

The play is acted in a casually and imaginatively designed setting by Lester Polakov that lets the action spill in and out of the kitchen and through the dooryard. In the long, immensely complicated part of the adolescent girl, Julie Harris, a very gifted young actress, gives an extraordinary performance—vibrant, full of anguish and elation by turns, rumpled, unstable, egotistic and unconsciously cruel.

As the Negro cook and symbol of maternity, Miss Waters gives one of those rich and eloquent performances that lay such a deep spell on any audience that sees her. Although the character has a physical base in Miss Waters' mountainous personality, it has exalted spirit and great warmth of sympathy.

Brandon De Wilde, who is seven and a half years old, plays the neighborhood boy with amazing imperturbability. This is a vastly humorous part, and Brandon won all the hearts in the audience last evening, for he is resourceful and self-contained; and Mr. Clurman, who has a special gift for the parts of children and young people, has staged these interludes tactfully and amusingly.

None of the other parts is extensive or important, for Miss McCullers merely uses the other characters to fill out the character sketches. But the parts are well played, particularly by William

Hansen, Harry Bolden and Henry Scott. In view of the rare quality of the writing and acting, the fact that *The Member of the Wedding* has practically no dramatic movement does not seem to be very important. It may not be a play, but it is art. That is the important thing.

Brooks Atkinson ON
Come Back, Little Sheba
BY William Inge

February 15, 1950

Booth Theatre

191 Performances

COME BACK, LITTLE SHEBA, a play in two acts and six scenes, by William Inge. Staged by Daniel Mann; produced by the Theatre Guild under the supervision of Lawrence Langner and Theresa Helburn; associate producer, Phyllis Anderson; setting and lighting designed by Howard Bay; costumes by Lucille Little.

Doc...Sidney Blackmer
Marie ....Joan Lorring
Lola...Shirley Booth
Turk ....Lonny Chapman
Postman...Daniel Reed
Mrs. Coffman..Olga Fabian
Milkman...John Randolph
Messenger..Arnold Schulman
Bruce...Robert Cunningham
Ed Anderson ....Wilson Brooks
Elmo Huston ....Paul Krauss

At last the Theatre Guild has got round to doing an original play. William Inge's *Come Back, Little Sheba,* which was acted at the Booth last evening, is straightforward and unhackneyed and, in its best moments, terrifyingly true. Having been a drama critic, Mr. Inge naturally knows more about more things than most people, including the sort of material worth writing about in the theatre.

In his second professionally produced drama he has poked into the agony of an alcoholic who is trying to escape the disaster of an intolerable life. Among the other useful things Mr. Inge knows is how to write two parts that Shirley Booth and Sidney Blackmer can act with a simple honesty that is pitiless and overwhelming.

Come Back, Little Sheba is a small play. During the first half of the evening Mr. Inge has kept it so slight that it verges on the monotonous. He is describing the dreary home life of a Middle Western chiropractor who is well along in a cure for alcoholism. Doc, which is the character's only name, lives in a messy house run by his good-natured but slovenly wife, who is sentimental, lazy and common.

Apparently Mr. Inge wants you to believe that Doc has been compensating himself through alcohol for marrying beneath his station. Since Doc is no great shakes himself, this column will reserve judgment on Mr. Inge's diagnosis pending further evidence of Doc's superiority.

Whatever the truth may be about the causes which Mr. Inge sketches very lightly and tentatively in the first act, the consequences are wild and frightening in the second act when Mr. Inge gets to work with his coat off. For the irritations and frustrations of a squalid home and tragic memories are more than Doc can stand. He goes off the deep end and wrecks all that is left. In a last forgiving scene Doc and his wife cling desperately together, afraid of the horrible things they know. Doc is not cured. But his wife and he understand each other and love each other. They can face the future—whatever the future turns out to be.

Under the direction of Daniel Mann, the Theatre Guild and its handservants have arranged a candid production and a splendid performance. Howard Bay has designed functional scenery that catches the dreariness as well as the hominess of an old house in a run-down neighborhood. And Lucille Little has provided costumes that portray the hopelessness of the old people and the shining self-confidence of some young people who run in and out without ever realizing the horrors that surround them.

The small parts are neatly played—Daniel Reed as postman, who knows how to listen to nonsense graciously; John Randolph as an athletic milkman; Olga Fabian as a warmhearted neighbor; Lonny Chapman and Robert Cunningham as suitors for a college girl who rooms in Doc's house; Wilson Brooks and Paul Krauss as cardholders in good standing with Alcoholics Anonymous. As the blond and self-centered college girl Joan Lorring gives a genuine and attractive performance.

But *Come Back, Little Sheba* is overweighted by the characters of Doc and his wife. Again Miss Booth is superb. She has the shuffle, the maddening garrulity and the rasping voice of the slattern, but withal she imparts to the role the warmth, generosity and valor of a loyal and affectionate woman. Mr. Blackmer gets through Doc's weak good-nature painlessly in the first act. In the second act he plays the scene of disaster like a thunderbolt, leaving the Theatre Guild subscribers pretty well stunned.

Mr. Inge's play is unnecessarily bare in view of the lives he is tampering with. The first act is hardly more than an outline. There must be more to the nightmare of Doc and his wife than Mr. Inge has reported. But when he is ready to plunge into the anguish in the second act, he writes with a kind of relentless frankness and compassion that are deeply affecting. Miss Booth and Mr. Blackmer know what he means and say it with extraordinary resourcefulness and veracity.

Brooks Atkinson ON
Guys and Dolls
BOOK BY Jo Swerling
AND Abe Burrows
MUSIC AND LYRICS BY Frank Loesser

November 24, 1950
Forty-sixth Street Theatre
1,144 Performances

Isabel Bigley and Robert Alda are the tourists in a Havana dance number for *Guys and Dolls*. EILEEN DARBY, GRAPHIC HOUSE

GUYS AND DOLLS, a musical fable of Broadway, based on a story ("The Idyll of Miss Sarah Brown") and characters by Damon Runyon. Music and lyrics by Frank Loesser. Book by Jo Swerling and Abe Burrows. Dances and musical numbers staged by Michael Kidd. Scenery and lighting by Jo Mielziner. Costumes by Alvin Colt. Musical director, Irving Actman. Orchestral arrangements, George Bassman and Ted Royal. Vocal arrangements and direction, Herbert Greene. Produced by Cy Feuer and Ernest H. Martin.

Nicely-Nicely Johnson.....................................Stubby Kaye
Benny Southstreet...Johnny Silver
Rusty Charlie...Douglas Deane
Sarah Brown ....Isabel Bigley
Arvide Abernathy...Pat Rooney Sr.
Calvin ....Paul Migan
Agatha...Margery Oldroyd

Priscilla	Christine Matsios
Harry the Horse	Tom Pedi
Lieut. Brannigan	Paul Reed
Nathan Detroit	Sam Levene
Angie the Ox	Tony Gardell
Miss Adelaide	Vivian Blaine
Sky Masterson	Robert Alda
Joey Biltmore	Bern Hoffman
Mimi	Beverly Tassoni
General Matilda B. Carstairs	Netta Packer
Big Jule	B. S. Pully
Drunk	Eddie Phillips
Waiter	Joe Milan

Out of the pages of Damon Runyon, some able artisans have put together a musical play that Broadway can be proud of. *Guys and Dolls* they call it out of one corner of the mouth. It opened at the Forty-sixth Street last evening. With a well-written book by Jo Swerling and Abe Burrows, and a dynamic score by Frank Loesser, it is a more coherent show than some that have higher artistic pretensions.

But you can count as its highest achievement the fact that it has preserved the friendly spirit of the Runyon literature without patronizing and without any show-shop hokum. It is the story of some gamblers and their unfortunate women who try to fit into the shifty pattern of Broadway life some of the stabilizing factors of marriage and love-making.

Let one playgoer remark in passing that there is something a little disconcerting about the casual attitude this story takes toward a religious mission which is trying to save a few souls in the neighborhood. But even this intrusion on the way of life of some street-corner salvationists is redeemed by the hearty camaraderie of all the characters of the book. Although they are gamblers, showgirls, cops and adult delinquents, they have their ethics, too, and live in a gaudy, blowzy world that is somehow warm and hospitable. After all, the Broadway culture is simple and sentimental but has a better heart than some cultures that are more literate.

Everyone concerned with *Guys and Dolls* has cast the show with relish and originality; and George S. Kaufman has never been in better form

in the director's box. As the executive officer of the oldest floating crap game in town, Sam Levene gives an excitable and hilarious performance. Vivian Blaine makes something comic out of the lively vulgarity of a nightclub leading lady, singing her honky-tonk songs in a shrill but earnest voice. Isabel Bigley does as well by a missionary sergeant who astonishes herself by falling in love with an itinerant gambler. She plays a few enticing tricks on one of Mr. Loesser's most rollicking songs—"If I Were a Bell." As the tall, dark and handsome gambler, Robert Alda keeps romance enjoyable, tough and surly.

The Runyon milieu is rich in startling types, and *Guys and Dolls* has the most flamboyant population of any show in town. Stubby Kaye, as a rotund sidewalk emissary; Johnny Silver, as a diminutive horse philosopher; B. S. Pully, as a big gun-and-blackjack man from Chicago—are sound, racy members of hallway society; and at last Tom Pedi has got a part that runs more than five minutes as Harry the Horse, executive secretary for a thug. No one could make a more lovable salvationist than Pat Rooney Sr., who sings "More I Cannot Wish" with cordial good-will.

Everything is all of a piece in this breezy fiction which has been organized as simply and logically as a Runyon story. Michael Kidd's comic ballets of night club production numbers and crap games belong to the production as intimately as Jo Mielziner's affable settings and Alvin Colt's noisy costumes. Mr. Loesser's lyrics and songs have the same affectionate appreciation of the material as the book, which is funny without being self-conscious or mechanical.

From the technical point of view we might as well admit that *Guys and Dolls* is a work of art. It is spontaneous and has form, style and spirit. In view of the source material, that is not astonishing. For Damon Runyon captured the spirit of an idle corner of the town with sympathetic understanding and reproduced it slightly caricatured in the sketches and stories he wrote. *Guys and Dolls* is gusty and uproarious, and it is not too grand to take a friendly, personal interest in the desperate affairs of Broadway's backroom society.

Brooks Atkinson ON
Laurence Olivier and Vivien Leigh's
Antony and Cleopatra

December 20, 1951

Ziegfeld Theatre

66 Performances

Vivien Leigh and Laurence Olivier starred in *Antony and Cleopatra* in 1951, performing Shakespeare's tragedy in repertory with Shaw's *Caesar and Cleopatra.* THE NEW YORK TIMES PHOTO ARCHIVES

ANTONY AND CLEOPATRA, a revival of Shakespeare's play. Staged by Michael Benthall; scenery by Roger Furse; costumes by Audrey Cruddas; music by Herbert Menges; sword-play by Clement McCallin; orchestra conducted by Jacques Singer; produced by Gilbert Miller.

Philo Candidius	David Greene
Cleopatra	Vivien Leigh
Antony	Laurence Olivier
Mardian	Harold Kasket
The Messenger	Alec McCowen
Scarus Dercetas	Clifford Williams
Charmian	Katharine Blake
Alexas Diomedes	Robert Beaumont
Lemprius Euphronius	Donald Pleasence
Enobarbus	Harry Andrews
Iras	Mairhi Russell
Octavius Caesar	Robert Helpmann
Lepidus	Wilfrid Hyde White
Maecenas	Jack Melford
Agrippa	Ronald Adam
Octavia	Elizabeth Kentish
Pompey	Niall MacGinnis
Menas	Max Gardiner
Attendant on Octavia	Pat Nye
Old Soldier	Anthony Pelly
Eros	Lyndon Brook
Dolabella	Dan Cunningham
Thydeus	Edmund Purdom
Nubian Messenger	Cy Grant
A Soldier of Caesar	Oliver Hunter

What the Oliviers began on Wednesday evening they completed last evening magnificently. In their scheme the Shaw play about Cleopatra is prologue to Shakespeare's romantic tragedy, *Antony and Cleopatra,* which opened at the Ziegfeld last evening and brought us a memorable experience in the theatre.

For Laurence Olivier as the reckless Antony and Vivien Leigh as the royal Cleopatra are perfectly matched in a production that conveys the richness, fire and majesty of Shakespeare. There has not been an *Antony and Cleopatra* to compare with this in New York in the last quarter of a century; and there have not been many productions of any Shakespearian play that have approached this exalted quality.

Shakespeare made *Antony and Cleopatra* difficult for the modern stage by writing it in so many brief acts and skipping rapidly over so vast a landscape. In the production directed by Michael Benthall it now looks easy and logical. Putting Roger Furse's vivid settings on a revolving stage, they move swiftly through the rosy corridors of Shakespeare's drama; and they have caught up all the details of an epochal love-story into great dramatic design. Audrey Cruddas' costumes are gorgeous. Herbert Menges' incidental score is pertinent and theatrical. Although the details of the production are multitudinous, the drama has the headlong simplicity of an integrated work of art.

Miss Leigh's Cleopatra is superb. We all knew that she would look glorious in the Egyptian costumes and that she would be every inch a queen. But it is a pleasure to report that she also has captured the infinite variety of the ruler of the Nile. She is smoldering and sensual, wily and treacherous, but she is also intelligent, audacious and courageous. And when destiny turns against her she does not go down whimpering but with pride and glory, looking grand in her regal vestments, looking cool, grave and triumphant.

Mr. Olivier's Antony is worthy of her mettle. He may be willful and selfish, but he is a man of breeding, with the authority of an old campaigner, as ready to carouse in a Roman naval ship as to buckle on his armor and plunge with confidence and joy into battle. Like Miss Leigh, Mr. Olivier has mastered all the qualities of a full-blooded human being; and their immortal affair in Egypt is a true mingling of passion, defiance and enjoyment; and where they are dead, you know that they have lived resolutely.

Wednesday's *Caesar and Cleopatra* proved that the Olivier troupe can play together with the harmony of a well-disciplined orchestra. Despite the variety of the characterizations, they also play together with easy grace in *Antony and Cleopatra*. Most of the characters are boldly defined as individuals and give the production a tart, stinging flavor.

Harry Andrews' swaggering, but shrewd and honest Enobarbus, Robert Helpmann's ascetic, petulant Octavius Caesar, Niall MacGinnis' belligerent though comradely Pompey are characters with strong personalities. They and their associates live every minute with vigor and awareness.

But they all blend into the sweeping, highly figured tapestry of Shakespeare's *Antony and Cleopatra*. The poetry is the speech of heroes. The action is real and the conclusion inevitable. It is as though *Antony and Cleopatra* never had been played before. Everything about the Olivier production is glowing or crackling with vitality.

Brooks Atkinson ON
The Crucible
BY Arthur Miller

January 22, 1953
Martin Beck Theatre
197 Performances

Arthur Kennedy and Beatrice Straight in *The Crucible*. Arthur Miller's drama about the Salem witch trials in 1692 spoke to political concerns of the 1950s.   FRED FEHL

THE CRUCIBLE, a play in a prologue and two acts, by Arthur Miller. Staged by Jed Harris; produced by Kermit Bloomgarden; scenery by Boris Aronson; costumes by Edith Lutyens; lullaby composed by Ann Ronnell.

Betty Parris	Janet Alexander
Tituba	Jacqueline Andre
Rev. Samuel Parris	Fred Stewart
Abigail Williams	Madeleine Sherwood
Susanna Wallcott	Barbara Stanton
Mrs. Ann Putnam	Jane Hoffman
Thomas Putnam	Raymond Bramley
Mercy Lewis	Dorothy Jolliffe
Mary Warren	Jenny Egan

John Proctor	Arthur Kennedy
Rebecca Nurse	Jean Adair
Giles Corey	Joseph Sweeney
Rev. John Hale	E. G. Marshall
Elizabeth Proctor	Beatrice Straight
Francis Nurse	Graham Velsey
Ezekiel Cheever	Don McHenry
John Willard	George Mitchell
Judge Hathorne	Philip Coolidge
Deputy-Gov. Danforth	Walter Hampden
Sarah Good	Adele Fortin
Hopkins	Donald Marye

Arthur Miller has written another powerful play. *The Crucible,* it is called, and it opened at the Martin Beck last evening in an equally powerful performance. Riffling back the pages of American history, he has written the drama of the witch trials and hangings in Salem in 1692. Neither Mr. Miller nor his audiences are unaware of certain similarities between the perversions of justice then and today.

But Mr. Miller is not pleading a cause in dramatic form. For *The Crucible,* despite its current implications, is a self-contained play about a terrible period in American history. Silly accusations of witchcraft by some mischievous girls in Puritan dress gradually take possession of Salem. Before the play is over good people of pious nature and responsible temper are condemning other good people to the gallows.

Having a sure instinct for dramatic form, Mr. Miller goes bluntly to essential situations. John Proctor and his wife, farm people, are the central characters of the play. At first the idea that Goodie Proctor is a witch is only an absurd rumor. But *The Crucible* carries the Proctors through the whole ordeal—first vague suspicion, then the arrest, the implacable, highly wrought trial in the church vestry, the final opportunity for John Proctor to save his neck by confessing to something he knows is a lie, and finally the baleful roll of the drums at the foot of the gallows.

Although *The Crucible* is a powerful drama, it stands second to *Death of a Salesman* as a work of art. Mr. Miller has had more trouble with this one, perhaps because he is too conscious of its implications. The literary style is cruder. The early moti-

vation is muffled in the uproar of the opening scene, and the theme does not develop with the simple eloquence of *Death of a Salesman.*

It may be that Mr. Miller has tried to pack too much inside his drama, and that he has permitted himself to be concerned more with the technique of the witch hunt than with its humanity. For all its power generated on the surface, *The Crucible* is most moving in the simple, quiet scenes between John Proctor and his wife. By the standards of *Death of a Salesman,* there is too much excitement and not enough emotion in *The Crucible.*

As the director, Jed Harris has given it a driving performance in which the clashes are fierce and clamorous. Inside Boris Aronson's gaunt, pitiless sets of rude buildings, the acting is at a high pitch of bitterness, anger and fear. As the patriarchal deputy Governor, Walter Hampden gives one of his most vivid performances in which righteousness and ferocity are unctuously mated. Fred Stewart as a vindictive parson, E. G. Marshall as a parson who finally rebels at the indiscriminate ruthlessness of the trial, Jean Adair as an aging woman of God, Madeleine Sherwood as a malicious town hussy, Joseph Sweeney as an old man who has the courage to fight the court, Philip Coolidge as a sanctimonious judge—all give able performances.

As John Proctor and his wife, Arthur Kennedy and Beatrice Straight have the most attractive roles in the drama and two or three opportunities to act them together in moments of tranquillity. They are superb—Mr. Kennedy clear and resolute, full of fire, searching his own mind; Miss Straight, reserved, detached, above and beyond the contention. Like all the members of the cast, they are dressed in the chaste and lovely costumes Edith Lutyens has designed from old prints of early Massachusetts.

After the experience of *Death of a Salesman* we probably expect Mr. Miller to write a masterpiece every time. *The Crucible* is not of that stature and it lacks that universality. On a lower level of dramatic history with considerable pertinence for today, it is a powerful play and a genuine contribution to the season.

Lewis Funke ON
Damn Yankees
BOOK BY George Abbott AND
Douglass Wallop
MUSIC AND LYRICS BY Richard Adler AND
Jerry Ross

May 5, 1955

Forty-sixth Street Theatre

1,019 Performances

Gwen Verdon, Ray Walston *(center)* and Stephen Douglass as they appear in a scene from *Damn Yankees*   TALBOT

DAMN YANKEES, a musical comedy, based on Douglass Wallop's novel *The Year the Yankees Lost the Pennant.* Book by George Abbott and Mr. Wallop. Music and lyrics by Richard Adler and Jerry Ross. Directed by Mr. Abbott; dances and musical numbers staged by Bob Fosse; scenery and costumes designed by William and Jean Eckart; musical direction by Hal Hastings; orchestrations by Don Walker; dance music arrangements by Roger Adams; presented by Frederick Brisson, Robert E. Griffith and Harold S. Prince, in association with Albert D. Taylor.

Meg	Shannon Bolin
Joe Boyd	Robert Shafer
Applegate	Ray Walston
Sister	Jean Stapleton
Doris	Elizabeth Howell
Joe Hardy	Stephen Douglass
Henry	Al Lanti
Sohovik	Eddie Phillips
Smokey	Nathaniel Frey
Vernon	Albert Linville
Van Buren	Russ Brown
Rocky	Jimmie Komack
Gloria	Rae Allen
Teen-Ager	Cherry Davis
Lynch	Del Horstmann
Welch	Richard Bishop
Lola	Gwen Verdon
Miss Weston	Janie Janvier
Guard	George Marcy
Commissioner	Del Horstmann
Postmaster	Albert Linville

As shiny as a new baseball and almost as smooth, a new musical glorifying the national pastime slid into the Forty-sixth Street Theatre last night. As far as this umpire is concerned you can count it among the healthy clouts of the campaign.

It is called *Damn Yankees* and it tells about how Casey Stengel's stalwarts are brought down to defeat by the Washington Senators in the final game of the season with the American League bunting the prize. But even the most ardent supporters of Mr. Stengel's minions should have a good time. And, as for that Dodger crowd, well you can just imagine.

Heading the board of strategy for this outfit is that shrewd manipulator of talent, George Abbott. He acts as general manager of the proceedings on the stage in addition to having collaborated on the book with Douglass Wallop, from whose novel, *The Year the Yankees Lost the Pennant,* this merry romp was taken.

To be sure, like any other manager in the course of a long season, Mr. Abbott has not been able to iron out all the kinks in his combination. In spite of his emphasis on speed afoot and timing there is a tendency every now and then for things to settle down a bit flatly on the ground. But the story of how Joe Boyd leases his soul to the Devil in order to become Joe Hardy, champion home-run hitter and inspiration of the Washington Senators, succeeds in being a sufficiently satisfactory vehicle on which to hang some highly amusing antics and utilize some splendid performers.

There is for instance that enchantress, Gwen Verdon, who socked a home run two years ago in *Can-Can.* Miss Verdon is the devil's handmaiden called upon to aid in sealing the fate of Joe Hardy's soul. It is difficult to understand how Joe was able to hold out for so long. For Miss Verdon is just about as alluring a she-witch as was ever bred in the nether regions. Vivacious, as sleek as a car on the showroom floor, and as nice to look at, she gives brilliance and sparkle to the evening with her exuberant dancing, her wicked, glistening eyes and her sheer delight in the foolery.

For the Devil there is the impeccable Ray Walston, a suave and sinister fellow who knows how to be disdainful of the good in man, whose pleasure, as you might expect, is to make humans squirm. Authoritative and persuasive, he does not overdo a role that easily could become irritating in less expert hands. Stephen Douglass, as Joe Hardy, is a completely believable athlete, clean-cut and earnest about his work. And, although it is impossible to spread the full credits to a large and vigorous cast, mention must be made of the effective contributions by Jean Stapleton as an autograph hound, Nathaniel Frey and Jimmie Komack as a couple of ball hawks, and Rae Allen as a nervy feminine sports writer.

In the music department Richard Adler and Jerry Ross have provided a thoroughly robust score to fit the occasion. The music has the spirit and brass that you'd expect to find out at the ball park and the lyrics are appropriate and smart. "Heart" is a humorous ode to the need for courage on the athletic field and it is done splendidly by Russ Brown, the sturdy manager of the Senators, along with the Messrs. Komack, Frey and Albert Linville. "The Game" is a humorous hymn to athletic abstinence. And "Shoeless Joe from Hannibal, Mo." sets the stage for a splendid hoe-down for Robert Fosse, who attended to the choreography.

Mr. Fosse, with Miss Verdon, is one of the evening's heroes. His dance numbers are full of fun and vitality. In "Whatever Lola Wants," there is a first-class gem in which music, lyrics and dance combine to make a memorable episode of the femme fatale operating on the hapless male. "Who's Got the Pain" involves Miss Verdon and Eddie Phillips in a mambo and "Two Lost Souls" puts on a torrid and rowdy bacchanal just to prove everyone's versatility.

William and Jean Eckart, assigned to the scenery and costume department, have decked out the whole affair handsomely. And in the baseball sets they have imparted complete authenticity. There is a considerable amount of talent in this entertainment and it makes up for some of the wide-open spaces that pop up every now and then. Looks like Mr. Abbott has another pennant winner.

Brooks Atkinson ON
The Diary of Anne Frank
BY Frances Goodrich AND Albert Hackett

October 5, 1955

Cort Theatre

717 Performances

THE DIARY OF ANNE FRANK, a play in two acts by Frances Goodrich and Albert Hackett, dramatized from the book, *Anne Frank: The Diary of a Young Girl;* staged by Garson Kanin; production designed by Boris Aronson; presented by Kermit Bloomgarden; costumes by Helene Pons; lighting by Leland Watson; production manager, William Hammerstein.

Mr. Frank.............................Joseph Schildkraut
Miep ....Gloria Jones
Mrs. Van Daan.........................Dennie Moore
Mr. Van Daan ....Lou Jacobi
Peter Van Daan ....David Levin
Mrs. Frank ....Gusti Huber
Margot Frank...........................Eva Rubinstein
Anne Frank.................................Susan Strasberg
Mr. Kraler...............................Clinton Sundberg
Mr. Dussel ....Jack Gilford

They have made a lovely, tender drama out of *The Diary of Anne Frank,* which opened at the Cort last evening. They have treated it with admiration and respect.

"They" are Frances Goodrich and Albert Hackett, who wrote the dramatization; Garson Kanin, who directed; Boris Aronson, who designed the setting, and a remarkable cast in which Joseph Schildkraut is the star. Strange how the shining spirit of a young girl now dead can filter down through the years and inspire a group of theatrical professionals in a foreign land.

Among them, not the least and perhaps the finest is Susan Strasberg, who plays the part of Anne. Although Miss Strasberg once appeared at the Theatre de Lys, this is her official Broadway debut, and it is worth particular notice. She is a slender, enchanting young lady with a heart-shaped face, a pair of burning eyes and the soul of an actress.

By some magic that cannot be explained, she has caught the whole character of Anne in a flowing, spontaneous, radiant performance. Anne is a girl—not the stage image of a girl—but a capricious, quick-tempered, loving maiden whose imagination is always running ahead of her experience. Whether that is Anne or Miss Strasberg it is hard to say at the moment, for they are blended into one being. It looks artless because Miss Strasberg has created it with so much purity from within.

From any practical point of view the job of making a play out of the diary of Anne Frank is impossible. Perhaps that is why Mr. and Mrs. Hackett have succeeded so well. They have not contrived anything; they have left the tool-kit outside the door of their workroom. They have absorbed the story out of the diary and related it simply.

It is the story of some Jews hidden in an Amsterdam garret during the Nazi occupation, fed by some friends and successfully secreted for a couple of years. Nothing momentously dramatic happens. It is a story of stealth, boredom, bickering, searching for comfort in other people, dreams, fears, hunger, anger and joy.

It is lightly bound together by the character of an adolescent girl who is on tip-toe before life. She is amusing and vexing. But also unconquerable because she is in love with life and squeezes the bitterness and sweetness of every moment that comes her way.

Everyone associated with the production has caught some of her spirit and has preserved her innocence and faith. The garret Mr. Aronson has designed glows with an elusive beauty. As Papa Frank, Mr. Schildkraut plays with taste and kindness. The members of the rather boorish Van Daan family are played with perception by Dennie Moore, Lou Jacobi and David Levin. Jack Gilford's nervous, crochety dentist is amusing and precise.

Gusti Huber's patient mother whose nerves are once unstrung and Eva Rubinstein's loyal, placid sister complete the closely knit Frank family. As the two people from outside, Clinton Sundberg and Gloria Jones bring into the play some of the freshness and also the anxieties of the normal world.

But it is Miss Strasberg who puts the clearest print of truth on the whole enterprise. Her Anne is the Anne that won so many hearts when the book was published. Out of the truth of a human being has come a delicate, rueful, moving drama.

Brooks Atkinson ON
My Fair Lady
BOOK AND LYRICS BY Alan Jay Lerner
MUSIC BY Frederick Loewe

March 15, 1956

Mark Hellinger Theatre

2, 717 Performances

MY FAIR LADY, a musical comedy adapted from George Bernard Shaw's *Pygmalion*. Book and lyrics by Alan Jay Lerner, with music by Frederick Loewe. Production staged by Moss Hart; presented by Herman Levin; choreography by Hanya Holm; scenery by Oliver Smith; costumes by Cecil Beaton; musical arrangements by Robert Russell Bennett and Phil Lang; lighting by A. H. Feder; dance music arranged by Trude Rittman; musical director, Franz Allers; production stage manager, Samuel Liff.

Mrs. Eynsford-Hill...Viola Roache
Eliza Doolittle..Julie Andrews
Freddy Eynsford-Hill ....John Michael King
Colonel Pickering...Robert Coote
Henry Higgins..Rex Harrison
Bartender ....David Thomas
Jamie ....Rod McLennan
Alfred P. Doolittle ....Stanley Holloway
Mrs. Pearce...Philippa Bevans
Mrs. Hopkins ....Olive Reeves-Smith
Mrs. Higgins ....Cathleen Nesbitt
Lord Boxington ....Gordon Dilworth
Zoltan Karpathy ....Christopher Hewett

Bulletins from the road have not been misleading. *My Fair Lady,* which opened at the Mark Hellinger last evening, is a wonderful show.

Alan Jay Lerner has adapted it from Shaw's *Pygmalion,* one of the most literate comedies in the language. Many other workmen have built the gleaming structure of a modern musical play on the Shaw fable. They are Frederick Loewe, the composer who collaborated with Mr. Lerner on *Brigadoon* and *Paint Your Wagon;* Oliver Smith, who has designed a glorious production; Cecil Beaton, who has decorated it with ravishingly beautiful costumes; Moss Hart, who has staged it with taste and skill.

Although their contributions have been bountiful, they will not object if this column makes one basic observation. Shaw's crackling mind is still the genius of *My Fair Lady.* Mr. Lerner has retained the same ironic point of view in his crisp adaptation and his sardonic lyrics. As Professor Higgins and Eliza Doolittle, Rex Harrison and Julie Andrews play the leading parts with the light, dry touch of top-flight Shavian acting.

My Fair Lady is staged dramatically on a civilized plane. Probably for the first time in history a typical musical comedy audience finds itself absorbed in the act of pronunciation and passionately involved in the proper speaking of "pain," "rain" and "Spain."

And yet it would not be fair to imply that *My Fair Lady* is only a new look at an old comedy. For the carnival version adds a new dimension; it gives a lift to the gaiety and the romance. In his robust score, Mr. Loewe has made the Covent Garden scenes more raffish and hilarious. Not being ashamed of old forms, he has written a glee-club drinking-song, and a mock hymn for Alfred Doolittle's wedding.

Not being afraid of melody, he has written some entrancing love music, and a waltz; and he has added something to Professor Higgins' characterization in a pettish song entitled "A Hymn to Him." All this is, no doubt, implicit in *Pygmalion.* But Mr. Loewe has given it heartier exuberance. Although the Old Boy had a sense of humor, he never had so much abandon. *Pygmalion* was not such a happy revel.

In the choreography and in the staging of the musical numbers, Hanya Holm has made a similar contribution. The "Ascot Gavotte" at the races is a laconic satire of British reserve in the midst of excitement, and very entertaining, too. "The Embassy Waltz" is both decorous and stunning. And to the rollicking tune of "Get Me to the Church on Time" there is a rowdy, festive dance that is vastly enjoyable.

Despite all the rag-tag and bobtail of a joyous musical show, Mr. Hart and his associates have never lost their respect for a penetrating comedy situation. Some things of human significance are at stake in *My Fair Lady,* and some human values are involved. Thanks to the discerning casting, the values have been sensitively preserved. As Professor Higgins' sagacious mother, Cathleen Nesbitt carries off her scenes with grace and elegance.

As Alfred P. Doolittle, the plausible rogue, Stanley Holloway gives a breezy performance that is thoroughly enjoyable. And Robert Coote is immensely comic as the bumbling Colonel Pickering.

But it is the acting of Miss Andrews and Mr. Harrison in the central roles that makes *My Fair Lady* affecting as well as amusing. Miss Andrews does a magnificent job. The transformation from street-corner drab to lady is both touching and beautiful. Out of the muck of Covent Garden something glorious blossoms, and Miss Andrews acts her part triumphantly.

Although Mr. Harrison is no singer, you will probably imagine that he is singing when he throws himself into the anguished lyrics of "A Hymn to Him" in the last act. By that time he has made Professor Higgins' temperament so full of frenzy that something like music does come out of him. Mr. Harrison is perfect in the part—crisp, lean, complacent and condescending until at last a real flare of human emotion burns the egotism away and leaves us a bright young man in love with fair lady. Mr. Harrison acts his part triumphantly, too.

It's a wonderful show. To Shaw's agile intelligence it adds the warmth, loveliness and excitement of a memorable theatre frolic.

Brooks Atkinson ON
Waiting for Godot
BY Samuel Beckett

April 19, 1956
John Golden Theatre
59 Performances

WAITING FOR GODOT, a tragicomedy in two acts by Samuel Beckett; staged by Herbert Berghof; presented by Michael Myerberg, by arrangement with Independent Plays, Ltd.; scenery by Louis Kennel; costumes by Stanley Simmons; production supervisor, John Paul.

Estragon (Gogo)..Bert Lahr
Vladimir (Didi)...E. G. Marshall
Lucky...Alvin Epstein
Pozzo ....Kurt Kasznar
A Boy ....Luchino Solito de Solis

Don't expect this column to explain Samuel Beckett's *Waiting for Godot,* which was acted at the John Golden last evening. It is a mystery wrapped in an enigma.

But you can expect witness to the strange power this drama has to convey the impression of some melancholy truths about the hopeless destiny of the human race. Mr. Beckett is an Irish writer who has lived in Paris for years, and once served as secretary to James Joyce.

Since *Waiting for Godot* has no simple meaning, one seizes on Mr. Beckett's experience of two worlds to account for his style and point of view. The point of view suggests Sartre—bleak, dark, disgusted. The style suggests Joyce—pungent and fabulous. Put the two together and you have some notion of Mr. Beckett's acrid cartoon of the story of mankind.

Literally, the play consists of four raffish characters, an innocent boy who twice arrives with a message from Godot, a naked tree, a mound or two of earth and a sky. Two of the characters are waiting for Godot, who never arrives. Two of them consist of a flamboyant lord of the earth and a broken slave whimpering and staggering at the end of a rope.

Since *Waiting for Godot* is an allegory written in a heartless modern tone, a theatregoer naturally rummages through the performance in search of a meaning. It seems fairly certain that Godot stands for God. Those who are loitering by the withered tree are waiting for salvation, which never comes.

The rest of the symbolism is more elusive. But it is not a pose. For Mr. Beckett's drama adumbrates—rather than expresses—an attitude toward man's experience on earth; the pathos, cruelty, comradeship, hope, corruption, filthiness and wonder of human existence. Faith in God has almost vanished. But there is still an illusion of faith flickering around the edges of the drama. It is as though Mr. Beckett sees very little reason for clutching at faith, but is unable to relinquish it entirely.

Although the drama is puzzling, the director and the actors play it as though they understand every line of it. The performance Herbert Berghof has staged against Louis Kennel's spare setting is triumphant in every respect. And Bert Lahr has never given a performance as glorious as his tatterdemalion Gogo, who seems to stand for all the stumbling, bewildered people of the earth who go on living without knowing why.

Although *Waiting for Godot* is an uneventful, maundering, loquacious drama, Mr. Lahr is an actor in the pantomime tradition who has a thousand ways to move and a hundred ways to grimace in order to make the story interesting and theatrical, and touching, too. His long experience as a bawling mountebank has equipped Mr. Lahr to represent eloquently the tragic comedy of one of the lost souls of the earth.

The other actors are excellent, also. E. G. Marshall as a fellow vagrant with a mind that is a bit more coherent; Kurt Kasznar as a masterful egotist reeking of power and success; Alvin Epstein as the battered slave who has one bitterly satirical polemic to deliver by rote; Luchino Solito de Solis as a disarming shepherd boy—complete the cast that gives this diffuse drama a glowing performance.

Although *Waiting for Godot* is a "puzzlement," as the King of Siam would express it, Mr. Beckett is no charlatan. He has strong feelings about the degradation of mankind, and he has given vent to them copiously. *Waiting for Godot* is all feeling. Perhaps that is why it is puzzling and convincing at the same time. Theatregoers can rail at it, but they cannot ignore it. For Mr. Beckett is a valid writer.

Brooks Atkinson ON
Long Day's Journey into Night
BY Eugene O'Neill

November 7, 1956

Helen Hayes Theatre

390 Performances

LONG DAY'S JOURNEY INTO NIGHT, a drama in four acts by Eugene O'Neill. Staged by José Quintero; setting by David Hays; lighting by Tharon Musser; costumes by Motley; production stage manager, Elliott Martin; presented by Leigh Connell, Theodore Mann and Mr. Quintero.

James Tyrone	Fredric March
Mary Cavan Tyrone	Florence Eldridge
James Tyrone Jr.	Jason Robards Jr.
Edmund Tyrone	Bradford Dillman
Cathleen	Katherine Ross

With the production of *Long Day's Journey into Night* at the Helen Hayes last evening, the American theatre acquires size and stature.

The size does not refer to the length of Eugene O'Neill's autobiographical drama, although a play three and three-quarter hours long is worth remarking. The size refers to his conception of theatre as a form of epic literature.

Long Day's Journey into Night is like a Dostoevsky novel in which Strindberg had written the dialogue. For this saga of the damned is horrifying and devastating in a classical tradition, and the performance under José Quintero's direction is inspired.

Twelve years before he died in 1953, O'Neill epitomized the life of his family in a drama that records the events of one day at their summer home in New London, Conn., in 1912. Factually it is a sordid story about a pathologically parsimonious father, a mother addicted to dope, a dissipated brother and a younger brother (representing Eugene O'Neill) who has TB and is about to be shipped off to a sanitarium.

Roughly, those are the facts. But the author has told them on the plane of an O'Neill tragedy in which the point of view transcends the material. The characters are laid bare with pitiless candor. The scenes are big. The dialogue is blunt. Scene by scene the tragedy moves along with a remorseless beat that becomes hypnotic as though this were life lived on the brink of oblivion.

Long Day's Journey into Night could be pruned of some of its excesses and repetitions and static looks back to the past. But the faults come, not from tragic posturing, but from the abundance of a great theatre writer who had a spacious point of view. This summing-up of his emotional and artistic life ranks with *Mourning Becomes Electra* and *Desire Under the Elms,* which this department regards as his masterpieces.

Like those dramas, it comes alive in the theatre. Although the text is interesting to read between covers, it does not begin to flame until the actors take hold of it. Mr. Quintero, who staged the memorable *The Iceman Cometh* in the Village, has directed *Long Day's Journey into Night* with insight and skill. He has caught the sense of a stricken family in which the members are at once fascinated and repelled by one another. Always in control of the turbulence of the material, he has also picked out and set forth the meaning that underlies it.

The performance is stunning. As the aging actor who stands at the head of the family, Fredric March gives a masterly performance that will stand as a milestone in the acting of an O'Neill play. Petty, mean, bullying, impulsive and sharp-tongued, he also has magnificence—a man of strong passions, deep loyalties and basic humility. This is a character portrait of grandeur.

Florence Eldridge analyzes the pathetic character of the mother with tenderness and compassion. As the evil brother, Jason Robards Jr., who played Hickey in *The Iceman Cometh,* gives another remarkable performance that has tremendous force and truth in the last act. Bradford Dillman is excellent as the younger brother—winning, honest, and both callow and perceptive in his relationship with the family. Katherine Ross plays the part of the household maid with freshness and taste.

All the action takes place inside David Hays' excellent setting of a cheerless living-room with dingy furniture and hideous little touches of unimaginative décor. The shabby, shapeless costumes by Motley and the sepulchral lighting by Tharon Musser, perfectly capture the lugubrious mood of the play.

Long Day's Journey into Night has been worth waiting for. It restores the drama to literature and the theatre to art.

Brooks Atkinson ON
West Side Story
BOOK BY Arthur Laurents
LYRICS BY Stephen Sondheim
MUSIC BY Leonard Bernstein

———

September 26, 1957

Winter Garden

732 Performances

WEST SIDE STORY, a musical comedy, based on a conception of Jerome Robbins, with book by Arthur Laurents, music by Leonard Bernstein and lyrics by Stephen Sondheim. Entire production directed and choreographed by Mr. Robbins; presented by Robert E. Griffith and Harold S. Prince, by arrangement with Roger L. Stevens; scenery by Oliver Smith; costumes by Irene Sharaff; lighting by Jean Rosenthal; co-choreographer, Peter Gennaro; production associate, Sylvia Druille; musical direction, Max Goberman; orchestrations by Mr. Bernstein, Sid Ramin and Irwin Kostal; production stage manager, Ruth Mitchell.

The Jets ....Riff, Mickey Calin; Gee-Tar, Tommy Abbott; Tony, Larry Kert; Mouth Piece, Frank Green; Action, Eddie Roll; Tiger, Lowell Harris; A-Rab, Tony Mordente; Graziella, Wilma Curley; Baby John, David Winters; Velma, Carole D'Andrea; Snowboy, Grover Dale; Minnie, Nanette Rosen; Clarice, Marilyn D'Honau; Big Deal, Martin Charnin; Pauline, Julie Oser; Diesel, Hank Brunjes; Anybodys, Lee Becker.

The Sharks ....Bernardo, Ken Le Roy; Juano, Jay Norman; Maria, Carol Lawrence; Toro, Erne Castaldo; Anita, Chita Rivera; Moose, Jack Murray; Chino, Jamie Sanchez; Rosalia, Marilyn Cooper; Pepe, George Marcy; Consuelo, Reri Grist; Indio, Noel Schwartz; Terestia, Carmen Guiterrez; Luis, Al De Sio; Francisca, Elizabeth Taylor; Anxious, Gene Gavin; Estella, Lynn Ross; Nibbles, Ronie Lee; Marguerita, Liane Plane.

The Adults ....Doc, Art Smith; Krupke, William Bramley; Schrank, Arch Johnson; Gladhand, John Harkins.

Although the material is horrifying, the workmanship is admirable.

Gang warfare is the material of *West Side Story,* which opened at the Winter Garden last evening, and very little of the hideousness has been left out. But the author, composer and ballet designer are creative artists. Pooling imagination and virtuosity, they have written a profoundly moving show that is as ugly as the city jungles and also pathetic, tender and forgiving.

Arthur Laurents has written the story of two hostile teen-age gangs fighting for supremacy amid the tenement houses, corner stores and bridges of the West Side. The story is a powerful one, partly, no doubt, because Mr. Laurents has deliberately given it the shape of *Romeo and Juliet.* In the design of *West Side Story* he has powerful allies. Leonard Bernstein has composed another one of his nervous, flaring scores that capture the shrill beat of life in the streets. And Jerome Robbins, who has directed the production, is also its choreographer.

Since the characters are kids of the streets, their speech is curt and jeering. Mr. Laurents has provided the raw material of a tragedy that occurs because none of the young people involved understands what is happening to them. And his contribution is the essential one. But it is Mr. Bernstein and Mr. Robbins who orchestrate it. Using music and movement they have given Mr. Laurents' story passion and depth and some glimpses of unattainable glory. They have pitched into it with personal conviction as well as the skill of accomplished craftsmen.

In its early scenes of gang skirmishes, *West Side Story* is facile and a little forbidding—the shrill music and the taut dancing movement being harsh and sinister. But once Tony of the Jets gang sees Maria of the Sharks gang, the magic of an immortal story takes hold. As Tony, Larry Kert is perfectly cast, plain in speech and manner; and as Maria, Carol Lawrence, maidenly soft and glowing, is perfectly cast also. Their balcony scene on the firescape of a dreary tenement is tender and affecting. From that moment on, *West Side Story* is an incandescent piece of work that finds odd bits of beauty amid the rubbish of the streets.

Everything in *West Side Story* is of a piece. Everything contributes to the total impression of wildness, ecstasy and anguish. The astringent score has moments of tranquillity and rapture, and occasionally a touch of sardonic humor. And the ballets convey the things that Mr. Laurents is inhibited from saying because the characters are so inarticulate. The hostility and suspicion between the gangs, the glory of the nuptials, the terror of the rumble, the devastating climax—Mr. Robbins has found the patterns of movement that express these parts of the story.

Most of the characters, in fact, are dancers with some images of personality lifted out of the whirlwind—characters sketched on the wing. Like everything also in *West Side Story,* they are admirable. Chita Rivera in a part equivalent to the Nurse in the Shakespeare play; Ken Le Roy as leader of The Sharks; Mickey Calin as leader of The Jets; Lee Becker as a hobble-dehoy girl in one gang—give terse and vigorous performances.

Everything in *West Side Story* blends—the scenery by Oliver Smith, the costumes by Irene Sharaff, the lighting by Jean Rosenthal. For this is one of those occasions when theatre people, engrossed in an original project, are all in top form.

The subject is not beautiful. But what *West Side Story* draws out of it is beautiful. For it has a searching point of view.

Brooks Atkinson ON
Look Back in Anger
BY John Osborne

October 1, 1957

Lyceum Theatre

407 Performances

LOOK BACK IN ANGER, a play in three acts, by John Osborne. Staged by Tony Richardson; presented by David Merrick; setting by Alan Tagg; costumes by Motley; scenery, lighting and costumes supervised by Howard Bay; music for songs by Tom Eastwood; stage manager, Howard Stone.

Jimmy Porter...Kenneth Haigh
Cliff Lewis ....Alan Bates
Alison Porter ....Mary Ure
Helena Charles ....Vivienne Drummond
Colonel Redfern...Jack Livesey

To see *Look Back in Anger* at the Lyceum, where it opened last evening, is to agree with the British who saw the original performance. John Osborne has written the most vivid British play of the decade.

Since we have had angry young men writing bitter plays for a quarter of a century, *Look Back in Anger* will not be the landmark here that it is already in London. But Mr. Osborne is a fiery writer with a sharp point of view and a sense of theatre. Under the direction of Tony Richardson, five British actors give his savage morality drama the blessing of a brilliant performance.

Mr. Osborne is in blind revolt against the England of his time. In a squalid attic somewhere in the Midlands three young people are railing against the world. They are Jimmy Porter, a tornado of venomous phrases; his wife, who is crushed by the barrenness of their life and the wildness of her husband's vocabulary, and Cliff Lewis, an unattached young man who is the friend of both.

Being in a state of rebellion, neither Mr. Osborne nor his chief character has a program or a reasonable approach to life. From any civilized point of view, they are both impossible. But Mr. Osborne has one great asset. He can write. The words come bursting out of him in a flood of satire and invective. They are cruel; they are unfair, and they leave nothing but desolation as they sweep along.

But they are vibrant and colorful; they sting the secondary characters in the play, to say nothing of the audience. You know that something is going on in the theatre, and that the British drama has for once said a long farewell to the drawing-room, the bookshelves, the fireplace and the stairway. If Mr. Osborne is disgusted with England today, he is also disgusted with the pallor of British drama.

Not that he does not have trouble with the form. After inveighing against everyone and his wife for two acts with a certain malevolent though tolerable logic, he switches to the craft of writing a play. At the curtain of the second act Helena, a girl who despises Jimmy and is despised by him and who has persuaded his wife to go back home to escape further torture, becomes his mistress, and takes over where the beaten wife leaves off. When the curtain goes up on the third act Helena is at the ironing-board, as the wife was in the first act. Everything has been turned upside down.

This is a bit too pat. During the first scene of the third act, Mr. Osborne finds himself more preoccupied with the job of keeping a play in motion than with hurling words at the world. But in the last scene he is in control again. He is back in top form—twisting and turning, sulking and groaning, turning civil morality inside out and doing other things he hadn't oughter. He is not the man for temperate statements.

If *Look Back in Anger* recovers its stride in the last scene, it is partly because the performance has so much pressure and passion. The acting is superb; it makes its points accurately with no waste motion. As Jimmy, Kenneth Haigh absorbs Mr. Osborne's furious literary style in an enormously skillful performance that expresses undertones of despair and frustration and gives the character a basis in humanity. This wild man is no impostor.

As the tormented wife, Mary Ure succeeds in retaining the pride of an intelligent young woman by filling her silences with unspoken vitality, by being alive and by glowing with youth in every sequence. Alan Bates gives a vigorous performance in a more fluid style as the mutual friend. Vivienne Drummond plays the more ambiguous part of the intruding female with charm and guile.

Everything occurs inside a cheerless, slatternly attic room well designed by Alan Tagg. Miserable though it is, it is sturdy enough to withstand Mr. Osborne's thunderbolts. With the lightning that goes with them, they shake quite a lot of complacency out of the theatre.

Brooks Atkinson ON

The Music Man

BOOK, MUSIC AND LYRICS BY

Meredith Willson

December 19, 1957

Majestic Theatre

1,375 Performances

Barbara Cook as Marian the librarian and Robert Preston as the fast-talking con man, Harold Hill, in *The Music Man*
FRIEDMAN-ABELES

THE MUSIC MAN, a musical comedy in two acts and sixteen scenes. Book, music and lyrics by Meredith Willson, based on a story by Mr. Willson and Franklin Lacey. Staged by Morton Da Costa; choreography by Onna White; scenery and lighting by Howard Bay; costumes by Raoul Péne du Bois; orchestrations by Don Walker; dance arrangements by Laurence Rosenthal; production associate, Sylvia Drulie; musical direction and vocal arrangements by Herbert Greene; hair styles by Ronald de Mann; production stage manager, Henri Caubisens; presented by Kermit Bloomgarden, with Mr. Green in association with Frank Productions, Inc.

Charlie Cowell	Paul Reed
Conductor	Carl Nicholas
Harold Hill	Robert Preston
Mayor Shinn	David Burns
Ewart Dunlop	Al Shea
Oliver Hix	Wayne Ward
Jacey Squires	Vern Reed
Olin Britt	Bill Spangenberg
Marcellus Washburn	Iggie Wolfington
Tommy Djilas	Danny Carroll
Marian Paroo	Barbara Cook
Mrs. Paroo	Pert Kelton
Amaryllis	Marilyn Siegel
Winthrop Paroo	Eddie Hodges
Eulalie Mackecknie Shinn	Helen Raymond
Zaneeta Shinn	Dusty Worrall
Gracie Shinn	Barbara Travis
Alma Hix	Adnia Rice
Maud Dunlop	Elaine Swann
Ethel Toffelmier	Peggy Mondo
Mrs. Squires	Martha Flynn
Constable Locke	Carl Nicholas

Dollars to doughnuts, Meredith Willson dotes on brass bands.

In *The Music Man,* which opened last evening at the Majestic, he has translated the thump and razzle-dazzle of brass-band lore into a warm and genial cartoon of American life. Since the style is gaudy and since David Burns plays a small town mayor with low-comedy flourishes, *The Music Man* is a cartoon and not a valentine.

But Mr. Willson's sophistication is skin-deep. His heart is in the wonderful simplicities of provincial life in Iowa in 1912, and his musical show glows with enjoyment. Mr. Willson's music is innocent; the beat is rousing and the tunes are full of gusto. The dances, improvised by Onna White, are rural and festive. Raoul Péne du Bois' country costumes are humorously hospitable. With Robert Preston in top form in the leading part, the cast is as exuberant as opening day at a county fair.

If Mark Twain could have collaborated with Vachel Lindsay, they might have devised a rhythmic lark like *The Music Man,* which is as American as apple pie and a Fourth of July oration.

It is the story of a traveling-salesman charlatan who cannot read music or play any instrument, but who sells the boys of River City a brass band and gorgeous uniforms. His motives are dishonest. But during the weeks when he is mulcting the customers, he transforms a dull town into a singing and dancing community. In the last scene the law is hot on his heels. But, don't worry, Mr. Willson approves of his charlatan as thoroughly as he loves the town librarian, the barber shop quartet, the kids, the ladies, the railroad, and the vitality of life in the Middle West.

In other hands, this could easily look like an assembly job, clever, smart and spurious. Serving as his own librettist, composer and lyric-writer, Mr. Willson has given it the uniformity of a well-designed crazy-quilt in which every patch blends with its neighbor. By some sort of miracle, his associates' have caught his point of view exactly. Morton Da Costa's droll, strutting direction; Don Walker's blaring orchestrations; Howard Bay's jovial scenery, including a racing locomotive that drowns the orchestra players in steam when the curtain goes up—these aspects of the production have Mr. Willson's own kind of gaiety.

As the infectious bunko man, Mr. Preston could hardly be improved upon. His expansive energy and his concentration on the crisis of the moment are tonic. Since the music is unpretentious, he has no trouble in making it sound hearty. When the music is romantic, Barbara Cook is on hand to sing it beautifully. She is also a beguiling actress in fresh and pleasant fashions.

But the cast is attractive in every instance. Pert Kelton as a harsh-voiced Irish widow; Iggie Wolfington as a breathless conspirator; little Eddie Hodges as a lisping youth and little Marilyn Siegel as a girl who can play cross-hand on the piano, Al Shea, Wayne Ward, Vern Reed and Bill Spangenberg as close-harmonizers—are immensely entertaining.

For Mr. Willson has given them lively, artless things to do, and they keep him good company. Like Richard Bissell, another Iowa playwright, Mr. Willson has a fresh slant on Americana. Although he does not take it seriously, he loves it with the pawkiness of a liberated native. *The Music Man* is a marvelous show, rooted in wholesome and comic tradition.

Brooks Atkinson ON
A Raisin in the Sun
BY Lorraine Hansberry

———

March 11, 1959
Ethel Barrymore Theatre
530 Performances

A RAISIN IN THE SUN, a drama by Lorraine Hansberry. Staged by Lloyd Richards; presented by Philip Rose and David J. Cogan; scenery and lighting by Ralph Alswang; costumes by Virginia Volland; production stage manager, Leonard Auerbach.

Ruth Younger	Ruby Dee
Travis Younger	Glynn Turman
Walter Lee Younger	Sidney Poitier
Beneatha Younger	Diana Sands
Lena Younger	Claudia McNeill
Joseph Asagai	Ivan Dixon
George Murchison	Louis Gossett
Bobo	Lonne Elder 3d
Karl Lindner	John Fiedler
Moving Men	Ed Hall, Douglas Turner

In *A Raisin in the Sun,* which opened at the Ethel Barrymore last evening, Lorraine Hansberry touches on some serious problems. No doubt, her feelings about them are as strong as any one's.

But she has not tipped her play to prove one thing or another. The play is honest. She has told the inner as well as the outer truth about a Negro family in the south-side of Chicago at the present time. Since the performance is also honest and since Sidney Poitier is a candid actor, *A Raisin in the Sun* has vigor as well as veracity and is likely to destroy the complacency of any one who sees it.

The family consists of a firm-minded widow, her daughter, her restless son and his wife and son. The mother has brought up her family in a tenement that is small, battered but personable. All the mother wants is that her children adhere to the code of honor and self-respect that she inherited from her parents.

The son is dreaming of success in a business deal. And the daughter, who is race-conscious, wants to become a physician and heal the wounds of her people. After a long delay the widow receives $10,000 as the premium on her husband's life insurance. The money projects the family into a series of situations that test their individual characters.

What the situations are does not matter at the moment. For *A Raisin in the Sun* is a play about human beings who want, on the one hand, to preserve their family pride and, on the other hand, to break out of the poverty that seems to be their fate. Not having any axe to grind, Miss Hansberry has a wide range of topics to write about—some of them hilarious, some of them painful in the extreme.

You might, in fact, regard *A Raisin in the Sun* as a Negro *The Cherry Orchard.* Although the social scale of the characters is different, the knowledge of how character is controlled by environment is much the same, and the alternation of humor and pathos is similar.

If there are occasional crudities in the craftsmanship, they are redeemed by the honesty of the writing. And also by the rousing honesty of the stage work. For Lloyd Richards has selected an admirable cast and directed a bold and stirring performance.

Mr. Poitier is a remarkable actor with enormous power that is always under control. Cast as the restless son, he vividly communicates the tumult of a highstrung young man. He is as eloquent when he has nothing to say as when he has a pungent line to speak. He can convey devious processes of thought as graphically as he can clown and dance.

As the matriarch, Claudia McNeil gives a heroic performance. Although the character is simple, Miss McNeil gives it nobility of spirit. Diana Sands' amusing portrait of the overintellectualized daughter; Ivan Dixon's quiet, sagacious student from Nigeria; Ruby Dee's young wife burdened with problems; Louis Gossett's supercilious suitor; John Fiedler's timid white man, who speaks sanctimonious platitudes—bring variety and excitement to a first-rate performance.

All the crises and comic sequences take place inside Ralph Alswang's set, which depicts both the poverty and the taste of the family. Like the play, it is honest. That is Miss Hansberry's personal contribution to an explosive situation in which simple honesty is the most difficult thing in the world. And also the most illuminating.

Brooks Atkinson ON

Gypsy

BOOK BY Arthur Laurents
LYRICS BY Stephen Sondheim
MUSIC BY Jule Styne

May 21, 1959
Broadway Theatre
702 Performances

Sandra Church *(left)*, Ethel Merman and Jack Klugman in *Gypsy* FRIEDMAN-ABELES

GYPSY, a musical fable, suggested by the memoirs of Gypsy Rose Lee. Book by Arthur Laurents, music by Jule Styne and lyrics by Stephen Sondheim. Directed and choreographed by Jerome Robbins; directorial assistant, Gerald Freedman; presented by David Merrick and Leland Hayward; sets and lighting by Jo Mielziner; costumes by Raoul Péne du Bois; musical direction, Milton Rosenstock; orchestrations, Sid Ramin and Robert Ginzler; dance music arrangements, John Kander; additional dance music, Petty Walberg; hair styles, Ernest Adler; production stage manager, Ruth Mitchell; production associate, Michael Mindlin Jr.; assistant to Mr. Merrick, Eduard Fuller.

Uncle Jocko	Mort Marshall
Baby Louise	Karen Moore
Baby June	Jacqueline Mayro
Rose	Ethel Merman
Pop	Erv Harmon
Weber	Joe Silver
Herbie	Jack Klugman
Louise	Sandra Church
June	Lane Bradbury
Tulsa	Paul Wallace
Yonkers	David Winters
Kringelein	Loney Lewis
Miss Cratchitt	Peg Murray
Agnes	Marilyn Cooper
Tessie Tura	Maria Karnilova
Mazeppa	Faith Dane
Electra	Chotzi Foley

Since Ethel Merman is the head woman in *Gypsy,* which opened at the Broadway last evening, nothing can go wrong. She would not permit *Gypsy* to be anything less than the most satisfying musical of the season.

She is playing the indomitable mother of Gypsy Rose Lee, a stripper with a difference; and Miss Merman, her pipes resonant and her spirit syncopated, struts and bawls her way through it triumphantly.

Ever since *Annie Get Your Gun,* it has been obvious that she is an actress in addition to being a singer. In the book Arthur Laurents has written for her (based on the memoirs of Gypsy Rose Lee) she is the female juggernaut who drives her two daughters into show business and keeps their noses to the grindstone until one of them is a star.

Gypsy is a musical tour of the hotel rooms and backstages of the seamy side of show business thirty years ago when vaudeville was surrendering to the strip-tease. Jo Mielziner has designed a savory production. Jule Styne has supplied a genuine show-business score, and Stephen Sondheim has set amusing lyrics to it.

Under the genial direction of Jerome Robbins, who is willing to take time to enjoy what he is doing, the performance is entertaining in all the acceptable styles from skulduggery to the anatomy of a termagant. There are some very funny scenes in the beginning when Jacqueline Mayro, as a baby star, makes all the clichés of juvenile performing wonderfully garish and plausible.

As Mother Rose's shoestring act sinks lower in the profession, *Gypsy* descends into the inferno of a burlesque joint where the grind sisters—notably Maria Karnilova and Faith Dane—contribute some ludicrous exercises in vulgarity. No one could improve much on the scene Mr. Robbins and Mr. Mielziner have devised to portray one of Minsky's most elegant show pieces. It fairly explodes with rhinestone splendor.

The cast is delightful. Lane Bradbury plays with gusto the part of June, the baby star who wrecks the act by running off to be married. Jack Klugman, kindly and worried, plays Herbie, the combination boy friend and booking agent. As Gypsy, Sandra Church gives a lovely performance. A slight young lady with small features and a delicate style of acting, she conveys with equal skill the shyness of the adolescent and the tough assurance of the lady who becomes a star.

But *Gypsy* is Miss Merman's show. Mr. Styne has given her some good greased-horn music, which she delivers with earthy magnificence in her familiar manner. There are some sticky scenes toward the end when *Gypsy* abandons the sleazy grandeur of show business and threatens to become belles-lettres. It deserts the body and starts cultivating the soul. Things look ominous in the last ten minutes.

But trust Ethel. She concludes the proceedings with a song and dance of defiance. Mr. Styne's music is dramatic. Miss Merman's performance expresses her whole character—cocky and aggressive, but also sociable and good-hearted. Not for the first time in her fabulous career, her personal magnetism electrifies the whole theatre. For she is a performer of incomparable power.

Gypsy is a good show in the old tradition of musicals. For years Miss Merman has been the queen.

Brooks Atkinson ON

The Fantasticks

BOOK AND LYRICS BY Tom Jones

MUSIC BY Harvey Schmidt

May 3, 1960

Sullivan Street Playhouse

16,999+ Performances

THE FANTASTICKS, a musical suggested by Edmond Rostand's *Les Romantiques.* Book and lyrics by Tom Jones. Music by Harvey Schmidt. Directed by Word Baker; presented by Lore Noto; associate producers, Shelly Baron, Dorothy Olim and Robert Alan Gold; musical direction and arrangements by Julian Stein; production designed by Ed Wittstein; production stage manager, Geoffrey Brown.

Narrator ....Jerry Orbach
Girl..Rita Gardner
Boy ....Kenneth Nelson
Boy's Father ....William Larsen
Girl's Father..Hugh Thomas
Actor ....Thomas Bruce
Man Who Dies ....George Curley
Mute ....Richard Stauffer
Handyman ....Jay Hampton
At the piano, Julian Stein; at the harp, Beverly Mann.

Having won a lot of admirers with a short version of *The Fantasticks,* Tom Jones has expanded it for the production that opened at the Sullivan Street Playhouse last evening.

Although it is ungrateful to say so, two acts are one too many to sustain the delightful tone of the first. After the intermission, the mood is never quite so luminous and gay.

The remark is ungrateful because the form of a masque seems original in the modern theatre. Harvey Schmidt's simple melodies with uncomplicated orchestrations are captivating and the acting is charming. Throughout the first act *The Fantasticks* is sweet and fresh in a civilized manner.

According to the program, it is based on Rostand's *Les Romantiques.* In the form of a dainty masque, designed in modern taste by Ed Wittstein, it is a variation on a Pierrot and Columbine theme. A boy and a girl, who are neighbors, are in love as long as a wall separates them and they believe that their fathers disapprove. Actually, their fathers want them to marry. To create an irresistible romantic mood, the fathers arrange a flamboyant abduction scene in the moonlight.

Although the story is slight, the style is entrancing in Word Baker's staging. It seems like a harlequinade in the setting of a masque. The characters are figures in a legend, acted with an artlessness that is winning. As the Narrator, the Girl and the Boy, Jerry Orbach, Rita Gardner and Kenneth Nelson, respectively, sing beautifully and act with spontaneity, not forgetting that they are participating in a work of make-believe.

After the intermission the author substitutes sunshine for moonlight. Disillusion destroys the rapture of the introductory scene. Pierrot and Columbine have combed the stardust out of their hair. But it seems to this theatregoer that the second act loses the skimming touch of the first. As an aging ham actor, Thomas Bruce is not so funny as he is in his first appearance, and the conceits of the staging become repetitious.

Perhaps *The Fantasticks* is by nature the sort of thing that loses magic the longer it endures. Any sign of effort diminishes it. But for the space of one act it is delightful. The music, played on piano and harp, has grace and humor. All the actors are thoroughbreds.

Howard Taubman ON

Rhinoceros

BY Eugene Ionesco

January 9, 1961

Longacre Theatre

240 Performances

RHINOCEROS, a play by Eugene Ionesco, translated by Derek Prouse. Staged by Joseph Anthony; presented by Leo Kerz, in association with Seven Arts Associates Corporation; costumes by Michael Travis; scenery and lighting by Mr. Kerz; production stage manager, Bill Ross; sound engineered by Saki Oura.

Waitress	Flora Elkins
Logician	Morris Carnovsky
Grocer	Dolph Sweet
Grocer's Wife	Lucille Patton
Housewife	Jane Hoffman
Berrenger	Eli Wallach
John	Zero Mostel
Old Gentleman	Leslie Barrett
Café Proprietor	Joseph Bernard
Daisy	Anne Jackson
Mr. Nicklebush	Philip Coolidge
Dribble	Mike Kellin
Shiftor	Michael Strong
Mrs. Ochs	Jean Stapleton
Fireman	Dolph Sweet

Don't look now, but those creatures throwing up dust and trumpeting primitively may be rhinoceroses debouching from the Longacre Theatre. Or better still, look and listen, for they are comic and they are serious, too.

They come from the vivid imagination of Eugene Ionesco and they inhabit his play, *Rhinoceros,* which opened here last night. It is an antic piece with overtones of gravity. And it has been staged and performed with a mad, inventive gusto that never loses sight of the important things behind the parody, horseplay and calculated illogicality.

In *Rhinoceros,* Mr. Ionesco is telling an allegory for our time, which has been beset by various, blighting uniformities. But he is not preaching. Nor is he concerned with the conventions of routine dramatic construction. He pokes fun unremittingly at conventional ideas, established institutions and all sorts of people, including himself. He cavorts and capers. He exaggerates wildly, and lets some of his notions run on too long. But just when he seems to be losing his touch, he discovers a new vein of fun.

Thanks to the play's success in a number of cities abroad, its subject may be familiar. If you have not heard of its contents, they may be summed up quickly. Mr. Ionesco imagines a city in which first one person, then a few, then all but a feckless clerk turn into rhinoceroses. His theme is a single motive, but he is fertile with delightful variations.

In working out his variations, Mr. Ionesco manages to say a good deal about the inconsistencies and irrationalities of human behavior. He ticks off the logician, the unionist, the straw boss, the ordinary run of men and women. He makes mincemeat of intellectual pretensions and then, of course, laughs at pompous simpletons.

Mr. Ionesco's mind is playful, full of quips and wanton wiles. Some of his jokes are obvious, no doubt deliberately. Others stem from a fresh view of the world. Mr. Ionesco has a fondness for the counterpoint of talk. In the first act he builds a pair of overlapping dialogues with a clever orchestrator's ingenuity. Then he follows with a discourse by the logician that is both humorous and satirical.

He is not above exchanges that are like Pat-and-Mike bits. Says one character of the office chief: "He turned into a rhinoceros." And the other responds: "He had such a good chance to become a vice president."

Is it Mr. Ionesco's final joke that his last man in a world of rhinoceroses is the weak, ineffectual clerk, Berrenger? If this is the playwright's intention, one cannot cavil. But if his moral is that the meek shall have to redeem the earth from its totalitarian follies, one would disagree violently. It requires courage, will and knowledge to hold fast to individuality—and to fight against mob psychology.

Joseph Anthony has caught Mr. Ionesco's wild, irreverent mood. To one who saw a rather stuffy, subdued version of *Rhinoceros* in London last

June, this production was a joyous revelation. The staging here has the knockabout high spirits of Mack Sennett comedy. Indeed, it carries this mood too far at times, settling for noise when ideas run thin. But like Mr. Ionesco's fancy, the staging repeatedly renews itself with fresh inventions.

As Berrenger, Eli Wallach gives a sustained, varied performance that remains in a low key. As his irascible, self-righteous friend John, Zero Mostel is a superb comedian, full of bouncing movement and roaring, cooing inflections. Anne Jackson turns Daisy, the girl Berrenger admires in his modest way, into a broadly stylized ingenue; her comic signature is the familiar gesture of a leg lifted backward archly. Morris Carnovsky, Mike Kellin and Michael Strong contribute soberly droll impersonations.

There are diverting, rowdy bits by Philip Coolidge, Jean Stapleton, Leslie Barrett, Jane Hoffman, Flora Elkins, Lucille Patton, Dolph Sweet and Joseph Bernard. They help to fill Leo Kerz' oddly rakish sets with motion and turmoil.

Mr. Ionesco may be an avant-gardist, but there is nothing recherché or difficult about *Rhinoceros*. Here he uses lighthearted means to remind human beings how easily they can turn beastly.

Howard Taubman ON
The Blacks
BY Jean Genet

May 4, 1961
St. Marks Playhouse
1,408 Performances

Ethel Ayler *(left)*, Godfrey Cambridge, wearing the mask, and Cynthia Belgrave in *The Blacks* THE NEW YORK TIMES PHOTO ARCHIVES

THE BLACKS, a play by Jean Genet, translated by Bernard Frechtman. Staged by Gene Frankel; presented by Sidney Bernstein, George Edgar and Andre Gregory, by arrangement with Geraldine Lust; scenery by Kim E. Swados; lighting by Lee Watson; costumes and masks by Patricia Zipprodt; movement by Talley Beatty; music supervised by Charles Gross; production associate, Alfred Manacher; production stage manager, Maxwell Glanville.

Archibald Wellington	Roscoe Lee Browne
Deodatus Village	James Earl Jones
Adelaide Bobo	Cynthia Belgrave
Edgar Alas Newport News	Louis Gossett
Augustus Snow	Ethel Ayler
Felicity Trollop Pardon	Helen Martin
Stephanie Virtue Diop	Cicely Tyson
Diouf	Godfrey M. Cambridge
Missionary	Lex Monson
Judge	Raymond St. Jacques
Governor	Jay J. Riley
Queen	Maya Angelou Make
Valet	Charles Gordone
Drummer	Charles Campbell

In writing and performance, Jean Genet's *The Blacks* at the St. Marks Playhouse is a brilliantly sardonic and lyrical tone poem for the theatre.

In form, it flows as freely as an improvisation, with fantasy, allegory and intimations of reality mingled into a weird, stirring unity. If you like your drama plain and naturalistic, *The Blacks* will leave you unsettled and disoriented. But if you are willing to venture into the diabolical chambers in which the French playwright conjures up his demons of the imagination, you will encounter one of the most original and stimulating evenings Broadway or Off Broadway has to offer.

If you wish an inkling of what M. Genet is up to, you must know the three sentences with which he prefaces his script. In the English of Bernard Frechtman, who has made the excellent translation of *The Blacks*, these sentences are:

"One evening an actor asked me to write a play for an all-black cast. But what exactly is a black? First of all, what's his color?"

M. Genet's investigation of the color of black begins where most plays on this burning theme of our time leave off. Using the device of performances within a performance, he evokes a group of players involved in a ceremony. On an upper level of the stage there is a court composed of a queen, valet, missionary, judge and governor. Below them is a group of ordinary mortals who weave in and out of a variety of impersonations that shift subtly and often abruptly.

All the players are dark-skinned. Those of the court wear white masks and for the greater part of the evening they represent the whites, the colonial masters, the dominant, superior race. While they roar, preen themselves and ultimately cringe, the illusion of their whiteness is meant to be transparent. By using Negro players in these roles M. Genet adds another level of bitter comment.

The ceremony is a trial for a murder that you eventually discover has not taken place. It occurs before a catafalque that turns out in the end to be merely a white sheet over a pair of chairs that the valet and missionary had complained about missing. But there is no mistaking the fierce motif that courses through M. Genet's furious flights of language encompassing obscenity and purity, violence and tenderness, hatred and love.

That motif is the meaning, in all its burden of the past and in the determination that shapes the future, of being a color that happens to be black. "Invent hatred," cries a character early in the drama. A little later comes an invocation to Africa and darkness and the hatred they have engendered. There is a ferociously satirical scene in which the Negroes below recite a "litany of the livid" as the devout in a church might intone the litanies of the Blessed Virgin.

In its conception *The Blacks* calls for an interpretation that summons most of the magic of the theatre but abjures its literalisms. Music including the minuet from *Don Giovanni* and the *Dies Irae,* the dance from the tribal movements of Africa to the sinuosities the Western world has grafted on it, architectural forms like platforms and curving ramps, acting and speaking that are formal and rhapsodic by turns—all these elements are required by M. Genet.

Gene Frankel has staged a performance that paces M. Genet's theatrical tone poem with humor and passion. The craftsmen and artists who have contributed to this interpretation deserve their meed of credit. So do the actors, who bring vibrancy and intensity to their performances. Read the names of all in the cast with respect, and remember with special warmth Roscoe Lee Browne, James Earl Jones, Cynthia Belgrave, Ethel Ayler, Helen Martin, Cicely Tyson and Godfrey M. Cambridge.

Theatregoers acquainted with M. Genet's *The Balcony* know that this vastly gifted Frenchman uses shocking words and images to cry out at the pretensions and injustices of our world. In *The Blacks* he is not only a moralist of high indignation but also a prophet of rage and compassion.

"Everything is changing," says Felicity, who speaks often like a high priestess. "Whatever is gentle and kind and good and tender will be black." So M. Genet has a Negro declare as if in a vision, but surely he looks for the day when these things will be all colors and no color.

Howard Taubman ON
The Caretaker
BY Harold Pinter

October 4, 1961

Lyceum Theatre

165 Performances

THE CARETAKER, a comedy-drama by Harold Pinter.
Staged by Donald McWhinnie; presented by Roger
L. Stevens, Frederick Brisson and Gilbert Miller;
scenery by Brian Currah; supervision and lighting by
Paul Morrison; production stage manager, Fred
Hebert.

Mick ....Alan Bates
Aston..Robert Shaw
Davies..Donald Pleasence

Out of a scabrous derelict and two mentally
unbalanced brothers Harold Pinter has woven a play of strangely compelling beauty and
passion. *The Caretaker,* which opened last night at
the Lyceum, proclaims its young English author
as one of the important playwrights of our day.

At first glance the materials of this play could
hardly be less promising. Two of the characters
are just this side of articulate, and the third spins a
glib, wild line about real estate, leases, interior
decoration and other common concerns. Yet Mr.
Pinter finds comedy, tenderness and heartbreak in
all three. He builds his spare elements into powerful drama with a climax that tears at the heart.

The Caretaker begins as if it will turn into sardonic comedy, beatnik style. An old bum receives
shelter in a cluttered room of an abandoned house.
His samaritan is a gentle young man whose kindness is so casual that he seems almost indifferent.
Dirty, tattered, unkempt, itching and scratching,
the tramp is by turns wheedling, truculent and full
of bravado.

This human jetsam, Davies or Jenkins or whatever his name may be, begins as a grossly comic
figure. He speaks the proud lingo of those who
have untold resources awaiting them at near-by
havens. He pronounces his meager phrases with

the exaggerated precision of one unaccustomed to
being heeded. He flails a fist into a palm or into
the air with the belligerence of a fighter no one
will ever corner. He associates himself with fastidious practices like soap as if they were his daily
habit. He is very funny—at first.

But the laughter shades increasingly into pity.
Like a cornered animal, he cannot believe anyone
means to be kind to him. He complains about the
hospitality he receives, and although it is impoverished, it clearly exceeds any recent comfort he has
known. He looks down on the blacks who live in
an adjacent abandoned house and is fearful that
they will share his lavatory. He hates foreigners.
He trusts no one, and fears everyone.

He alienates the two brothers who separately
have offered him a job as caretaker of the premises. Their offers and the job itself become themes
with subtle overtones. For Aston, the samaritan,
lives in personal and emotional isolation, tinkering with gadgets and dreaming of building a shed
out in the yard. And Mick, who carries on like a
man of affairs, inhabits a dream world that resembles an extrovert's nightmares.

Mr. Pinter has been vehement in his assertions
that his play is not more than the story it tells. But
he cannot prevent his audiences from finding it in
a modern parable of derisive scorn and bitter sorrow. Who will take care of Davies, the caretaker?
Even the demented cannot endure the scrofulous
old vagrant. If it is possible for one such as Davies
to have a Gethsemane, this play at last brings him
to it.

Donald Pleasence gives an unforgettable performance as Davies. He exudes a sense of degradation. He speaks in a strangled voice and then
shouts with the anger of the frightened. He is
comic and pathetic and, in his facing up to what
seems his last agony, shattering. A very distinguished actor.

Robert Shaw is enormously touching as Aston,
particularly in a long soliloquy at the end of the
second act. Alan Bates brilliantly manages the eager geniality and the mad intensity of Mick. Donald McWhinnie's staging in Brian Currah's
imaginatively cluttered set has the strength of

character to begin patiently and to build with cumulative force.

A work of rare originality, *The Caretaker* will tease and cling to the mind. No matter what happens in the months to come, it will lend luster to this Broadway season.

Howard Taubman ON
Who's Afraid of Virginia Woolf?
BY Edward Albee

October 13, 1962

Billy Rose Theatre

664 Performances

WHO'S AFRAID OF VIRGINIA WOOLF?, a play by Edward Albee. Staged by Alan Schneider; presented by Richard Barr and Clinton Wilder; production designed by William Ritman; stage manager, Mark Wright.

Martha ....Uta Hagen
George ....Arthur Hill
Honey...Melinda Dillon
Nick.......................................George Grizzard

Thanks to Edward Albee's furious skill as a writer, Alan Schneider's charged staging and a brilliant performance by a cast of four, *Who's Afraid of Virginia Woolf?* is a wry and electric evening in the theater.

You may not be able to swallow Mr. Albee's characters whole, as I cannot. You may feel, as I do, that a pillar of the plot is too flimsy to support the climax. Nevertheless, you are urged to hasten to the Billy Rose Theater, where Mr. Albee's first full-length play opened Saturday night.

For *Who's Afraid of Virginia Woolf?* is possessed by raging demons. It is punctuated by comedy, and its laughter is shot through with savage irony. At its core is a bitter, keening lament over man's incapacity to arrange his environment or private life so as to inhibit his self-destructive compulsions.

Moving onto from off Broadway, Mr. Albee carries along the burning intensity and icy wrath

that informed *The Zoo Story* and *The American Dream*. He has written a full-length play that runs almost three and a half hours and that brims over with howling furies that do not drown out a fierce compassion. After the fumes stirred by his witches' caldron are spent, he lets in, not sunlight and fresh air, but only an agonized prayer.

Although Mr. Albee's vision is grim and sardonic, he is never solemn. With the instincts of a born dramatist and the shrewdness of one whose gifts have been tempered in the theater, he knows how to fill the stage with vitality and excitement.

Sympathize with them or not, you will find the characters in this new play vibrant with dramatic urgency. In their anger and terror they are pitiful as well as corrosive, but they are also wildly and humanly hilarious. Mr. Albee's dialogue is dipped in acid, yet ripples with a relish of the ludicrous. His controlled, allusive style grows in mastery.

In *Who's Afraid of Virginia Woolf?* he is concerned with Martha and George, a couple living in mordant, uproarious antagonism. The daughter of the president of the college where he teaches, she cannot forgive his failure to be a success like her father. He cannot abide her brutal bluntness and drive. Married for more than twenty years, they claw each other like jungle beasts.

In the dark hours after a Saturday midnight they entertain a young married pair new to the campus, introducing them to a funny and cruel brand of fun and games. Before the liquor-sodden night is over, there are lacerating self-revelations for all.

On the surface the action seems to be mostly biting talk. Underneath is a witches' revel, and Mr. Albee is justified in calling his second act "Walpurgisnacht." But the means employed to lead to the denouement of the third act, called "The Exorcism," seems spurious.

Mr. Albee would have us believe that for twenty-one years his older couple have nurtured a fiction that they have a son, that his imaginary existence is a secret that violently binds and sunders them and that George's pronouncing him dead may be a turning point. This part of the story does not ring true, and its falsity impairs the credibility of his central characters.

If the drama falters, the acting of Uta Hagen and Arthur Hill does not. As the vulgar, scornful, desperate Martha, Miss Hagen makes a tormented harridan horrifyingly believable. As the quieter, tortured and diabolical George, Mr. Hill gives a superbly modulated performance built on restraint as a foil to Miss Hagen's explosiveness.

George Grizzard as a young biologist on the make shades from geniality to intensity with shattering rightness. And Melinda Dillon as his mousy, troubled bride is amusing and touching in her vulnerable wistfulness.

Directing like a man accustomed to fusing sardonic humor and seething tension, Mr. Schneider has found a meaningful pace for long—some too long—passages of seemingly idle talk, and has staged vividly the crises of action.

Who's Afraid of Virginia Woolf? (the phrase is sung at odd moments as a bitter joke to the tune of the children's play song, "Mulberry Bush") is a modern variant on the theme of the war between the sexes. Like Strindberg, Mr. Albee treats his women remorselessly, but he is not much gentler with his men. If he grieves for the human predicament, he does not spare those lost in its psychological and emotional mazes.

His new work, flawed though it is, towers over the common run of contemporary plays. It marks a further gain for a young writer becoming a major figure of our stage.

Howard Taubman on
Beyond the Fringe
by Alan Bennett, Peter Cook, Jonathan Miller and Dudley Moore

October 27, 1962
John Golden Theater
667 Performances

BEYOND THE FRINGE, a revue. Written and acted by Alan Bennett, Peter Cook, Jonathan Miller and Dudley Moore. Staged by Alexander H. Cohen; presented by Mr. Cohen, by arrangement with William Donaldson and Donald Albery; original London production staged by Eleanor Fazan; scenery by John Wyckham; lighting by Ralph Alswang; production associates, André Goulston and Gabriel Katzka; production stage manager, Alan Hall.

In a time of peril, try laughing. Look in on *Beyond the Fringe* and try not laughing.

You won't escape the crises and alarums that roil our planet. But under the guidance of the four keen-witted, riotous young Englishmen who brought their satirical sketches to the John Golden Theater Saturday night, the world's troubles, though still critical, no longer seem grave.

Paralyzed by fear of the H-bomb? Attend a Civil Defense briefing as Alan Bennett, Peter Cook and Jonathan Miller preside with the comforting casualness of a garden party and as Dudley Moore represents the public with a chipper air of a chap who has just won a few bob on a long shot. If they won't allay your terror of the awful menace, they'll have you shaking so hard with laughter that you'll forget momentarily to tremble with fear.

Blond, bespectacled Mr. Bennett, whose north-country twang could slice a London fog, is in the chair and begins the discourse. At his left the tall, red-haired Mr. Miller, whose long limbs seem jointless and whose face has a pixie's innocence, draws on his pipe with foolish complacency. Sober, owlish Mr. Cook, the other panelist, continues the discussion with the dogged patience of a man getting things straight himself.

"Get out of the danger area," he advises with the imperturbability of a regular at the corner pub ruminating on the weather. To make his meaning unmistakable, he explains, "That's where the bomb drops," and adds with unsmiling dispassion, "If you're out of it, you're well out of it; if you're in it, you're well in it."

The small, sanguine Mr. Moore, perched in the balcony with the audience, pops an eager question: "Please, panel, following the holocaust, when will public services be resumed?" The bumbling Mr. Cook replies reassuringly that all is provided for but warns that at first it may only be "a skeleton service."

The four who have written and perform *Beyond the Fringe* mask their malevolence with a benign air, and their performances alternate between deadpan dryness and wild impishness. Since their entertainment is British in provenance, their targets cover their native heath. Indeed, several numbers are so stubbornly home-grown that you may want a glossary or a trip to England. Mostly, however, their ridicule is aimed at topics perfectly understandable on 45th Street—or anywhere on a grim globe badly in need of a smile.

Swift skits touch lightly or savagely on politics, statesmen, royalty, international affairs, racialism and a variety of urgent matters. Mr. Cook devastatingly takes off on Prime Minister Macmillan reporting on a journey of state. Mr. Bennett, as a lecturer on the world situation, narrowly avoids embarrassment on an inflamed subject when he adverts to Cuba but extricates himself by advising Americans "to imitate our splendid effort at Suez" and admonishing Bertrand Russell to stick to thinking.

In a TV discussion program Mr. Miller dares to impersonate a Negro politician from Africa and manages to make him as mendaciously bland and comic as pompous politicians anywhere.

But the public affairs are not the only game tracked in *Beyond the Fringe*. These lads are like serpents striking at any succulently pretentious prey in sight, and their fangs are envenomed.

Mr. Miller, wandering with the angular, disjointed charm of a Danny Kaye, muses maliciously on pornography. Mr. Bennett, his tones dripping with nasality, delivers a sermon that should make meandering preachers of all denominations look to their pulpits. Mr. Moore, the musician of the foursome, bravely begins a concert piece at the piano and, like a virtuoso in a nightmare, finds himself trapped in endless closing chords.

Mr. Cook, as a dimwitted miner, explains in a slow, unrancorous monotone why he failed of his desire to be a judge and why he wouldn't mind enjoying something other than "the trappings of poverty." There are times when *Beyond the Fringe* cuts painfully close to the bone.

A long emotional sequence recalled in no tranquillity is a biting as well as funny recollection of the war. A spoof of two philosophers indulging in their high-domed jargon is murderously droll. Four hee-hawing Englishmen inarticulately met for lunch has the ring of truth.

The most uninhibited hilarious number wreaks havoc on Shakespeare and Shakespearean hams. Wearing wildly exaggerated headpieces, mouthing portentous pentameters like demented princes and jesters, and mincing and posturing like comedians and tragedians rabid with high art, the four make a hash of bardolatry. When Mr. Miller, mortally wounded, expires in an extravagance of staggering, crawling and careening in and out of the wings, he is not merely a satirist but a knockabout comic of the highest order.

At the end the four sit on a mountain top waiting for the last trumpet to sound and the final mighty wind to blow. The only end is the show's. What a pity one must return to the real world of disputatious winds and alarming trumpets, where wonderfully talented Englishmen or Americans or Russians are not roaring with joyous irreverence.

Hello, Dolly!

BOOK BY Michael Stewart

MUSIC AND LYRICS BY Jerry Herman

January 16, 1964

St. James Theater

2,844 Performances

David Burns and Carol Channing as the resourceful match-maker Dolly Levi in *Hello, Dolly!* EILEEN DARBY, GRAPHIC HOUSE

HELLO, DOLLY!, a new musical comedy suggested by Thornton Wilder's *The Matchmaker*. Book by Michael Stewart; music and lyrics by Jerry Herman; scenery by Oliver Smith; costumes by Freddy Wittop; lighting by Jean Rosenthal; musical direction and vocal arrangements by Shepard Coleman; orchestrations by Philip Lang; dance and incidental music arranged by Peter Howard; directed and choreographed by Gower Champion, assisted by Lucia Victor; presented by David Merrick.

Mrs. Dolly Gallagher Levi	Carol Channing
Ernestina	Mary Jo Catlett
Ambrose Kemper	Igors Gavon
Horse	Jan LaPrade, Bonnie Mathis
Horace Vandergelder	David Burns
Ermengarde	Alice Playten
Cornelius Hackl	Charles Nelson Reilly
Barnaby Tucker	Jerry Dodge
Irene Molloy	Eileen Brennan
Minnie Fay	Sondra Lee
Mrs. Rose	Amelia Haas
Rudolph	David Hartman
Judge	Gordon Connell
Court Clerk	Ken Ayers

As a play Thornton Wilder's *The Matchmaker* vibrated with unheard melodies and unseen dances. Michael Stewart, Jerry Herman and Gower Champion apparently heard and saw them, and they have conspired ingeniously to bring them to shining life in a musical shot through with enchantment.

Hello, Dolly!, which blew happily into the St. James Theater last night, has qualities of freshness and imagination that are rare in the run of our machine-made musicals. It transmutes the broadly stylized mood of a mettlesome farce into the gusto and colors of the musical stage. What was larger and droller than life has been puffed up and gaily tinted without being blown apart. *Hello, Dolly!* is the best musical of the season thus far.

It could have been more than that. Were it not for lapses of taste, it could have been one of the notable ones. But Mr. Champion, whose staging and choreography abound in wit and invention, has tolerated certain cheapnesses, like the vulgar accent of a milliner's clerk, like the irritating wail of a teen-ager crying for her beau, like the muddled chase in the midst of a series of tableaux vivants. Mr. Stewart's book has settled for some dull and cheap lines the musical would not miss.

It is a pity because *Hello, Dolly!* does not need such crutches. One can understand, of course, why offenses against taste creep into an essentially imaginative musical. The stakes are so high that there is a tendency to whip things up, as if the public could not be trusted. But only musicals without ideas or talent must resort to desperate measures, which don't help anyhow.

But enough of peevishness. Let us rejoice in the blessings *Hello, Dolly!* bestows.

The conception as a whole, despite an occasional excess of exuberance that turns into turbulence, is faithful to the spirit of Mr. Wilder's broad, chuckling jest. Mr. Stewart's book holds fast to Mr. Wilder's atmosphere and style even if it trots off into Broadwayese now and then. Mr. Herman's songs are brisk and pointed and always tuneful.

Mr. Champion's direction at its happiest darts and floats on stylized, yet airborne patterns of choreography. Oliver Smith's sets with their backdrops that unroll like screens have the elegance of pen-and-ink drawings and the insouciance of a rejuvenated old New York. Freddy Wittop's costumes join Mr. Smith's designs in an extravagance of period styles and colors.

The basic story, deliberately calculating in its simplicity, is unchanged. Here in a shrewdly mischievous performance by Carol Channing is the endlessly resourceful widow, Mrs. Dolly Gallagher Levi, matchmaker and lady-of-all-trades, who sets her enormous bonnet crested by a huge pink bird for the half-millionaire, Vandergelder, and lands him on her pleasure-loving terms.

Miss Channing's Dolly is all benevolent guile. She can talk faster than a con man without losing her big-eyed innocent gleam. She can lead Vandergelder to the widow Molloy and manage to rub noses with him enticingly.

She can teach "Dancing" to Mr. Herman's gliding three-four muse. Resplendent in scarlet gown embroidered with jewels and a feathered headdress, and looking like a gorgeous, animated kewpie doll, she sings the rousing title song with earthy zest and leads a male chorus of waiters and chefs in a joyous promenade around the walk that circles the top of the pit.

Here is David Burns as the curmudgeon Vandergelder, bellowing nasally like W. C. Fields redivivus. His intransigence in the face of warmth and kindness is a comfort in a Polyanna world. When he roars that he is "rich, friendless and mean, which in Yonkers is as far as you can go," you are bound to share his pride. And when, standing on a dismantled parade float that is being pulled out of sight, he roars, "Where are you taking me?", he has the righteous wrath of a Horatius defending a sinking bridge.

Charles Nelson Reilly and Jerry Dodge as two of Vandergelder's oppressed clerks loose on the town sing and dance agreeably, and their buffoonery would be funnier if it were toned down. Eileen Brennan is as pretty and desirable a Widow Molloy as one could wish—with a voice, too. Igors Gavon is another performer with a big, resonant voice.

What gives *Hello, Dolly!* its special glow is its amalgamation of the lively theater arts in the musical numbers. Mr. Champion has provided fragments of dance for the overture-less opening that are all the more attractive because they are spare and unexpectedly spaced.

When he fills the stage for the ebullient "Put on Your Sunday Clothes" at the Yonkers Depot and has his lavishly garbed cast promenading along the oval runway out front, the theater throbs with vitality. As if to put a cherry on the sundae, the stage magicians have provided a railroad car pulled by an engine that spits smoke and ashes.

For a 14th Street parade Mr. Champion has deployed his forces in a cheerful old New York version of medieval guilds. To a bouncing gallop by Mr. Herman, Mr. Champion has set a corps of waiters with trays, spits and jeroboams at the ready, dancing a wild, vertiginous rout. To Mr. Herman's lightly satirical "Elegance," Mr. Champion has fashioned a delightfully mannered routine for his quartet of singers—Miss Brennan, Sondra Lee, Mr. Reilly and Mr. Dodge.

Making the necessary reservations for the unnecessary vulgar and frenzied touches, one is glad to welcome *Hello, Dolly!* for its warmth, color and high spirits.

Howard Taubman ON
The Blood Knot
BY Atholl Fugard

March 2, 1964

Cricket Theater

239 Performances

THE BLOOD KNOT, a play by Atholl Fugard. Staged by John Berry; presented by Sidney Bernstein and Lucille Lortel Productions, Inc.; production associate, Michael Perloff; scenery by John Bury; lighting by Harold Baldridge; costumes by Martha Gould; production stage manager, Ed Cambridge.
Morris Pieterson...J. D. Cannon
Zachariah Pieterson..............................James Earl Jones

No play in town is simpler and more penetrating, tenderer and more bruising than *The Blood Knot*, which arrived last night at the Cricket Theater.

Its author is Atholl Fugard, a new voice from South Africa. Himself a white man, Mr. Fugard has told a story that bares the anguish of his native land, where white men and dark-skinned men now live in a state of raw, abrasive suspicion and hostility.

On the surface *The Blood Knot* is transparently direct and touching. It has only two characters, sons of the same mother, but one is black and the other white. They live in a miserable corrugated-tin shack in the colored section of Korsten on the outskirts of South Africa's Port Elizabeth. In their empty, dull lives they go through routines and act out games that reveal their distrust and need of each other.

But *The Blood Knot* is a good deal more than it seems, for it is a parable about South Africa today. While the black brother appears to be as simple-minded as a child, he seethes inwardly with hatred. While the white brother is considerate, well-spoken and content to let the other toil for him, he is restless and torn with fear.

Mr. Fugard is neither portentous nor solemn about his symbolism. Although there is fervor in his viewpoint, he knows how to let emotion rise from the simplest of touches. Each brother is a warmly realized human being. The swift changes in their relationship from harmony to conflict are described in homely, comic, affecting terms.

As the play begins, Morris, the white brother, waits for his Zachariah to return from his long day's labor in the hot sun. He has water heated for the tired man's foot bath, and he has two kinds of salts to assuage his aching feet. A plain, meager supper is ready.

But the colored brother is restive in the Eden that the white man has tried to make out of the shack. He refuses to be pacified with a dream of a farm that their savings will buy. He is explosive with desire, and the white brother cajoles him into believing that a female pen pal will do as well as a woman here and now.

The pen pal becomes for a time the serpent in this shabby paradise. In the reaction of the brothers to her first letter *The Blood Knot* begins to dig deeply into what it must feel like to be a colored man in South Africa. And as the play develops, Mr. Fugard strips away the protective coverings of playfulness and fraternity that the brothers wear for each other. At the end one sees them in a desperate struggle, which cannot be won or ended.

Under John Berry's imaginative and powerful direction, J. D. Cannon and James Earl Jones are giving *The Blood Knot* the brilliant performance it deserves. Mr. Jones plays Zachariah with a rare grasp of his slow simplicity with its warmth and slyness, and he brings tension and fury to the bitter, explosive scenes. Mr. Cannon is patient and artful with this difficult brother, and he summons a searing intensity for his passages of terror.

With its two characters *The Blood Knot* looks like a small package, but it packs a larger charge than most of the plays we get on or off Broadway. And don't think that what Mr. Fugard reveals of the souls of white and black brothers living uneasily together involves only South Africa.

Howard Taubman ON

Funny Girl

BOOK BY Isobel Lennart

LYRICS BY Bob Merrill

MUSIC BY Jule Styne

March 26, 1964

Winter Garden

1,348 Performances

FUNNY GIRL, a musical. Book by Isobel Lennart. Music by Jule Styne. Lyrics by Bob Merrill. Staged by Garson Kanin; presented by Ray Stark, in association with Seven Arts Productions; associate producer, Al Goldin; production supervised by Jerome Robbins; associate director, Lawrence Kasha; choreographed by Carol Haney; scenery and lighting by Robert Randolph; costumes by Irene Sharaff; musical director, Milton Rosenstock; orchestrations by Ralph Burns; vocal arrangements by Buster Davis; dance orchestrations by Luther Henderson; production stage manager, Richard Evans.

Fanny Brice	Barbra Streisand
Emma	Royce Wallace
Mrs. Brice	Kay Medford
Mrs. Strakosh	Jean Stapleton
Mrs. Meeker	Lydia S. Fredericks
Mrs. O'Malley	Joyce O'Neil
Tom Keeney	Joseph Macaulay
Eddie Ryan	Danny Meehan
Snub Taylor	Buzz Miller
Trombone Smitty	Blair Hammond
Five Finger Finney	Alan E. Weeks
Nick Arnstein	Sydney Chaplin
Florenz Ziegfeld Jr.	Roger De Koven
Mimsie	Sharon Vaughn
Ziegfeld Tenor	John Lankston
Ziegfeld Lead Dancer	George Reeder
Mr. Renaldi	Marc Jordan

Who wouldn't want to resurrect Fanny Brice? She was a wonderful entertainer.

Since Fanny herself cannot be brought back, the next best thing is to get Barbra Streisand to sing and strut and go through comic routines à la Brice. Miss Streisand is well on her way to becoming a splendid entertainer in her own right,

and in *Funny Girl* she goes as far as any performer can toward recalling the laughter and joy that were Fanny Brice.

If the new musical that arrived last night at the Winter Garden were dedicated entirely to the gusto and buffoonery of Fanny Brice, all would be well nigh perfect this morning. But *Funny Girl* also is intent on telling the story of how Fanny loved and lost Nick Arnstein, and part of the time it oozes with a thick helping of sticky sentimentality.

But that's show-business sagas for you. They rarely can untrack themselves from the hokum and schmaltz that authors and, for all one knows, show people consider standard operating procedure. As for the public, it often is a pushover for the glamour of the stage and the romances of show folk. Say for *Funny Girl* that it has not reached to be neck deep in show business. It has every right to be there.

Funny Girl is most fun when it is reveling in Fanny's preoccupation with show business. Miss Streisand as a young Brice bursting with energy and eagerness to improve her routines is an impudent dancing doll who refuses to run down. Miss Streisand imagining herself in a radiant future in "I'm the Greatest Star," an appealingly quirky song, is not only Fanny Brice but all young performers believing in their destinies.

Then there are the production numbers that recall the theater before World War I. Miss Streisand and a wildly agitated chorus, set loose in a pattern designed by Carol Haney, do the explosive "Cornet Man" in a way that would startle the music halls of old but does not betray their spirit.

For an evocation of the stately Ziegfeld *Follies,* which Miss Brice brightened with her exuberance, there are two big nostalgic numbers. One glorifies the bride, with beautiful girls, draped and undraped, fixed in the scenery and rippling on a lofty flight of stairs topped by candelabra, and with Miss Streisand turning the overblown "His Love Makes Me Beautiful" into a spoof. The other, using the same stairway, shoots soldiers and soldierettes into a furious drill to a military "Rat-Tat-Tat-Tat," with Miss Streisand doing her bit as a comic veteran.

Fanny's friends making merry with a block party on Henry Street after her debut in the *Follies* are festive company. And Miss Streisand as Fanny hamming it up in her first rendezvous with Sydney Chaplin in a private room in a swank restaurant is almost as funny as the funny girl herself might have been. She uses a fan with mock coyness; she arranges herself on a chair like a rachitic femme fatale; she walks across the room with a wiggle Mae West would envy.

These maneuvers, nevertheless, to a Brice or a Streisand, are the small tricks of the clown's trade. What makes Miss Streisand's manipulation of them in this scene particularly impressive is that she conveys a note of honest emotion underneath the clowning. Indeed, at this point the romance of Fanny and Nick is as charming as young love.

Isobel Lennart's book skirts sentimentality reasonably well until Fanny and Nick turn serious, get married and run into troubles. By the end *Funny Girl* is drenched in tears.

Fortunately, Miss Streisand can make a virtue out of suffering, if she is allowed to sing about it. Jule Styne, who has written one of his best scores, has provided her with bluesy tunes like "Who Are You Now?" and she turned them into lyrical laments.

Miss Streisand can also draw rapture from the yearning "People." For a change of pace she makes her raffish share of "You Are Woman," for which Bob Merrill has done smiling lyrics, worthy of the performer she impersonates.

Mr. Chaplin is a tall, elegant figure as Nick, gallant in courting and doing his best when he must be noble. Kay Medford, who seems to be a stage mother every time you see her in a musical, is dry and diverting as Fanny's shrewd parent. Danny Meehan is agreeable as a hoofer who befriends the young Fanny.

Garson Kanin gets credit for being the director and Jerome Robbins for being the production supervisor, and only they and the company know what their contributions were. Say for both of them that *Funny Girl* behaves as if it takes its hokum seriously and that its show-business sequences framed in Robert Randolph's cheerful sets move at a pace hard to resist.

It's the authentic aura of show business arising out of Fanny Brice's luminous career that lights up *Funny Girl*. Much of the spoken humor is homespun—that is, East Side homespun. The true laughter in this musical comes from the sense of truth it communicates of Fanny Brice's stage world. And Fanny's personality and style are remarkably evoked by Miss Streisand. Fanny and Barbra make the evening. Who says the past cannot be recaptured?

Howard Taubman ON
Richard Burton's *Hamlet*

April 9, 1964
Lunt-Fontanne Theater
137 Performances

Richard Burton as Hamlet in 1964, with Eileen Herlie as Gertrude   FRIEDMAN-ABELES

HAMLET, Shakespeare's tragedy. Staged by John Gielgud; presented by Alexander H. Cohen with Frenman Productions; production associates, Gabriel Katzka and Andre Goulston; production designed by Ben Edwards; lighting by Jean Rosenthal; clothes by Jane Greenwood; production manager, Jean Barrere.
Francisco ....Michael Ebert
Marcellus..Barnard Hughes

Horatio	Robert Milli
Claudius	Alfred Drake
Voltimand	Philip Coolidge
Laertes	John Cullum
Polonius	Hume Cronyn
Hamlet	Richard Burton
Gertrude	Eileen Herlie
Ophelia	Linda Marsh
Ghost	John Gielgud
Reynaldo	Dillon Evans
Rosencrantz	Clement Fowler
Guildenstern	William Redfield
Player King	George Voskovec
Lucianus	Geoff Garland
First Gravedigger	George Rose

The first and most important thing to be said about the *Hamlet* that opened last night at the Lunt-Fontanne Theater is that it is Shakespeare, not a self-indulgent holiday for a star.

Richard Burton dominates the drama, as Hamlet should. For his is a performance of electrical power and sweeping virility. But it does not burst the bounds of the framework set for it by John Gielgud's staging. It is not so much larger than life that it overwhelms the rest of the company. Nor does it demand attention so fiercely for itself that the shape and poetry of the play are lost to the audience.

Mr. Gielgud has pitched the performance to match Mr. Burton's range and intensity. The company for the most part has been well-chosen, though it is not and cannot be expected everywhere to approach the crispness of the Hamlet's attack, the scope of his voice, the peaks of his fury and remorse.

Mr. Gielgud's own Hamlet years ago was much different—more sinuous and refined. It is his merit that he has found a new way to look at the play to be in keeping with Mr. Burton's style and view of the role. This is no melancholy *Hamlet,* no psychoanalytical or Oedipal *Hamlet,* no effete or lack-luster *Hamlet.*

It is designed to look like a final runthrough. The stage is bare, its brick walls and columns visible. A platform and a series of steps plus a few bits of furniture provide the setting. A clothes rack holding costumes—for some other *Hamlet,* no doubt—is at the side and becomes the curtain behind which Polonius and the king hide and later the arras through which Polonius is gored.

The actors are in working clothes. Hamlet wears a black V-necked shirt and black trousers. Claudius and Polonius have on jackets and ties. The other men are in formal jackets, windbreakers, sweaters, slacks and jeans. Gertrude and Ophelia are in blouses and long skirts. Only the strolling players wear costumes when they are enacting the murder of Gonzago—a recognition that some differentiation in attire is useful.

Does this liberate the production from the weight of the customary trappings? If Mr. Burton and his companions think so, one should not quibble. My preference is for costumes, for there is a jarring note at the outset as the majestic Elizabethan language does not consort properly with rehearsal clothes. But as the performance progresses, one forgets about dress and moves into Shakespeare's magnificent imaginative world.

As for the lack of colorful scenery, one does not cavil. We have grown accustomed in recent years to open stages with little or no painted canvas, and the absence of the trumpery and machinery of lavish productions need not be mourned.

For it is liberating to the audience's imagination as well as the actor's to do without the gaudy stuff—at least when you have a play of the magnitude of *Hamlet.* But it must be added that an uncluttered proscenium stage is not nearly the same thing as an open stage that becomes one with the audience.

It is clear early on that Mr. Burton means to play Hamlet with all the stops out—when the power is wanted. He is aware of the risk of seeming to rant. For it is he who warns that the players must not tear a passion to tatters. But he is unafraid—and he is right.

I do not recall a Hamlet of such tempestuous manliness. In the first two soliloquies Mr. Burton does not hesitate to cry out as if his very soul were in torment, and the thunderous, wrenching climaxes do not ring false. But he reads the "To be or not to be" soliloquy with subdued anguish, like a man communing painfully with himself. Then in the scene that follows with Ophelia, he begins by being ineffably tender, but when he rails at her to get to a nunnery, his rage bespeaks his hatred for himself as well as for a base world.

Mr. Burton's Hamlet is full of pride and wit and mettle. He is warm and forthright with Horatio. As he listens to Polonius's windy craftiness, a look of shrewd contempt hoods his eye. He trades quips with the First Gravedigger with gusto.

Mr. Burton's voice is not mellifluous like those of a few highly cultivated classic actors. It has a hearty ring and a rough edge, attributes that suit his interpretation. He does not, however, scant the poetry. He has a fine sense of rhythm. It is very much his own, with a flair for accenting words and phrases in unexpected ways. But the result, while personal, does no violence to sound or sense.

One has reservations about details. Hamlet prowls too restlessly during the performance of the players. His grabbing of the goblet from Claudius's hand is an effect that disturbs one's eagerness to believe. His standing with sword raised high only inches from the praying Claudius is another liberty that strikes at credibility.

Worthy of being on the stage with this Hamlet is Hume Cronyn's superbly managed and richly fatuous Polonius. Alfred Drake is a little too bland as Claudius, but achieves intensity in the prayer scene. Eileen Herlie is a persuasive Gertrude, especially affecting in the closet scene. George Rose lights up the stage in his brief turn as the First Gravedigger.

George Voskovec as the Player King, Clement Fowler as Rosencrantz, William Redfield as Guildenstern, John Cullum as Laertes, Robert Milli as Horatio, and the dark, sepulchral voice of Mr. Gielgud as the Ghost contribute impressively. Linda Marsh is a little over her head as Ophelia, but manages the Mad Scene with a touch of rue.

As one sits through a long evening that seems all too short, one is humbled afresh by the surge of Shakespeare's poetry, by his tenderness and by his disillusioned awareness of man and his ways. It is the grandeur of *Hamlet*, not of an actor or director, that prevails.

Howard Taubman ON
Fiddler on the Roof
BOOK BY Joseph Stein
LYRICS BY Sheldon Harnick
MUSIC BY Jerry Bock

September 22, 1964
Imperial Theater
3,242 Performances

A rehearsal session from *Fiddler on the Roof*
THE NEW YORK TIMES

FIDDLER ON THE ROOF, a musical based on Sholem Aleichem's stories. Book by Joseph Stein. Music by Jerry Bock. Lyrics by Sheldon Harnick. Staged and choreographed by Jerome Robbins; presented by Harold Prince; scenery by Boris Aronson; costumes by Patricia Zipprodt; lighting by Jean Rosenthal; orchestrations by Don Walker; musical direction and vocal arrangements by Milton Greene; dance music arranged by Betty Walberg; production stage manager, Ruth Mitchell.

Tevye	Zero Mostel
Golde	Maria Karnilova
Tzeitel	Joanna Merlin
Hodel	Julia Migenes
Chava	Tanya Everett
Shprintze	Marilyn Rogers
Bielke	Linda Ross
Motel	Austin Pendleton
Perchik	Bert Convy
Yente	Beatrice Arthur

Lazar Wolf..Michael Granger
Morche...Zyee Scooler
Rabbi...Gluck Sandor
Mendel...Leonard Frey
Avram...Paul Lipson
Nachum...Maurice Edwards
Grandma Tzeitel..Sue Babel
Fruma-Sarah..Carol Sawyer
Constable...Joseph Sullivan
Fyedka..Joe Ponazecki
Shandel ....Helen Verbit
Bottle Dancers ....Louis Genevrino, Mitch Thomas,
                                        Duane Bodin, John C. Attle
Fiddler ....Gino Conforti

It has been prophesied that the Broadway musical theater would take up the mantle of meaningfulness worn so carelessly by the American drama in recent years. *Fiddler on the Roof* does its bit to make good on this prophecy.

The new musical, which opened last night at the Imperial Theater, is filled with laughter and tenderness. It catches the essence of a moment in history with sentiment and radiance. Compounded of the familiar materials of the musical theater—popular song, vivid dance movement, comedy and emotion—it combines and transcends them to arrive at an integrated achievement of uncommon quality.

The essential distinction of *Fiddler on the Roof* must be kept in mind even as one cavils at a point here or a detail there. For criticism of a work of this caliber, it must be remembered, is relative. If I wish that several of the musical numbers soared indigenously, if I find fault with a gesture that is Broadway rather than the world of Sholem Aleichem, if I deplore a conventional scene, it is because *Fiddler on the Roof* is so fine that is deserves counsels toward perfection.

But first to the things that are marvelously right. The book that Joseph Stein has drawn from the richly humorous and humane tales of Sholem Aleichem, the warm-hearted spokesman of the poor Jews in the Russian villages at the turn of the century, is faithful to its origins.

It touches honestly on the customs of the Jewish community in such a Russian village. Indeed, it goes beyond local color and lays bare in quick, moving strokes the sorrow of a people subject to sudden tempests of vandalism and, in the end, to eviction and exile from a place that had been home.

Although there is no time in a musical for a fully developed gallery of human portraits, *Fiddler on the Roof* manages to display several that have authentic character. The most arresting, of course, is that of Tevye, the humble dairyman whose blessings included a hardworking, if sharp-tongued, wife, five daughters and a native philosophical bent.

If Sholem Aleichem had known Zero Mostel, he would have chosen him, one is sure, for Tevye. Some years ago Mr. Mostel bestowed his imagination and incandescence on Tevye in an Off-Broadway and television version of Sholem Aleichem's stories. Now he has a whole evening for Tevye, and Tevye for him. They were ordained to be one.

Mr. Mostel looks as Tevye should. His full beard is a pious aureole for his shining countenance. The stringy ends of his prayer shawl hang from under his vest; the knees of his breeches are patched, and his boots are scuffed. On festive occasions he wears a skull cap and a kaftan that give him an appearance of bourgeois solidity. But he is too humble to put on airs.

A man of goodwill, Mr. Mostel often pauses to carry on a dialogue with himself, arguing both sides of a case with equal logic. He holds long conversations with God. Although his observations never are disrespectful, they call a spade a spade. "Send us the cure," he warns the Lord, "we got the sickness already."

When Maria Karnilova as his steadfast but blunt wife breaks in on one of these communions with a dry greeting, "Finally home, my breadwinner!", he is polite enough for a parting word to God, "I'll talk to You later."

Mr. Mostel does not keep his acting and singing or his walking and dancing in separate compartments. His Tevye is a unified, lyrical conception. With the exception of a grimace or a gesture several times that score easy laughs, Tevye stays in character.

The scope of this performance is summed up best in moments made eloquent through music and movement. When Mr. Mostel sings "If I Were a Rich Man," interpolating passages of cantillation in the manner of prayer, his Tevye is both devout and pungently realistic. When Tevye chants a prayer as the good Golde tries to convey an item of vital news, Mr. Mostel is not only comic but evocative of an old way of life. When Tevye hears the horrifying word that his third daughter has run away with a gentile, Mr. Mostel dances his anguish in a flash of savage emotion.

The score by Jerry Bock and the lyrics by Sheldon Harnick at their best move the story along, enrich the mood and intensify the emotions. "Sabbath Prayer" is as hushed as a community at its devotions. "Sunrise, Sunset" is in the spirit of a traditional wedding under a canopy. When Tevye and Golde after twenty-five years of marriage ask themselves, "Do You Love Me?", the song has a touching angularity. But several of the other romantic tunes are merely routine.

Jerome Robbins has staged *Fiddler on the Roof* with sensitivity and fire. As his own choreographer, he weaves dance into action with subtlety and flaring theatricalism. The opening dance to a nostalgic song, "Tradition," has a ritual sweep. The dances at the wedding burst with vitality. A dream sequence is full of humor. And the choreographed farewells of the Jews leaving their Russian village have a poignancy that adds depth to *Fiddler on the Roof.*

Boris Aronson's sets provide a background that rings true; they give the work an unexpected dimension of beauty in scenes like "Sabbath Prayer," the wedding and the epilogue.

Joanna Merlin, Julia Migenes, Tanya Everett as three of the daughters, Beatrice Arthur as a busybody of a matchmaker, Austin Pendleton as a poor tailor, Bert Convy as a young radical, Michael Granger as a well-to-do butcher and Joe Ponazecki as the gentile suitor are among those who sing and act with flavor.

Richness of flavor marks *Fiddler on the Roof.* Although it does not entirely eschew the stigmata of routine Broadway, it has an honest feeling for another place, time and people. And in Mr. Mostel's Tevye it has one of the most glowing creations in the history of the musical theater.

Howard Taubman ON
The Odd Couple
BY Neil Simon

———

March 10, 1965
Plymouth Theater
964 Performances

Walter Matthau as the slovenly Oscar *(left)* and Art Carney as the compulsively neat Felix in Neil Simon's *The Odd Couple* FRIEDMAN-ABELES

THE ODD COUPLE, a comedy by Neil Simon. Staged by Mike Nichols; presented by Saint Subber; scenery by Oliver Smith; lighting by Jean Rosenthal; costumes by Ann Roth; production stage manager, Harvey Medlinsky.

Speed	Paul Dooley
Murray	Nathaniel Frey
Vinnie	John Fiedler
Oscar Madison	Walter Matthau
Felix Unger	Art Carney
Gwendolyn Pigeon	Carole Shelley
Cecily Pigeon	Monica Evans

The opening scene in *The Odd Couple,* of the boys in their regular Friday night poker game, is one of the funniest card sessions ever held on a stage.

If you are worried that there is nothing Neil Simon, the author, or Mike Nichols, his director, can think of to top that scene, relax. The main business of the new comedy, which opened last night at the Plymouth Theater, has scarcely begun, and Mr. Simon, Mr. Nichols and their excellent cast, headed by Art Carney and Walter Matthau, have scores of unexpected ways prepared to keep you smiling, chuckling and guffawing.

Mr. Simon has hit upon an idea that could occur to any playwright. His odd couple are two men, one divorced and living in dejected and disheveled splendor in a eight-room apartment and the other about to be divorced and taken in as a roommate.

One could predict the course of this odd union from its formation in misery and compassion through its disagreements to its ultimate rupture. Mr. Simon's way of writing comedy is not to reach for gimmicks of plot; he probably doesn't mind your knowing the bare outline of his idea.

His skill—and it is not only great but constantly growing—lies in his gift for the deliciously surprising line and attitude. His instinct for incongruity is faultless. It nearly always operates on a basis of character.

Begin with that poker game. Mr. Matthau, the slovenly host, is off stage in the kitchen fixing a snack while Nathaniel Frey, John Fiedler, Sidney Armus and Paul Dooley are sitting around the table on a hot summer night, sweating and grousing at the luck of the cards. The burly Mr. Frey is shuffling awkwardly, "for accuracy, not speed," and the querulous Mr. Fiedler, the big winner, talks of quitting early.

The cards are dealt. Mr. Matthau walks in with a tray of beer and white and brown sandwiches. They're brown in his scheme of housekeeping because they're either new cheese or very old meat. As he opens the beer cans, sending sprays of lager over his guests (surely a Nichols touch), the dealer inquires whether he intends to look at his cards. "What for," Mr. Matthau, the big loser, grumbles, "I'm gonna bluff anyhow."

The sixth member of the Friday night regulars, Mr. Carney, is missing. Evidently he has been away from his known haunts for twenty-four hours and a phone call from his wife informs his friends that she hopes he never turns up. Since they know that he is a man who takes such blows seriously, they fear that he will do something violent to himself.

With Mr. Carney's arrival as Felix, the discarded husband, the principal action begins. Mr. Carney is truly bereaved, a man of sorrows. His eyes are stricken, his lips quiver, his shoulders sag. Even poker gives way before his desolation. The players are too concerned about possible moves by Felix toward self-destruction. When at last they go home, they depart softly and gravely like chaps leaving a sick room.

Mr. Matthau as Oscar, the host, consoles Felix, massaging away the spasms in his neck and enduring the moose calls with which the unfortunate fellow clears ears beset by allergies. Nothing much happens during the rest of the act except that these two inevitably blunder into a domestic alliance, but there is scarcely a moment that is not hilarious.

The unflagging comedy in the remainder of the play depends on the fundamental switch—of the odd couple. Felix is a compulsive house keeper, bent on cleaning, purifying the air and cooking. When the gang assembles for its poker game, Felix has special treats ready for snacks.

Mr. Carney handles the housewifely duties with a nice, delicate, yet manly verve. But he is strict. When he serves a drink to Mr. Frey, he wants to know where the coaster is. The answer—and this is Mr. Simon, the marksman at firing droll lines—is, "I think I bet it."

Mr. Matthau for his part is wonderfully comic as a man who finds his companion's fussy habits increasingly irksome. He walks about with a bearish crouch that grows more belligerent as his domestic situation becomes both familiar and oppressive. There is a marvelous scene in which he and Mr. Carney circle each other in mutual distaste—Mr. Matthau looking like an aroused animal about to spring and Mr. Carney resembling a paper tiger suddenly turned neurotic and dangerous.

To vary the humors of the domestic differences, Mr. Simon brings on two English sisters named Pigeon—yes, Pigeon, Gwendolyn and Cecily—for a date with Oscar and Felix. The girls induce more laughter than their names promise. Carole Shelley and Monica Evans are a delight as the veddy British and dumb Pigeons.

Mr. Nichols's comic invention, like Mr. Simon's, shines through this production and the comfortable Riverside Drive apartment invoked by Oliver Smith's set. Just a sample: Mr. Carney left alone with the Pigeons is as nervous as a lad on his first date. When one of the girls takes out a cigarette, he hastens to her with his lighter and comes away with the cigarette clamped in its mechanism.

The Odd Couple has it made. Women are bound to adore the sight of a man carrying on like a little homemaker. Men are sure to snicker at a male in domestic bondage to a man. Kids will love it because it's funny. Homosexuals will enjoy it—for obvious reasons. Doesn't that take care of everyone?

Howard Taubman ON
Marat/Sade
BY Peter Weiss

December 27, 1965
Martin Beck Theater
144 Performances

Ian Richardson as the revolutionary Marat *(left),* Clifford Rose and Patrick Magee as the Marquis de Sade
MORRIS NEWCOMBE

THE PERSECUTION AND ASSASSINATION OF MARAT AS PERFORMED BY THE INMATES OF THE ASYLUM OF CHARENTON UNDER THE DIRECTION OF THE MARQUIS DE SADE, a play by Peter Weiss. Staged by Peter Brook; presented by the David Merrick Arts Foundation, by arrangement with the Governors of the Royal Shakespeare Theatre, Stratford-on-Avon; English version by Geoffrey Skelton; verse adaptation by Adrian Mitchell; scenery and properties by Sally Jacobs; costumes by Gunilla Palmstierna-Weiss; choreography by Malcolm Goddard; lighting and design supervision by Lloyd Burlingame; music by Richard Peaslee; assistant to the director, Ian Richardson; stage manager, Christine Staley.

Coulmier	Clifford Rose
Mrs. Coulmier	Brenda Kempner
Miss Coulmier	Ruth Baker
Herald	Michael Williams
Cucurucu	Freddie Jones
Kokol	Hugh Sullivan
Polooch	Jonathan Burn
Rossignol	Jeanette Landis

Jacques Roux...Robert Lloyd
Charlotte Corday ....Glenda Jackson
Jean-Paul Marat.....................................Ian Richardson
Simonne Evrard...................................Susan Williamson
Marquis de Sade...Patrick Magee
Duperret...John Steiner
Abbott ....Mark Jones
Mad animal ....Morgan Sheppard
Schoolmaster...James Mellor
Military representative..Ian Hogg
Mother ....Mark Jones
Father ....Henry Woolf
Newly rich lady ....John Hussey
Voltaire..John Harwood
Lavoisier..Leon Lissek

Imagination has not vanished from the stage. Nor intelligence. For proof see Peter Weiss's play, which opened last night at the Martin Beck Theater.

The exceptional length of the play's title is not caprice. The play reverberates with overtones even as its name is crowded with words and syllables: *The Persecution and Assassination of Marat as Performed by the Inmates of the Asylum of Charenton Under the Direction of the Marquis de Sade.*

Mr. Weiss has written a play within a play, and in both there are unexpected resonances of comment and meaning. He has used the techniques of Brecht, invoking verse, music and speeches to the audience to produce an effect of standing apart, but has orchestrated them in his own way. In the end one is involved as one stands apart; one thinks when one should feel and feels when one should think.

There is hardly anything conventional about the play. But Mr. Weiss's novel devices are not employed for the sake of novelty. His primary purpose, if one may dare to isolate one aim as the chief one, is to examine the conflict between individualism carried to extreme lengths and the idea of a political and social upheaval.

Spokesman for this sort of individualism is Sade; the voice of upheaval is Marat. But Mr. Weiss has gone beyond a simple confrontation. He has achieved a remarkable density of impression and impact by locating his conflict, in the course of his play within a play, in a mental institution.

The result is a vivid work that vibrates on wild, intense, murmurous and furious levels. It is sardonic and impassioned, pitiful and explosive. It may put you off at times with its apparent absurdity, or it may shock you with its allusions to violence and naked emotions. But it will not leave you untouched.

As the play begins on the wide, lofty uncurtained stage, furnished with a few planks, benches and several pits, the inmates of Charenton wander in. They wear rough, tattered rags, and some are twisted in body and limbs as well in mind. The director of the asylum and two of his ladies in their elegant clothes arrive, and he explains that he has encouraged Sade to direct the inmates in this play for its therapeutic value.

Mr. Weiss has not invented this point. Sade, who was an inmate at Charenton, did write and stage plays there in the early years of the nineteenth century. What Mr. Weiss has invented is the play that Sade has chosen to write and direct, though certain details of the Marat story used in Sade's play are facts of history.

The play unfolds in a series of episodes. The basic action involves the events leading up to the slaying of Marat by Charlotte Corday. But the episodes do not follow an ordinary continuity. Songs, scenes that at first view seem irrelevant, the unpredictable movements and sounds of the patients, weave around the main action to provide a remarkable richness of texture.

Marat, his body angry and blotched with a feverish ailment, sits in his bathtub, a bandage on his head and a sheet over his shoulders, but the tormenting pains and memories cannot be appeased. Since Marat is played by a Charenton paranoiac, his fierce outbursts have a deepened anguish. Sade, of course, is Sade, but despite his worn, faded finery, he is also an inmate, and the fury of his worship of self becomes both heightened and oddly pathetic.

They are both rebels. Sade is in revolt against accepted notions because he needs to believe in and explore himself. Marat is the social revolutionary. Their ideas clash, but Mr. Weiss does not choose between them.

He lets passionate, burning truths emerge from

their feverish preoccupations. Out of the mouths and actions of other inmates in this madhouse come other insights.

Mr. Weiss, a German who fled Nazism and who now lives in Sweden, has written in a kind of singsong vernacular, which rises often to eloquence. Geoffrey Skelton's English version and Adrian Mitchell's verse adaptation establish the flavor of the playwright's style.

This is a work, that demands all the theater's arts and artifices, and this production by Great Britain's Royal Shakespeare Company, staged with savage brilliance by Peter Brook, translates Mr. Weiss's writing into throbbing theatrical terms.

The images of life in a mental institution are weird and moving. An inmate who raves like a mad animal and utters searing truths is not an oddity; he freezes the blood. Inmates going through a make-believe guillotining and falling pell-mell into a pit are horrifying and piteous. A quartet of inmates done up as clowns caper and cavort amusingly and piercingly. Even the whipping of Sade by Charlotte Corday with her long hair, though not literally painful, stings.

Mr. Brook has used sound like a conjurer. There is not only Richard Peaslee's evocative, simple music for the songs and for the band, dressed like inmates and seated in boxes on opposite sides of the house. There are also the clanging of chains, the pounding of boards, the eerie moans of the inmates.

The visitors from Britain are performing Mr. Weiss's play with conviction and intensity, in taut, colorful ensemble. The entire company deserves to be noticed, but there is time only to speak admiringly of Ian Richardson's flaming Marat, Patrick Magee's cold, sinous Sade, Glenda Jackson's wild Corday, Clifford Rose's elegantly superficial asylum director, and Michael Williams's subtle Herald.

Mr. Weiss's play expresses a fresh, probing sensibility in original stage terms. Like its title, it will give you pause, stir your imagination and provoke your mind. It is good to encounter a playwright who dares to challenge the theater and its audience to full participation.

Walter Kerr ON
Cabaret
BOOK BY Joe Masteroff
LYRICS BY Fred Ebb
MUSIC BY John Kander

———

November 20, 1966
Broadhurst Theater
1,165 Performances

Lotte Lenya and Jack Gilford in a scene from the musical *Cabaret*   FRIEDMAN-ABELES

CABARET, a musical based on the play by John van Druten and stories by Christopher Isherwood. Book by Joe Masteroff; music by John Kander; lyrics by Fred Ebb; dances and cabaret numbers by Ronald Field; settings by Boris Aronson; costumes by Patricia Zipprodt; lighting by Jean Rosenthal; musical direction by Harold Hastings; orchestrations by Don Walker; dance arrangements by David Baker; directed by Harold Prince. Presented by Mr. Prince in association with Ruth Mitchell.

Master of Ceremonies ....Joel Grey
Clifford Bradshaw ....Bert Convy
Ernst Ludwig...Edward Winter
Custom Official..Howard Kahl
Fraulein Schneider ....Lotte Lenya
Herr Schultz ....Jack Gilford
Fraulein Kost..Peg Murray
Telephone Girl ....Tresha Kelly
Kit Kat Band ....Maryann Burns, Janice Mink, Nancy Powers, Viola Smith

Maitre D'..Frank Bouley
Max ....John Herbert
Bartender...Ray Baron
Sally Bowles...Jill Haworth
Two Ladies ....Mary Ehara, Rita O'Connor
German Soldiers.............Bruce Becker, Steven Boockvor,
	Roger Briant, Edward Nolfi
Frau Wendel ....Mara Landi
Herr Wendel.......................................Eugene Morgan
Frau Kruger.............................Miriam Lehmann-Haupt
Herr Erdmann...Sol Frieder
Kit Kat Girls:
Maria ....Pat Gosling
Lulu ....Lynn Winn
Rosie...Bonnie Walker
Fritzie ....Marianne Seibert
Texas ....Kathie Dalton
Frenchie...Barbara Alston
Bobby..Jere Admire
Victor...Bert Michaels
Greta..Jayme Mylroie
Felix ....Robert Sharp

Cabaret is a stunning musical with one wild wrong note. I think you'd be wise to go to it first and argue about that startling slip later.

The first thing you see as you enter the Broadhurst is yourself. Designer Boris Aronson, whose scenery is so imaginative that even a gray green fruit store comes up like a warm summer dawn, has sent converging strings of frosted lamps swinging toward a vanishing point at upstage center. Occupying the vanishing point is a great geometric mirror, and in the mirror the gathering audience is reflected. We have come for the floor show, we are all at tables tonight, and anything we learn of life during the evening is going to be learned through the tipsy, tinkling, angular vision of sleek rouged-up clowns, who inhabit a world that rains silver.

This marionette's-eye view of a time and place in our lives that was brassy, wanton, carefree and doomed to crumble is brilliantly conceived. The place is Berlin, the time the late twenties when Americans still went there and Hitler could be shrugged off as a passing noise that needn't disturb dedicated dancers. Adapted by Joe Masteroff from the Christopher Isherwood-John van Druten materials that first took dramatic form as *I Am a Camera,* the story line is willing to embrace

everything from Jew baiting to abortion. But it has elected to wrap its arms around all that was troubling and all that was intolerable with a demonic grin, an insidious slink, and the painted-on charm that keeps revelers up until midnight making false faces at the hangman.

Master of Ceremonies Joel Grey bursts from the darkness like a tracer bullet, singing us a welcome that has something of the old *Blue Angel* in it, something of Kurt Weill, and something of all the patent-leather nightclub tunes that ever seduced us into feeling friendly toward sleek entertainers who twirled canes as they worked. Mr. Grey is cheerful, charming, soulless and conspiratorially wicked. In a pink vest, with sunburst eyes gleaming out of a cold-cream face, he is the silencer of bad dreams, the gleeful puppet of pretended joy, sin on a string.

No matter what is happening during the evening, he is available to make light of it, make sport of it, make macabre gaiety of it.

Perhaps an amoral chanteuse with the mind of a lightning bug ("I guess I am a really strange and extraordinary person") is installing herself without warning in the rented apartment of an American writer, ready to share bed and bread but not for long. Perhaps the landlady is shyly and ruefully succumbing to a proposal of marriage from a Jewish grocer (she is rueful because she is old now, singing "When you're as old as I—is anyone as old as I?") and perhaps the Jewish grocer is beginning to feel the bite of things to come. Precisely as a brick is hurled through her suitor's shop window, Mr. Grey comes bouncing from the portals to grab a gorilla in rose tulle. The two spin into a hesitation waltz with the prim and stately delicacy of partners well-met. Let the world lose its mind, let the waltz go on.

Under choreographer Ronald Field's beautifully malicious management, Mr. Grey is superb, as are the dancers, the four girls who bang at instruments and call themselves the Kit Kat Klub Kittens (even the piano seems to wear feathers), and the unending supply of tenors to give an Irish lilt ("Tomorrow Belongs to Me") to a contrapuntal pause in the tacky, rattling, bizarre and bankrupt goings-on. With the exception of an unlucky last song for landlady Lotte Lenya, the John Kander-Fred Ebb tunes snatch up the melodic desperation of an era and make new, sprightly, high-voltage energy of it, providing the men of the company with a table-to-table telephone song that comes to seem rhythm in a state of shock, and offering Miss Lenya several enchantingly throaty plaints, notably a winning acceptance of the way things are, called "So What?"

Miss Lenya has never been better, or if she has been, I don't believe it. Suitor Jack Gilford, with just enough hair left to cross his forehead with spitcurls and gamely spinning his partner in spite of clear signs of vertigo, makes his first-act wrap-up, a rapid-fire comic turn called "Meeskite," one of the treasures of the occasion. Bert Convy, as the American with a small whirlwind on his hands, not only acts well but opens his throat for "Why Should I Wake Up?" with the belief and the urgency of a singer who'd never given acting a second thought.

We are left now with the evening's single, and all too obvious, mistake. One of the cabaret tables is empty, the table reserved for heroine Sally Bowles. Sally Bowles, as the narrative has it, is a fey, fetching, far-out lassie with a head full of driftwood and a heart she'd rather break than shackle. She is a temperament, and she needs a temperament to play her.

Producer-director Harold Prince, in a totally uncharacteristic lapse of judgment, has miscast a pretty but essentially flavorless ingénue, Jill Haworth, in the role. Miss Haworth has certain skills and may be able to use them in other ways. Wrapped like a snowball in white fur and sporting that pancake tam that girls of the twenties used to wear whenever they were going to be photographed having snowball fights, she succeeds— at some angles—in looking astonishingly like Clara Bow. But her usefulness to this particular project ends there. She is trim but neutral, a profile rather than a person, and given the difficult things *Cabaret* is trying to do, she is a damaging presence, worth no more to the show than her weight in mascara.

The damage is deeply serious and must be stressed. With the kooky heroine canceled out, the tangled love story vanishes. Its disappearance is scarcely noticed during the striking first half, because Miss Lenya and Mr. Gilford are there to take over. But the second act must account for a botched romance and build to a disillusion ending on it and that's a bad time to watch the emotional air being steadily drained from a show that takes its style and its subject matter seriously.

The style is there, though, driven like glistening nails into the musical numbers, and I think you'll find they make up for what's missing.

Clive Barnes ON
Rosencrantz and Guildenstern Are Dead
BY Tom Stoppard

October 16, 1967
Alvin Theater
420 Performances

Brian Murray *(left)* and John Wood in Tom Stoppard's *Rosencrantz and Guildenstern Are Dead*   MARTHA SWOPE

ROSENCRANTZ AND GUILDENSTERN ARE DEAD, play by Tom Stoppard; staged by Derek Goldby; setting and costumes by Desmond Heeley; lighting by Richard Pilbrow; music by Marc Wilkinson; production stage manager, Mitchell Erickson. Presented by David Merrick Arts Foundation by arrangement with the National Theater of Great Britain; associate producer, Samuel Liff.

Rosencrantz	Brian Murray
Guildenstern	John Wood
The Player	Paul Hecht
Alfred	Douglas Norwick
Tragedians	Roger Kemp, Dino Laudicina, B. J. DeSimone, Ray Lozano
Hamlet	Noel Craig
Ophelia	Patricia McAneny
Claudius	Roger Hamilton
Gertrude	Anne Meacham
Polonius	Ralph Drischell
Soldier	Alexander Courtney
Ambassador	Carl Jacobs
Horatio	Michael Holmes

It is not only Hamlet who dies in *Hamlet*. They also serve who only stand and wait. Tom Stoppard's play *Rosencrantz and Guildenstern Are Dead,* which opened last night at the Alvin Theater, is a very funny play about death. Very funny, very brilliant, very chilling; it has the dust of thought about it and the particles glitter excitingly in the theatrical air.

Mr. Stoppard uses as the basis for his play a very simple yet telling proposition; namely that although to Hamlet those twin-stemmed courtiers Rosencrantz and Guildenstern are of slight importance, and that to an audience of Shakespeare's play they are little but functionaries lent some color by a fairly dilatory playwright, Rosencrantz and Guildenstern are very important indeed to Rosencrantz and Guildenstern.

This then is the play of *Hamlet* not seen through the eyes of Hamlet, or Claudius, or Ophelia or Gertrude, but a worm's-eye view of tragedy seen from the bewildered standpoint of Rosencrantz and Guildenstern.

We first see them on a deserted highway. They have been summoned to the King's palace; they do not understand why. They are tossing coins to pass the time of day. The ordinary laws of chance appear to have been suspended. Perhaps they have been. Destiny that has already marked out Hamlet for such a splendid, purple satin death, is keeping a skimpy little piece of mauve bunting for poor Guildenstern and gentle Rosencrantz. They are about to get caught up in the action of a play.

Their conversation, full of Elizabethan school logic and flashes of metaphysical wit, is amusing but deliberately fatuous. Rosencrantz and Guildenstern are fools. When you come to think of it, they would have to be. Otherwise they might have been Hamlet.

As they talk, the suspicion crosses the mind (it is a play where you are encouraged to stand outside the action and let suspicions, thoughts, glimmers and insights criss-cross your understanding) that Mr. Stoppard is not only paraphrasing *Hamlet,* but also throwing in a paraphrase of Samuel Beckett's *Waiting for Godot* for good measure. For this is antic lunacy with a sad, wry purpose.

Like Beckett's tramps, these two silly, rather likable Elizabethan courtiers are trying to get through life with a little human dignity and perhaps here and there a splinter of comprehension. They play games with each other and constantly question not their past (probably only heroes can afford that luxury) but their present and their future. Especially their future.

On the road they meet the strolling players, also, of course, for the plot is a mousetrap seen from the other side of the cheese, on the road to Elsinore. The leading Player, a charming, honest and sinister man, invites the two to participate in a strolling play. They, with scruples, refuse, but in fact they cannot refuse—because in life this precisely is what they have done.

Mr. Stoppard seems to see the action of his play unfolding like a juicy onion with strange layers of existence protectively wrapped around one another. There are plays here within plays—and Mr. Stoppard never lets us forget that his courtiers are not only characters in a life, but also characters in a play. They are modest—they admit that they are only supporting players. But they do want to see something of the script everyone else is working from.

It is one of Mr. Stoppard's cleverest conceits of

stagecraft that the actors re-enacting the performance of *Hamlet* that is, in effect, dovetailed into
the main section of the play, use only Shakespeare's words. Thus while they are waiting in the
tattered, drafty antechamber of the palace for
something to happen, we in the audience know
what is happening on the other side of the stage.
As one of them says, "Every exit is an entry somewhere else."

Finally reduced to the terminal shrifts of unbe-
lief, it seems that Rosenkrantz and Guildenstern
realize that the only way they can find their identity
is in their "little deaths." Although on the final,
fateful boat they discover the letter committing
them to summary execution in England, they go
forward to death, glad, even relieved.

It is impossible to re-create the fascinating verbal tension of the play—Mr. Stoppard takes an
Elizabethan pleasure in the sound of his own actors—or the ideas, suggestive, tantalizing, that
erupt through its texture. Nor, even most unfortunately, can I suggest the happy, zany humor of
even the lovely figures of speech, such as calling
something "like two blind men looting a bazaar
for their own portraits." All this is something you
must see and hear for yourself.

When the play had its first professional production in London in April of this year it was
staged by the British National Theater, and to an
extent this version has been reproduced here by its
original and brilliant director, Derek Goldby.
Helped by the tatterdemalion glories of Desmond
Heeley's setting, the richness of his costumes, and
Richard Pilbrow's tactfully imaginative lighting,
the play looks very similar. But whereas the supporting players in London—the Hamlet, Claudius
and the rest—could well have played their roles in
Shakespeare as well as in Stoppard, here there is
understandably less strength.

However, the mime roles of the players (expertly devised by Claude Chagrin) are superbly
done, Paul Hecht is remarkably good as the chief
Player (although I would have welcomed a touch
more menace) and Brian Murray and John Wood
provide virtuoso portrayals as Rosencrantz and
Guildenstern.

Mr. Murray, blandly exuding a supreme lack of
confidence, and Mr. Wood, disturbed, perhaps
more intellectually than viscerally, play against
each other like tennis singles champions. And
luckily this is a game where neither needs to win
and both can share the trophy.

This is a most remarkable and thrilling play. In
one bound Mr. Stoppard is asking to be considered as among the finest English-speaking writers
of our stage, for this is a work of fascinating distinction. Rosencrantz and Guildenstern LIVE!

Clive Barnes ON
The Boys in the Band
BY Mart Crowley

April 14, 1968
Theater Four
1,000 Performances

Reuben Greene makes a painful phone call in *The Boys in
the Band*, as Cliff Gorman *(center)* and Kenneth Nelson
watch. FRIEDMAN-ABELES

THE BOYS IN THE BAND, play by Mart Crowley. Staged by Robert Moore; setting by Peter Harvey; stage manager, Charles Kindl. Presented by Richard Barr and Charles Woodward Jr.

Michael	Kenneth Nelson
Donald	Frederick Combs
Emory	Cliff Gorman
Larry	Keith Prentice
Hank	Laurence Luckinbill
Bernard	Reuben Greene
Cowboy	Robert La Tourneaux
Alan	Peter White
Harold	Leonard Frey

As the conventional thing to say about Mart Crowley's *The Boys in the Band* will be something to the effect that it makes Edward Albee's *Who's Afraid of Virginia Woolf?* seem like a vicarage tea party, let me at least take the opportunity of saying it first.

The play, which opened last night at Theater Four, is by far the frankest treatment of homosexuality I have ever seen on the stage. We are a long way from *Tea and Sympathy* here. The point is that this is not a play about a homosexual, but a play that takes the homosexual milieu, and the homosexual way of life, totally for granted and uses this as a valid basis of human experience. Thus it is a homosexual play, not a play about homosexuality.

Just as you do not have to be Negro to appreciate a play about the Negro experience, you do not have to be homosexual to appreciate *The Boys in the Band*. On the other hand, it would be equally idle to pretend that, just as a Negro will see the plays of LeRoi Jones differently from the way I do, so some of my best friends (as Alan Brien wrote in *The Sunday Times* of London the other week, "some of the best homosexuals are my friends") will be able to identify with its specifics more closely than I can myself.

Yet wherever we stand, sit or lie on the sliding scale of human sexuality, I have a feeling that most of us will find *The Boys in the Band* a gripping, if painful, experience. I know I did. It is about a long, bloody and alcoholic party; but only the superficial (and perhaps the suspiciously easily shocked) will see it as a pack of youngish middle-aged fairy queens shouting bitchicisms at one another down the long night.

The similarity between Albee's *Virginia Woolf* and *The Boys in the Band* is striking. Both are concerned with the breaking down of pretenses, with the acceptance of reality. Both plays achieve that purpose by using the flame throwers of a cruel, excoriating wit. The victims are flayed alive, and even the persecutors are victims.

The Boys in the Band starts out as a birthday party for Harold, an ugly, pock-marked queer. Michael, a man of thirty with no visible means of support but the possessor of a handsome duplex apartment, is giving the party, and all Harold's friends, homosexual to the last, are there to eat, drink and be gay, if not merry.

The preparations for the party are disturbed slightly when a friend of Michael's, an old college friend named Alan, telephones in distress and asks to see him at once. Alan is straight (married, and with a couple of kids) and would clearly be out of place with the boys of the band.

He arrives anyway, and at first Michael and his friends try to pretend that everything is normal; but the truth soon emerges. What also soon emerges is a strong doubt about the heterosexuality of Alan.

As the party proceeds, Michael, getting drunker all the time, seems impelled to play crueler and crueler jokes on his companions until he introduces a game in which all the contestants have to telephone the person they most love in the world and tell them they love them. The results are rather different from those Michael envisaged, but to a greater or lesser extent everyone is wounded—even a $20 contemptuously mocked dumb-ox of a hustler who has been bought for $20 as a special birthday gift for Harold.

This is Mr. Crowley's first play, and here and there it betrays signs of inexperience. The opening exposition of theme, for example, when Michael gratuitously has to explain who and what he is to one of his closest friends, is a little clumsily contrived, and some of the dialogue is certainly overwritten.

The special self-dramatization and the frightening self-pity—true I suppose of all minorities, but I think especially true of homosexuals—is all the same laid on too thick at times.

There is also the question of camp or homosexual humor. Like Jewish humor, it is an acquired taste; and in both instances every adult New Yorker I know has acquired them. (Indeed, the New York wit, famous the world over, is little more than a mixture of Jewish humor and homosexual humor seen through the bottom of a dry martini glass.) But camp humor—relentless, overpolished and heartless—can after a time prove a little too much.

The play is often screamingly funny as well as screamingly fag, but this camp, always-be-prepared wit is too personally vituperative, too lacking in a sense of pure fun or even a sense of comic perspective, not to pall after a time. The bitter jokes lose their savor—but perhaps they are meant to.

The power of the play, which I saw at one of its press previews, is the way in which it remorselessly peels away the pretensions of its characters and reveals a pessimism so uncompromising in its honesty that it becomes in itself an affirmation of life.

The best thing I can say of both the acting and Robert Moore's almost invisible but clearly most effective direction is that, not only were they completely at one with the play, but also there were times when I all but expected the audience to answer back to the actors. It would be unfair to mention individual members of the cast—all nine names are listed above, and they all have my praise. This is one of the best acted plays of the season.

It is also a very attractive production visually. With the bold use of photomontages, the designer, Peter Harvey, has precisely conveyed in black and white a slightly flashy, yet believable, New York apartment.

A couple of years ago, my colleague Stanley Kauffmann, in a perceptive but widely misunderstood essay, pleaded for a more honest homosexual drama, one where homosexual experience was not translated into false, pseudoheterosexual terms. This I think *The Boys in the Band*, with all its faults, achieves. It is quite an achievement.

Clive Barnes ON
Hair
BOOK AND LYRICS BY Gerome Ragni
AND James Rado
MUSIC BY Galt MacDermot

April 29, 1968
Biltmore Theater
1,750 Performances

HAIR, love-rock musical. Book and lyrics by Gerome Ragni and James Rado; music by Galt MacDermot. Staged by Tom O'Horgan; dance director, Julie Arenal; musical director, Galt MacDermot. Costumes by Nancy Potts; setting by Robin Wagner; lighting by Jules Fisher; sound by Robert Kiernan; production stage manager, Fred Reinglas. Presented by Michael Butler; Bertrand Castelli, executive producer.

Ron	Ronald Dyson
Claude	James Rado
Berger	Gerome Ragni
Woof	Steve Curry
Hud	Lamont Washington
Sheila	Lynn Kellogg
Jeanie	Sally Eaton
Dionne	Melba Moore
Crissy	Shelley Plimpton
Mother	Sally Eaton, Jonathan Kramer, Paul Jabara
Father	Robert I. Rubinsky, Suzannah Norstrand, Lamont Washington
Tourist Couple	Jonathan Kramer, Robert I. Rubinsky
General Grant	Paul Jabara
Young Recruit	Jonathan Kramer
Sergeant	Donnie Burks
Parents	Diane Keaton, Robert I. Rubinsky

What is so likable about *Hair,* that tribal-rock musical that last night completed its trek from downtown, via a discothèque, and landed, positively panting with love and smelling of sweat and flowers, at the Biltmore Theater? I think it is simply that it is so likable. So new, so fresh and so unassuming, even in its pretensions.

When *Hair* started its long-term joust against Broadway's world of Sigmund Romberg it was at Joseph Papp's Public Theater. Then its music came across with a kind of acid-rock, powerhouse lyricism, but the book, concerning the life and times of hippie protest was as rickety as a knock-kneed centipede.

Now the authors of the dowdy book—and brilliant lyrics—have done a very brave thing. They have in effect done away with it altogether. *Hair* is now a musical with a theme, not with a story. Nor is this all that has been done in this totally new, all lit-up, gas-fired, speed-marketed Broadway version. For one thing it has been made a great deal franker. In fact it has been made into the frankest show in town—and this has been a season not noticeable for its verbal or visual reticence.

Since I have had a number of letters from people who have seen previews asking me to warn readers, and, in the urbanely quaint words of one correspondent, "Spell out what is happening on stage," this I had better do. Well, almost, for spell it out I cannot, for this remains a family newspaper. However, a great many four-letter words, such as "love," are used very freely. At one point—in what is later affectionately referred to as "the nude scene"—a number of men and women (I should have counted) are seen totally nude and full, as it were, face.

Frequent references—frequent approving references—are made to the expanding benefits of drugs. Homosexuality is not frowned upon—one boy announces that he is in love with Mick Jagger, in terms unusually frank. The American flag is not desecrated—that would be a Federal offense, wouldn't it?—but it is used in a manner that not everyone would call respectful. Christian ritual also comes in for a bad time, the authors approve enthusiastically of miscegenation, and one enterprising lyric catalogues somewhat arcane sexual practices more familiar to the pages of the *Kama Sutra* than *The New York Times*. So there—you have been warned. Oh yes, they also hand out flowers.

The show has also had to be adapted to its new proscenium form—and a number of new songs have been written, apparently to fill in the gaps where the old book used to be. By and large these new numbers are not quite the equal of the old, but the old ones—a few of them sounding like classics by now—are still there, and this is a happy show musically. Galt MacDermot's music is merely pop-rock, with strong soothing overtones of Broadway melody, but it precisely serves its purpose, and its noisy and cheerful conservatism is just right for an audience that might wince at "Sergeant Pepper's Lonely Hearts Club Band," while the Stones would certainly gather no pop moss.

Yet with the sweet and subtle lyrics of Gerome Ragni and James Rado, the show is the first Broadway musical in some time to have the authentic voice of today rather than the day before yesterday. It even looks different. Robin Wagner's beautiful junk-art setting (a blank stage replete with broken-down truck, papier-mâché Santa Claus, juke box, neon signs) is as masterly as Nancy Potts's cleverly tattered and colorful, turned-on costumes. And then there is Tom O'Horgan's always irreverent, occasionally irrelevant staging—which is sheer fun.

Mr. O'Horgan has worked wonders. He makes the show vibrate from the first slow-burn opening—with half-naked hippies statuesquely slow-parading down the center aisle—to the all-hands-together, anti-patriotic finale. Mr. O'Horgan is that rare thing: a frenetic director who comes off almost as frequently as he comes on. Some of his more outlandish ideas were once in a while too much, but basically, after so many musicals that have been too little, too much makes a change for the good.

But the essential likability of the show is to be found in its attitudes and in its cast. You probably don't have to be a supporter of Eugene McCarthy to love it, but I wouldn't give it much chance among the adherents of Governor Reagan. The theme, such as it is, concerns a dropout who freaks in, but the attitudes are those of protest and alienation. As the hero says at one point: "I want to eat mushrooms. I want to sleep in the sun."

These attitudes will annoy many people, but as long as Thoreau is part of America's heritage, others will respond to this musical that marches to a different drummer.

You don't have to approve of the Yip-Yip-

Horray roaring boys to enjoy *Hair,* any more than you have to approve of the Royal Canadian Mounted Police to enjoy *Rose Marie,* and these hard-working and talented actors are in reality about as hippie as Mayor Lindsay—no less. But the actors are beguiling. It would be impossible to mention them all, so let me content myself with Mr. Rado and Mr. Ragni, actors and perpetrators both, Lynn Kellogg and Shelley Plimpton—one of the comparatively few holdovers from the original production—who does marvels with a lovely Lennon and McCartney–like ballad, "Frank Mills."

Incidentally, the cast washes. It also has a delightful sense of self-mockery.

Clive Barnes ON
The Living Theatre's
Frankenstein

October 2, 1968
Brooklyn Academy of Music

FRANKENSTEIN, created by The Living Theater Company, based on the Mary Shelley novel. Under the direction of Julian Beck and Judith Malina. Setting by Julian Beck; mechanical sound direction by Luke Theodore; costumes by Birgit Knabe; chief technical supervision by Jim Anderson, Echnation and Rod Beere. Performed by the members of the Living Theater Company. Presented by the Brooklyn Academy of Music, 30 Lafayette Avenue.

It may not be at all true, but—just let us consider the possibility—the playwright may be a disappearing species like the buffalo. The thought came idly last night—it was an evening when thoughts had the time to be idle—at the Brooklyn Academy of Music, where the Living Theater after, as Barnum would say, triumphs the seven seas over, opened its New York season. God bless it and God help it.

It opened with *Frankenstein,* the title of which is taken from the nineteenth-century novel of the same name by Mary Shelley, and why not? What I presume is happening here is the development of the theater as a place of wonderment and miracles, a circus-like home of rituals to be celebrated by a generation that has lost the time and the place for ritual.

This is essentially a non-verbal theater. With its emphasis on spectacle and movement, its concern with visual rather than intellectual images, it is a type of theater that will be most readily immediate to the dance-oriented. It is also a theater of action—political action. It is a theater of protest, as, historically, probably most good theater is.

The author in *Frankenstein* has been totally eliminated. The play—or perhaps drama would be a more appropriately ambiguous word—is carefully described as "created by the Living Theater Company under the direction of Julian Beck and Judith Malina." It is, I presume, a very carefully rehearsed improvisation: an exercise in dramatic collage in which are to be found movement, noise (the actors may not have much to say but they sure do grunt and wheeze a lot), and the intellectual debris of Western civilization.

The piece opens with a yoga ritual followed by a systematic murder. From the murder comes the second ritual of rebirth and the first attempt at creating the monster. In a second act, Frankenstein feeds information into the monster's brain—myth, learning, emotion. At the end of the act the embryo monster is arrested.

The third act is a pantomime of violence. Actors are arrested in the audience by other actors, pulled on stage, fingerprinted and passed into a cagelike prison on three levels. It is a ballet out of Kafka, culminating in a jail-break, a fire and, in a fantastic physical tableau of bodies, the final creation of the monster.

The evening is at times repetitious, at times banal, here and there (and only here and there) a little boring. But the overwhelming impression is of a new physical style of theater, raw, gutsy and vital.

The methods are fascinating. Visual images such as the Four Horsemen of the Apocalypse are slipped in with the same freedom as arcane references to mystic rituals or—and here is a perfect example of the company's collage method—ship-wrecked sailors singing Shakespeare's "Full Fathom Five" to the melody of the last movement of Beethoven's *Choral Symphony*.

When the actors speak they speak in mufti with the flat, slightly embarrassed non-voices of nonactors. But when they move they move with the discipline and purposefulness of trained dancers. Perhaps this is more of an exercise for the theater than a theater itself. Perhaps. Or perhaps it is the beginning of a new type of dance-theater. In any case it is very much what is happening.

Clive Barnes ON
The Great White Hope
BY Howard Sackler

October 3, 1968

Alvin Theater

556 Performances

James Earl Jones as the first black world champion boxer and Jane Alexander in *The Great White Hope*. THE NEW YORK TIMES PHOTO ARCHIVES

THE GREAT WHITE HOPE, a play by Howard Sackler. Staged by Edwin Sherin; setting by Robin Wagner; costumes by David Toser; lighting by John Gleason; music arranged by Charles Gross; production stage manager, William Dodds. Presented by Herman Levin.
PRINCIPALS............James Earl Jones, Jane Alexander, George Matthews, Lou Gilbert, Jon Cypher, Jimmy Pelham, George Ebeling, Peter Masterson, Marlene Warfield, Hilda Haynes, Eugene R. Wood.

Howard Sackler's play *The Great White Hope* came into the Alvin Theater last night like a whirlwind, carrying with it, triumphantly, James Earl Jones. Indeed, to be honest I'm not sure that the whirlwind was not on the other foot, and that it was Mr. Jones who was doing some of the carrying—but about the triumph make no mistake.

Mr. Sackler has written a great part—a tragic hero, cheated, degraded and at last brutally beaten. But more than this, Mr. Sackler has used his hero, Jack Jefferson, a figure based closely on the first black heavyweight champion of the world, Jack Johnson, as a symbol in part of black aspiration. And white audiences are bound to feel white guilt—a guilt hardly lessened by the treatment meted out to the present Black Muslim heavyweight champion, Muhammed Ali.

The play has an epic scope and range to it. It is spread over 3 acts, 19 scenes and a few assorted monologues. It picks up the Johnson story soon after that Australian day in 1908 when Johnson whipped Tommy Burns to win the championship and takes it to Havana in 1915, when Jess Willard, the great white hope, won it back for the whites—at least for a time.

Very properly Mr. Sackler does not stick to the letter of history—at the end, for example, his hero, all but battered to a pulp, is fairly and squarely beaten, having resisted offers to throw the fight. Certainly Willard did not beat the real Johnson so effectively, yet Mr. Sackler is here dealing with playwriting and not prizefighting and he is right.

He has also whitewashed his hero, and it is here perhaps a fault of the play that, apart from his pride, Jack Jefferson is almost too good, too noble, to be true. And while we are fault-picking, the play—although trimmed a little since I first saw it at the Arena Stage in Washington—is still too long, and sprawlingly constructed. But this now hardly matters at all in the face of the play's tempestuous merits, and the opportunities it gives not only to its baffled bull of a hero but also to the white girl who chooses to share his degradation.

It is in this relationship, warm and yet finally corrosive, that the play finds its heart, for it lies at the nub of Jack's anger and rejection. This forbidden love is also the visible gesture of defiance that Jack throws out to the white world and—through a Mann Act prosecution—his downfall.

Mr. Sackler, at the end of the most harrowing and tense scene in the play, where Jack spurns the girl, completely sums up the tragedy after the girl has committed suicide and her mud-spattered body is brought in. It is laid on Jack's massage table, and Jack, tortured with a grief too much for a race to bear, let alone a man, sobs out: "What Ah done to ya . . . what you done honey . . . honey, what dey done to us. . . ." This is a tremendous moment in the theater—one of those moments when the heart rushes up not just to the players, but to that almost mystic note of communication and understanding that is perhaps the theater's most potent miracle.

The play moves faster and crisper than it did in Washington, although the director, Edwin Sherin (who shares fully in the triumph with Mr. Sackler and Mr. Jones) is the same, as, very rightly, is much of the cast. The changes then are minimal, but their effect is sufficient to make a very interesting if not entirely successful play into a theatrical experience that should not be willingly missed. (In fairness to Washington, I must admit that I too was quicker on my toes on this occasion and, having had the chance to read the play, was, I think, more understanding and receptive.)

It is Mr. Sherin's sheer skill that keeps the play interlocking so neatly, adding up to a fast series of something like cinematic takes, and he uses this pace to build up a fine and oddly convincing picture of America and Americans at the beginning of the century. With Mr. Sackler's digressions in Europe he can do little, but in general both play-

wright and director do provide a boldly if not finely drawn backcloth against which to display the contestants, and whether the play moves to a Chicago ghetto, or to a London courtroom or, finally, to a striking scene outside the fight ring in Havana, Mr. Sherin and his actors find the right style.

Of the vast supporting cast—the play is the size of a musical—two splendid characterizations stand out, Lou Gilbert as the seedy but decent little Jewish manager and, most remarkably, Jane Alexander as Jack's girl Ellie. Miss Alexander, as bright as a sparrow and with an almost spiritual beauty, makes a wonderful foil for Mr. Jones, a kind of frail and defiantly loving Desdemona to this twentieth-century Othello.

As I was leaving the theater Mr. Jones was receiving a standing ovation of the kind that makes Broadway history. If I had had the time I would have stayed to cheer, he deserved it.

Mr. Jones pounded into the role, spitting and shouting. He rolled his eyes, he stamped on the ground, he beat his chest, he roared with pain and when he even chuckled it seemed like thunder. Here was Jack, larger than life, good-natured and with a bitter, mocking ghetto humor that was always turned in upon itself. Here too was the all but unbreakable pride of a man, stiff, unyielding, stubborn, and yet also that very gentle softness you find so often in very big men. If anyone deserves to become that occasional thing, a star overnight, then Mr. Jones deserves no less.

Clive Barnes ON
Promises, Promises
BOOK BY Neil Simon
LYRICS BY Hal David
MUSIC BY Burt Bacharach

December 1, 1968

Shubert Theater

1,281 Performances

PROMISES, PROMISES, a musical. Book by Neil Simon, based on the screenplay, *The Apartment*, by Billy Wilder and I. A. L. Diamond; music by Burt Bacharach; lyrics by Hal David; settings by Robin Wagner; costumes by Donald Brooks; lighting by Martin Aronstein; musical direction and dance arrangements by Harold Wheeler; orchestrations by Jonathan Tunick; musical numbers staged by Michael Bennett; staged by Robert Moore; production stage manager, Charles Blackwell. Presented by David Merrick; associate producer, Samuel Liff.

Chuck Baxter	Jerry Orbach
J. D. Sheldrake	Edward Winter
Fran Kubelik	Jill O'Hara
Bartender Eddie	Ken Howard
Mr. Dobitch	Paul Reed
Sylvia Gilhooley	Adrienne Angel
Mr. Kirkeby	Norman Shelly
Mr. Eichelberger	Vince O'Brien
Vivien Della Hoya	Donna McKechnie
Dr. Dreyfuss	A. Larry Haines
Marge MacDougall	Marian Mercer
Jesse Vanderhof	Dick O'Neill
Dentist's Nurse	Rita O'Connor
Company Doctor	Gerry O'Hara
Company Nurse	Carole Bishop
Peggy Olson	Millie Slavin
Lum Ding Hostess	Baayork Lee
Waiter	Scott Pearson
Madison Sq. Gdn. Attendant	Michael Vita

Yes, of course, yes! The Neil Simon and Burt Bacharach musical *Promises, Promises* came to the Sam S. Shubert Theater last night and fulfilled them all without a single breach. In fact it proved to be one of those shows that do not so much open as start to take root, the kind of show where you feel more in the mood to send it a congratulatory telegram than write a review.

Neil Simon has produced one of the wittiest books a musical has possessed in years, the Burt Bacharach music excitingly reflects today rather than the day before yesterday, and the performances, especially from Jerry Orbach as the put-upon and morally diffident hero, contrive, and it's no easy feat, to combine zip with charm.

Also it is a "new musical" that does, for once, seem entitled to call itself "new." To an extent the new element is to be found in the book, for although ancestors can be found for the story in *How to Succeed in Business* and *How Now, Dow Jones,* the intimacy of the piece is fresh. Even more, there is the beat of the music; this is the first musical where you go out feeling rhythms rather than humming tunes.

The story is based upon the screenplay by Billy Wilder and I. A. L. Diamond for the film *The Apartment,* starring Jack Lemmon and Shirley MacLaine, that has the perhaps enviable reputation of being either one of the most immoral films ever made or else a slashing satire against the American way of business life.

The hero is not a nice man. In fact he is a kind of mouse-fink, who decides to sleep his way to the top in business without really lying. The sleeping is done—in a manner of speaking—not by him but by the senior executives in the life insurance firm in which he works. He gives them the key to his apartment and they give him the key to the executive washroom. They find a haven for their girls, and he finds a haven for his aspirations.

Curiously enough, deep down where it matters he has a kind of battered integrity that suffers from nothing so much as moral color-blindness. Then he falls in love. He falls in love with a girl who is on visiting terms with his apartment but not with him. Guess what happens? You are right the first time.

Mr. Simon's play (and revealingly I find myself thinking of it as much as a play with music as a musical) crackles with wit. The jokes cling supplely to human speech so that they never seem contrived. The whole piece has a sad and wry humanity to it, to which the waspishly accurate wisecracks are only a background.

It is also interesting to see how Mr. Simon wins our sympathy, even our empathy, for his morally derelict hero. In a dramatic trick half as old as time, or at least half as old as Pirandello, he has this dubious young man address the audience direct. The same dubious young man—he must have been great at selling life insurance—takes us so far into his lack of confidence that we feel sorry for him. We even forgive his half-baked way of talking to invisible audiences. Mr. Simon, you see, is a very resourceful man, and persuasive. He wouldn't even have to sell you the Brooklyn Bridge; you would be prepared to rent it.

The music is modern pop and delightful. Mr. Bacharach—always helped by Hal David's happily colloquial lyrics—is no musical revolutionary. Yet the score does have a new beat. It is tense rather than lyrical, and it is fond of bolero rhythms and hidden celestial choirs.

It is Mr. Bacharach who gives the musical its slinky, fur-coated feel of modernity, but it is certainly a feel that has been taken up and even exploited by the staging. Robin Wagner's settings are so architecturally and decoratively perfect for time, place and period that they seem to absorb the characters like the blotting paper–style backgrounds of top class advertisements, while Donald Brooks's costumes look so apt that they will probably need to be changed every three months to keep up.

Even more considerable is the success of Robert Moore, who has directed his first musical with all the expertise of a four-armed juggler. He has dovetailed Michael Bennett's most imaginatively staged musical numbers into the whole, and given the musical notable pace and style.

The cast was virtually perfect. Mr. Orbach has the kind of wrists that look as though they are about to lose their hands, and the kind of neck that seems to be on nodding acquaintanceship with his head. He makes gangle into a verb, because that is just what he does. He gangles. He also sings most effectively, dances most occasionally, and acts with an engaging and perfectly controlled sense of desperation.

Jill O'Hara, sweet, tender and most innocently beddable, looks enchanting and sings like a slightly misty lark, and Edward Winter is handsome and satisfyingly caddish as the man who betrays her, and is finally given his deserts by our worm-turning hero.

Of the rest, I enjoyed Paul Reed, Norman Shelly, Vince O'Brien and Dick O'Neill as a quartet of tired business men hoping to get themselves tireder, and two beautifully judged character performances from A. Larry Haines as a doctor in a more than usually general practice, and Marian Mercer as a tiny-voiced hustler with a heart as big as a saloon. I liked finally the girl, Donna McKechnie, who led the dance number at the end of the first act with the power and drive of a steam hammer in heat.

Clive Barnes ON
Oh! Calcutta!

June 17, 1969
Eden Theater
5,959 Performances

OH! CALCUTTA! an entertainment with music. Devised by Kenneth Tynan; conceived and staged by Jacques Levy; contributors: Samuel Beckett, Jules Feiffer, Dan Greenburg, John Lennon, Mr. Levy, Leonard Melfi, David Newman and Robert Benton, Sam Shepard, Kenneth Tynan, Sherman Yellen; music and lyrics by the Open Window; choreography by Margo Sappington; setting by James Tilton; lighting by David Segal; costumes by Fred Voelpel; projected media designed by Gardner Compton and Emile Ardolino; still photography by Michael Childers; audio design by Robert Liftin; production supervisor, Michael Thoma; stage manager, John Actman. Presented by Hillard Elkins in association with Michael White and Gordon Crowe, associate producer, George Platt.
Principals ...Raina Barrett, Mark Dempsey, Katie Drew-Wilkinson, Boni Enten, Bill Macy, Alan Rachins, Leon Russom, Margo Sappington, Nancy Tribush, George Welbes; and the Open Window: Robert Dennis, Peter Schickele, Stanley Walden.

Voyeurs of the city, unite, you have nothing to lose but your brains. During *Oh! Calcutta!*, which I saw at the final preview and which opened last night at the Eden Theater, a member of the cast—barebacked as it were—announces with a simple but euphoric pride: "Gee, this makes *Hair* seem like *The Sound of Music.*"

On the contrary, my friend. I assure you *Oh! Calcutta!* makes *The Sound of Music* seem like *Hair.* There is no more innocent show in town—and certainly none more witless—than this silly little diversion, devised by Kenneth Tynan, produced by Hillard Elkins and destined to make the shrewd entrepreneurs the crock of gold that lies there somewhere over the rainbow.

Innocent it is, completely. It is childlike when they strip—and the stripping, dancing and staging are the only tolerable parts of the evening for the "mature audiences" to whom the producers are somewhat foolhardily addressing their sales pitch—and childish when they talk. The sketches are unbelievably weak. The sex joke, I must protest, has not in reality sunk so low. This is the kind of show to give pornography a dirty name.

I have enormous respect for Ken Tynan, as critic, social observer and man of the theater. But what a nice dirty-minded boy like him is doing in a place like this, I fail to understand.

I thought we were to be offered a little pleasant erotic dramatic literature and a few neatly turned bawdy jokes. It was, I imagined, not to be the kind of evening for everyone, but for those who wanted it, a diverting place not to take your maiden aunt to.

The authors, gathered together (although their individual contributions remain unidentified), are formidable. Listen to them—Samuel Beckett, Jules Feiffer, Dan Greenburg, John Lennon, Jacques Levy, Leonard Melfi, David Newman and Robert Benton (they wrote *Bonnie and Clyde* although which wrote which I am not sure), Sam Shepard, Mr. Tynan himself and Sherman Yellen. But personally I think the butler did it, and that none of these fine and worthy men are really guilty.

It is curious how anti-erotic public nudity, as opposed to private nudity, is. There is a clinical lack of mystery about it that, speaking for myself, makes me disconcertingly think pure and beautiful thoughts. Other people of course may have other reactions. For students of form, I should point out that while Margo Sappington (an ex-Joffrey dancer of great promise I always expected to see more of, although hardly as much as this) has devised pleasant choreography, it is not very original. The San Francisco Dance Workshop does the nude bit better and prettier.

In sum, *Oh! Calcutta!* is likely to disappoint different people in different ways, but disappointment is the order of the night. To be honest, I think I can recommend the show with any vigor only to people who are extraordinarily underprivileged either sexually, socially or emotionally. Now is your chance to stand up and be counted.

ETYMOLOGICAL NOTE: Perhaps the only witty joke of the evening is the title *Oh! Calcutta!* This is not a reference to the black hole of Indian mutiny fame, but is the title of a painting by the contemporary French artist Clovis Trouille that shows the tattooed behind of a well-endowed young lady.

The title is a pun. It suggests in French: *Oh! Quelle – – – t'as!* The dashes represent a three-letter French argot word that *Le Monde* would not dream of publishing. Or, freely translated: "What a lovely – – – – you have!" The dashes represent a slightly longer Anglo-Saxon word the English language edition of *Le Monde* would not dream of publishing. Yes, Virginia, that really was the best joke.

For the humor is so doggedly sophomoric and soporific that from internal evidence alone I would go to court and testify that in my opinion such highly literate men could not have been responsible. Luckily at the preview I saw, the audience appeared to be moderately unsophisticated, and modestly grateful for anything.

The jokes are prissy and silly—depending for their effectiveness, such as it is, on their naive attempts at being daring. My seven-year-old son recently went through a phase where he kept on trying to shock my young daughter with one of the more vital and active Anglo-Saxon swear words. For a day or so he succeeded—but I hasten to add that my daughter is only five, and was not really a "mature audience" for him. Eventually he failed to shock, and now seems to have accepted the advisibility of restricting such language to private moments of considerable stress.

But, I hear you asking yourself, is all the written material stale, flat and merely profitable. The answer is no. One sketch—called "Delicious Indignities"—was very funny indeed and had a genuine literary feel to it. Wait till they do it on television—you'll scream. I also admit I was very amused by a burlesque-style skit, a few years after Dr. Kronkheit, on human sexual response. It wasn't witty, it wasn't clever, but it made me laugh immoderately.

The failure here is almost exclusively a failure of the writers and the producers. The director, Jacques Levy, has done his best with the weak material at hand. The opening—a group-spoof strip-tease—has just the right touch of erotic sophistication, but regrettably it is a touch never again repeated in the show.

However, the nude scenes, while derivative, are attractive enough. The best effects—including the rather sweet grope-in immediately after the intermission—have been taken from Robert Joffrey's ballet *Astarte,* and the show uses the same projected media designers, Gardner Compton and Emile Ardolino and, of course, rock music, here provided by the Open Window. The Joffrey Ballet version was not only better but also far, far sexier.

Clive Barnes ON
No, No, Nanette
BOOK BY Otto Harbach AND Frank Mandel
LYRICS BY Irving Caesar AND Otto Harbach
MUSIC BY Vincent Youmans

January 19, 1971
Forty-sixth Street Theater
861 Performances

NO, NO, NANETTE, revival of the 1925 musical. Book by Otto Harbach and Frank Mandel; music by Vincent Youmans; lyrics by Irving Caesar and Otto Harbach; setting by Raoul Péne du Bois; lighting by Jules Fisher; musical direction and vocal arrangements by Buster Davis; orchestrations by Ralph Burns; dance music arranged and incidental music composed by Luther Henderson; dances and musical numbers staged by Donald Saddler; adapted and directed by Burt Shevelove; sound created by Jack Shearing; tap supervisors, Mary Ann Niles and Ted Cappy; stage manager, Robert Schear; production supervised by Busby Berkeley. Presented by Pyxidium Ltd.

Pauline	Patsy Kelly
Lucille Early	Helen Gallagher
Sue Smith	Ruby Keeler
Jimmy Smith	Jack Gilford
Billy Early	Bobby Van
Tom Trainor	Roger Rathburn
Nanette	Susan Watson
Flora Latham	K. C. Townsend
Betty Brown	Loni Zoe Ackerman
Winnie Winslow	Pat Lysinger

Nostalgia may prove to be the overriding emotion of the seventies, with remembrance of things past far more comfortable than the realization of things present. For everyone who wishes the world were fifty years younger—and particularly, I suspect, for those who remember it when it was fifty years younger—the revival of the 1925 musical *No, No, Nanette* should provide a delightful, carefree evening. It also has a certain amount of taste and imagination.

The resuscitation of operettas and musical comedies is a tricky operation, and the producers here have gone about their task with skill. It is described as adapted by Burt Shevelove, who is also the director, and although I do not know the original book by Otto Harbach and Frank Mandel, I would take a fair-sized bet that Mr. Shevelove's adaptation has been fairly extensive.

What emerges at the Forty-sixth Street Theater is something like one of the new modish put-ons, such as *Dames at Sea* or *Curley McDimple,* but with the original music and lyrics, and, of course, much more of the original spirit. This is far closer to a musical of the twenties than anything New York has seen since the twenties, but it is seen through a contemporary sensibility.

Time-travelers of all ages will revel in the simplicity of Vincent Youmans's music. It is music to hum, and particularly music to dance to. Its rhythms suggest their own dancing feet, and the melodies are light, cheerful and exuberant, so that even the blues are not too blue.

There are a number of standards, and near-standards in the score, most notably "I Want to Be Happy" and "Tea for Two," and they emerge fresh but with reverberations of the past. They have also been cleverly arranged and orchestrated, so that while they sound familiar they don't sound quite familiar enough to be impertinent.

Note also the lyrics by Irving Caesar and Mr. Harbach. These are as neat as a playful kitten, and on occasion as daring as a trapeze star. Youmans specialized in short musical phrases, which set his lyricists special technical problems. Those are surmounted with a dexterity that deserves a place in any museum of American musical comedy, and yet live wonderfully today. I doubt whether we will encounter any cleverer or more purely musical lyrics than these all this season.

It seems that the books of most musicals in the twenties were not especially important. The boy met the girl, lost her and found her in time for the finale. At the drop of a hat, or the click of a cane, the stage would be invaded by a horde of happy dancing boys and girls, who would sing and tap in the background. There were also comedy scenes, but dream ballets were to come later.

In *No, No, Nanette* the story is of Jimmy Smith, a manufacturer of Bibles who wants a belt. He philanders in a gentlemanly way with three young ladies (he does not lay a hand on them, it says) and has to pay them off, in an intrigue that involves his young lawyer, who, in the way of young lawyers of the day, would obviously do anything for money. How times have changed. Such nostalgia!

Nanette is the little girl to whom everyone says "No," until she escapes to an Atlantic City not yet made famous by Monopoly. There, of course, she gets engaged to Mr. Right. It all ends happily.

One of the show's many charms is the amount of dancing—not unexpected, when it is remembered that the production has been supervised by the great Busby Berkeley, who once made Hollywood a world fit for tap dancers, and stars Ruby Keeler, who, way back when, was sent on that stage by Warner Baxter, an unknown, and came back a star. Ruby still is a star.

Admittedly Miss Keeler is making acting into one of the arts of conversation, but she dances like a trouper and wears indomitability shyly like a badge of service. She is just enormously likable. Jack Gilford is also enormously likable, even though he has fewer opportunities to be liked, and Patsy Kelly, a formidable lady who specializes in maids who have not only given notice but also taken notice, sucks up every scene she is in with the impressive suction of the vacuum cleaner she herself wields with such masterly expertise.

In this kind of show juveniles are juveniles. Susan Watson (a really pretty girl) and Roger Rathburn were less juvenile than most. But for my money the best performances came from Bobby Van as the suave, debonair dancing lawyer (the man is a superb tap dancer—the program says he has never had a lesson; where would he be now with lessons?) and the adorable Helen Gallagher as his short-suffering wife. When Miss Gallagher sings the blues of a lovelorn wife with piece of chiffon and a chorus of properly epicene tailor's dummies, she makes the good old days come alive once more.

The staging by Mr. Shevelove and the supervision by Mr. Berkeley seemed attractively tongue-in-cheek (where else, by the way, do people put tongues?) and the choreography by Donald Saddler was creatively the most important new element in the show. This choreography dazzled—I had forgotten tap-dancing could be so much fun. Less need be said of the designing by Raoul Péne du Bois, which like everything else was highly popular with the audience, also seemed to take kitsch down to new depths.

One wonders what else lies in store for us. They revived *The Desert Song* in London a few years back and it did surprisingly well with theater parties.

Clive Barnes ON
Peter Brook's
A Midsummer Night's Dream

January 20, 1971

Billy Rose Theater

62 Performances

A MIDSUMMER NIGHT'S DREAM, the Royal Shakespeare Company production of Shakespeare's comedy. Directed by Peter Brook; settings and costumes by Sally Jacobs; music by Richard Peaslee; lighting by Lloyd Burlingame. Presented by the David Merrick Arts Foundation.

Theseus/Oberon	Alan Howard
Hippolyta/Titania	Sara Kestelman
Philostrate/Puck	John Kane
Egeus/Quince	Philip Locke
Bottom	David Waller
Flute	Glynne Lewis
Starveling	Phillip Manikum
Snout	Patrick Stewart
Snug	Barry Stanton
Hermia	Mary Rutherford
Lysander	Terence Taplin
Helena	Frances de la Tour
Demetrius	Ben Kingsley
Fairies:	
Cobweb	Hugh Keays Byrne
Moth	Ralph Cotterill
Peaseblossom	Celia Quicke
Mustardseed	John York

Many people have seen magic in Shakespeare's *A Midsummer Night's Dream*, the magic of moonshine and fairyland, and—since no Shakespearean play has been so foully encrusted over with nineteenth-century romanticism—the magic of Mendelssohn and bosky scenery looking good enough to eat. Peter Brook has also seen magic in the *Dream*, but it is the magic of man. His production of the play, first seen last summer at Stratford-on-Avon and now gloriously come to the Billy Rose Theater, is also full of the magic of the theater.

It is a celebration of life and fancy, of man and his imagination, his fate, and the brevity of his brief candle in the light of the world. Shakespeare gave us "the lunatic, the lover and the poet," and Brook smilingly added the acrobat.

This is without any equivocation whatsoever the greatest production of Shakespeare I have ever seen in my life—and for my joys and my sins I have seen literally hundreds. Its greatness lies partly in its insight into man, and best of all its remarkable insight into Shakespeare. But it also lies in its originality. It is the most genuinely and deeply original production of Shakespeare in decades.

So-called original Shakespeare often is enough to make sensitive and sensible men squirm. It usually means strange texts, outlandish readings, battered phrases, rude glosses and impertinent additions. Here it means no such thing. Here it means merely that Brook has forgotten—not really forgotten, for on occasion he jokes about it—or at least ignored, that scaly accretion of time called a classic's performing tradition. Brook has behaved as if *A Midsummer Night's Dream* had been written just last midsummer by a young man with an archaic turn of phrase, an immortal gift for poetry, and no ability whatsoever to write stage directions.

He has taken this script and staged it with regard for nothing but its sense and meaning. He has collaborated with Shakespeare, not twisted his arm or blinded his senses, not tried to be superior, but just helped him out to get this strange play on stage.

Helped by the designer Sally Jacobs, Brook has placed the play within three white and gleaming walls. Across the back are two white doors, and on top of the walls are battlements where musicians can play, actors run or wait, or even on occasion dangle scenery into the playing cockpit below. Its purpose? And for that matter, the purpose of an Oberon on a trapeze, a Puck who juggles with plates or dashes across the scene on Tarzan rope or runs on stilts? Why all this? Are they merely the tricks of Brook's fertile imagination; conjurations to while the time, and limn out a little talent? Emphatically no.

Brook has taken this play as pristine new and samite white. But he also knows that we take to the play our expectations taken from schoolhouse and playhouse. He wants, I think, to surprise us into listening to these lute-songs of the spirit with new ears and unencumbered intelligences.

His one liberty—and this has been taken in some circles as a mere literary conceit—has been to combine the roles of Theseus and Hippolyta with those of Oberon and Titania, that of Philostrate with Puck and that of Egeus with Quince. What sounds perverse in theory, in practice serves to emphasize the playwright's purpose. Shakespeare should have done such a combination himself. For a rare once, the director knows best.

For now the play takes on the shape of an allegory of love, with the actors, and their plays within plays, whether they be mechanicals or poets, all pointed toward some explanation of sudden love and eventual mortality. "What fools these mortals be," muses Puck. But here Puck too is mortal, and fairyland is only a dimension of love, for Theseus, Oberon and, yes, even, the comically tragic Pyramus, all are lovers.

Brook takes the elements of the theater and mixes them as if he were a chef trying out a recipe. Circus tricks, Indian chants, flamenco guitar, children's streamers, paper plates, mock and mocked Mendelssohn, all are thrown into some eclectic broth. Only the text is sacred, to be illuminated, or like some holy child, cosseted, and once in a while cuffed behind the ear, to show a proper religious irreverence.

The superb actors seem as dedicated to Brook as Brook is to Shakespeare. Alan Howard, humorous and compassionate as the Theseus/Oberon, Sara Kestelman, sensual and womanly as the Hippolyta/Titania, John Kane's supremely amused Puck, David Waller's humanistic and appealing Bottom, the Quince of Philip Locke, the lovers of Mary Rutherford, Frances de la Tour, Terence Taplin and Ben Kingsley are all masterly in the natural way of men and women surprised in life rather than actors caught acting.

If you have any interest in the theater, in life or in your fellow men, I think you will be transfixed by this *Dream*. And, if you haven't, well, even so, you might appreciate still the fun and the juggling. As Shakespeare would surely be the first to admit, jugglers have their place.

Clive Barnes ON
Follies
BOOK BY James Goldman
MUSIC AND LYRICS BY Stephen Sondheim

———

April 4, 1971

Winter Garden

521 Performances

FOLLIES, a musical. Book by James Goldman; music and lyrics by Stephen Sondheim; choreography by Michael Bennett; setting by Boris Aronson; costumes by Florence Klotz; lighting by Tharon Musser; musical direction by Harold Hastings; orchestrations by Jonathan Tunick; dance music arrangements by John Berkman; production directed by Harold Prince and Michael Bennett; production stage manager, Fritz Holt. Presented by Harold Prince in association with Ruth Mitchell.

Major-Domo	Dick Latessa
Sally Durant Plummer	Dorothy Collins
Young Sally	Marti Rolph
Christine Crane	Ethel Barrymore Colt
Willy Wheeler	Fred Kelly
Stella Deems	Mary McCarty
Max Deems	John J. Martin

Heidi Schiller	Justine Johnston
Chauffeur	John Grigas
Meredith Lane	Sheila Smith
Chet Richards	Peter Walker
Roscoe	Michael Bartlett
Deedee West	Helon Blount
Sandra Donovan	Sonja Levkova
Hattie Walker	Ethel Shutta
Young Hattie	Mary Jane Houdina
Emily Whitman	Marcie Stringer
Theodore Whitman	Charles Welch
Vincent	Victor Griffin
Vanessa	Jayne Turner
Young Vincent	Michael Misita
Young Vanessa	Graciela Daniele
Solange LaFitte	Fifi D'Orsay
Carlotta Campion	Yvonne De Carlo
Phyllis Rogers Stone	Alexis Smith
Benjamin Stone	John McMartin
Young Phyllis	Virginia Sandifur
Young Ben	Kurt Peterson
Buddy Plummer	Gene Nelson
Young Buddy	Harvey Evans
Dimitri Weismann	Arnold Moss
Kevin	Ralph Nelson
Young Heidi	Victoria Mallory
Party Musicians	Taft Jordan, Aaron Bell, Charles Spies, Robert Curtis

The musical *Follies,* which opened last night at the Winter Garden, is the kind of musical that should have its original cast album out on 78s. It carries nostalgia to where sentiment finally engulfs it in its sickly maw. And yet—in part—it is stylish, innovative, it has some of the best lyrics I have ever encountered, and above all it is a serious attempt to deal with the musical form.

A theater is being torn down. Between the wars—tap, tap, tap, slurp, slurp, slurp—it was the home of Weismann's *Follies* where, it seems, that every pretty girl was so much like a melody that the melodies themselves did not matter too much.

Weismann, himself retired and seeing the theater about to take its place among the more attractive parking lots of New York City, throws a first and last reunion party—and all the Weismann girls out of the graveyard and the geriatric ward get together for one final bash. They sing a few of their old numbers and open up a few of their old sores.

Among them are Buddy and Sally, and Ben and Phyllis. Years ago, in 1941, Buddy loved Sally, Sally loved Ben, Phyllis loved Ben, and Ben loved Ben. Buddy married Sally, Ben married Phyllis, but their marriages are not working out. (They rarely do in Stephen Sondheim musicals.)

Now meeting again after thirty years, the girls have left show business, and Buddy is a moderately unsuccessful salesman, while, so far as I can tell, Ben is a world-famous Foundation head who has just written a coffee-table book about someone called Wilson. He has made a fortune and he and his wife bask in Braques, Utrillos and Georgian silver. Their lives though are empty. The other pair's are also empty but in a smaller size.

For a moment it looks as though intellectual Ben will take off with silly little Sally, but they then get involved in some *Follies* extravaganza and all four end up going off into the bleak Broadway dawn to live unhappily ever after, with their lawful spouses.

James Goldman's book is well enough written; indeed one of its problems is that the writing is far better than the shallow, narrow story, raising expectations that are never fulfilled. When, to give this all-too-eternal quadrilateral dramatic dimension, Mr. Goldman first has their lives intercut with the ghosts of their earlier selves, and finally puts all eight of them into an ironic *Follies* routine that is meant to comment on their personal and marital plights—by the faded beard of Pirandello he has gone too far.

Mr. Sondheim's music comes in two flavors—nostalgic and cinematic. The nostalgic kind is for the pseudo-oldie numbers, and I must say that most of them sound like numbers that you have almost only just forgotten, but with good reason. This non-hit parade of pastiche trades on camp, but fundamentally gives little in return. It has all the twists and turns of yesteryear, but none of the heart—and eventually the fun it makes of the past seems to lack something in affection. The cinematic music is a mixture of this and that, chiefly that. I doubt whether anyone will be parodying it in thirty or forty years' time.

The lyrics are as fresh as a daisy. I know of no better lyricist in show-business than Mr. Sondheim—his words are a joy to listen to, even when his music is sending shivers of indifference up your spine. The man is a Hart in search of a Rodgers, or even a Boito in search of a Verdi.

The production has been directed by Harold Prince and Michael Bennett, the latter also arranging the *Late Late Show*–style dances. It is all very stylish, with Boris Aronson's beautifully decrepit scenery moving in and out like a TV studio, and Florence Klotz having provided the best costumes to be seen on Broadway.

The first-night audience—which someone should hire intact for openings—adored many of the old-timers. Fifi D'Orsay, Mary McCarty and Ethel Shutta all stopped the show with their gutsy Broadway routines, but although I admired all three, I also felt a little uncomfortable at the nature of my admiration.

It is a carefully chosen cast—which, oddly enough, performed better when I first saw the show Wednesday afternoon—that works very hard. Gene Nelson, who injured himself and last night was unable to perform his flashily effective thirties-style acrobatic dance solo, makes an attractively battered loser out of Buddy; Dorothy Collins, with a simmering torch-song to end, is woebegonely flighty as Sally; John McMartin makes a rakishly and seedily convincing Ben, and Yvonne De Carlo was blowsily adorable as a surviving movie star who had seen better days and worse nights.

My personal favorite was Alexis Smith, however. She looks wonderful—O.K., let's say it, she still looks wonderful—and she has a mixture of ice and vitality that is tantalizingly amusing. She also sings and dances with style and acts with commanding serenity.

There are many good things here—I think I enjoyed it better than the Sondheim/Prince last torn-marriage manual, *Company,* and obviously everyone concerned here is determined to treat the musical seriously as an art form, and such aspiration must be encouraged.

Yet perhaps too many little old ladies are passing by just lately. Before we know it Broadway will be awash with nostalgia and that special sensibility toward former film stars that Mart Crowley once so memorably summed up in *The Boys in the Band.* "Maria Montez," shrilled one of his characters, "was a *good* woman."

Clive Barnes ON

The Basic Training of Pavlo Hummel

BY David Rabe

May 20, 1971

Newman/Public Theater

365 Performances

William Atherton, sniffing glue, and Albert Hall, in uniform, in *The Basic Training of Pavlo Hummel*
SY FRIEDMAN, ZODIAC

THE BASIC TRAINING OF PAVLO HUMMEL, a play by David W. Rabe. Directed by Jeff Bleckner; setting by David Mitchell; costumes by Theoni V. Aldredge; lighting by Martin Aronstein; stage manager, Dean Compton. Presented by the New York Shakespeare Festival, Joseph Papp, producer, Bernard Gersten, associate producer.

Pavlo Hummel	William Atherton
Yen	Victoria Racimo
Ardell	Albert Hall
First Sergeant Tower	Joe Fields
Captain Saunders	Edward Cannan
Corporal Ferrara	Anthony R. Charnota
Parker	Peter Cameron
Burns	Stephen Clarke
Ryan	John Walter Davis
Hall	Bob Delegall
Grennel	Tom Harris
Hinkle	Edward Hermann
Kress	Earl Hindman
Pierce	Robert Lehman
Hendrix	D. Franklyn Lenthall
Mrs. Hummel	Sloane Shelton
Mickey	Frederick Coffin
Sergeant Brisbey	Lee Wallace
Corporal Jones	Garrett Morris
Mamasan	Christal Kim
Small Boy	Hoshin Seki
Sergeant Wall	John Benson
Parham	Bob Delegall
Linh	Hoshin Seki
Zung	Victoria Racimo

David Rabe's play, *The Basic Training of Pavlo Hummel,* at the New York Shakespeare Festival Public Theater, which opened last night at the Newman Theater, introduces a new and authentic voice to our theater. What Mr. Rabe is saying—war is hell, especially when it is in Vietnam—is not at all original, and this is the play's major defect, but he does have a persuasive way of saying things.

Pavlo Hummel is a regular soldier. We see him go through his misfitted primary training to his death in a Saigon whorehouse, blown up by a grenade thrown by an Army sergeant he had insulted.

Hummel is something different. He has a slight mental disturbance, he tells lying stories, and he cannot relate to his fellow rookies who distrust him, and eventually beat him up. Yet he finally does make a sort of soldier, and in Vietnam, although he is wounded three times, he finds a sad, brief manhood before he finds death.

The subject matter of the play is familiar enough—sadly so. There are few surprises here, from recruit training to death, but what interested me was the playwright's sense of what people

really say and his obvious feel for the dynamics of character confrontation.

There are a number of incidents here, such as Hummel taunting his bullying oppressor, who had failed his basic training and was being kept for a further eight weeks, until a fight that Hummel must lose, inevitably starts. Or the man, with no legs, and one arm in a hospital bed—"a stump of a man," as he calls himself—pleading for a gun to shoot himself with and railing at the world with a corrosive irony. Here are small truths.

The character of Hummel himself, a gawky, born loser, struggling with a mad mother and a personality out of joint with his circumstances, has a dramatic power to it. Hummel is an interesting man.

The play's form is deliberately diffuse. The First Sergeant, bullying, menacing and not really cruel, and saved by a tough humor, is up on a pedestal drilling his recruits, exhorting them, trying to instill military discipline and love of country. He is the focus of the play.

Against this central theme of training and warfare stands Hummel and his education. Hummel has been provided with some kind of mysterious conscience figure, called Ardell, who lurks around him. He is an army officer, who at times identifies with the army but at times does not. This device never quite works—Ardell is ambiguous enough, but his chorus-like commentary never really adds much to the play's movement or even texture.

Jeff Bleckner's direction helps stress the fluidity and pace of the play and yet also emphasizes the author's anecdotal material which gives the play its tone of reportage. The performances are extremely good.

All the minor roles are very carefully played, and the three principal parts have all been perfectly cast. Joe Fields as the First Sergeant, an amiably honey-voiced tyrant, is very impressive, as is Albert Hall as the elusive Ardell, both mocking and humane.

However, a great deal of the play's effectiveness depends on Hummel himself, and here William Atherton had a distinct personal success. Raw-boned and awkward, good-natured but stupid, Hummel goes through the play like a stifled cry of pain, going to his death like a slaughtered lamb.

Mel Gussow ON
Much Ado About Nothing
BY William Shakespeare

August 17, 1972

Delacorte Theater

136 Performances

MUCH ADO ABOUT NOTHING, the Shakespeare play. Directed by A. J. Antoon; setting by Ming Cho Lee; costumes by Theoni V. Aldredge; lighting by Martin Aronstein; music by Peter Link; dances by Donald Saddler; stage manager, John Beven. Presented by the New York Shakespeare Festival, Joseph Papp, producer; associate producer, Bernard Gersten.

Leonato ....Mark Hammer
A Reporter ....Charles Bartlett
Beatrice ....Kathleen Widdoes
Hero ....April Shawhan
Benedick...Sam Waterston
Claudio ....Glenn Walken
Don Pedro ....Douglas Watson
Don John ....Jerry Mayer
Antonio ....Lou Gilbert
Conrade ....Jack Gianino
Borachio ....Frederick Coffin
Margaret..Jeanne Hepple
Balthasar ....Marshall Efron
Ursula ....Bette Henritze
Dogberry ....Barnard Hughes
Verges..Will Mackenzie
First Watch ....George Guglcotti
Second Watch..David Lenthall
Other Watches..............David Anderson, James McGill, John Michalski
Friar Francis..Tom McDermott
Sexton..Charles Bartlett
Townspeople ....David Anderson, Anna Brennen, J.J. Lewis, James McGill, John Michalski, Lynne Taylor and Nina Jordan
Musicians...................................Charles Lewis—trumpet; Henry (Bootsie) Normand—banjo; Sam Pilatian—tuba; Peter Phillips—piano; Aaron Sacks—sax; Jimmy Young—drums.

A. J. Antoon, the director, has said that theater for him is an invitation to the audience to come into his kitchen and eat. By that measure, Antoon's *Much Ado About Nothing,* which opened Wednesday night at the Delacorte Theater in Central Park, is a feast.

Antoon has transposed Shakespeare's Messina to a small town in Middle America. This is a pre-World War I America—marked by chauvinism, self-confidence and suddenly requited love. The gentlemen wear spats and carry pocket flasks. The ladies sneak a shared cigarette, and clear the smoke away before the father of the house enters. Almost everyone is inhibited by social conventions—yet everyone is having a glorious time. As sparklers flare, the couples dance Donald Saddler dances by the light of Japanese lanterns—and the Central Park moon could be part of the set.

Does this sound more like *No, No, Nanette* than like *Much Ado About Nothing*? For Antoon, the nostalgia is intentional. Happily, Middle America is not a forced concept for *Much Ado,* but a comfortable setting—a place in which to play the comedy, to give it more relevance to its audience. This, like *Two Gentlemen of Verona,* is Shakespeare for the contemporary masses.

What makes it such an entertaining evening is not just Antoon's imaginative direction, but, of course, the play's intelligence and urbanity. In *Much Ado* Shakespeare raises persiflage and badinage to a high art.

The cast, drawn mostly from Joseph Papp's deep-welled reserve of actors who have worked with him before, is splendid—particularly Sam Waterston as Benedick.

He is a boyish—but not immature—Benedick. He is sharp-tongued and headstrong, never losing sight of the character's propulsively romantic nature. It is a long step from the misogyny of "What, my dear Lady Disdain! are you yet living?" to the love-sickness of "When I said I would die a bachelor, I did not think I would live till I married," but Waterston leaps it with enormous grace and agility. This is a superb comic performance.

Kathleen Widdoes is a lovely foiler as Beatrice. She is a paragon for Woman's Lib—strong and acidulous but never dropping her femininity. She is not a shrew, but as Beatrice should be, a thoroughly merry woman. Even as the two parry insults, there is never any doubt about the magnetism of the mutual attraction.

Also outstanding is Douglas Watson as Don Pedro—breezily assured and always orchestrating his followers. As Hero and Claudio, outwardly but not actually the focus of the play, April Shawhan and Glenn Walken manage to portray innocence without seeming foolish.

Before the play begins, a blue-jacketed brass band marches on stage, interspersing foot-tapping Peter Link tunes with Scott Joplin rags. Later, the band underscores the action—there are very few actual songs in this show. Love scenes, for example, are played against a background of sentimental ballads.

Insouciantly, the director shifts some of the scenes from the original settings. Waterston soliloquizes while paddling a canoe, then upturns the vessel and hides behind it as his friends discuss Beatrice's supposed love for him. He is hilarious as he flashes looks of unconcealed pleasure.

Most of the switches in time and place work, but occasionally Antoon's theatrical exuberance carries him into small errors and excesses. The play begins awkwardly—and for no reason—with a portrait photographer, instead of a messenger, bringing news of Don Pedro's return.

The bastard Don John is turned into a sneering, almost Hitlerian villain and his followers are dressed like Chicago gangsters. Dogberry and his provincial constabulary are Keystone Kops, and despite Barnard Hughes's amusing performance as Dogberry, the scenes are too farcical and too long.

But these are minor demurrers in an otherwise disarming evening. In addition to the major beneficences, this *Much Ado* is a good excuse for Theoni V. Aldredge to broaden her canvas of costumes, for Ming Cho Lee to create a set that is a bright collage of early century Americana, and for Henry (Bootsie) Normand's band to play beer-and-pretzel music loud enough to drown out the rival Schaeffer Music Festival in Central Park.

Suitably, the show ends not with Shakespeare's "Strike up, pipers!" but with Antoon's "Strike up the band!"

Clive Barnes ON
Butley
BY Simon Gray

October 31, 1972

Morosco Theater

135 Performances

BUTLEY, a play by Simon Gray. Directed by James Hammerstein; setting by Eileen Diss; lighting and costumes by Neil Peter Jampolis, production stage manager, Harry Young. Presented by Lester Osterman Productions (Lester Osterman–Richard Horner), in association with Michael Cooron.

Ben Butley	Alan Bates
Joseph Keyston	Hayward Morse
Miss Heasman	Geraldine Sherman
Edna Shatt	Barbara Lester
Anne Butley	Holland Taylor
Reg Nuttall	Roger Newman
Mr. Gardner	Christopher Hastings

Ben Butley—tattered, battered super-anti-hero of Simon Gray's play *Butley*—is coming adrift as his moorings. Desk lamps don't work for him, bananas and warm whisky have lost their kick, his wife has left him for another man and his roommate and protégé has—well—also left him for another man. This English play, with Alan Bates in the softly bravura, underplayed virtuoso role of his career, opened last night at the Morosco Theater.

Butley is a mess. His suit is trampled, his hair untidy, his breath halitosic, his eyes bloodshot. He is a professor of English at the University of London. He was once a sort of authority on T. S. Eliot. In recent years, however, he has devoted his career to bitchery and Beatrix Potter. He is overeducated, underemployed, lazy, foolish, bitter and witty. His is a literary sensibility adrift on a sea of despair, with nothing but a donnish urbanity and antic irony to keep it afloat. Butley is a very interesting man, and his tragedy is beautifully and crisply funny.

Mr. Gray has written about this half-baked academic with astonishing compassion. Butley goes around "spreading futility." He slouches like a lost soul, and yet uses his wit like a sledgehammer to ward off the world and reality. And despite his glorious and desperate faults, he remains oddly likable and strangely sympathetic. Even his pompousness and mad egotism have been made in some way attractive.

Mr. Gray has devised his comedy with considerable adroitness. Butley is caught at the very pinpoint moment of his final deflation. His life is subsiding around him. Where Mr. Gray has been particularly clever is to give his declining slob all the funny lines. He fights against all comers like a cornered Bugs Bunny full of wisecracks and with a splenetic humor. You can see the tarnished brilliance of the man, the fallen hopes, the eroding self-distrust that spews out a fine comic bitterness upon the world. Unfulfilled and unforgiving, Butley makes his last stand with style and venom.

What the play has caught is a specific mood and style. Here is the spiteful humor of a university common room combined with a rootlessness and lack of purpose that seem currently endemic among the foolishly wise. Even Butley's sexual leanings are, at the very least, ambivalent, and he rails at the world to no purpose. He hates himself in a very chilly climate.

Although Mr. Gray conceived the part, wrote it and sent it out on the world, Mr. Bates gives it life. Mr. Bates is offering a boisterous and yet most vivid performance. He never puts a rumple out of place. His high-pitched voice is strung out to the very edge of hysteria, his hair is tousled in an almost defiant and jaunty defeat and he slouches out against his oppressors with a bullying gallantry.

It would have been so easy to have made Butley either a prissy academic or a simple slob with dirty fingernails and stained morals. But Mr. Bates will have none of this. Perhaps almost going beyond the play, he seems to insist that we all share something of Butley's failure to realize life's expectations. At times desk lamps fail for us all.

In London, where it was the hit of last season and is still running, the play was staged, with exquisite precision, by Harold Pinter. Here it has been restaged by James Hammerstein, and although I miss the infinite delicacy of Pinter's original, it now provides a freer framework for Mr. Bates's performance, which is, perhaps as a result, all the more spontaneous and natural.

Butley never leaves the stage from beginning of the play till its end, but Joseph Keyston, his departing roommate and junior colleague, shares a little of his limelight. Hayward Morse in this role was sharp and sensitive, providing the perfect balance to Bates's Butley. The remainder of the cast was fine, particularly the husky insecurity of Barbara Lester as an academic too long in the academy.

Butley is no major contribution to dramatic literature, but it is that sadly rare thing—a literate and literary comedy with a heart. I reveled in every minute of it, and not least in Mr. Bates's performance, which is so nonchalantly superlative.

Mel Gussow on
The Hot L Baltimore
by Lanford Wilson

February 7, 1973

2307 Broadway

1,166 Performances

Judd Hirsch and Trish Hawkins in *The Hot L Baltimore*
ABNER SYMONS

THE HOT L BALTIMORE, a play by Lanford Wilson.
Directed by Marshall W. Mason; settings by Ronald
Radice; costume coordination by Dina Costa; stage
manager, Howard McBride. Presented by the Circle
Theater Company.

Bill	Judd Hirsch
Girl	Trish Hawkins
Millie	Helen Stenborg
Mrs. Bellotti	Trinity Thompson
Postman	John Heuer
April	Conchata Ferrell
Mr. Morse	Rob Thirkield
Jackie	Mari Gorman
Jamie	Zane Lasky
Mr. Katz	Antony Tenuta
Suzy	Stephanie Gordon
Friend	Burke Pearson
Paul Granger 3d	Jonathan Hogan
Mr. Oxenham	Louis Clay
Rogers	Peter Tripp
Hack man	Howard McBride
Delivery boy	Marcial Gonzales

In his new play, *The Hot L Baltimore,* Lanford Wilson writes with understanding and sensitivity about unwanted people. His characters are locked in interior worlds, clinging to solitary, futile dreams—and stubborn about not being defeated.

The play is filled with runaways—a brother and sister pair of urchins with a fantasy about organic farming in Utah, a young wanderer seeking a grandfather he has never met, a waif who can individually identify the far-off whistle of trains.

These characters and many more—from adolescence to senility—sit in, and pass through, the lobby of the condemned Hotel Baltimore, a hotel so derelict that the "e" has dropped out of its marquee (giving the play its title). Like the hotel itself, the characters belong to an immutable past where trains were on time and where playwrights could afford to be sentimental and unfashionable.

There are moments in this play (and in his others) when Wilson—with his passion for idiosyncratic characters, atmospheric details and invented homilies—reminds me of William Saroyan and Thornton Wilder. The comparison is not at all to his disadvantage. He, too, is a very American playwright, with a nostalgic longing for a lost sensibility.

The Baltimore slowly awakens, not, as in *Grand Hotel,* with international intrigue and high romance, but with everyday encounters and human comedy. The play unfolds until we feel the pace of the hotel and the pulse of the characters. As he had done before, the playwright overlaps conversations. Two, even three couples talk simultaneously—as in life. The dialogues start and stop together giving the play a musical flow.

The play seems to meander—it is a full three acts—and eventually a few of the guests become repetitive. There is little plot or action, but there is emotion. A brief altercation over a checkerboard becomes the sum of a generational conflict. At the playwright's invitation we share lives that are both comic and wistful. This is a play to be savored and to be cherished.

Wilson began his career off Off Broadway and

since then he has had many plays produced on and off Broadway and in regional theaters.

As if fulfilling a dream of one of his characters, he has returned to his off Off Broadway roots—as a resident playwright at the Circle Theater. He has bestowed his new play on the Circle, and Marshall W. Mason, co-founder of the company and the most frequent interpreter of Wilson, has responded with a harmonious production.

Together with the set designer, Ronald Radice, Mason has turned the stage at the theater (comfortably refurbished since my last visit) into an authentically seedy hotel lobby, complete with buzzing switchboard, potted plants and what appears to be a marble staircase—a reminder of the Baltimore's elegant past.

The actors rise to the occasion. There is excellent work from, among others, Mari Gorman and Zane Lasky as the brother and sister, Judd Hirsch and Antony Tenuta as the harassed hotel manager, and Conchata Ferrell and Stephanie Gordon as contrasting resident whores. The pivotal character in this group portrait, the girl with the train fixation, is played with vivacity by Trish Hawkins. Listen to her recite the American cities she has visited, making each name sound freshly minted and bracing.

Clive Barnes ON
A Moon for the Misbegotten
BY Eugene O'Neill

December 30, 1973
Morosco Theater
313 Performances

Jason Robards and Colleen Dewhurst in *A Moon for the Misbegotten* MARTHA SWOPE/TIME, INC.

A MOON FOR THE MISBEGOTTEN, a play by Eugene O'Neill. Directed by José Quintero; setting and lighting by Ben Edwards; costumes by Jane Greenwood; production stage manager, Jane E. Neufeld. Presented by Elliot Martin and Lester Osterman Productions (Lester Osterman–Richard Horner).

Josie Hogan	Colleen Dewhurst
Mike Hogan	Edwin J. McDonough
Phil Hogan	Ed Flanders
James Tyrone Jr.	Jason Robards
T. Stedman Harder	John O'Leary

There are some performances in the theater, just a few, that surge along as if they were holding the whole world on a tidal wave. I felt that surge, that excitement, that special revealed truth while watching Eugene O'Neill's *A Moon for the Misbegotten,* which on Saturday night officially opened a limited run at the Morosco Theater.

This is a landmark production that people are going to talk about for many years. The play has been staged by José Quintero, making a directorial comeback as assured as it is welcome, and stars Jason Robards, Colleen Dewhurst and Ed Flanders. It seemed to me to be an ideal, vibrant cast—a cast that listened acutely to the realities and tonalities of O'Neill's voice—in one of the great plays of the twentieth century.

O'Neill is a playwright with two distinct reputations, and this is becoming more apparent as time goes on. The first is as the major American playwright of his time—and this is a reputation that has perhaps been underestimated. But then there is the O'Neill of the last four plays (for oddly enough I count the one-act *Hughie* in with the big three), for which he can be considered one of the great playwrights of the modern theater.

O'Neill is a poetic realist. His best plays enclose you within the dimensions of their own world. You believe that you are listening to life, yet at the end you have intimations of something beyond naturalism. Indeed, if you have given yourself to O'Neill's spare and sometimes clumsy language, you have found an insight into the business of living as a walking casualty, as a flesh and blood hostage to death.

A Moon for the Misbegotten is probably the most immediate of the last plays. Superficially it is a sequel to *Long Day's Journey into Night,* as its autobiographical sources, much amended, tell of the final crisis of O'Neill's elder brother, Jamie. Jamie, the unsuccessful actor, unsuccessful drunk and unsuccessful son.

O'Neill never makes judgments in his plays—he is almost Shakespearean in his ambivalence to character. You will find no judgments in *A Moon for the Misbegotten.*

It is an encounter between two people under a moon. They are two people who should be in love and almost certainly are. They are two people who represent the only possibility, each for the other,

of happiness and earthly redemption. But fears are too much for them, and they part on their ways to separate deaths.

This is a most telling production. Ben Edwards has provided a very open and free setting, and his lighting, so absolutely essential to this diurnal travel of the day, is carefully sensitive to mood and occasion. A fair word too for Jane Greenwood's costumes—yes, this did look like 1923, and those clothes did look like those people.

Mr. Quintero plays his cards unerringly. You could take a temperature chart of his staging, and it would be the same as the play itself. He never exaggerates, falsifies; indeed, he never cheats on the playwright's scoring. And in this play, much more than any other, O'Neill seemed to know exactly what he wanted.

The cast is engaged and beautiful. Colleen Dewhurst as Josie, the virgin earth-mother, with common sense shining through her eyes like stars, and love clinging to her big red hands, was so beautiful. She spoke O'Neill as if it were being spoken for the first time—and not the first time in a theater (you always hope for that) but for the first time in a certain New England farm, on a certain September night in 1923.

Of course the real part, the whirlpool part, in the play is that of James Tyrone, and it is here that Mr. Robards—with his diffidently cocky stance, his map-lined face a stark report of suffering, and yet also an odd recollection of pictures of O'Neill himself—lays bare the simple secret of the Tyrones. It is simply their impossible embrace of guilt. But Mr. Robards finds a significance in the way he lights a match, or in his post-drunken recognition of a bonded whisky—with a glance, a grimace and gesture he showed that O'Neill and Proust knew the same terrible revelations about remembrance.

But how can you write about performances you are going to talk about for years? Watch the technical skill with which Miss Dewhurst gasps while taking whisky down the wrong way, or the Pietà suggestions—thanks to Mr. Quintero—of James in Josie's arms.

And I have not yet even mentioned Ed Flanders's sprightly O'Casey and playboy-of-the-Eastern-world performance as Josie's father, Phil. This is O'Neill at his most Irish, and Mr. Flanders is a nimble, loving rogue of Abbey Theater vintage. You can see him doing Joxer—and, perhaps surprisingly, this is right. Edwin J. McDonough and John O'Leary gave their contrived cameo sketches with very decent conviction.

O'Neill is the whipping boy for our souls. We all feel guilt, we all juggle with pipe-dreams, and we all play footsie with reality. O'Neill knew this. And you can gather this for yourself in this touching and splendid production of *A Moon for the Misbegotten.*

Mel Gussow ON

Short Eyes

BY Miguel Piñero

January 7, 1974

156 Performances

Joseph Carberry, Ben Jefferson and Johnny Johnson in
Short Eyes FRIEDMAN-ABELES

SHORT EYES, a play by Miguel Piñero. Directed by Marvin Felix Camillo; setting by Lee A. Goldman; lighting by Alan M. Beck; sound by Thomas Mark Edlun; costumes by Pamela Dendy; technical production supervisor, William Higgins; production stage manager, Denise Kasell. Presented by the Theater of the Riverside Church, Arthur Bartow, producer. At Riverside Drive and 120th Street.

Juan Otero ....Bimbo
Julio (Cupcakes) Mercado........................Andrew Butler
Charlie (Longshoe) Murphy ....Joseph Carberry
Clark Davis..William Carden
John (Ice) Wicker.......................................Ben Jefferson
William (El Raheem) Johnson ....Johnny Johnson
Fredrick Nett...Robert Maroft
Omar Blinker...Kenny Steward
Paco Pasqual...Felipe Torres
Captain Allard ....H. Richard Young

Miguel Piñero is a twenty-seven-year-old playwright and poet who has spent seven years in prison. The first time I saw his work was in 1972 during a visit to Sing Sing (the Ossining Correctional Facility), where a number of his short skits and street plays were performed by him and other inmates. Mr. Piñero's work was remarkable for its humor, perception and theatricality.

After his release from Sing Sing, Mr. Piñero became director of Third World Projects for Theater of the Riverside Church, where his first full-length play, *Short Eyes,* recently had its world premiere. It will run at Riverside through January 20.

Short Eyes proves that Mr. Piñero's prison sketches were no fluke. He is an original writer for the theater, whose plays we will be anticipating and witnessing for many years to come.

In this production, his director, Marvin Felix Camillo, also reveals a rare talent for taking raw material (the cast as well as the play) and, without distorting its essential nature, giving it dramatic stage life.

If the team of Mr. Piñero and Mr. Camillo could be utilized in America's prisons, they would probably work wonders of rehabilitation. This production is significant not only as a theatrical event but also as an act of social redemption.

Only one actor in the cast is a member of Actors Equity. Half of the others have acted with

"The Family," Mr. Camillo's company of former inmates and former addicts. Most members of the cast have served time in prison, which explains their authenticity, but not their talent for expression.

Because of the cast's performing inexperience (and also the theater's acoustics), occasionally the dialogue is inaudible, but the actors are not self-conscious—and they *are* playing characters, ranging from street-wise criminals to a religious fanatic. Several of them, particularly Bimbo as a reluctant jailhouse confessor, clearly are actors in the making.

The play is, as the subtitle indicates, about "The Killing of a Sex Offender by the Inmates of the House of Detention Awaiting Trial." That offender—"short eyes" in prison slang—is white. All but one of the other inmates are black or Puerto Rican (the actual killer is the other white prisoner, the psychotic Charlie "Longshoe" Murphy). Despite their own records, they think of the sex offender as the true criminal—an object of disgust.

Except for the murder, there is little physical brutality in the play, but there is a sense of emotional deprivation. These are stunted lives, and prison as well as society, bears the responsibility. The prison becomes a microcosm of that hostile society, and the inmates retreat into cells within their cells. The demarcation among races is rigid, the prison codes inflexible—a source of comedy as well as of conflict.

Short Eyes is not a perfect play. At moments its plotting is too tricky. But in it we learn the intricacies and the rituals of the prison system as it is practiced by the prisoners as well as by the jailers. This personal statement—from inside—is instructive and provocative.

Clive Barnes ON
Equus
BY Peter Shaffer

October 24, 1974
Plymouth Theater
1,209 Performances

Peter Firth and Everett McGill in *Equus*   VAN WILLIAMS

EQUUS, a play by Peter Shaffer. Directed by John Dexter; setting and costumes by John Napier; lighting by Andy Phillips; sound by Marc Wilkinson; mime by Claude Chagrin; American supervision of scenery and lighting by Howard Bay; costumes by Patricia Adshead; production stage manager, Robert L. Borod. Presented by Kermit Bloomgarden and Doris Cole Abrahams, in association with Frank Milton.

Martin Dysart	Anthony Hopkins
Alan Strang	Peter Firth
Nurse	Mary Doyle
Hester Salomon	Marian Seldes
Frank Strang	Michael Higgins
Dora Strang	Frances Sternhagen
Horseman	Everett McGill
Harry Dalton	Walter Mathews
Horses/Customers	Gus Kaikkonen, Philip Kraus, Gabriel Oshen, David Ramsey, John Tyrrell
Jill Mason	Roberta Maxwell

A bare stage, a few actors, a standing ovation, and quite clearly Broadway had gotten a new popular success in Peter Shaffer's play *Equus,* and a new star in the shock-headed, twenty-one-year-old Peter Firth. Both play and star emerged last night at the Plymouth Theater.

Mr. Shaffer's play does an unusual thing. It asks why? Most plays tell us how. *Equus* is a psychological inquiry into a crime, a journey into someone's mind. It is a kind of highbrow suspense story, a psychic and mythic thriller, but also an essay in character and motive. It is the documentation of a crime.

One night in England—and the story has been based by Mr. Shaffer on a flimsily documented but apparently true incident—a young stable hand attacked six horses in their stable. He systematically put their eyes out. It seems motiveless. He loved horses. He almost worshiped them—yet one night, one by one, in a disgusting, purposeless scene of violence he blinded them. Why? The boy was sick. Of course, he was sick, but why?

The disturbed boy is placed in an institution under the care of a psychiatrist. The boy has perpetrated a crime that is not only senseless but also bizarre. The pattern of the crime runs not just contrary to nature but contains elements of grotesque fantasy. Why blind horses? A madman might kill them, wound them in some crazed passion, but to carefully if frenziedly blind six horses suggests a certain method in the madness.

The young criminal is obviously alienated. When he first meets the psychiatrist he refuses to answer any questions—his only response is to gabble-sing advertising jingles with a mocking despair. His mind is closed up by the secret of his tragedy. The psychiatrist decides to unclam it—to exorcise the ghost.

This is the story of the play. The psychiatrist painfully has to unravel the boy's background. He not only has to win his confidence, he also has to sustain his interest. First what was his family like? What were the events leading up to this obscene violence? Slowly the doctor investigates the facts and the circumstances, and pieces together the anatomy of an outrage. He does not have to judge.

He is merely seeking the truth in the hope of freeing the boy from a demon.

The play Mr. Shaffer has created from all this is richly rewarding on a number of levels. It is by no means a clinical documentary, though it does have elements of this about it. Yet its nub is to be found in the doctor's relationship with the boy, and his growing realization that the boy has a fantasy love for horses. For it is a love, he actually finds in horses the spirit that Mr. Shaffer calls Equus, a deification of the horse as a life force, and the boy has entered realms of passion and, in a sense, reality, that his own humdrum existence has never known. He has an unkissed wife, an antiquarian interest in Greek relics and a whole tally of little, medium boredoms. He lives, as he recognizes, to a small if safe scale.

He comes to realize the uniqueness of the boy. "That boy," he says, "has known a passion more intense than any I felt all my life." He does not excuse, of course, the horrific results of that passion, but he is sheerly impressed by the Dionysiac strength of its existence. He can patch up the boy's tortured mind and psyche, and send it out on the street. But what will be lost in spiritual energy? "Passion can be destroyed by a doctor, it cannot be created."

The play is quite different from anything Mr. Shaffer has written before, and has, to my mind, a quite new sense of seriousness to it. It has all of Mr. Shaffer's masterly command of the theater.

He has his theater set up here as a kind of bull-ring with a section of the audience actually sitting on stage, like confident graduate students watching a class. And most adroitly, he runs through many of the patterns of clinical psychiatry, from elementary hypnotism to the abreaction, whereby the patient re-enacts circumstances of his trauma.

Mr. Shaffer was always a great juggler of the theater, whether it was in making his well-made play, such as *Five Finger Exercises* or constructing a musicless Verdi spectacular in *The Royal Hunt of the Sun.* But in *Equus* he has found a different métier. It is still a popularly intended play—it is essentially a Broadway vehicle for star actors—but it has a most refreshing and mind-opening intellectualism. It has the power of thought to it. Take one: "A child is born into a world of phenomena, all equal in their power to enslave." This, just as sample, has a quality of thoughtfulness to it that is rare in the contemporary popular theater.

John Dexter has directed it beautifully. The staging catches just the right element of court drama, mystery thriller and philosophical exposition. The direction holds all the elements of the play together with consummate skill, and I was also impressed by the mimetic conception of the horses devised by Claude Chagrin. It is not easy to present men playing horses on stage without provoking giggles—here the horses live up to their reputed godhead.

The performances blaze with theatrical life. Oddly—and perhaps intentionally—Mr. Firth's performance as the victim-assailant is set apart from the rest, keyed into a kind of naturalism the others do not attempt.

It is a marvelous performance by a young man who has the makings of a great actor.

The rest are the background, yes, even the psychiatrist who by any count has the most important role, if only because it represents the playwright himself coming to terms with alienation. Anthony Hopkins, articulate and troubled, is superb in opposition to the unyielding suspicion and wary tenseness of Mr. Firth. It is a virtuoso performance gauged to a fraction.

The casting was exemplary, with Michael Higgins and Frances Sternhagen as the worried, guilty but uncomprehending parents, Roberta Maxwell as the young girl who involuntarily triggers the tragedy, and Marian Seldes as an admonishing psychiatrist.

This is a very fine and enthralling play. It holds you by the root of drama, and it adds immeasurably to the fresh hopes we have for Broadway's future.

Clive Barnes ON
A Chorus Line
BOOK BY James Kirkwood AND
Nicholas Dante
LYRICS BY Edward Kleban
MUSIC BY Marvin Hamlisch

May 21, 1975
Newman/Public Theater
6,137 Performances

A CHORUS LINE, conceived, choreographed and directed by Michael Bennett. Book by James Kirkwood and Nicholas Dante; music by Marvin Hamlisch; lyrics by Edward Kleban; co-choreographer, Bob Avian; setting by Robin Wagner; costumes by Theoni V. Aldredge; lighting by Tharon Musser; orchestrations by Bill Byers, Hershy Kay and Jonathan Tunick; music coordinator, Robert Thomas; music direction and vocal arrangements by Don Pippin; production stage manager, Jeff Hamlin. Presented by the New York Shakespeare Festival Public Theater, Joseph Papp, producer, Bernard Gersten, associate producer.
With Scott Allen, Renée Baughman, Carole Bishop, Pamela Blair, Wayne Cilento, Chuck Cissel, Clive Clerk, Kay Cole, Ronald Dennis, Donna Drake, Brandt Edwards, Patricia Garland, Carolyn Kirsch, Ron Kuhlman, Nancy Lane, Baayork Lee, Priscilla Lopez, Robert LuPone, Cameron Mason, Donna McKechnie, Don Percassi, Michael Serrecchia, Michel Stuart, Thomas J. Walsh, Sammy Williams and Crissy Wilzak.

The conservative word for *A Chorus Line* might be tremendous, or perhaps terrific. Michael Bennett's new-style musical opened at the Newman Theater of the New Shakespeare Festival Public Theater on Lafayette Street last night, and the reception was so shattering that it is surprising if, by the time you read this, the New York Shakespeare Festival has got a Newman Theater still standing in its Public Theater complex on Lafayette Street. It was that kind of reception, and it is that kind of a show.

We have for years been hearing about innovative musicals; now Mr. Bennett has really innovated one. *A Chorus Line* takes a close, hard squint at Broadway babies on parade—here and now. The scene is a Broadway gypsy encampment—and the chorus, and how to get into it, is the line of battle.

It is easy to see from where *A Chorus Line* evolved. It is in direct succession to Harold Prince's *Company,* and, to a lesser extent, *Cabaret* and *Follies.* The debt is unmistakable, but it has been paid in full. What makes *A Chorus Line* so devastatingly effective is its honesty of subject matter—so that even its faults can work for it.

Show-business musicals always start with a certain advantage. Even their clichés can pass for justifiable observation of the form, and Mr. Bennett was obviously aware of this when he had his idea. But the idea is bright—indeed, it glows like a beacon heavenward. Like most great ideas it is simple. It is nothing but the anatomy of a chorus line. And the gypsies themselves—those dear, tough, soft-bitten Broadway show dancers, who are the salt and the earth of the small white way—are all neatly dissected as if they were a row of chickens. Their job-hunger, their sex lives, their failures (because even the best of them never thought of themselves forever in the chorus but 99 per cent of them will be there until they drop or drop out), their feeling toward dancing, why they started and what they might do when they stop—all is under a coruscatingly cruel microscope.

Of course, the show—which has been brilliantly written by James Kirkwood and Nicholas Dante—has a long streak of sentimentality where its heart might have been, but this is show business, baby, and even the sentimentality is true to form. We accept it—and rightly so—as part of the scene. For Mr. Bennett has found a marvelous set-up for his exploration into the life and times of the contemporary show dancer. It is an audition.

The director of a new show has whittled down his choice of twenty-three people to seventeen. The seventeen are lined up before him. He needs eight, or what he calls "four and four." Four boys and four girls—and "how about us women?" as one of the girls says. One by one—as he calls them out—he has them step from the line and talk. Talk about themselves—what they are doing there in that rehearsal hall on that morning. It is psychological striptease, and slowly the kids undress in a series of sad if funny vignettes. There is the girl who wanted to be a ballerina, the boy who discovered he was homosexual, the girl who flunked Stanislavsky motivation at the High School of Performing Arts and the somewhat elderly Puerto Rican boy who never had his father call him son until he found him working in a drag show. (Try to get the Stanislavsky motivation for that one—it is beyond me.)

Even the director has a story to tell. His girl, fearful of the saccharine smell of his success, walked out on him, and now, after failure and heartbreak in Los Angeles, she is back, in the audition, trying to win a way back onto the chorus line. Yet somehow all the hokum works—because it is undisguised and unapologetic.

The music by Marvin Hamlisch is occasionally hummable and often quite cleverly drops into a useful buzz of dramatic recitative. Mr. Hamlisch is not such a good composer as he was in the movie *The Sting* when he was being helped out by Scott Joplin, but he can pass, and the lyrics by Edward Kleban do more than that, they pass with a certain distinction, while the look of the show (an explosion of mirrors that may owe something to the *Cabaret* set but is still food for reflection) and the cast is 105 per cent marvelous.

One simply must mention a few—Donna McKechnie as the prodigal Chorine, for example, is wonderfully right, as are Clive Clerk as the reluctant drag artist, Priscilla Lopez as the histrionic dropout, Carole Bishop as the fast-talking brunette who wasn't even born the day before yesterday, and Robert LuPone as the uptight director, who, like all the others, could be a portrait, or a composite portrait, of so many failed successes. For honesty is the policy of Mr. Bennett's show, and from opening to the stupendous closing chorus, it is, stamped indelibly, as Mr. Bennett's show.

His choreography and direction burn up

superlatives as if they were inflammable. In no way could it have been better done.

It is in a small theater and here, at last, is the intimate big musical. Everything is made to work. The groupings are always faultless, the dances have the right Broadway surge, and two numbers, the mirror-dance for Miss McKechnie and the Busby Berkeley–inspired finale deserve to become classics of musical staging. And talking of classics, while there will be some to find fault, perhaps with a certain reason, with the hard-edged glossiness of *A Chorus Line,* it is a show that must dance, jog and whirl its way into the history of the musical theater. *Oklahoma!* it isn't, but no one with strength to get to the box office should willingly miss it. You will talk about it for weeks.

Clive Barnes ON
For Colored Girls . . .
BY Ntozake Shange

June 1, 1976
Anspacher/Public Theater
742 Performances

The playwright Ntozake Shange *(right rear)* also acted in her lyric drama of black sisterhood, *For Colored Girls Who Have Considered Suicide / When the Rainbow Is Enuf.*
SY FRIEDMAN

FOR COLORED GIRLS WHO HAVE CONSIDERED SUICIDE/WHEN THE RAINBOW IS ENUF, by Ntozake Shange. Directed by Oz Scott; choreography by Paula Moss; costumes by Judy Dearing; lighting by Vitor En Yu Tan; mural by Ifa Iyaun; music by Diana Wharton; stage manager, John Beven. Presented by the New York Shakespeare Festival, Joseph Papp, producer.

Lady in Rose	Janet League
Lady in Yellow	Aku Kadago
Lady in Red	Trazana Beverley
Lady in Green	Paula Moss
Lady in Purple	Rise Collins
Lady in Blue	Laurie Carlos
Lady in Orange	Ntozake Shange

Black sisterhood. That is what Ntozake Shange's totally extraordinary and wonderful evening at Joseph Papp's Anspacher Theater, in the Lafayette Street Public Theater complex, is all about. It has those insights into life and living that make the theater such an incredible marketplace for the soul. And simply because it is about black women—not just blacks and not just women—it is a very humbling but inspiring thing for a white man to experience.

To be black and to be a woman is a kind of double infirmity that must be faced with courage. Miss Shange's evening of prose and poetry—it is given by seven brilliant black actresses, including herself—is a lyric and tragic exploration into black woman's awareness. Not that Miss Shange is sorry for herself or any of her sisters, she is angry and contemptuous. At the end, the seven women sing, it is a kind of chant, "I found God in myself and I loved Her—fearlessly." It was an inspiring moment of theater, and a real gesture of life.

The play, the evening, whatever, is called *For Colored Girls Who Have Considered Suicide/When the Rainbow Is Enuf.* In a sense the title tells it all—and with the same, tense poetic beauty that characterizes the play's statement and its writing.

The writing flies into the air like dark swallows. Miss Shange can describe Harlem as "six blocks of cruelty piled up on itself," and her own situation as "I couldn't stand being colored and sorry at the same time—it seems redundant in the modern world."

The evening is composed of poems and stories

that go deeply, profoundly and lovingly into what it is like to be black and not beautiful. Of course Miss Shange writes with such exquisite care and beauty that anyone can relate to her message. Fundamentally—if we have any sensitivity or sensibility at all—we all feel the same things. We just need poets and other strangers to point them out to us. She says, "I survive on intimacy and tomorrow," and most of us do, or, more dramatically perhaps, "I will tell all of your secrets into your face." That is beautiful, pungent, accurate writing. It has leanness and accuracy to it that purges the mind.

This collage of a black woman's existence is never for a moment maudlin or sentimental. The woman is tough and together and as funny as a comic strip. She has a way of striking to the heart of a situation with both perception and skepticism. The tone of the writing might be expressed by her wistful yet still demanding phrase, "I was missing something promised." That is the mood of this black on black, canary-colored evening.

She will tell a story of a man getting a woman pregnant—the actress in the role plays both the man and the woman—and demanding to marry her. And yet the woman doesn't want to. The man is a mental rapist. As blackmail, he takes their two children and holds them out the window. The woman lives on the fifth floor. And then he drops them. Yet even to this story there is a rugged, jail-yard humor, and always—with such an almost, but not quite, evident melodrama—a total sense of reality. The reality of a woman who has been there, cried a little and taken notes.

This is true folk poetry. It springs from the earth with the voice of people talking with that peculiarly precise clumsiness of life. It is the gaucheness of love. It is the jaggedness of actuality.

The play has been directed by Oz Scott as if he had not had to direct it at all—which is the ultimate achievement—and the actresses are simply wonderful. Just watch the way they react to one another, smile or look away, this is ensemble playing of great quality. The actresses were Trazana Beverley, Laurie Carlos, Rise Collins, Aku Kadago, Janet League, Paula Moss, and Miss Shange.

Mr. Papp last year gave us *A Chorus Line,* for which we are grateful. But this, while it may prove caviar to the general, is much more important. It could very easily have made me feel guilty at being white and male. It didn't. It made me feel proud at being a member of the human race, and with the joyous discovery that a white man can have black sisters.

Clive Barnes ON
The Cherry Orchard
BY Anton Chekhov

February 17, 1977
Vivian Beaumont Theater
48 Performances

Irene Worth as Madame Ranevskaya and Raul Julia as Lopakhin in Chekhov's *The Cherry Orchard* SY FRIEDMAN

THE CHERRY ORCHARD, a comedy by Anton Chekhov, new English version by Jean-Claude van Itallie. Directed by Andrei Serban; setting and costumes by Santo Loquasto; lighting by Jennifer Tipton; incidental music by Elizabeth Swados; dance arranged by Kathryn Posin; production manager, Andrew Mihok. Presented by the New York Shakespeare Festival, Joseph Papp, producer, Bernard Gersten, associate producer.

Yermolay Alexeyevich Lopakhin......................Raul Julia
Dunyasha ....Meryl Streep
Semyon Panteleyevich Yepikhodov ....Max Wright
Anya..Marybeth Hurt
Lyubov Andreyevna Ranevskaya ....Irene Worth
Leonid Andreyevich Gayev ....George Voskovec

Charlotta Ivanovna ....Cathryn Damon
Simeonov-Pischik.....................................C. K. Alexander
Yasha ....Ben Masters
Firs...Dwight Marfield
Pyotor Sergeyevich Trofimov................Michael Cristofer
Vagrant...Jon De Vries
Stationmaster ....William Duff-Griffin

To stage a classic is an easy thing but to restore that classic to the hands, mind and blood of its creator is in itself an act of creativity. And that is precisely what Andrei Serban and his team of collaborators and clowns have done with their production of Anton Chekhov's *The Cherry Orchard,* which opened last night at the Vivian Beaumont Theater. It is a celebration of genius, like the cleaning of a great painting, a fresh exposition of an old philosophy.

We in the English-speaking world have frequently been accused of disregarding Chekhov's comedy, and of permitting even his sternly satirical political purpose to get lost in some kind of undertow of romantic sentiment. This *Cherry Orchard* will have none of that; indeed, it is not only a comedy, it is a comedy played as a tragic farce. And what makes it a tragic farce is the political understanding brought to it by the director and adaptor, Jean-Claude van Itallie, who has taken liberties in the cause of freedom and justice.

It is a play, basically and simplistically, about the death of a civilization described in the metaphor of the death of a house. In this house are those who regret the civilization passing, those who do not understand such a development, those who accept it and those who even mock it. Because the players in this charade of decaying death are people rather than puppets you are touched, and because they are even clowns rather than people you are amused. When you are both amused and touched something very special happens to our hearts—they are uplifted to the giddy, bitter laughter of the gods.

Mr. Van Itallie has certainly taken some freedom with the text—not only with its tone, which is refreshingly idiomatic, but with the words themselves. In that great revolutionary scene where that eternal flame of a student, Trofimov, is trying to give the young girl, Anya, a vision of a new future for Russia, this translation has him say of her society: "You are living at the expense of the people who were your slaves."

Now the more conventional, and more readily poetic, translation I have before me as I write puts it: "Now think, Anya, your grandfather, your great-grandfather, and all your ancestors were serf-owners, proprietors of living souls." The change may not seem very significant, but the accumulation of such changes places the play into more immediate focus than is usual.

Mr. Serban's direction is, generally speaking, content to leave politics to the text. He presents the play as a ritual of change. He will, here and there, use political symbols—a frieze of laboring peasants lumbering across the backcloth, while more fortunate souls enter giggling—yet mostly it is the gracious decline and fall of old Russia that seems to intrigue him, and he makes this into a moving picture of hearts in transition.

Mr. Seban employs the Beaumont stage as it has never been used before—although in fairness, Ellis Rabb came close to it in his staging of *The Merchant of Venice* many years ago. The idea is to use it merely as height and depth, allowing the theatrical space, which most directors find so tricky to assess in this theater to take care of itself, indeed simply to be defined by the movement.

Apart from the ballroom scene, the designer, Santo Loquasto (here surpassing even himself), has arranged for no setting as such. There is a vast white carpet, the suggestion of white walls at the side and a huge curtain across the back of the stage, flown right up to the flies. There are sometimes light projections behind this curtain—marvelous lighting, by the way, from Jennifer Tipton—but for the most part it is a spectral backdrop to various props and bits of furniture.

What is the theater of ritual? It is difficult to describe in ten minutes or so, but for Mr. Serban it involves the use of choreographic masses, carefully posed sculptural groups and, within this ritualistic patterning, a specific style of acting—which here is enormously inventive but broad farce. Mr. Serban and his friends make a pratfall into a sonnet and a flutter into a joke.

This technique enables the many-layered texture of the play to make its full effect—so we see the pattern, watch the jokes, and listen to the sadly abrasive poetry of a civilization that has lost its moorings and is about to float out into the never-never sea of history.

Before mentioning the actors—space does not let me do justice to them—let me just tip my typewriter in salute to the incidental music by Elizabeth Swados and the Ballroom Dance arranged by Kathryn Posin. The actors should be taken out in alphabetical order, stood against a wall and have roses thrown at them.

Where does one start—of course, with Irene Worth, as Madame Ranevskaya, who was peerless among her set of peers. The range and cadences of her voice have the serenity of accepted sadness, and she moves across the stage as if it were the living room of her heart.

The others all sensitively grasped the intense physicality of the production, its visual speed and daring, its contacts with people and objects. How good, for example, was Meryl Streep as a sexy maid, or Cathryn Damon as a bizarre Fellini-style governess, or George Voskovec as Madame Ranevskaya's brother, or Raul Julia as a gracefully clumsy Lopakhin, or Max Wright as the clumsily graceful clerk, or C. K. Alexander as an impoverished landowner, or Marybeth Hurt and Priscilla Smith as two kinds of hopeful youth, or Ben Masters and Dwight Marfield as two kinds of servant, or Michael Cristofer as a student with his feet in the past and his eye on the future. How good they were.

At the very end, when Firs comes to die—he pushes his way through the curtain, finds no one in the house, and curls up fetus-fashion for the final touch of death—suddenly, a young girl rushes in at the back bearing flowers, and the symbolic picture of the new, industrialized Russia lights up dimly at the back. That is theater—if only it were also modern Russia. But this lyric poem of Russia on the eve of revolution has never been funnier, more tragic or more moving. Not in my experience. The State Department should send it instantly to its spiritual home—the Moscow Art Theater.

Richard Eder ON
Uncommon Women and Others
BY Wendy Wasserstein

November 21, 1977
Marymount Manhattan Theater
22 Performances

UNCOMMON WOMEN AND OTHERS by Wendy Wasserstein. Directed by Steven Robman; setting and lighting by James Tilton; costumes by Jennifer von Mayrhauser; production stage manager, Tom Aberger. Presented by the Phoenix Theater, T. Edward Hambleton, managing director; Daniel Freudenberger, artistic director.

Kate Quin	Jill Eikenberry
Samantha Stewart	Ann McDonough
Holly Kaplan	Alma Cuervo
Muffet DiNicola	Ellen Parker
Rita Altabel	Swoosie Kurtz
Mrs. Plumm	Josephine Nichols
Susie Friend	Cynthia Herman
Carter	Anna Levine
Leilah	Glenn Close

Wendy Wasserstein has satirical instincts and an eye and ear for the absurd, but she shows signs of harnessing these talents to a harder discipline.

Her play *Uncommon Women and Others,* which the Phoenix Theater opened last night at its Marymount Manhattan stage, is exuberant to the point of coltishness. Miss Wasserstein, who is young, uses her very large gift for being funny and acute with a young virtuosity that is often self-indulgent.

But there is more. Unexpectedly, just when her hilarity threatens to become gag-writing, she blunts it with compassion. She blunts her cleverness with what, if it is not yet remarkable wisdom, is a remarkable setting-out to look for it. She lets her characters—some of them, anyway—get away from her and begin to live and feel for themselves.

Uncommon Women is about women in a time of changing traps: new ones, set and hidden in the same current of feminine consciousness and liberation that is springing the old ones. Although the play deals with feminist ideas, it is not so much interested in the traps as in the women. It does not disassociate itself from the march but it concerns itself with blisters.

The women are a group of friends at Mount Holyoke, one of the Seven Sisters colleges. We see them in flashbacks that take off from a reunion they hold six years after graduation. Only a small part of the focus is upon the changes that have taken place since; the time has not been long enough for them to be very great. The main emphasis is upon the lacerations, hopes, despairs and confusions that the times inflict upon these students at a hatchery for "uncommon women," where walls have turned porous and let all the winds blow through.

The institution is caricatured to a degree, largely through the personage of Susie—not a member of the group—who upholds such school traditions as folding one's napkin in a floral pattern, and Elves. These are seniors who slip chocolate kisses anonymously into freshmen's mailboxes to make them feel loved.

Susie, played with dismaying bounciness by Cynthia Herman, is a comic cartoon, very funny but hardly believable. So is her opposite, Carter, a genius freshman who sits catatonically on the floor practicing typing to the rhythm of the "Hallelujah" Chorus and plans to make a movie about Wittgenstein. Anna M. Levine, looking like a Jules Feiffer drawing, is wonderfully woozy in the part, particularly when she dances the Dying Swan to a calypso tape.

These two caricatures mingle awkwardly with the more rounded and believable figures of the students who are the heart of the play. There is Kate, handsome, active, programmed for success as a future lawyer but terrified by it. There is Muffet, who is torn between being liberated and wanting to find her Prince. There is Rita, quirky, funny and appealing, with her detailed obsession with the sexual aspects of liberation and her determination to be a fantastic person by the time she is thirty. And there is Holly, rich, overweight, full of longing and indecision.

A terror of choices and the future afflicts all of them, and Miss Wasserstein has made this anguish most movingly real, amid all the jokes and the knowing sophistication.

On the other hand, Samantha has made her choice. She is a sunny and exuberant character, recognizes the limits that her emotions place upon her, and announces that she is getting married. There is a fine, buried sharpness in her character—"A closet wit," someone calls her—and her choice is respected by the others who cannot command the same simplicity. "Walking into Samantha's room is like walking into a clean sheet," Muffet complains, but affectionately.

If the characters, in their outlines, represent familiar alternatives and contradictions, Miss Wasserstein has made each of them most real. They do not stay within what they represent: In the reunion scene, set in the present, each has softened or shifted and they will go on doing so. Miss Wasserstein's is an interim report and a convincing one.

Her gifts for characterization are supported by Steven Robman's supple and inventive direction, and by splendid acting. Jill Eikenberry makes elegance and grace seem like a trap as the overachieving Kate. Ellen Parker is wry and cheerful as Muffet, with a hidden threat of a future breakout. Ann McDonough sometimes overdoes Samantha's bubbliness, but she puts a sting into it.

Swoosie Kurtz transforms the part of Rita, which lacks definition in the writing. Miss Kurtz is anguish propelling a graceful oddity; her electric restlessness—her tongue revolves and sets her wrist revolving; the wrist sets off the ankle until all is loops and loopiness—keeps the stage continuously alive.

Alma Cuervo plays Holly with a melancholy that won't be pinned down or sympathized with. She makes a hopeful, hysterical and finally heartbreaking telephone call to a man she has met casually; gives up finally, and covers herself with her raccoon coat. It is the play's most luminous and heartbreaking scene.

Uncommon Women contains enough specific sex talk to cover the walls of every women's lavatory in the World Trade Center. It is believable, sometimes funny and sometimes touching, but it becomes excessive. One has only to imagine this to be a play about men to realize just how excessive.

Richard Eder ON
Ain't Misbehavin'

May 9, 1978
Longacre Theater
1,604 Performances

Nell Carter *(left),* Andre De Shields and Armelia McQueen in *Ain't Misbehavin'* MARTHA SWOPE

AIN'T MISBEHAVIN' a musical, based on an idea by Murray Horwitz and Richard Maltby Jr. Music supervision and pianist, Luther Henderson; associate director, Murray Horwitz; orchestrations and arrangements by Mr. Henderson; vocal arrangements by William Elliott and Jeffrey Gutcheon; settings by John Lee Beatty; costumes by Randy Barcelo; lighting by Pat Collins; musical numbers staged by Arthur Faria; conceived and directed by Mr. Maltby; production stage manager, Richard Evans. Presented by Emanuel Azenberg, Dasha Epstein, the Shubert Organization, Jane Gaynor and Ron Dante. With Nell Carter, Andre De Shields, Armelia McQueen, Ken Page and Charlaine Woodward.

What whistles, hoots, throws off sparks and moves at about 180 miles an hour, even though it is continually stopped?

Ain't Misbehavin'.

This musical re-creation of Fats Waller, the jazz singer and pianist, is a whole cluster of marvels. No self-respecting audience could let it go on without interrupting it continually, and if the audience at the Longacre Theater, where it opened last night, was self-respecting to start off, it ended up in a state of agitated delight.

There are approximately thirty numbers in the show, conceived and directed by Richard Maltby Jr. with a lot of help from some extraordinary talented friends. Most were written by Fats (Thomas) Waller, who died in 1943 on the Super Chief after whizzing through the twenties and thirties. Others were songs he recorded, and there are a few purely musical numbers to which Mr. Maltby has set lyrics.

A whole series of the jazz worlds of the time, uptown and downtown, raffish and posh—the posh had an edge of mockery to it—funny and startlingly beautiful, came to life. We are conducted through it by five singers, a gentle-fingered, garter-sleeved pianist named Luther Henderson, and a small band in the background.

The set, by John Lee Beatty, is simple: concentric red arches that concentrate the action on the Longacre's relatively small stage. If the five performers, all of them talented and three of them magnificent, ever flagged in holding the stage, there was always the piano. Tall and ornate as a small cathedral, it had an engaging way of moving around.

When Mr. Henderson got into his most vigorous stride—a two-beat rhythm: bass-note, chord, bass-note, chord—the piano sidled sideways as if being pumped. At the end of the first act, when the cast cake-walked off-stage, the piano bobbed along after them.

The company warms up with the show's title song, engagingly performed. This is ground-level, relatively speaking, pleasant as it is. It leads up to one of the half-dozen totally charged, hair-raising numbers that lift the show from merely delightful to electrifying.

This first peak is "Honeysuckle Rose." Rather, it is Ken Page, portly, loose-jointed and gravel-voiced, holding his stomach so it won't get away and belting out one note that he holds past resuscitation. Having held it, he tastes it, wrinkles his mouth, and looks rueful. And into his arms, like a large parcel mailing itself, sidles Nell Carter. Round-faced and rounder-bodied, she establishes beyond doubt and with metallic lyric conviction that she is unquestionably the honeysuckle rose that all the fuss is about.

Without waiting for the dust to settle they exit, giving the piano a casual twirl, it turns a half-turn, and there, plastered to the back, is the show's third star, Armelia McQueen. She is not merely round but spherical, and she smiles a demure smile that looks as if maggots had broken in overnight and laid eggs in it. Her high, breathy "Squeeze Me" is hilarious parody; she is the baby-doll to put an end to the species.

Nell Carter comes back and with a blaring "OW!" starts "I've Got a Feeling I'm Falling," one of the show's most devastating numbers. Miss Carter can blare like a trumpet, moan like a muted trumpet, and do a hundred variations on breathiness. Her "Mean to Me" is sung quietly, but with a silvery, delicate pungency—her round face suddenly becomes a prism of shifting expressions—that could lead an army.

Some of the songs are performed as skits, and some of these are very funny. "How Ya Baby" is a crackling dance performed by Andre De Shields and Charlaine Woodward, who juggles her thin frame as if she were six hoops all in the air at once. Mr. Page has the show's funniest number, "Your Feet's Too Big," delivered in high indignation and top form.

By comparison with Miss Carter, Miss McQueen and Mr. Page, the other two performers are weaker. Miss Woodward moves marvelously, but she is not a very interesting singer; and it is pure singing that is the heart of this show. Mr. De Shields is quite out of place; he is bland and mannered and his skill lacks the besotted conviction that makes *Ain't Misbehavin* behave so beautifully. His "The Viper's Drag," a long number about a man stoned on reefers, is the show's one real failure.

There are two or three other numbers that fall rather flat. Mr. Maltby's lyrics in a couple of pieces—"The Jitterbug Waltz" and "Lounging at the Waldorf"—are too wordy, and they overload the musical line. On the other hand his "Handful of Keys," where the singers vocalize the piano's stride effect, is charming.

These are small faults. They are hard to remember after the show's next-to-last number. The five singers sit perfectly still, hands folded, and break into "Black and Blue." But the plangent harmonies, the polyphonic quality, the majesty of this setting—the hallucinatory arrangement is by William Elliott—could be a spiritual, a Gesualdo madrigal, or any other musical work that operates on pure spirit. It is the heart of this heart-stopping *Ain't Misbehavin'*.

Richard Eder ON
Buried Child
BY Sam Shepard

November 6, 1978
Theater for the New City
152 Performances

Tom Noonan inspects the fur jacket worn by Mary McDonnell in *Buried Child.*   SHIRLEY HERZ

BURIED CHILD by Sam Shepard. Directed by Robert
  Woodruff; lighting by John P. Dodd; setting by
  David Gropman; costumes by Jess Goldstein. Presented by Bartenieff/Field, Theater for the New City,
  162 Second Avenue.

Dodge ....Richard Hamilton
Halie..Jacqueline Brookes
Tilden ....Tom Noonan
Bradley..Jay Sanders
Shelly..Mary McDonnell
Vince..Christopher McCann
Father Dewis..Bill Wiley

Sam Shepard does not merely denounce chaos
and anomie in American life, he mourns over
them. His corrosive images and scenes of absurdity never soften to concede the presence of a
lament, but it is there all the same.

Denunciation that has no pity in it is pamphle-
teering at best and a striking of fashionable attitudes at worst, and it is fairly common on the
contemporary stage. Mr. Shepard is an uncommon
playwright and uncommonly gifted and he does
not take denouncing for granted. He wrestles with
it at the risk of being thrown.

Recently he has been writing about families.
Curse of the Starving Class used the image of
physical hunger as a symbol of moral starvation.
It was a fierce, funny, unmanageable play whose
imagery never quite worked.

Buried Child, now at the Theater for the New
City, takes the same theme. As a piece of writing,
it may be less interesting but it seems to work far
better on the stage. In the very gifted production
directed by Robert Woodruff, it manages to be
vividly alive even as it is putting together a surreal
presentation of American intimacy withered by
rootlessness.

It takes the form of a homecoming. Vince, who
has been away for six years, comes home bringing
his saxophone and his Los Angeles girlfriend.
Home is an Illinois farm where his grandparents
live. It was flourishing once and he comes with the
most bucolic memories and a determination to get
to know his family and his roots.

What he finds is a house of the dying, full of
grotesques clinging to guilty secrets. His grandmother preaches morality and goes out on all-night
bashes with the local clergyman. His grandfather is
a bitter, self-absorbed drunk who, as it turns out,
has murdered an unwanted child. Vince's father,
Tilden, is half-crazed; he keeps bringing in arm-
loads of corn and carrots that grow even though
nobody has planted them. Finally, there is a brutal
uncle who has lost a leg to a chain saw.

It is a far cry from the apple pie, turkey, and
kindly old relatives that Shelly, the girl, has been
told to expect. By the time the visit is over she has
been insulted, assaulted, set to peel Tilden's supernatural carrots, and generally abused. Vince,
who had thought of the visit as a voyage through
memory, fares even worse. His memories don't remember him. His relatives ignore him or send him
out to buy whisky.

Dodge, the fierce, dying grandfather who is the
shattered heart of this American household, has no
use for progeny or for any future.

"You're all alike, you hopers," he tells Shelly, and clings to his whisky, his television and a battered baseball cap. The future is meaningless to him and the past is even more meaningless. "I'm descended from a long line of corpses," he says, "and there's not a living soul behind me." Shepard's America has poisoned its roots and destroyed its life.

But onstage each of these grotesques has as much individuality and vitality as the worst of William Faulkner's Snopeses. The director, Robert Woodruff, has seen to it that the play's judgments never eclipse their humanity. Each character is played in such a way that the symbolic function grows out of a very concrete humanity. We do not always understand these figures but we are almost always affected by them.

Richard Hamilton plays Dodge as if he were a scrawny old fighting cock. He sits feebly under his blanket, but one fierce hand whips out a whisky flask with the speed of a cobra's strike the moment the coast is clear. His eye glitters; it is mostly fixed in a senile introspection, but when it flashes upon another character it is like a spotlight.

Tom Noonan makes the hulking, inchoate Tilden a moving and powerful figure. He, more than any of the others, is the victim of the family's rootlessness; he dumbly reflects the play's mute compassion. So does Shelly, the girl. Mary McDonnell gives a splendid performance, making her grow from shallowness to experience with a tough and winning vitality. Jay Sanders, Jacqueline Brookes, Christopher McCann and Bill Wiley are all good in the somewhat less interesting roles of the cripple, the grandmother, Vince, and the clergyman.

Richard Eder ON
Sweeney Todd
BOOK BY Hugh Wheeler
MUSIC AND LYRICS BY Stephen Sondheim

March 1, 1979

Uris Theater

557 Performances

SWEENEY TODD, musical, with book by Hugh Wheeler; music and lyrics by Stephen Sondheim, based on *Sweeney Todd* by Christopher Bond; directed by Harold Prince; settings by Eugene Lee; costumes by Franne Lee; lighting by Ken Billington; orchestrations by Jonathan Tunick; musical direction by Paul Gemignani; production stage manager, Alan Hall. Presented by Richard Barr, Charles Woodward, Robert Fryer, Mary Lea Johnson and Martin Richards in association with Dean and Judy Manos; associate producer, Marc Howard.

Anthony Hope ....Victor Garber
Sweeney Todd ....Len Cariou
Beggar Woman ....Merle Louise
Mrs. Lovett ....Angela Lansbury
Judge Turpin ....Edmund Lyndeck
Beadle...Jack Eric Williams
Johanna ....Sarah Rice
Tobias Ragg ....Ken Jennings
Pirelli...Joaquin Rornaguera
Jonas Fogg ....Robert Ousley
The Company ....Duane Bodin, Walter Charles, Carole Doscher, Nancy Eaton, Mary-Pat Green, Cris Groenendaal, Skip Harris, Marthe Ihde, Betsy Joslyn, Nancy Killmer, Frank Kopyc, Spain Logue, Craig Lucas, Pamela McLernon, Duane Morris, Robert Ousley, Richard Warren Pugh, Maggie Task, Heather B. Withers and Robert Hendersen.

The musical and dramatic achievements of Stephen Sondheim's black and bloody *Sweeney Todd* are so numerous and so clamorous that they trample and jam each other in that invisible but finite doorway that connects a stage and its audience; doing themselves some harm in the process.

That is a serious reservation, and I will get back to it. But it is necessary to give the dimensions of the event. There is more of artistic energy, creative personality and plain excitement in *Sweeney Todd,* which opened last night at the enormous Uris Theater and made it seem like a cottage, than in a dozen average musicals.

It is in many ways closer to opera than to most musicals; and in particular, and sometimes too much for its own good, to the Brecht-Weill *Three-penny Opera.* Mr. Sondheim has composed an endlessly inventive, highly expressive score that works indivisibly from his brilliant and abrasive lyrics.

It is a powerful, coruscating instrument, this muscular partnership of words and music. Mr. Sondheim has applied it to making a Grand Guignol opera with social undertones. He has used a legend commemorated in broad-sheets, and made into a half-dozen nineteenth-century play versions; and most recently into a modern version written by Christopher Bond and shown in London in the early seventies.

It is the story of a barber, unjustly convicted and transported to Australia by a wicked judge who coveted his wife. Upon his return the barber takes the name Sweeney Todd, and takes his general and particular revenge by slitting the throats of his clients, who are then turned into meat pies by his industrious associate, Mrs. Lovett.

Mr. Sondheim and his director, Harold Prince, have taken this set of rattle-trap fireworks and made it into a glittering, dangerous weapon. With the help of Hugh Wheeler, who adapted the book from Mr. Bond's play, they amplify every grotesque and exaggerated detail and step up its horsepower.

The set, a great contraption like a foundry with iron beams, moving bridges, and clanking wheels and belts, is grim and exuberant at the same time. When a back panel, a festering mass of rusty corrugated iron, lifts, a doleful scene of industrial London is exposed.

In stylized attitudes, and gutter costumes, a whole London underworld appears, serving, in the manner of *The Three-penny Opera,* as populace and as sardonic chorus. In cut-off, laconic phrases they sing verses of the "Sweeney Todd Ballad"; a

work whose musical strength is deliberately bitten off until it swells out in the bloody finale.

Sweeney, played by Len Cariou, appears from a hole in the ground. He is lit throughout like a corpse. Mr. Cariou, his eyes sad and distracted, his hair parted foppishly in the middle, dresses and carries himself like a seedy failure; but a failure illuminated by a vision.

Mr. Cariou is to some degree the prisoner of his anguish: he slits throats with lordly abstraction but his role as deranged visionary doesn't give him much variety. He is such a strong actor, and such a fine singer, though, that he makes up for it with a kind of glow.

Angela Lansbury has more opportunities as Mrs. Lovett, and she makes towering use of them. Her initial number, in which she sings of selling the worst pies in London, while pounding dough and making as many purposefully flailing gestures as a pinwheel, is a triumph.

Her songs, many of them rapid patter songs with awkward musical intervals; and having to be sung while doing five or ten other things at once, are awesomely difficult and she does them awesomely well. Her voice is a visible voice; you can follow it amid any confusion; it is not piercing but piping. Her face is a comic face; her eyes revolve three times to announce the arrival of an idea; but there is a blue sadness blinking behind them.

Mr. Sondheim's lyrics can be endlessly inventive. There is a hugely amusing recitation of the attributes given by the different professions— priest, lawyer, and so on—to the pies they contribute to. At other times the lyrics have a black, piercing poetry to them.

His score is extraordinary. From the pounding "Sweeney Todd Ballad," to a lovely discovery theme given to Todd's young friend, Anthony, in various appearances, to the most beautiful "Green Finch and Linnet Bird" sung by Johanna, Todd's daughter, and through many others, Mr. Sondheim gives us all manner of musical strength.

He has strength to burn, in fact. Two marvelous songs, constructed in the style of early nineteenth-century ballads, are virtually throw-aways. Mr. Sondheim disciplines his music, insisting that it furnish power to the work as a whole and not function separately. Sometimes we wish he would let go a little; the "Green Finch" song, so lovely, is imprisoned in its own activity.

Mr. Prince has staged the unfolding story in a series of scenes, contrasting with each other, but sharing the central tone of comedy laid over grimness. Mr. Prince's effects are always powerful, and sometimes excessively so. The throat cuttings, for example, repeated half a dozen times, are simply too bloody. They are used on us like beatings.

Besides Mr. Cariou and Miss Lansbury, Victor Garber is most attractive as Anthony, Ken Jennings is strong and touching as Tobias, a hapless apprentice, and Jack Eric Williams is funny and sings beautifully as the villainous Beadle.

There is very little in *Sweeney Todd* that is not, in one way or other, a display of extraordinary talent. What keeps all its brilliance from coming together as a major work of art is a kind of confusion of purpose.

For one thing, Mr. Sondheim's and Mr. Prince's artistic force makes the Grand Guignol subject matter work excessively well. That is, what needs a certain disbelief to be tolerable—we have to be able to laugh at the crudity of the characters and their actions—is given too much artistic power. The music, beautiful as it is, succeeds, in a sense, in making an intensity that is unacceptable.

Furthermore, the effort to fuse this Grand Guignol with a Brechtian style of sardonic social commentary doesn't work. There is, in fact, no serious social message in *Sweeney;* and at the end, when the cast lines up on the stage and points to us, singing that there are Sweeneys all about; the point is unproven.

These are defects; vital ones; but they are the failures of an extraordinary, fascinating, and often ravishingly lovely effort.

Frank Rich ON
Sister Mary Ignatius Explains It All for You
BY Christopher Durang

October 21, 1981
947 Performances

Mark Stefan and Elizabeth Franz in a scene from *Sister Mary Ignatius Explains It All for You* SUSAN COOK

SISTER MARY IGNATIUS EXPLAINS IT ALL FOR YOU and THE ACTOR'S NIGHTMARE, by Christopher Durang; directed by Jerry Zaks; set designer, Karen Schulz; costume designer, William Ivey Long; lighting designer, Paul Gallo; sound design, Aural Fixation. Presented by Playwrights Horizons, 416 West 42d Street.

THE ACTOR'S NIGHTMARE
George Spelvin ....Jeff Brooks
Meg ....Polly Draper
Sarah Siddons ....Elizabeth Franz
Dame Ellen Terry ....Mary Catherine Wright
Henry Irving..Timothy Landfield
and
SISTER MARY IGNATIUS EXPLAINS IT ALL FOR YOU
Sister Mary Ignatius ....Elizabeth Franz

Thomas...Mark Stefan
Diane Symonds...Polly Draper
Gary Sullavan ....Timothy Landfield
Philomena Rostovitch.................Mary Catherine Wright
Aloysius Benheim ....Robert Joy

Anyone can write an angry play—all it takes is an active spleen. But only a writer of real talent can write an angry play that remains funny and controlled even in its most savage moments. *Sister Mary Ignatius Explains It All for You* confirms that Christopher Durang is just such a writer. In this one-act comedy he goes after the Catholic Church with a vengeance that might well have shocked the likes of either Paul Krassner or Lenny Bruce, and yet he never lets his bitter emotions run away with his keen theatrical sense.

Sister Mary Ignatius, the second half of a Durang double bill that opened at the Playwrights Horizons last night, is both the most consistently clever and deeply felt work yet by the author of *A History of the American Film* and *Beyond Therapy*. Originally produced by the Ensemble Studio Theater two years ago, it has the sting of a revenge drama, even as it rides waves of demonic laughter. The play is also terribly honest, for Mr. Durang knows better than to give himself a total victory over his formidable antagonist. With pointed rue, he must finally leave the church bloodied but unbowed.

Sister Mary Ignatius (Elizabeth Franz) is an aging teacher conducting an assembly in the auditorium of Our Lady of Perpetual Sorrows School. She seems, at first, a reasonably kindly pedant. As she lectures her students on the "physical torments" of hell, her voice quivers with self-contentment, her mouth curls heavenward in a self-righteous smile. Nor is her *Going My Way* demeanor challenged by the impish student questions she reads from file cards. "Was Jesus effeminate?" asks one of her charges. "Yes!" replies Miss Franz, cheerily closing off any further debate.

For about half the play's length, Mr. Durang uses his glibly dissembling protagonist to illustrate what he regards as church hypocrisies. Sister Mary must do some fancy and unconvincing foot-

work to explain how supposedly "infallible" dogma could have been changed overnight by her least favorite Pope, John XXIII. She instructs her star pupil, the seven-year-old Thomas (Mark Stefan), to read "a partial list" of sinners going to hell—and the roll call includes Zsa Zsa Gabor, Christine Keeler, David Bowie, Betty Comden and Adolph Green. The nun also tends to fondle little Thomas just a shade too playfully—thus allowing Mr. Durang to score his wicked points about the hidden sexual quotient of ostensibly sinless celibacy.

Eventually, however, we see that there is one question that *does* throw Sister Mary: "If God is all powerful, why does He allow evil in the world?" And the playwright forces the nun to confront that issue when four grown-up former students show up to stage a Joseph-and-Mary pageant, complete with camel, for her current flock. The visitors all hated their despotic teacher; they soon try to settle the score by making her defend God and His rules in a world where rape and cancer seem to justify such sins as abortion and agnosticism.

Mr. Durang successfully escalates this comic confrontation to a literally violent climax that strips the nun's moral authority bare even as it allows her to retain her crippling psychological power over her students, past and present. As the playwright sees his villainess, she will tolerate no failings in others—but will gladly use church law to rationalize even murder when it suits her own authoritarian purposes. In making his extreme case, Mr. Durang receives strong help from the director, Jerry Zaks, who wisely keeps his actors in realistic bounds. The entire cast is first-rate, including Mr. Stefan's catechism-reciting choirboy, and Miss Franz is brilliant. After her real— and insane—personality is revealed, she still remains all too frighteningly human.

Mr. Zaks and company also do very well by the evening's curtain-raiser, *The Actor's Nightmare*. In this sketch, the playwright gives us what his title promises—a hero, appropriately named George Spelvin (Jeff Brooks), who suddenly finds himself on stage in a play he has never rehearsed.

The premise lets Mr. Durang show off his gift for theatrical and show-biz satire, for the play-within-the-play proves to be an ever-changing amalgam of *Private Lives, Hamlet, A Man for All Seasons* and the collected works of Beckett. Who but this writer would imagine that Godot *will* someday arrive—reeking of garlic and telling stewardess jokes?

The nebbishy, deadpan Mr. Brooks may be the least likely melancholy Dane since Jack Benny in *To Be or Not to Be;* he is most amusing as he calls on *Kiss Me, Kate* lyrics and other half-remembered theatrical lines to ad lib his way through his jam. Like the playwright and cast, the designers—Karen Schulz, William Ivey Long and Paul Gallo—run joyously amok plundering the styles of four centuries of theater. If *The Actor's Nightmare* finally runs out of jokes too early and fails in its effort to deepen its hero, it gets us as ready as possible for the unstoppably virulent comic nightmare that's soon to come.

Frank Rich ON
Dreamgirls
BOOK AND LYRICS BY Tom Eyen
MUSIC BY Henry Krieger

December 20, 1981
Imperial Theater
1,522 Performances

Jennifer Holliday *(left),* Sheryl Lee Ralph *(center)* and Loretta Devine in *Dreamgirls*   MARTHA SWOPE

DREAMGIRLS, book and lyrics by Tom Eyen; music by Henry Krieger; directed and choreographed by Michael Bennett; co-choreographer, Michael Peters; scenic design, Robin Wagner; costume design, Theoni V. Aldredge; lighting design, Tharon Musser; sound design, Otts Munderloh; musical supervision and orchestrations by Harold Wheeler; musical director, Yolanda Segovia; vocal arrangements, Cleavant Derricks. Presented by Michael Bennett, Bob Avian, Geffen Records and the Shubert Organization.

The Stepp Sisters	Deborah Burrell, Vanessa Bell, Tenita Jordan and Brenda Pressley
Charlene	Cheryl Alexander
Joanne	Linda Lloyd
Marty	Vondie Curtis-Hall
Curtis Taylor Jr.	Ben Harney
Deena Jones	Sheryl Lee Ralph
The M.C. and Mr. Morgan	Larry Stewart
Tiny Joe Dixon and Jerry	Joe Lynn
Lorrell Robinson	Loretta Devine
C.C. White	Obba Babatunde

Effie Melody White ....Jennifer Holliday
Little Albert and the Tru-Tones ....Wellington Perkins,
    Charles Bernard, Jamie Patterson, Charles Randolph-
                    Wright and Weyman Thompson
James Thunder Early ....Cleavant Derricks
Edna Burke ....Sheila Ellis
The James Early Band ....Charles Bernard, Jamie
    Patterson, Wellington Perkins, Scott Plank, Charles
              Randolph-Wright and Weyman Thompson
Wayne ....Tony Franklin
Dave and the Sweethearts ....Paul Binotto, Candy
                    Darling and Stephanie Eley
Frank ....David Thome
Michelle Morris ....Deborah Burrell
The Five Tuxedos ....Charles Bernard, Jamie
    Patterson, Charles Randolph-Wright, Larry Stewart
                            and Weyman Thompson
Les Style ....Cheryl Alexander, Tenita Jordan,
                    Linda Lloyd and Brenda Pressley
Film Executives ....Paul Binotto, Scott Plank and
                                Weyman Thompson
Announcers, Fans, Reporters, Stagehands, Party Guests
    and Photographers ....Cheryl Alexander,
    Phylicia Ayers-Allen, Vanessa Bell, Charles Bernard,
    Paul Binotto, Candy Darling, Ronald Dunham,
    Stephanie Eley, Sheila Ellis, Tenita Jordan, Linda
    Lloyd, Joe Lynn, Frank Mastrocola, Jamie Patter-
    son, Wellington Perkins, Scott Plank, Brenda Press-
    ley, David Thome, Charles Randolph-Wright, Larry
    Stewart and Weyman Thompson.

When Broadway history is being made, you can feel it. What you feel is a seismic emotional jolt that sends the audience, as one, right out of its wits. While such moments are uncommonly rare these days, I'm here to report that one popped up at the Imperial last night. Broadway history was made at the end of the first act of Michael Bennett's beautiful and heartbreaking new musical, *Dreamgirls*.

Dreamgirls is the story of a black singing group that rises from the ghetto to national fame and fortune during the 1960s. Like the Supremes, to which they bear more than a passing resemblance, the Dreams have their share of obstacles to overcome on the way up. At the end of Act I, the heroines are beginning to make it in Las Vegas, but there's some nasty business to be dealt with backstage. The act's hard-driving manager, Curtis (Ben Harney), has come into the Dreams' dressing room to inform Effie, who is both his lover and the group's best singer, that she is through.

Effie is through because the Dreams are at last escaping the showbiz ghetto of rhythm and blues to cross over into the promised and lucrative land of white pop. To take the final leap, the Dreams must change their image—to a new, more glamorous look and a "lighter" sound. Effie no longer fits: she's fat, and her singing is anything but light. And Curtis's bad news does not end there. Not only does he have a brand-new, svelte Dream in costume, ready to replace Effie on stage, but he also has chosen another Dream to replace Effie in his bed.

It's at this point that Jennifer Holliday, the actress who plays Effie, begs Curtis to let her stay, in a song titled "And I Am Telling You I'm Not Going." Miss Holliday is a young woman with a broad face and an ample body. Somewhere in that body—or everywhere—is a voice that, like Effie herself, won't take no for an answer. As Miss Holliday physically tries to restrain her lover from leaving, her heart pours out in a dark and gutsy blues; then, without pause, her voice rises into a strangled cry.

Shortly after that, Curtis departs, and Miss Holliday just keeps riding wave after wave of painful music—clutching her stomach, keeling over, insisting that the scoundrel who has dumped her is "the best man I'll ever know." The song can end only when Mr. Bennett matches the performer's brilliance with a masterstroke of his own—and it's a good thing that Act I of *Dreamgirls* ends soon thereafter. If the curtain didn't fall, the audience would probably cheer Jennifer Holliday until dawn.

And, with all due respect to our new star, there's plenty more to cheer. If Miss Holliday's Act I solo is one of the most powerful theatrical coups to be found in a Broadway musical since Ethel Merman sang "Everything's Coming Up Roses" at the end of Act I of *Gypsy,* so *Dreamgirls* is the same kind of breakthrough for musical stagecraft that *Gypsy* was.

In *Gypsy,* the director-choreographer Jerome Robbins and his collaborators made the most persuasive case to date (1959) that a musical could be an organic entity—in which book, score and staging merged into a single, unflagging dramatic force. Mr. Bennett has long been Mr. Robbins's Broadway heir apparent, as he has demonstrated in two previous *Gypsy*-like backstage musicals, *Follies* (which he staged with Harold Prince) and *A Chorus Line*. But last night the torch was passed, firmly, unquestionably, once and for all. Working with an unusually gifted new composer, Henry Krieger, and a clever librettist, the playwright Tom Eyen—as well as with a wholly powerhouse cast and design team—Mr. Bennett has fashioned a show that strikes with the speed and heat of lightning.

He has done so in a most imaginative way. *Dreamgirls* is full of plot, and yet it has virtually no spoken scenes. It takes place in roughly twenty locations, from Harlem to Hollywood, but it has not one realistic set. It is a show that seems to dance from beginning to end, yet in fact has next to no dance numbers.

How is this magic wrought? *Dreamgirls* is a musical with almost forty numbers, and virtually everything, from record-contract negotiations to lovers' quarrels, is sung. More crucially, Mr. Krieger has created an individual musical voice for every major player and interweaves them all at will: in one cathartic backstage confrontation ("It's All Over"), the clashing of seven characters is realized entirely in musical terms.

What's more, the score's method is reinforced visually by Robin Wagner's set. Mr. Wagner has designed a few mobile, abstract scenic elements—aluminum towers and bridges—and keeps them moving to form an almost infinite number of configurations. Like the show's voices, the set pieces—gloriously abetted by Tharon Musser's lighting and Theoni V. Aldredge's costumes—keep coming together and falling apart to create explosive variations on a theme.

Linking everything together is Mr. Bennett. He keeps *Dreamgirls* in constant motion—in every conceivable direction—to perfect his special brand of cinematic stage effects (montage, dissolve, wipe). As if to acknowledge his historical

debt to Mr. Robbins, he almost pointedly re-creates moments from *Gypsy* before soaring onward in his own original way.

Some of his images are chilling. In Act I, an exchange of payola money between two men blossoms into a surreal panorama of mass corruption that finally rises, like a vision out of hell, clear to the roof of the theater. Throughout the show, Mr. Bennett uses shadows and klieg lights, background and foreground action, spotlighted figures and eerie silhouettes, to maintain the constant tension between the dark and bright sides of his Dreamgirls' glittery dreams.

And in that tension is the emotional clout of the show. Like its predecessors among backstage musicals, *Dreamgirls* is about the price of success. Some of that price is familiar: broken love affairs, broken families, broken lives. But by telling the story of black entertainers who make it in white America, this musical's creators have dug into a bigger, more resonant drama of cultural assimilation. As the Dreams blunt the raw anger of their music to meet the homogenizing demands of the marketplace, we see the high toll of guilt and self-hatred that is inflicted on those who sell their artistic souls to the highest bidder. If "dreams" is the most recurrent word in the show, then "freedom" is the second, for the Dreams escape their ghetto roots only to discover that they are far from free.

This upsetting theme is woven into the evening's very fabric. Mr. Krieger gives the Dreams songs that perfectly capture the rhythm-and-blues music of the fifties, and then replays them throughout the evening to dramatize (and satirize) the ever-changing, ever-more-emasculated refining of the Motown sound. (Indeed, the Dreams' signature number is used to clock their personal and esthetic progression much as "Let Me Entertain You" was used in *Gypsy*.) Mr. Eyen has supplied ironic, double-edge lyrics (notably in a song called "Cadillac Car"), and Harold Wheeler's subtle, understated orchestrations are sensitive to every delicate nuance of the Dreams' advance through recent pop-music history.

Perhaps inevitably the cast's two standouts are

those who play characters who do not sell out and who suffer a more redemptive form of anguish: Miss Holliday's Effie and Cleavant Derricks, as a James Brown–like star whose career collapses as new musical fashions pass him by. Like Miss Holliday, Mr. Derricks is a charismatic singer, who conveys wounding, heartfelt innocence. When, in Act II, he rebels against his slick new Johnny Mathis-esque image by reverting to his old, untamed Apollo shenanigans during a fancy engagement, he gives *Dreamgirls* one of its most crushing and yet heroic solo turns. But everyone is superb: Mr. Harney's Machiavellian manager, Sheryl Lee Ralph's Diana Ross–like lead Dream, Loretta Devine and Deborah Burrell as her back-ups, Obba Babatunde as a conflicted songwriter and Vondie Curtis-Hall as a too-honest agent.

Is *Dreamgirls* a great musical? Well, one could quarrel with a few lapses of clarity, some minor sags, the overpat and frantic plot resolutions of Act II. But Mr. Bennett and Miss Holliday have staked their claim to greatness. And if the rest of *Dreamgirls* isn't always quite up to their incredible level, I'm willing to suspend judgment until I've sampled the evidence another four or five times.

Frank Rich ON

Cats

MUSIC BY Andrew Lloyd Webber

October 7, 1982

Winter Garden

7, 485 Performances

CATS, music by Andrew Lloyd Webber; based on *Old Possum's Book of Practical Cats* by T. S. Eliot; directed by Trevor Nunn; orchestrations by David Cullen and Mr. Lloyd Webber; production musical director, Stanley Lebowsky; musical director, René Wiegert; sound design by Martin Levan; lighting design by David Hersey; designed by John Napier; associate director and choreographer, Gillian Lynne; executive producers, R. Tyler Gatchell Jr. and Peter Neufeld. Presented by Cameron Mackintosh, The Really Useful Company Ltd., David Geffen and the Shubert Organization.

Alonzo...Hector Jaime Mercado
Bustopher Jones, Asparagus and
    Growltiger..Stephen Hanan
Bombalurina ....Donna King
Carbucketty ....Steven Gelfer
Cassandra ....René Ceballos
Coricopat and Mungojerrie ....René Clemente
Demeter.......................................Wendy Edmead
Etcetera and Rumpleteazer ....Christine Langer
Grizabella ....Betty Buckley
Jellylorum and Griddlebone ....Bonnie Simmons
Jennyanydots...............................Anna McNeely
Mistoffolees................................Timothy Scott
Munkustrap ....Harry Groener
Old Deuteronomy..............................Ken Page
Plato, Macavity and Rumpus Cat ....Kenneth Ard
Pouncival ....Herman W. Sebek
Rum Tum Tugger ....Terrence V. Mann
Sillabub......................................Whitney Kershaw
Skimbleshanks................................Reed Jones
Tantomile ....Janet L. Hubert
Tumblebrutus...............................Robert Hoshour
Victoria ....Cynthia Onrubia
Cat Chorus ....Walter Charles, Susan Powers, Carol
                            Richards and Joel Robertson.

There's a reason why *Cats*, the British musical which opened at the Winter Garden last night, is likely to lurk around Broadway for a long time—and it may not be the one you expect.

It's not that this collection of anthropomorphic variety turns is a brilliant musical or that it powerfully stirs the emotions or that it has an idea in its head. Nor is the probable appeal of *Cats* a function of the publicity that has accompanied the show's every purr since it first stalked London seventeen months ago. No, the reason why people will hunger to see *Cats* is far more simple and primal than that: it's a musical that transports the audience into a complete fantasy world that could only exist in the theater and yet, these days, only rarely does. Whatever the other failings and excesses, even banalities, of *Cats*, it believes in purely theatrical magic, and on that faith it unquestionably delivers.

The principal conjurers of the show's spell are the composer Andrew Lloyd Webber, the director Trevor Nunn and the designer John Napier. Their source material is T. S. Eliot's one volume of light verse, *Old Possum's Book of Practical Cats*. If the spirit of the Eliot poems is highly reminiscent of Edward Lear, the playful spirit of *Cats* is Lewis Carroll, refracted through showbiz. Mr. Nunn and Mr. Napier in particular are determined to take us to a topsy-turvy foreign universe from the moment we enter the theater, and they are often more extravagantly successful at that here than they were in the West End *Cats* or in their collaboration on *Nicholas Nickleby*.

Certainly the Winter Garden is unrecognizable to those who knew it when. To transform this house into a huge nocturnal junkyard for Eliot's flighty jellicle cats, Mr. Napier has obliterated the proscenium arch, lowered the ceiling and stage floor and filled every cranny of the place with a Red Grooms-esque collage of outsized rubbish (from old Red Seal records to squeezed-out toothpaste tubes) as seen from a cat's eye perspective. Well before the lights go down, one feels as if one has entered a mysterious spaceship on a journey through the stars to a cloud-streaked moon. And once the show begins in earnest, Mr. Napier keeps his Disneyland set popping until finally he and his equally gifted lighting designer, David Hersey, seem to take us through both the roof and back wall of the theater into an infinity beyond.

The cast completes the illusion. Luxuriantly outfitted in whiskers, electronically glowing eyes, mask-like makeup and every variety of feline costume—all designed by Mr. Napier as well—a topnotch troupe of American singer-dancers quickly sends its fur flying in dozens of distinctive ways. It's the highest achievement of Mr. Nunn and his associate director-choreographer, Gillian Lynne, that they use movement to give each cat its own personality even as they knit the entire company into a cohesive animal kingdom. (At other, less exalted times, Mr. Nunn shamelessly recycles *Nickleby* business, as when he has the cast construct a train—last time it was a coach—out of found objects.)

The songs—and *Cats* is all songs—give each cat his or her voice. If there is a point to Eliot's catcycle, it is simply that "cats are much like you and me." As his verses (here sometimes garbled by amplification) personify all manner of cat, so do the tuneful melodies to which Mr. Lloyd Webber has set them. The songs are often pastiche, but cleverly and appropriately so, and, as always with this composer, they have been orchestrated to maximum effect. Among many others, the eclectic musical sources include swing (for the busy Gumbie cat), rock (the insolent Rum Tum Tugger), Richard Rodgers-style Orientalism (a pack of Siamese) and Henry Mancini's detective-movie themes (Macavity, the Napoleon of crime).

But while the songs are usually sweet and well sung, *Cats* as a whole sometimes curls up and takes a catnap, particularly in Act I. The stasis is not attributable to the music or the energetic cast, but to the entire show's lack of spine. While a musical isn't obligated to tell a story, it must have another form of propulsion (usually dance) if it chooses to do without one. As it happens, *Cats* does vaguely attempt a story, and it also aspires to become the first British dance musical in the Broadway tradition. In neither effort does it succeed.

If you blink, you'll miss the plot, which was inspired by some unpublished Eliot material. At the beginning the deity-cat, Old Deuteronomy (an owlishly ethereal Ken Page), announces that one cat will be selected by night's end to go to cat heaven—"the heaviside layer"—and be reborn. Sure enough, the only obvious candidate for redemption is chosen at the climax, and while the audience goes wild when the lucky winner finally ascends, it's because of Mr. Napier's dazzling *Close Encounters* spaceship, not because we care about the outcome of the whodunit or about the accompanying comic-book spiritualism.

As for Miss Lynne's profuse choreography, its quantity and exuberance do not add up to quality. Though all the cat clawings and slitherings are wonderfully conceived and executed, such gestures sit on top of a repetitive array of jazz and ballet clichés, rhythmically punctuated by somersaults and leaps.

It's impossible not to notice the draggy passages in a long number like "The Jellicle Ball," or the missed opportunities elsewhere. To a tinkling new music-hall melody that Mr. Lloyd Webber has written for Mungojerrie and Rumpleteazer, Miss Lynne provides only standard strutting. The stealthy Macavity number looks like shopworn Bob Fosse, and the battle of the Pekes and the Pollicles in Act I could be an Ice Capades reject. For the conjuring cat, Mr. Mistoffolees, Miss Lynne's acrobatics never match the superhuman promise of either the lyrics or the outstanding soloist, Timothy Scott.

It's fortunate for *Cats* that Miss Lynne is often carried by the production design and, especially, by her New York cast. At the risk of neglecting a few worthy names, let me single out such additional kitties as Anna McNeely's jolly Jennyanydots, Donna King's sinuous Bombalurina, Bonnie Simmons's tart Griddlebone, Reed Jones's railroad-crazed Skimbleshanks and Harry Groener's plaintive Munkustrap. Aside from the dubious intermingling of British and American accents—which is not justified by the uniformly English references in the lyrics—the only real flaw in this large company is Terrence V. Mann's Rum Tum Tugger, who tries to imitate Mick Jagger's outlaw sexuality and misses by a wide mark.

By virtue of their songs, as well as their talent, there are two other performers who lend *Cats* the emotional pull it otherwise lacks. Stephen Hanan, singing Gus the Theater Cat to the show's most lilting melody, is a quivering bundle of nostalgia and dormant hamminess who touchingly springs back to life in an elaborate flashback sequence. (He also contributes a jolly cat about town, Bustopher Jones, earlier on.) To Betty Buckley falls the role of Grizabella the Glamour Cat and the task of singing "Memory," the Puccini-scented ballad whose lyrics were devised by Mr. Nunn from great noncat Eliot poems, notably "Rhapsody on a Windy Night." Not only does Miss Buckley's coursing delivery rattle the rafters, but in her ratty, prostitute-like furs and mane she is a poignant figure of down-and-out catwomanhood.

One wishes that *Cats* always had so much feeling to go with its most inventive stagecraft. One wishes, too, that we weren't sporadically jolted from Eliot's otherworldly catland to the vulgar precincts of the videogame arcade by the overdone lightning flashes and by the mezzanine-level television monitors that broadcast the image of the offstage orchestra conductor (the excellent Stanley Lebowsky). But maybe it's asking too much that this ambitious show lift the audience—or, for that matter, the modern musical—up to the sublime heaviside layer. What *Cats* does do is take us into a theater overflowing with wondrous spectacle—and that's an enchanting place to be.

Frank Rich ON
Plenty
BY David Hare

———

October 21, 1982
Newman/Public Theater
137 Performances

Edward Herrmann and Kate Nelligan in a scene from
Plenty   MARTHA SWOPE

PLENTY, written and directed by David Hare; scenery by John Gunter; lighting by Arden Fingerhut; costumes by Jane Greenwood; incidental music by Nick Bicat. A New York Shakespeare Festival Production presented by Joseph Papp.

Alice Park ....Ellen Parker
Susan Traherne ....Kate Nelligan

Raymond Brock	Edward Herrmann
CodenameLazar	Kelsey Grammer
Frenchman No. 1	Ken Meseroll
Leonard Darwin	George Martin
Mick	Daniel Gerroll
Louise	Johann Carlo
M. Aung	Conrad Yama
Mme. Aung	Ginny Yang
Dorcas Frey	Madeleine Potter
John Begley	Stephen Mellor
Sir Andrew Charleson	Bill Moor
Frenchman No. 2	Dominic Chianese

It's not until late in Act II that the audience hears the noise of breaking glass in David Hare's *Plenty,* but long before then, we've become terribly familiar with the harrowing sound of things going smash. A partial list of the evening's casualties would include at least three lives, one empire (the British), the egalitarian ideals of a generation and many of the conventions of the traditional narrative play.

But if this sounds reckless, Mr. Hare is no indiscriminate vandal. Out of the bloody shards of the ruins, this young British playwright has meticulously erected an explosive theatrical vision of a world that was won and lost during and after World War II.

Plenty, which was first produced by England's National Theater in 1978, received its New York premiere last night at the Public's Newman Theater, where it brings this stillborn theatrical autumn to stunning life. Like the original production, the current one has been directed by the author and stars Kate Nelligan. It couldn't be any other way. Working with a largely American cast, Mr. Hare has staged his work with a precise and chilling lyricism that perfectly complements his disquieting writing. As for Miss Nelligan, the Canadian-born actress known for her screen role in *The Eye of the Needle,* mere adjectives are beside the point. Only a fool would hold his breath waiting to see a better performance this season.

The star, who is onstage throughout, plays Susan Traherne, an Englishwoman who, at seventeen, served as a courier for the French Resistance behind German lines. *Plenty* is about what happens to Susan during the war and in the two disillusioning decades to come. Convinced that the heroic values of the Resistance would carry over to the "New Europe" of peacetime, Susan soon finds herself traipsing through mindless jobs and destructive relationships in a declining England that is choking on "plenty" but has lost its moral rudder. Intolerant of both her society and intimates, she drifts into madness and takes her innocent, loving husband, a Foreign Service officer played by Edward Herrmann, down with her.

Mr. Hare tells Susan's tale in a dozen scenes that are ripped out of chronological order. His play's structure, which can be slightly confusing, employs flashback, flashforward and in medias res. While it's a jigsaw puzzle that only comes together at the end, it's no gimmick: Mr. Hare has found a visceral theatrical embodiment for the central tension in his heroine's soul. The France of the 1940s is always as much in focus as the modern England of Suez and rampant commercialization; we constantly see each setting refracted through the other.

The liberated chronology also allows the author to crystallize his highly selective story and character details; he strips away psychological, plot and ideological exposition to achieve a concentrated naturalism. Susan, like the Hedda Gabler she sometimes resembles (gun included), is an incandescent, troubling force who doesn't have to be explained away: we see her in context and she just is. As Miss Nelligan says to Mr. Herrmann in their first meeting, "I tell you nothing—I just say look at me and make a judgment." That complicated judgment, which is ultimately asked from all of us, is the incendiary crux of the play.

The writing's jagged fractionalization further gives *Plenty* a hallucinatory, nightmarish quality that makes it feel more like a disorienting Nicholas Roeg film than John Osborne's *Look Back in Anger.* The mood of mystery is heightened by Nick Bicat's subtly ominous music and the superb physical production.

John Gunter's sets float like haunted Magritte rooms within the stage's walls, which are papered with a ghostly black-and-gray mural of a bygone romantic England. Jane Greenwood's costumes, meanwhile, anchor the characters in vivid social reality. The lighting designer, Arden Fingerhut, gives the gloom of contemporary London a remarkable variety of dreamlike textures even as she creates the dangerous, pulse-quickening glow of a nocturnal war-torn France where parachutes plummet from the stars.

The dialogue within each scene is often a tour de force interweaving subliminal rage, ellipses and caustic wit. Mr. Hare doesn't waste words, and the ones he uses are crackling, whether they deal with the dreary English climate (even "passion comes down at you through a blocked nose") or the internecine politics of a Foreign Service that requires six thousand officers to dismantle an empire that once only took six hundred men to run. In the play's most remarkable scene—a diplomatic party in the midst of the Suez debacle—a grueling marital fight is blended in with an anguished political debate, comical small talk about an Ingmar Bergman film and the hilarious malapropisms of a sycophantic Burmese ambassador (Conrad Yama).

The mostly exemplary supporting cast begins with Mr. Herrmann, who may be giving the performance of his career as Susan's husband, a moneyed, generous, self-reproachful man who sadly pursues his diplomatic calling because, as he plaintively asks, "What other world do I have?" His sputtering collapse is preceded by one brave and rending effort to break through his cheery reserve and jolt Susan back into reality.

No less brilliant is George Martin, who provides a tragic yet funny, Graham Greene-esque version of the farcical, fussbudget British bureaucrat he performed in Harold Pinter's *The Hothouse* last season. There is also flawless work from Ellen Parker as Susan's best friend, a bohemian who survives her alienation as the heroine does not, and from Daniel Gerroll, as an amiable working-class fellow who is pitifully gored by Susan's sexual manipulations.

Miss Nelligan's performance can be admired in a multitude of ways: for its unflagging intensity, for its lack of mannerisms in delineating a neurotic character, for the seamlessness with which it blends the clear-eyed, rosy-cheeked Susan of seventeen with the feverish, slow-burning firecracker of a woman who follows. In the play's middle stretches—when she's tossing out sardonic wisecracks about her advertising copywriter's job or calmly plotting to have a child by a man she "barely knows"—the actress manages to show us how a deeply disturbed woman could appear completely lucid, even dazzlingly self-possessed.

Later on Miss Nelligan provides "a psychiatric cabaret"—first when she lashes out with unprovoked obscenities at Mr. Herrmann in public circumstances, then when she levitates into drugged hysteria while meeting a revered but now pathetic old Resistance comrade (Kelsey Grammer) for a nostalgic assignation in a seedy Blackpool hotel room. Yet, as magnetic and moving as Miss Nelligan is, she never neglects the selfishness and cruelty of a woman who makes the wrong people pay for the failings of a civilization.

That's important, because, in Mr. Hare's view, Susan is perhaps more responsible for those failings than anyone around her. If the author believes that idealists have a right to "a kind of impatience" with a world that betrays their noble, hardwon victories, he also seems to feel that Susan should have struggled anew for those ideals rather than "lose control" by giving in to bitterness and cynicism. And, of course, his perspective applies not only to World War II Resistance fighters, but also to the endless waves of defeated idealists who came before and after.

That's why the sharp edges of this relentlessly gripping play reach beyond its specific milieu to puncture our conscience. It's also why *Plenty* pointedly ends not with its heroine's defeat, but with a blazing tableau in which the young, innocent Susan of 1944 climbs a bucolic hill to "get a better view" of the newly liberated France that once promised her a utopian future. In *Plenty,* Mr. Hare asks that we, too, climb up to reclaim a "better view"—but not before he has shaken us violently at the bottom of that hill, not before he's forced us to examine just how we choose to live in our own world of plenty right now.

Frank Rich ON
Moose Murders
BY Arthur Bicknell

February 22, 1983
Eugene O'Neill Theater
1 Performance

MOOSE MURDERS, by Arthur Bicknell; directed by
John Roach; scenery by Marjorie Bradley Kellogg;
lighting by Pat Collins; costumes by John Carver
Sullivan; sound design by Chuck London Media/
Stewart Werner; dance coordinator, Mary Jane
Houdina; stage violence by Kent Shelton; associate
producer, Ricka Kanter Fisher; production stage
manager, Jerry Bihm. Presented by Force Ten Productions Inc.

Snooks Keene ....June Gable
Howie Keene ....Don Potter
Joe Buffalo Dance....................................Jack Dabdoub
Nurse Dagmar....................................Lisa McMillan
Hedda Holloway ....Holland Taylor
Stinky Holloway ....Scott Evans
Gay Holloway ....Mara Hobel
Lauraine Holloway Fay..........................Lillie Robertson
Nelson Fay ....Nicholas Hormann
Sidney Holloway......................................Dennis Florzak

From now on, there will always be two groups
of theatergoers in this world: those who have
seen *Moose Murders,* and those who have not.
Those of us who have witnessed the play that
opened at the Eugene O'Neill Theater last night
will undoubtedly hold periodic reunions, in the
noble tradition of survivors of the *Titanic.* Tears
and booze will flow in equal measure, and there
will be a prize awarded to the bearer of the most
outstanding antlers. As for those theatergoers who
miss *Moose Murders*—well, they just don't rate.
A visit to *Moose Murders* is what will separate the
connoisseurs of Broadway disaster from mere
dilettantes for many moons to come.

The play begins in the exact manner of *Who-
dunnit*—itself one of the season's drearier offer-
ings, though at the time of its opening we didn't
realize how relatively civilized it was. There's a
loud thunderclap, and the curtain rises to reveal an
elaborate, two-level, dark wood set. Amusingly designed by Marjorie Bradley Kellogg, the set represents a lodge in the Adirondacks and is profusely
decorated with the requisite stuffed moose heads.
Though the heads may be hunting trophies, one
cannot rule out the possibility that these particular
moose committed suicide shortly after being
shown the script that trades on their good name.

The first human characters we meet—if "human" is the right word—are "the singing Keenes."
The scantily clad Snooks Keene bumps her back-
side in the audience's face and sings "Jeepers
Creepers" in an aggressively off-key screech
while her blind husband, Howie, pounds away on
an electric hand organ. Howie's plug is soon mercifully pulled by the lodge's beefy middle-aged
caretaker, Joe Buffalo Dance, who wears Indian
war paint and braids but who speaks in an Irish
brogue.

This loathsome trio is quickly joined by a
whole crowd of unappetizing clowns. The wealthy
Hedda Holloway, the lodge's new owner, arrives
with her husband, Sidney, a heavily bandaged
quadriplegic who is confined to a wheelchair and
who is accurately described as "that fetid roll of
gauze." Sidney's attendant, Nurse Dagmar, wears
revealing black satin, barks in Nazi-ese and likes
to leave her patient out in the rain. The Holloway
children include Stinky, a drug-crazed hippie who
wants to sleep with his mother, and Gay, a little
girl in a party dress. Told that her father will always be "a vegetable," Gay turns up her nose and
replies, "Like a lima bean? Gross me out!" She
then breaks into a tap dance.

For much of Act I, this ensemble stumbles
about mumbling dialogue that, as far as one can
tell, is only improved by its inaudibility. Just before intermission, Stinky breaks out a deck of
cards to give the actors, if not the audience, something to do.

The lights go out in mid-game, and when they
come up again, one of the characters has been
murdered. Such is the comatose nature of the production that we're too busy trying to guess which
stiff on stage is the victim to worry about guessing
the culprit.

Even Act I of *Moose Murders* is inadequate preparation for the ludicrous depths of Act II. I won't soon forget the spectacle of watching the mummified Sidney rise from his wheelchair to kick an intruder, unaccountably dressed in a moose costume, in the groin. This peculiar fracas is topped by the play's final twist, in which Hedda serves her daughter, Gay, a poison-laced vodka martini. As the young girl collapses to the floor and dies in the midst of another Shirley Temple-esque buck-and-wing, her mother breaks into laughter and applause.

The ten actors trapped in this enterprise, a minority of them of professional caliber, will not be singled out here. I'm tempted to upbraid the author, director and producers of *Moose Murders,* but surely the American Society for the Prevention of Cruelty to Animals will be after them soon enough.

Frank Rich ON
Glengarry Glen Ross
BY David Mamet

March 25, 1984

John Golden Theater

378 Performances

GLENGARRY GLEN ROSS, by David Mamet; directed by Gregory Mosher; lighting by Kevin Rigdon; costumes by Nan Cibula; sets by Michael Merritt. Presented by Elliot Martin, the Shubert Organization, Arnold Bernhard and the Goodman Theater.

Shelly Levene..Robert Prosky
John Williamson...J. T. Walsh
Dave Moss ....James Tolkan
George Aaronow ....Mike Nussbaum
Richard Roma..Joe Mantegna
James Lingk ....Lane Smith
Baylen ....Jack Wallace

The only mellifluous words in David Mamet's new play are those of its title—*Glengarry Glen Ross*. In this scalding comedy about small-time, cutthroat real-estate salesmen, most of the language is abrasive—even by the standards of the author's *American Buffalo*. If the characters aren't barking out the harshest four-letter expletives, then they're speaking in the clammy jargon of a trade in which "leads," "closings" and "the board" (a sales chart) are the holiest of imperatives. There's only one speech in which we hear about such intimacies as sex and loneliness—and that speech, to our shock, proves to be a prefabricated sales pitch.

Yet the strange—and wonderful—thing about the play at the Golden is Mr. Mamet's ability to turn almost every word inside out. The playwright makes all-American music—hot jazz and wounding blues—out of his salesmen's scatological native lingo. In the jagged riffs of coarse, monosyllabic words, we hear and feel both the exhilaration and sweaty desperation of the huckster's calling. At the same time, Mr. Mamet makes his work's musical title into an ugly symbol of all that is hollow and vicious in the way of life his characters gallantly endure. The salesmen—middle-class bloodbrothers of the penny-ante Chicago hustlers of *American Buffalo*—are trying to unload worthless tracts of Florida land to gullible victims. It's the cruelest cut of all that that real estate is packaged into developments with names like *Glengarry Highlands* and *Glen Ross Farms*.

Mr. Mamet's talent for burying layers of meaning into simple, precisely distilled, idiomatic language—a talent that can only be compared to Harold Pinter's—is not the sum of *Glengarry Glen Ross*. This may well be the most accomplished play its author has yet given us. As Mr. Mamet's command of dialogue has now reached its most dazzling pitch, so has his mastery of theatrical form. Beneath the raucous, seemingly inane surface of *Glengarry,* one finds not only feelings but a detective story with a surprise ending. And there's another clandestine story, too, bubbling just underneath the main plot: Only as the curtain falls do we realize that one of the salesmen, brilliantly played by Robert Prosky, has traveled through an anguished personal history almost as complex as Willy Loman's.

So assured and uncompromising is Mr. Mamet's style that one must enter his play's hermetically sealed world completely—or risk getting lost. Taken at face value, the actual events, like the vocabulary, are minimal; the ferocious humor and drama are often to be found in the pauses or along the shadowy periphery of the center-stage action. But should this work fail to win the large public it deserves—a fate that has befallen other Mamet plays in their first Broadway outings—that won't be entirely because of its idiosyncratic form. *Glengarry,* which was initially produced at London's National Theater last fall, is being seen here in a second production, from Chicago's Goodman Theater. Mr. Prosky's contribution aside, this solid but uninspired staging isn't always up to the crackling tension of the script.

In the half-hour-long first act, that tension is particularly Pinteresque. We watch three successive two-character confrontations that introduce the salesmen as they conduct business in the Chinese restaurant that serves as their hangout and unofficial office. The dialogue's unfinished sentences often sound like code; one whole scene turns on the colloquial distinction the characters draw between the phrases "speaking about" and "talking about."

But these duologues in fact dramatize primal duels for domination, power and survival, and, as we penetrate that argot, we learn the Darwinian rules of the salesmen's game. Those who sell the most "units" receive a Cadillac as a bonus; those who hit "bad streaks" are denied access to management's list of "premier leads" (appointments with likely customers). Worse, this entrepreneurial system is as corrupt as it is heartless. The losing salesmen can still get leads by offering kickbacks to the mercurial young manager (J. T. Walsh) who administers the business for its unseen owners.

When the characters leave the dark restaurant for the brighter setting of the firm's office in Act II, Mr. Mamet's tone lightens somewhat as well. The office has been ransacked by burglars, and a detective (Jack Wallace) arrives to investigate. Even as the salesmen undergo questioning, they frantically settle fratricidal rivalries and attempt to

bamboozle a pathetic, tearful customer (Lane Smith) who has arrived to demand a refund. As written (though not always as staged), Act II is farce in Chicago's *Front Page* tradition—albeit of a blacker contemporary sort. While we laugh at the comic cops-and-robbers hijinks, we also witness the unraveling of several lives.

The play's director is Gregory Mosher, Mr. Mamet's long-time Chicago collaborator. Mr. Mosher's work is often capable, but sometimes he italicizes Mr. Mamet's linguistic stylization: Whenever the actors self-consciously indicate the exact location of the text's hidden jokes and meanings, they cease being salesmen engaged in do-or-die warfare. This is not to say that the actors are inept—they're good. But, as we've seen with other Mamet works, it takes a special cast, not merely an adequate one, to deliver the full force of a play in which even the word "and" can set off a theatrical detonation.

The actors do succeed, as they must, at earning our sympathy. Mr. Mamet admires the courage of these salesmen, who are just as victimized as their clients; the only villain is Mr. Walsh's manager—a cool deskman who has never had to live by his wits on the front lines of selling. Among the others, there's particular heroism in Mike Nussbaum, whose frightened eyes convey a lifetime of blasted dreams, and in Joe Mantegna, as the company's youngest, most dapper go-getter. When Mr. Mantegna suffers a critical reversal, he bravely rises from defeat to retighten his tie, consult his appointments book and march back to the Chinese restaurant in search of new prey.

Mr. Prosky, beefy and white-haired, is a discarded old-timer: in the opening scene, he is reduced to begging for leads from his impassive boss. Somewhat later, however, he scores a "great sale" and expands in countenance to rekindle his old confidence: Mr. Prosky becomes a regal, cigar-waving pontificator, recounting the crude ritual of a contract closing as if it were a grand religious rite.

Still, this rehabilitation is short-lived, and soon Mr. Prosky is trying to bribe his way back into his employer's favor. As we watch the bills spill from his pockets onto a desk, we at last see greenery that both befits and mocks the verdant words of the play's title. But there's no color in the salesman's pasty, dumbstruck face—just the abject terror of a life in which all words are finally nothing because it's only money that really talks.

Mel Gussow ON
The Mystery of Irma Vep
BY Charles Ludlam

October 3, 1984

Charles Ludlam's latest Ridiculous Theatrical Company escapade, *The Mystery of Irma Vep,* begins at Mandacrest on the moors, in the manner of *Rebecca,* then, after wuthering heights of hilarity, it slinks off to Egypt for scenes spliced from *The Mummy's Curse.* The evening winds up with a howler, courtesy of *The Wolf Man.* Naturally, the entire collage is filtered through the eclectic memory and perfervid imagination of Mr. Ludlam as author, director and star.

Even if this were the usual Ludlam yarn as performed by his resident troupe of zanies, *Irma Vep* would be a romp. What makes it singular is that every one of the myriad characters—men and women, more than six, less than twelve—is played by Mr. Ludlam and Everett Quinton.

The two actors quick-change costumes, characters and genders, diving in and out of disguises and doors with lightning-flash dexterity. Each actor often barely misses meeting himself on stage, although sometimes offstage voices collide. Behind the scenery, the cast (and crew) may be in a frenzy, but what we see at 1 Sheridan Square looks effortless. Between them, in performance, Mr. Ludlam and Mr. Quinton turn this self-styled "penny dreadful" into a double tour de force.

Blink your eyes, and the Boy Scoutish bravado of Mr. Quinton's master of the manse has been replaced by his Agnes Moorehead maidservant hiding her jealousy—and biding her time—behind a mask of self-sacrifice. The actor demonstrates here, as he has in other Ridiculous jaunts, that he has a genuine comic talent for pretending to be female.

As for Mr. Ludlam, he shifts from an ominous, one-legged haunter of the heath to the new mistress of Mandacrest. In one slightly offstage, extremely offcenter scene, he simultaneously plays both the heroine and her assailant, changing profiles and voices like a hermaphroditic ventriloquist.

Despite all the dastardy, the playwright has an underlying affection for all his characters, even for the misunderstood vampire. That poor fellow simply cannot help himself and always seems to be on the lookout for a rising full moon. In the Egyptian crypt, the atmosphere turns frighteningly funny. That journey to archeological depths is led by Mr. Ludlam as a guide-guru outfitted with a Peter Sellers accent. Together with Mr. Quinton as an ace Egyptologist, Mr. Ludlam ransacks the past for missing tombs, pronounced "tombas." The imaginary descent of the grave robbers into the tombas is itself a stunt worthy of a fakir.

While the two actors are the entire Ridiculous foreground, the background—scenery artfully designed by Mr. Ludlam—is triggered for trickery, including an animated portrait of the first Lady Hillcrest (the former Irma Vep), a Sphinx, a false-bottomed sarcophagus and not so cryptic hieroglyphics. To keep everything equal, Mr. Quinton designed the ornate costumes, cleverly fashioned for split-second doffing. In all respects, this is a highly polished production.

In common with the play itself, Peter Golub's musical score is a Gothic movie patchwork. At one point, the actors—for the fun of it—take time out from skullduggery to sit before the hearth like twinned club ladies and strum a sweet duet for dulcimers.

The script veers crazily from Brontë, borrows a bit of du Maurier and recycles Shakespeare while remaining firmly resident in the land of Ludlamania. Though Mr. Ludlam, in his various guises, has allowed himself a few easy jokes, even a bouquet of wolfsbane could not keep laughter from the door.

Ma Rainey's Black Bottom

BY August Wilson

October 11, 1984

Cort Theater

275 Performances

MA RAINEY'S BLACK BOTTOM, by August Wilson;
directed by Lloyd Richards; costumes by Daphne
Pascucci; setting by Charles Henry McClennahan;
lighting by Peter Maradudin; music direction by
Dwight Andrews; sound by Jan Nebozenko; production stage manager, Mortimer Halpern; associate
producers, Bart Berman, Hart Productions and
William P. Suter. The Yale Repertory Theater production presented by Ivan Bloch, Robert Cole and
Frederick M. Zollo.

Sturdyvant	John Carpenter
Irvin	Lou Criscuolo
Cutler	Joe Seneca
Toledo	Robert Judd
Slow Drag	Leonard Jackson
Levee	Charles S. Dutton
Ma Rainey	Theresa Merritt
Dussie Mae	Aleta Mitchell
Sylvester	Scott Davenport-Richards
Policeman	Christopher Loomis

Late in Act I of *Ma Rainey's Black Bottom,* a
somber, aging band trombonist (Joe Seneca)
tilts his head heavenward to sing the blues. The
setting is a dilapidated Chicago recording studio
of 1927, and the song sounds as old as time. "If I
had my way," goes the lyric, "I would tear this old
building down."

Once the play has ended, that lyric has almost
become a prophecy. In *Ma Rainey's Black Bottom,*
the writer August Wilson sends the entire history
of black America crashing down upon our heads.
This play is a searing inside account of what white
racism does to its victims—and it floats on the
same authentic artistry as the blues music it celebrates. Harrowing as *Ma Rainey's* can be, it is also
funny, salty, carnal and lyrical. Like his real-life
heroine, the legendary singer Gertrude (Ma)
Rainey, Mr. Wilson articulates a legacy of un-

speakable agony and rage in a spellbinding voice.

The play is Mr. Wilson's first to arrive in New
York, and it reached here, via the Yale Repertory
Theater, under the sensitive hand of the man who
was born to direct it, Lloyd Richards. On Broadway, Mr. Richards has honed *Ma Rainey's* to its
finest form. What's more, the director brings us an
exciting young actor—Charles S. Dutton—along
with his extraordinary dramatist. One wonders if
the electricity at the Cort is the same that audiences felt when Mr. Richards, Lorraine Hansberry
and Sidney Poitier stormed into Broadway with *A
Raisin in the Sun* a quarter-century ago.

As *Ma Rainey's* shares its director and Chicago
setting with *Raisin,* so it builds on Hansberry's
themes: Mr. Wilson's characters want to make it
in white America. And, to a degree, they have. Ma
Rainey (1886–1939) was among the first black
singers to get a recording contract—albeit with a
white company's "race" division. Mr. Wilson
gives us Ma (Theresa Merritt) at the height of her
fame. A mountain of glitter and feathers, she has
become a despotic, temperamental star, complete
with a retinue of flunkies, a fancy car and a kept
young lesbian lover.

The evening's framework is a Paramount-label
recording session that actually happened, but
whose details and supporting players have been
invented by the author. As the action swings between the studio and the band's warm-up room—
designed by Charles Henry McClennahan as if
they might be the festering last-chance saloon of
The Iceman Cometh—Ma and her four accompanying musicians overcome various mishaps to
record "Ma Rainey's Black Bottom" and other
songs. During the delays, the band members
smoke reefers, joke around and reminisce about
past gigs on a well-traveled road stretching
through whorehouses and church socials from
New Orleans to Fat Back, Arkansas.

The musicians' speeches are like improvised
band solos—variously fizzy, haunting and mournful. We hear how the bassist Slow Drag (Leonard
Jackson) got his nickname at a dance contest, but
also about how a black preacher was tortured by
being forced to "dance" by a white vigilante's

gun. Gradually, we come to know these men, from their elusive pipe dreams to their hidden scars, but so deftly are the verbal riffs orchestrated that we don't immediately notice the incendiary drama boiling underneath.

That drama is ignited by a conflict between Ma and her young trumpeter, Levee, played by Mr. Dutton. An ambitious sport eager to form his own jazz band, Levee mocks his employer's old "jug-band music" and champions the new dance music that has just begun to usurp the blues among black audiences in the urban North. Already Levee has challenged Ma by writing a swinging version of "Ma Rainey's Black Bottom" that he expects the record company to use in place of the singer's traditional arrangement.

Yet even as the battle is joined between emblematic representatives of two generations of black music, we're thrust into a more profound war about identity. The African nationalist among the musicians, the pianist Toledo (Robert Judd), argues that "We done sold ourselves to the white man in order to be like him." We soon realize that, while Ma's music is from the heart, her life has become a sad, ludicrous "imitation" of white stardom. Levee's music is soulful, too, but his ideal of success is having his "name in lights"; his pride is invested in the new shoes on which he's blown a week's pay.

Ma, at least, senses the limits of her success. Though she acts as if she owns the studio, she can't hail a cab in the white city beyond. She knows that her clout with the record company begins and ends with her viability as a commercial product: "When I've finished recording," she says, "it's just like I'd been some whore, and they roll over and put their pants on." Levee, by contrast, has yet to learn that a black man can't name his own terms if he's going to sell his music to a white world. As he plots his future career, he deceives himself into believing that a shoeshine and Uncle Tom smile will win white backers for his schemes.

Inevitably, the promised door of opportunity slams, quite literally, in Levee's face, and the sound has a violent ring that reverberates through the decades. Levee must confront not just the collapse of his hopes but the destruction of his dignity. Having played the white man's game and lost to its rigged rules, he is left with less than nothing: Even as he fails to sell himself to whites, Levee has sold out his own sense of self-worth.

Mr. Dutton's delineation of this tragic downfall is red-hot. A burly actor a year out of Yale, he is at first as jazzy as his music. With his boisterous wisecracks and jumpy sprinter's stance, he seems ready to leap into the stratosphere envisioned in his fantasies of glory. But once he crash-lands, the poison of self-hatred ravages his massive body and distorts his thundering voice. No longer able to channel his anger into his music, he directs it to God, crying out that a black man's prayers are doomed to be tossed "into the garbage." As Mr. Dutton careens about with unchecked, ever escalating turbulence, he transforms an anonymous Chicago bandroom into a burial ground for a race's aspirations.

Mr. Dutton's fellow band members are a miraculous double-threat ensemble: They play their instruments nearly as convincingly as they spin their juicy monologues. Aleta Mitchell and Lou Criscuolo, as Ma's gum-chewing lover and harried white manager, are just right, and so is Scott Davenport-Richards, as Ma's erstwhile Little Lord Fauntleroy of a young nephew. It's one of the evening's more grotesquely amusing gags that Ma imperiously insists on having the boy, a chronic stutterer, recite a spoken introduction on her record.

Miss Merritt is Ma Rainey incarnate. A singing actress of both wit and power, she finds bitter humor in the character's distorted sense of self: When she barks her outrageous demands to her lackeys, we see a show business monster who's come a long way from her roots. Yet the roots can still be unearthed. In a rare reflective moment, she explains why she sings the blues. "You don't sing to feel better," Miss Merritt says tenderly. "You sing because that's a way of understanding life."

The lines might also apply to the play's author. Mr. Wilson can't mend the broken lives he unravels in *Ma Rainey's Black Bottom*. But, like his heroine, he makes their suffering into art that forces us to understand and won't allow us to forget.

Frank Rich ON
Les Misérables

ORIGINAL FRENCH TEXT BY
Alain Boublil AND Jean-Marc Natel
ENGLISH LYRICS BY Herbert Kretzmer
MUSIC BY Claude-Michel Schonberg

March 12, 1987

Broadway Theater

5,948+ Performances

Colm Wilkinson *(left)* as the fugitive Jean Valjean and Terrence Mann as the relentless police inspector in *Les Misérables*   JACK MITCHELL/THE NEW YORK TIMES

LES MISÉRBLES, by Alain Boublil and Claude-Michel Schonberg, based on the novel by Victor Hugo; adapted and directed by Trevor Nunn and John Caird; music by Mr. Schonberg; lyrics by Herbert Kretzmer; original French text by Mr. Boublil and Jean-Marc Natel; additional material by James Fenton; orchestral score by John Cameron; musical supervision and direction by Robert Billig; sound by Andrew Bruce/Autograph; executive producers, Martin McCallum and Richard Jay-Alexander; designed by John Napier; lighting by David Hersey; costumes by Andreane Neofitou. Presented by Cameron Mackintosh.

Jean Valjean...Colm Wilkinson
Javert...Terrence Mann
Fantine...Randy Graff
Thenardier ....Leo Burmester
Éponine ....Frances Ruffelle
With Cindy Benson, Jane Bodle, David Bryant, Jennifer

Butt, Jesse Corti, Anthony Crivello, Ann Crumb, Braden Danner, John Dewar, Joanna Glushak, Susan Goodman, Paul Harman, Kelli James, Gretchen Kingsley-Weihe, Joseph Kolinski, Judy Kuhn, Norman Large, Marcus Lovett, Michael Maguire, Kevin Marcum, Chrissie McDonald, John Norman, Alex Santoriello, Marcie Shaw, Steve Shocket and Donna Vivino.

If anyone doubts that the contemporary musical theater can flex its atrophied muscles and yank an audience right out of its seats, he need look no further than the Act I finale of *Les Misérables.*

At that point in the gripping pop opera at the Broadway, the strands of narrative culled from Victor Hugo's novel of early-nineteenth-century France intertwine in a huge undulating tapestry. The unjustly hounded fugitive Jean Valjean (Colm Wilkinson) is once more packing his bags for exile on the "never-ending road to Calvary," even as his eternal pursuer, the police inspector Javert (Terrence Mann), plots new malevolent schemes. The young lovers Marius and Cosette are exchanging tearful farewells while Marius's unrequited admirer, Éponine, mourns her own abandonment. And everywhere in the Paris of 1832 is the whisper of insurrection, as revolutionary students prepare to mount the barricade.

Were *Les Misérables* unfolding as a novel—or in one of its many film adaptations—these events would be relayed sequentially, or through literary or cinematic cross-cutting. But in the musical theater at its most resourceful, every action can occur on stage at once. Such is the thunderous coup that brings down the Act I curtain. The opera-minded composer Claude-Michel Schonberg, having earlier handed each character a gorgeous theme, now brings them all into an accelerating burst of counterpoint titled "One Day More." The set designer John Napier and lighting designer David Hersey peel back layer after layer of shadow—and a layer of the floor as well—to create the illusion of a sprawling, multilayered Paris on the brink of upheaval. Most crucially, the directors Trevor Nunn and John Caird choreograph the paces of their players on a revolving stage so that spatial relationships mirror both human relationships and the pressing march of history.

The ensuing fusion of drama, music, character, design and movement is what links this English adaptation of a French show to the highest tradition of modern Broadway musical production. One can hardly watch the Act I finale without thinking of the star-crossed lovers and rival gangs preparing for the rumble in the "Tonight" quintet of *West Side Story*—or of the revolving-stage dispersal of Tevye's shtetl following the pogrom in *Fiddler on the Roof.* In *Les Misérables,* Mr. Nunn and Mr. Caird have wedded the sociohistorical bent, unashamed schmaltz and Jerome Robbins staging techniques from those two American classics with the distinctive directorial style they've developed on their own at the Royal Shakespeare Company. This production is the Nunn-Caird *Nicholas Nickleby* gone gloriously show biz—which is to say, with conviction, inspiration and taste.

The evening may not appeal to those enraptured by the 1,300-page edition of Hugo. The musical thinks nothing of condensing chapters of exposition or philosophical debate into a single quatrain or unambiguous confrontation; encyclopedic digressions and whole episodes are thrown out. Unlike *Nicholas Nickleby,* which slavishly attempted to regurgitate its entire source, *Les Misérables* chooses sweeping and hurtling motion over the savoring of minute details. That artistic decision, however arguable, is in keeping with the difference between Hugo and Dickens as writers, not to mention the distinction between musicals and plays as theatrical forms.

While facts and psychological nuances are lost and even the plot is often relegated to a program synopsis, the thematic spirit of the original is preserved. Sequence after sequence speaks of Hugo's compassion for society's outcasts and his faith in God's offer of redemption. When the poor Fantine is reduced to "making money in her sleep," her downtrodden fellow prostitutes are apotheosized in golden light as their predatory clients circle in menacing shadows. When the story's action moves from the provinces to Paris, two hulking wooden piles of domestic bric-a-brac converge to form an abstract representation of a mean slum, bordered on every side by the shuttered windows of a city coldly shunning its poor. In a subsequent and dazzling transition, the towers tilt to form an enormous barricade. Later still, the barricade twirls in mournful silence to become a charnel house—*Guernica* re-imagined as a Dada sculpture—crammed with the splayed corpses of a revolution that failed.

Except for that uprising's red flag, Mr. Napier's designs, all encased in a dark, beclouded prison of a proscenium, are drained of color. *Les Misérables* may be lavish, but its palette, like its noblest characters, is down-to-earth—dirty browns and cobblestone grays, streaked by Mr. Hersey with the smoky light that filters down to the bottom of the economic heap. The proletarian simplicity of the design's style masks an incredible amount of theatrical sophistication. In one three-dimensional zoom-lens effect, Valjean's resolution of a crisis of conscience is accompanied by the sudden materialization of the courtroom where the moral question raised in his song ("Who Am I?") must be answered in deed. *Les Misérables* eventually takes us from the stars where Inspector Javert sets his metaphysical perorations to the gurgling sewers inhabited by the parasitic innkeeper, Thenardier—and in one instance even simulates a character's suicidal fall through much of that height.

Mr. Schonberg's profligately melodious score, sumptuously orchestrated by John Cameron to straddle the eras of harpsichord and synthesizer, mixes madrigals with rock and evokes composers as diverse as Bizet (for the laborers) and Weill (for their exploiters). Motifs are recycled for ironic effect throughout, allowing the story's casualties to haunt the grief-stricken survivors long after their deaths. The resourceful lyrics—written by the one-time London drama critics Herbert Kretzmer and James Fenton, from the French of Alain Boublil and Jean-Marc Natel—can be as sentimental as Hugo in translation. Yet the libretto has been sharpened since London, and it is the edginess of the cleverest verses that prevents the Thenardiers' oom-pah-pah number, "Master of the House," from sliding into *Oliver!*

It's New York's good fortune that Mr. Wilkinson has traveled here with his commanding London performance as Valjean intact. An actor of pugilistic figure and dynamic voice, he is the heroic everyman the show demands at its heart—convincingly brawny, Christlike without being cloying, enraged by injustice, paternal with children. Mr. Wilkinson anchors the show from his first solo, in which he runs away from his identity as paroled prisoner 20601 with a vengeance that burns his will into the inky void around him. He is symbiotically matched by Mr. Mann's forceful Javert, who at first acts with his sneering lower lip but soon gains shading in the soliloquy that passionately describes the authoritarian moral code driving him to stalk the hero obsessively for seventeen years.

Though uniformly gifted as singers, the American supporting cast does not act with the consistency of its West End predecessors. Randy Graff delivers Fantine's go-for-the-throat "I Dreamed a Dream" like a Broadway belter handed a showstopper rather than a pathetic woman in ruins. David Bryant, as Marius, brings fervor to a touching hymn to dead comrades ("Empty Chairs at Empty Tables"), but not before he's proved a narcissistic romantic lead. Jennifer Butt plays the funny but cruel Mme. Thenardier as if she were the toothlessly clownish orphanage matron of *Annie*.

Other roles fare better. Frances Ruffelle, the production's second London émigrée, is stunning as the bedraggled Éponine: She's an angel with a dirty face and an unrelenting rock balladeer's voice. Leo Burmester's moldy-looking Thenardier really metamorphoses into the vicious, dog-eat-dog social carnivore his lyrics claim him to be. Judy Kuhn's lovely Cosette and Michael Maguire's noble rebel, Enjolras, are also first-rate. Donna Vivino, the young Cosette, and Braden Danner, the urchin Gavroche, tower over most child actors, however diminutively.

That *Les Misérables* easily overrides its lesser performers, candied romantic tableaux and early Act II languors is a testament to the ingenuity of the entire construction. This show isn't about individuals, or even the ensemble, so much as about how actors and music and staging meld with each other and with the soul of its source. The transfiguration is so complete that by evening's end, the company need simply march forward from the stage's black depths into a hazy orange dawn to summon up Hugo's unflagging faith in tomorrow's better world. The stirring sentiments belong to hallowed nineteenth-century literature, to be sure, but the fresh charge generated by this *Misérables* has everything to do with the electrifying showmanship of the twentieth-century musical.

Frank Rich ON
Frankie and Johnny in the Clair de Lune
BY Terrence McNally

October 27, 1987

Stage 1, City Center

533 Performances

FRANKIE AND JOHNNY IN THE CLAIR DE LUNE, by Terrence McNally; directed by Paul Benedict; sets by James Noone; costumes by David Woolard; lighting by David Noling; sound by John Gromada; production stage manager, Pamela Singer. Presented by the Manhattan Theater Club, Lynne Meadow, artistic director; Barry Grove, managing director.
Frankie ....Kathy Bates
Johnny.......................................Kenneth Welsh

When we first meet the title characters of Terrence McNally's provocative new play, *Frankie and Johnny in the Clair de Lune,* they are grunting through an orgasm on a Murphy bed in a dreary Hell's Kitchen walk-up. But Frankie (Kathy Bates) and Johnny (Kenneth Welsh) are hardly sweethearts. They are fellow employees of a greasy spoon—she a waitress, he a recently hired short-order cook—and this is their first and quite possibly their last date. They've been to a movie. They've made small talk. Now they've had sex. What else can they give one another? As the couple's panting subsides, Frankie hopes only that Johnny will get dressed and get out so she can resume her usual nightly ritual of watching television and eating ice cream in peace.

Yet Johnny refuses to leave. A nonstop talker and meddler, he repeatedly proclaims his undying love for the dumpy, sarcastic waitress even as she rudely mocks his ludicrously overblown compliments and points him toward the door. The exasperated Frankie thinks Johnny is "too needy" and worries he may be a creep. "You just don't decide to fall in love with people out of the blue," she says. Johnny argues back that Frankie, much wounded by other men, is simply too fearful of rejection to accept true affection when it comes her way. "Pretend we're the only two people in the world," he says, insisting that he and Frankie, both middle-aged and "not beautiful," have only this one last chance "to connect." Should they fail to seize the moment, they'll never know more than the isolation and loneliness that already is their lot—a life of merely "bumping into bodies."

Frankie and Johnny in the Clair de Lune, which opens the main-stage season of the Manhattan Theater Club, has the timeless structure of romantic comedies: Will there be a second night to this odd couple's problematic one-night-stand? As one expects from Mr. McNally, the author of *Bad Habits* and *It's Only a Play,* the evening often floats by on bright and funny conversation, some of it dotted, however parenthetically, with jaundiced references to show business (*The Sound of Music, Looking for Mr. Goodbar,* Kathleen Turner). But there has always been another side to Mr. McNally's highly lacquered sophistication: even his raucous gay-bath sex farce, *The Ritz,* had something poignant to say about transitory romantic attachments. In *Frankie and Johnny in the Clair de Lune,* the playwright examines his characters' connections with a new forthrightness and maturity, and it's just possible that, in the process, he's written the most serious play yet about intimacy in the age of AIDS.

To be sure, *Frankie and Johnny* is not about AIDS per se. There is only one vague reference to

the disease, and its characters do not belong to high-risk groups. Still, there's a pointed end-of-the-world feel to James Noone's drab tenement set and to the blank, Edward Hopper-esque solitude of the couple's existence. Mr. McNally seems to be taking stock of what's really important in a society where life can be "cheap and short," where sexual marauding can no longer pass as its own reward, where emotional defenses are so well fortified that human contact is harder to achieve than ever.

The persistent, nosy Johnny is as obnoxious a suitor as Frankie says he is—he's the kind of guy who picks at any visible scab—but his relentless battering does make her and us think about how much of love is fleeting chemistry and how much is merely a willingness to overcome the inertia of detachment and engage in hard work. Perhaps Johnny is right when he says his and Frankie's only hope is that they somehow forget "the million reasons they don't love each other" and build instead on the few reasons that did bring them together, if only for an hour and by chance, on one desperate moonlit night. Perhaps, too, the durability of their bond will have less to do with their various similarities and differences of personality than with their ability to remember the "music" of their first, hungry romantic passion. Music—from that alluded to in the title to bits of Bach, Wagner and Frederick Loewe—figures throughout *Frankie and Johnny.* The play's offstage third character is a pretentious FM disk jockey who would "still like to believe in love."

Mr. McNally may or may not still believe in love himself, but he has dexterously managed to avoid the tragic denouement of folklore's Frankie and Johnny (and of his last and thematically related play, *The Lisbon Traviata*) as well as the guaranteed happy endings of boulevard comedies. In *Frankie and Johnny,* it's enough of a victory for the hero and heroine to share un-self-consciously the intimate domestic activity of brushing their teeth. But if the playwright avoids the trap of reaching for a definitive final curtain, he sometimes exerts too firm a controlling hand along the way. The hash-slinging characters both seem like second-hand William Inge–style Middle Americans—as if they were archetypal figures contrived to enact a parable rather than people drawn freely from life. Sometimes their credibility is further compromised by their slips into knowing badinage reminiscent of Mr. McNally's upscale Manhattanites.

Under the fine direction of Paul Benedict, two excellent actors supply the spontaneity and conviction needed to override the moments of contrivance in their roles. Mr. Welsh keeps us guessing as to whether Johnny is merely sickeningly sincere or a weirdo, finally allowing us to see and understand all the pieces of a complex, damaged man. While Ms. Bates's Frankie superficially resembles the suicidal daughter she played in *'Night, Mother,* the actress creates a wholly new character—a tough waitress whose wisecracks mask not a sentimental heart but an unsparing vision of the world. When Johnny tells her that he's a romantic who likes seeing things in a shadowy light, she typically snaps back that his idea of romance is her idea of "hiding something." As it happens, we can understand both points of view in a play that brings fresh illumination to the latest phases of that old lovers' moon.

Frank Rich ON
Six Degrees of Separation
BY John Guare

June 14, 1990
Mitzi E. Newhouse Theater
640 Performances

Stockard Channing *(left),* James McDaniel *(center),* and John Cunningham in *Six Degrees of Separation*
BRIGITTE LACOMBE

SIX DEGREES OF SEPARATION by John Guare; directed by Jerry Zaks; sets, Tony Walton; costumes, William Ivey Long; lighting, Paul Gallo; sound, Aural Fixation; production manager, Jeff Hamlin. Presented by Lincoln Center Theater, Gregory Mosher, director; Bernard Gersten, executive producer.

Ouisa	Stockard Channing
Flan	John Cunningham
Geoffrey	Sam Stoneburner
Paul	James McDaniel
Hustler	David Eigenberg

Kitty	Kelly Bishop
Larkin	Peter Maloney
Detective	Brian Evers
Tess	Robin Morse
Woody	Gus Rogerson
Ben	Anthony Rapp
Dr. Fine	Stephen Pearlman
Doug	Evan Handler
Policeman/Doorman	Philip LeStrange
Trent	John Cameron Mitchell
Rick	Paul McCrane
Elizabeth	Mari Nelson

Ouisa Kittredge, the Upper East Side hostess at the center of John Guare's *Six Degrees of Separation,* delights in the fact that it only takes a chain of six people to connect anyone on the planet with anyone else. But what about those who are eternally separated from others because they cannot find the right six people? Chances are that they, like Ouisa, live in chaotic contemporary New York, which is the setting for this extraordinary high comedy in which broken connections, mistaken identities and tragic social, familial and cultural schisms take the stage to create a hilarious and finally searing panorama of urban America in precisely our time.

For those who have been waiting for a masterwork from the writer who bracketed the 1970s with the play *House of Blue Leaves* and the film *Atlantic City,* this is it. For those who have been waiting for the American theater to produce a play that captures New York as Tom Wolfe did in *Bonfire of the Vanities,* this is also it. And, with all due respect to Mr. Wolfe, *Six Degrees of Separation* expands on that novel's canvas and updates it. Mr. Guare gives as much voice to his black and female characters as to his upper-crust white men, and he transports the audience beyond the dailiness of journalistic storytelling to the magical reaches of the imagination.

Though the play grew out of a 1983 newspaper account of a confidence scheme, it is as at home with the esthetics of Wassily Kandinsky as it is with the realities of Rikers Island. The full sweep of the writing—ninety nonstop minutes of cyclonic action, ranging from knockabout farce to hallucinatory dreams—is matched by Jerry Zaks's ceaselessly inventive production at Lincoln Center's Mitzi E. Newhouse Theater. A brilliant ensemble of seventeen actors led by Stockard Channing, John Cunningham and James Mc-Daniel is equally adept at fielding riotous gags about Andrew Lloyd Webber musicals and the shattering aftermath of a suicide leap. As elegantly choreographed by Mr. Zaks, the action extends into the auditorium and rises through a mysterious two-level Tony Walton set that is a fittingly abstract variation on the designer's *Grand Hotel.*

The news story that sparked *Six Degrees of Separation* told of a young black man who talked his way into wealthy white Upper East Side households by purporting to be both Sidney Poitier's son and the Ivy League college friend of his unwitting hosts' children. In Mr. Guare's variation, the young man (Mr. McDaniel), who calls himself Paul Poitier, lands in the Fifth Avenue apartment of Ouisa (Ms. Channing) and her husband, Flan (Mr. Cunningham), a high-rolling art dealer. Paul is a charming, articulate dissembler on all subjects who has the Kittredges in thrall. He is also a petty thief who invites a male hustler into the guest room he occupies while waiting for his "father" to take up residence at the Sherry-Netherland Hotel.

Much as this situation, a rude twist on *Guess Who's Coming to Dinner,* lends itself to the satirical mayhem Mr. Wolfe inflicted on white liberals in *Radical Chic,* Mr. Guare has not written a satire about race relations. Paul, the black man whose real identity the Kittredges never learn, becomes the fuse that ignites a larger investigation of the many degrees of separation that prevent all the people in the play from knowing one another and from knowing themselves.

It is not only blacks and whites who are estranged in Mr. Guare's New York. As the action accelerates and the cast of characters expands, the audience discovers that the Kittredges and their privileged friends don't know their alienated children, that heterosexuals don't know homosexuals, that husbands don't know their wives, that art dealers don't know the art they trade for millions.

The only thing that everyone in this play's Manhattan has in common is the same American malady that afflicted the working-class Queens inhabitants of *House of Blue Leaves*—a desire to bask in the glow of the rich and famous. Here that hunger takes the delirious form of a maniacal desire to appear as extras in Sidney Poitier's purported film version of *Cats,* a prospect Paul dangles in front of his prey. Yet these people hunger for more as well, for a human connection and perhaps a spiritual one. It is Paul, of all people, who points the way, by his words and his deeds. In a virtuoso monologue about *Catcher in the Rye,* he decries a world in which assassins like Mark David Chapman and John W. Hinckley Jr. can take Holden Caulfield as a role model—a world in which imagination has ceased to be a means of self-examination and has become instead "something outside ourselves," whether a handy excuse for murderous behavior or a merchandisable commodity like van Gogh's *Irises* or an escapist fashion promoted by *The Warhol Diaries.* Intentionally or not, Paul helps bring Ouisa into a reunion with her imagination, with her authentic self. His trail of fraud, which ultimately brushes against death, jolts his hostess out of her own fraudulent life among what Holden Caulfield calls phonies so that she might at last break through the ontological paralysis separating her from what really matters.

Among the many remarkable aspects of Mr. Guare's writing is the seamlessness of his imagery, characters and themes, as if this play had just erupted from his own imagination in one perfect piece. "There are two sides to every story," says a comic character, a duped New York Hospital obstetrician (Stephen Pearlman), and every aspect of *Six Degrees of Separation,* its own story included, literally or figuratively shares this duality, from Paul's identity to a Kandinsky painting that twirls above the Kittredge living room to the meaning of a phrase like "striking coal miners." The double vision gives the play an airy, Cubist dramatic structure even as it reflects the class divisions of its setting and the Jungian splits of its characters' souls.

Mr. Guare is just as much in control of the brush strokes that shift his play's disparate moods: In minutes, he can take the audience from a college student who is a screamingly funny personification of upper-middle-class New York Jewish rage (Evan Handler) to a would-be actor from Utah (Paul McCrane) of the same generation and opposite temperament. Though Mr. Guare quotes Donald Barthelme's observation that "collage is the art form of the twentieth century," his play does not feel like a collage. As conversant with Cezanne and the Sistine Chapel as it is with Sotheby's and *Starlight Express,* this work aspires to the classical esthetics and commensurate unity of spirit that are missing in the pasted-together, fragmented, twentieth-century lives it illuminates. That spirit shines through. Great as the intellectual pleasures of the evening may be, it is Mr. Guare's compassion that allows his play to make the human connections that elude his characters. The people who walk in and out of the picture frames of Mr. Walton's set are not satirical cartoons but ambiguous, full-blooded creations. There's a Gatsby-like poignance to the studied glossy-magazine aspirations of Mr. McDaniel's Paul, a Willy Loman-ish sadness to the soiled idealism of Mr. Cunningham's art dealer. As the one character who may finally see the big picture and begin to understand that art of living, the wonderful Ms. Channing steadily gains gravity as she journeys flawlessly from the daffy comedy of a fatuous dinner party to the harrowing internal drama of her own rebirth.

"It was an experience," she says with wonder of her contact with the impostor she never really knew. For the author and his heroine, the challenge is to hold on to true experience in a world in which most human encounters are bogus and nearly all are instantly converted into the disposable anecdotes, the floating collage scraps that are the glib currency of urban intercourse. In *Six Degrees of Separation,* one of those passing anecdotes has been ripped from the daily paper and elevated into a transcendent theatrical experience that is itself a lasting vision of the humane new world of which Mr. Guare and his New Yorkers so hungrily dream.

May 4, 1993

Walter Kerr Theater

367 Performances

ANGELS IN AMERICA: MILLENNIUM AP-
PROACHES by Tony Kushner; directed by George
C. Wolfe; sets by Robin Wagner; costumes by Toni-
Leslie James; lighting by Jules Fisher; music by Anthony Davis; additional music by Michael Ward;
sound by Scott Lehrer; production supervisors, Gene
O'Donovan and Neil A. Mazzella; production stage
manager, Perry Cline. Produced in association with
the New York Shakespeare Festival. Associate pro-
ducers, Dennis Grimaldi, Marilyn Hall, Ron Kastner,
Hal Luftig/126 Second Avenue Corporation and Suki
Sandler; executive producers, Benjamin Mordecai
and Robert Cole. Presented by Jujamcyn Theaters
and Mark Taper Forum/Gordon Davidson, with
Margo Lion, Susan Quint Gallin, Jon B. Platt, the
Baruch-Frankel-Viertel Group and Frederick Zollo,
in association with Herb Alpert.
Rabbi Chemelwitz, Henry, Hannah Pitt and Ethel
Rosenberg ....Kathleen Chalfant
Roy Cohn and Prior 2 ....Ron Leibman
Joe Pitt, Prior 1 and the Eskimo ..David Marshall Grant
Harper Pitt and Martin Heller ....Marcia Gay Harden
Mr. Lies and Belize ....Jeffrey Wright
Louis Ironson ....Joe Mantello
Prior Walter and Man in the Park.........Stephen Spinella
Emily, Ella Chapter, the Woman in the South Bronx
and the Angel ....Ellen McLaughlin

"History is about to crack open," says Ethel
Rosenberg, back from the dead, as she confronts a cadaverous Roy Cohn, soon to die of
AIDS, in his East Side town house. "Something's
going to give," says a Brooklyn housewife so addicted to Valium she thinks she is in Antarctica.
The year is 1985. It is fifteen years until the next
millennium. And a young man drenched in death
fevers in his Greenwich Village bedroom hears a
persistent throbbing, a thunderous heartbeat, as if
the heavens were about to give birth to a miracle
so that he might be born again.

This is the astonishing theatrical landscape, intimate and epic, of Tony Kushner's *Angels in
America,* which made its much-awaited Broadway debut at the Walter Kerr Theater last night.
This play has already been talked about so much
that you may feel you have already seen it, but believe me, you haven't, even if you actually have.
The new New York production is the third I've
seen of *Millennium Approaches,* as the first,
self-contained, three-and-a-half-hour part of *Angels in America* is titled. (Part 2, *Perestroika,* is to
join it in repertory in the fall.) As directed with
crystalline lucidity by George C. Wolfe and ignited by blood-churning performances by Ron
Leibman and Stephen Spinella, this staging only
adds to the impression that Mr. Kushner has written the most thrilling American play in years.

Angels in America is a work that never loses its
wicked sense of humor or its wrenching grasp on
such timeless dramatic matters as life, death and
faith even as it ranges through territory as far-
flung as the complex, plague-ridden nation Mr.
Kushner wishes both to survey and to address.
Subtitled "A Gay Fantasia on National Themes,"
the play is a political call to arms for the age of
AIDS, but it is no polemic. Mr. Kushner's convic-
tions about power and justice are matched by his
conviction that the stage, and perhaps the stage
alone, is a space large enough to accommodate
everything from precise realism to surrealistic hal-
lucination, from black comedy to religious revelation. In *Angels in America,* a true American work
in its insistence on embracing all possibilities in
art and life, he makes the spectacular case that
they can all be brought into fusion in one play.

At center stage, *Angels* is a domestic drama,
telling the story of two very different but equally
troubled young New York couples, one gay and
one nominally heterosexual, who intersect by
chance. But the story of these characters soon
proves inseparable from the way Mr. Kushner tells
it. His play opens with a funeral led by an Orthodox rabbi and reaches its culmination with what
might be considered a Second Coming. In between,

it travels to Salt Lake City in search of latter-day saints and spirals into dreams and dreams-within-dreams where the languages spoken belong to the minority American cultures of drag and jazz. Hovering above it all is not only an Angel (Ellen McLaughlin) but also an Antichrist, Mr. Leibman's Roy Cohn, an unreconstructed right-wing warrior who believes that "life is full of horror" from which no one can escape.

While Cohn is a villain, a hypocritical closet case and a corrupt paragon of both red-baiting and Reagan-era greed, his dark view of life is not immediately dismissed by Mr. Kushner. The America of *Angels in America* is riddled with cruelty. When a young WASP esthete named Prior Walter (Mr. Spinella) reveals his first lesions of Kaposi's sarcoma to his lover of four years, a Jewish clerical worker named Louis Ironson (Joe Mantello), he finds himself deserted in a matter of weeks. Harper Pitt (Marcia Gay Harden), pill-popping housewife and devout Mormon, has recurrent nightmares that a man with a knife is out to kill her; she also has real reason to fear that the man is her husband, Joe (David Marshall Grant), an ambitious young lawyer with a dark secret and aspirations to rise high in Ed Meese's Justice Department.

But even as Mr. Kushner portrays an America of lies and cowardice to match Cohn's cynical view, he envisions another America of truth and beauty, the paradise imagined by both his Jewish and Mormon characters' ancestors as they made their crossing to the new land. *Angels in America* not only charts the split of its two central couples but it also implicitly sets its two gay men with AIDS against each other in a battle over their visions of the future. While the fatalistic, self-loathing Cohn ridicules gay men as political weaklings with "zero clout" doomed to defeat, the younger, equally ill Prior sees the reverse. "I am a gay man, and I am used to pressure," he says from his sick bed. "I am tough and strong." Possessed by scriptural visions he describes as "very Steven Spielberg" even when in abject pain, Prior is Mr. Kushner's prophet of hope in the midst of apocalypse.

Though Cohn and Prior never have a scene together, they are the larger-than-life poles between which all of *Angels in America* swings. And they could not be more magnetically portrayed than they are in this production. Mr. Leibman, red-faced and cackling, is a demon of Shakespearean grandeur, an alternately hilarious and terrifying mixture of chutzpah and megalomania, misguided brilliance and relentless cunning. He turns the mere act of punching telephone buttons into a grotesque manipulation of the levers of power, and he barks out the most outrageous pronouncements ("I brought out something tender in him," he says of Joe McCarthy) with a shamelessness worthy of history's most indelible monsters.

Mr. Spinella is a boyish actor so emaciated that when he removes his clothes for a medical examination, some in the audience gasp. But he fluently conveys buoyant idealism and pungent drag-queen wit as well as the piercing, open-mouthed cries of fear and rage that arrive with the graphically dramatized collapse of his health. Mr. Spinella is also blessed with a superb acting partner in Mr. Mantello, who as his callow lover is a combustible amalgam of puppyish Jewish guilt and self-serving intellectual piety.

The entire cast, which includes Kathleen Chalfant and Jeffrey Wright in a variety of crisply observed comic cameos, is first rate. Ms. Harden's shattered, sleepwalking housewife is pure pathos, a figure of slurred thought, voice and emotions, while Mr. Grant fully conveys the internal warfare of her husband, torn between Mormon rectitude and uncontrollable sexual heat. When Mr. Wolfe gets both of the play's couples on stage simultaneously to enact their parallel, overlapping domestic crackups, *Angels in America* becomes a wounding fugue of misunderstanding and recrimination committed in the name of love.

But *Angels in America* is an ideal assignment for Mr. Wolfe because of its leaps beyond the bedroom into the fabulous realms of myth and American archetypes, which have preoccupied this director and playwright in such works as *The Colored Museum* and *Spunk*. Working again with Robin Wagner, the designer who was an essential collaborator on *Jelly's Last Jam,* Mr. Wolfe makes the action fly through the delicate, stylized heaven that serves as the evening's loose scenic environment, yet he also manages to make some of the loopier scenes, notably those involving a real-estate agent in Salt Lake City and a homeless woman in the South Bronx, sharper and far more pertinent than they have seemed before.

What has really affected *Angels in America* during the months of its odyssey to New York, however, is not so much its change of directors as Washington's change of administrations. When first seen a year or so ago, the play seemed defined by its anger at the reigning political establishment, which tended to reward the Roy Cohns and ignore the Prior Walters. Mr. Kushner has not revised the text since—a crony of Cohn's still boasts of a Republican lock on the White House until the year 2000—but the shift in Washington has had the subliminal effect of making *Angels in America* seem more focused on what happens next than on the past.

This is why any debate about what this play means or does not mean for Broadway seems, in the face of the work itself, completely beside the point. *Angels in America* speaks so powerfully because something far larger and more urgent than the future of the theater is at stake. It really is history that Mr. Kushner intends to crack open. He sends his haunting messenger, a spindly, abandoned gay man with a heroic spirit and a ravaged body, deep into the audience's heart to ask just who we are and just what, as the plague continues and the millennium approaches, we intend this country to become.

David Richards ON
Twilight: Los Angeles, 1992
BY Anna Deavere Smith

March 23, 1994
Newman/Public Theater
85 Performances

TWILIGHT: LOS ANGELES, 1992, conceived, written and performed by Anna Deavere Smith; directed by George C. Wolfe; sets by John Arnone; costumes by Toni-Leslie James; lighting by Jules Fisher and Peggy Eisenhauer; sound by John Gromada; projections and video by Batwin and Robin Production; production stage manager, William Joseph Barnes. Presented by the New York Shakespeare Festival, Mr. Wolfe, producer; Jason Steven Cohen, managing director; Rosemarie Tichler and Kevin Kline, associate producers.

Anna Deavere Smith is the ultimate impressionist: she does people's souls. She is so good at the task that to describe *Twilight: Los Angeles, 1992* as a one-woman show is patently ridiculous. Probing the riots that erupted in April of that year, after the first Rodney King trial, she gives an epic accounting of neighborhoods in chaos, a city in anguish and a country deeply disturbed by the violent images, live and in color, coming over the nightly airwaves.

She does so by portraying nearly four dozen real-life individuals. Some were participants in the riots, others mere onlookers. A few were made momentarily famous by the media; a number still clutch their anonymity about them as if it were a security blanket. To each, however, Ms. Smith brings her penetrating eye and a voracious need to know what lurks in the depths of the human heart. Her subject may be daunting, but the scale of her investigation isn't. One person at a time, one idea at a time, one temperament at a time, she builds up a rich, panoramic canvas of a national trauma.

By every measurement, *Twilight: Los Angeles, 1992,* which opened last night at the Joseph Papp

Public Theater in a sleek multi-media production directed by George C. Wolfe, is bigger than *Fires in the Mirror: Crown Heights, Brooklyn and Other Identities,* the 1992 show that made Ms. Smith's reputation. Her method remains unaltered, though. Armed with a tape recorder and a manner that must invite frank confession, she interviews a wide cross-section of people connected with a significant current event, as any enterprising journalist might. Then the actress takes over. The tape-recorded testimony is transformed into roles to be played in quick and often startling juxtaposition.

This time, the triggering incidents are the savage 1991 beating of Mr. King by the Los Angeles police, captured on videotape and witnessed by millions of Americans, and the trial and acquittal of four of the officers, who maintained they were only acting in the line of duty. But other equally brutal events fuel the fear and fury coursing through Ms. Smith's piece: the assault on the truck driver Reginald Denny by rioters, also horrifyingly caught on videotape; the fatal shooting of Latasha Harlins by a Korean grocer who believed the fifteen-year-old girl was shoplifting; and the second trial of the Los Angeles police officers, not to mention the long history of uneasy relations among black, white, Asian and Mexican Americans in the palm-fringed crucible that is South-Central Los Angeles.

Although much of this is still seared on the nation's consciousness, explanatory subtitles are regularly flashed on the proscenium. And on a screen behind Ms. Smith, a dazzling swirl of projections and videotape, including that of the King and Denny beatings, periodically explodes to the wail of sirens and the hollow rat-a-tat-tat of machine-gun fire.

We are a far cry from the essentially bare stage that housed the performer's inquiry into the 1991 racial confrontations in Crown Heights. This production, which has glide-on, glide-off scenery by John Arnone and disco lighting by Jules Fisher and Peggy Eisenhauer, goes for a lot of the glossy, adrenaline-generating pizazz you expect of a Broadway musical. Ms. Smith, possessed of un-

common conviction and unflinching concentration, holds her ground magnificently.

Her living portraits range from Daryl F. Gates, the former chief of the Los Angeles Police Department, who tries to justify his presence at a fund raiser on the very night the riots were "blossoming," to Elaine Brown, the acerbic onetime head of the Black Panther Party, who, from her vantage point in France, differentiates between "strategy and swashbuckling" and advises hotheaded blacks that "if you just want to die and become a poster, go ahead." Mr. Denny, beaming a bit goofily, insists he harbors no bitterness whatsoever and talks about building "a happy room" in his house to display all the loving notes and memorabilia he has received from around the world.

In the sort of coincidence that makes Ms. Smith's pieces so revelatory, Paul Parker, who headed the defense committee for Mr. Denny's assailants, also talks about setting aside a room in his house. "It's gonna be my No Justice, No Peace room," he says, venting his implacable hatred for the white power structure.

Ms. Smith backs off from no one, even if it means assuming the majesty of the mezzo-soprano Jessye Norman and the oratorical pomp of Senator Bill Bradley, delivering some of her monologues in Korean and Spanish or plunging into the frazzled minds of inarticulate street people who desperately want to be heard. Yet in so much diversity, there is unity. Their perspectives may be wildly different, but all these people in their fashion are struggling to put sense into senselessness and find the justice in what looks like injustice run rabid. By the end, the piece has transcended specifics and become an expression of the eternal search for order in an anarchic world.

Varying her basic outfit of black slacks and blouse with the odd accessory—a tie, a pair of rhinestone glasses, a baseball cap—the actress changes identities primarily by changing her vocal rhythms and thought patterns. The words she's speaking remake not only her features but her sex and race as well. In two instances, *Twilight* allows Ms. Smith to venture even further and act out what could be self-contained mini-dramas.

The first is the story of Elvira Evers, a cashier from Panama who was pregnant and near delivery when struck by a random bullet. How she made it to the hospital and gave birth to a girl and what saved both their lives is the stuff of *Ripley's Believe It or Not.* As Ms. Smith tells it, sweetly and simply, it makes for a triumphant monologue about love and acceptance, in which the dark forces of chance work in favor of humanity for once.

The evening's other standout is Maria, Juror No. 7 in the second trial of the four police officers. Recounting what went on behind closed doors, complete with devilish impersonations of her fellow jurors, she proves a regular live wire with a low tolerance for sham. In this case, how deliberations, weighted down in a morass of prejudice and personal guilt, got unstuck makes for triumph of a different kind. Ms. Smith does both women proud.

Twilight: Los Angeles, 1992, which was seen in an earlier version last year at the Mark Taper in Los Angeles, is largely sold out for its run at the Public. On April 10, however, it moves to the Cort Theater on Broadway for a 16-week run. For its restless intelligence and passionate understanding, it will be welcome. For its appreciation of the singular voice in the howling throng, it should be treasured.

Ben Brantley ON

Rent

BOOK, MUSIC AND LYRICS BY

Jonathan Larson

February 13, 1996

2,213+ Performances

RENT by Jonathan Larson; directed by Michael Greif; musical director, Tim Weil; choreography by Marlies Yearby; sets by Paul Clay; costumes by Angela Wendt; lighting by Blake Burba; sound by Darron L. West; dramaturge, Lynn M. Thomson; musical arranger, Steve Skinner; assistant director, Martha Banta; original concept and additional lyrics, Billy Aronson; film, Tony Gerber; production manager, Susan R. White; production stage manager, Crystal Huntington; assistant stage manager, Catherine J. Haley. New Director/New Directions Series. Presented by New York Theater Workshop, James C. Nicola, artistic director; Nancy Kassak Diekmann, managing director. At 79 East Fourth Street, East Village.

Mark Cohen..Anthony Rapp
Roger Davis...Adam Pascal
Tom Collins...Jesse L. Martin
Benjamin Coffin 3d ....Taye Diggs
Joanne Jefferson ....Fredi Walker
Angel Schunard.......................Wilson Jermaine Heredia
Mimi Marquez...................................Daphne Rubin-Vega
Maureen Johnson...Idina Menzel
With Kristen Lee Kelly, Byron Utley, Gwen Stewart, Timothy Britten Parker, Gilles Chiasson, Rodney Hicks and Aiko Nakasone.

The subject of the work is death at an early age. And in one of the dark dramatic coincidences theater occasionally springs on us, its thirty five-year-old author died only weeks before its opening. Yet no one who attends Jonathan Larson's *Rent,* the exhilarating, landmark rock opera at the New York Theater Workshop, is likely to mistake it for a wake.

Indeed, this vigorous tale of a marginal band of artists in Manhattan's East Village, a contemporary answer to *La Bohème,* rushes forward on an electric current of emotion that is anything but morbid. Sparked by a young, intensely vibrant cast directed by Michael Greif and sustained by a glittering, inventive score, the work finds a transfixing brightness in characters living in the shadow of AIDS. Puccini's ravishingly melancholy work seemed, like many operas of its time, to romance death; Mr. Larson's spirited score and lyrics defy it.

Rent inevitably invites reflections on the incalculable loss of its composer, who died of an aortic aneurysm on January 25, but it also shimmers with hope for the future of the American musical. Though this production still has its bumps, most visibly in its second act, Mr. Larson has proved that rock-era song styles can be integrated into a character-driven story for the stage with wildly affecting success. (Only the Broadway version of the Who's *Tommy* has supported that premise in recent years, and its characters were more icons than real people.)

Actually, while Mr. Larson plays wittily with references to Puccini's masterpiece, the excitement around *Rent* more directly recalls the impact made by a dark-horse musical Off Broadway in 1967: *Hair.* Like that meandering, genial portrait of draft-dodging hippies, this production gives a pulsing, unexpectedly catchy voice to one generation's confusion, angst and anarchic, pleasure-seeking vitality.

The setting has shifted east, from Washington Square to St. Mark's Place; the drug of choice is now heroin, not L.S.D.; and the specter that gives its characters' lives a feverish, mordant edge isn't the Vietnam War but H.I.V.

And Mr. Larson has provided a story line and ambitious breadth of technique miles away from *Hair,* with its funky, loosely plotted patchwork of countercultural ditties and ballads. But both works, in a way, are generational anthems, not so much of protest, finally, but of youthful exuberance, even (or especially) when the youth in question is imperiled.

The denizens of Mr. Larson's bohemian landscape are directly descended from their Puccini prototypes but given a hip, topical spin. The poet Rodolfo becomes Roger (Adam Pascal), a songwriter who has shut down emotionally after the suicide of his girlfriend. The painter Marcello is now Mark (Anthony Rapp), a video artist who shares an abandoned industrial loft with Roger on Avenue B.

Mark has recently been thrown over by his lover, Maureen (Idina Menzel), the show's answer to Musetta and a performance artist who has left him for another woman, the lawyer Joanne (Fredi Walker). And Puccini's frail, tubercular Mimi sheds her passivity to be reincarnated as Mimi Marquez (Daphne Rubin-Vega), a tough stray kitten of a woman who dances in an S-and-M club.

The plot is a peppery hash of lovers' quarrels and reconciliations, with a slightly labored subplot in which the men's landlord, Benjamin (Taye Diggs), a former confrere gone Yuppie, padlocks their building while trying to evict a colony of homeless people next door.

Obviously, poverty is less picturesque in Mr. Larson's world than in Puccini's. (The moon, in the most inspired touch in Paul Clay's gritty set, is only an oversize Japanese lantern.) This show's equivalent of the Latin Quarter café scene, with its jolly parade of children and vendors, is an angry Christmas Eve vignette set among bag people on St. Mark's Place. And this Mimi has cold hands because she needs a fix.

Moreover, Mimi, who is H.I.V.-positive, isn't the only candidate for an early death. Roger and his friends, Tom Collins (Jesse L. Martin), a self-styled computer-age philosopher, and Angel (Wilson Jermaine Heredia), a transvestite sculptor, also carry the virus. Accordingly, the leitmotif of the show is the image of time evaporating; its credo, quite unabashedly, "Seize the day."

Mr. Larson gives refreshingly melodic life to these sentiments with a score of breathtaking eclecticism, lovingly and precisely interpreted by the production's excellent five-member band, led by Tim Weil.

The styles include not only electric rock but salsa, Motown, be-bop and reggae, with a firm nod to Stephen Sondheim and even a passing one to Burt Bacharach. There is also a disarmingly dexterous use of operatic, multi-voiced counterpoint and of duets that range from the exquisite (the candle-lit meeting of Roger and Mimi) to the two-fistedly comic (Musetta's waltz becomes "Tango: Maureen").

An alternately agile and baldly declarative lyricist with a tireless knack for all manner of rhymes, Mr. Larson, like his characters, is clearly a child of postmodernism. (This, after all, is a show that rhymes "curry vindaloo" with "Maya Angelou.") But he ultimately avoids the style of brittle, defensive irony, with everything framed in quotation marks, that has become the hallmark of downtown theater in recent years.

In fact, on one level, *Rent* is about breaking through the self-protective detachment, here embodied by both Roger and Mark, of a generation weaned on the archness of David Letterman and the blankness of Andy Warhol. Like such other recent works as Mr. Sondheim's *Passion* and Nicky Silver's *Raised in Captivity,* this show directly addresses the idea of being cut off from feelings by fear.

This is definitely not a problem for Mr. Larson. Indeed, one forgives the show's intermittent lapses into awkwardness or cliché because of its overwhelming emotional sincerity. And when the whole ensemble stands at the edge of the stage, singing fervently about the ways of measuring borrowed time, the heart both breaks and soars.

It should also be pointed out that Mr. Greif lets his cast come to the edge of the stage to serenade the audience entirely too often. He is also guilty of staging that obscures crucial plot elements. And he and his choreographer, Marlies Yearby, don't make the most of the varied possibilities of the score. Only the heady, intricately rhymed "Vie Boheme" banquet number, which concludes the first act, and the erotically staged death of Angel really match the inventive sweep of the music.

The cast, however, is terrific, right down to the last ensemble member, and blessed with voices of remarkable flexibility and strength. The unflaggingly focused Mr. Rapp gives the show its energetic motor; the golden-voiced Mr. Pascal its meditative soul and Ms. Rubin-Vega its affirmative sensuality. Mr. Martin, Ms. Walker, Mr. Here-

dia and Ms. Menzel are all performers of both wit and emotional conviction.

It is the latter trait that lifts *Rent* well above the synthetic, cleverly packaged herd of Broadway musical revivals and revues. Along with George C. Wolfe and Savion Glover's *Bring in da Noise, Bring in da Funk,* this show restores spontaneity and depth of feeling to a discipline that sorely needs them. People who complain about the demise of the American musical have simply been looking in the wrong places. Well done, Mr. Larson.

Ben Brantley ON

Bring in da Noise, Bring in da Funk

BOOK BY Reg E. Gaines

MUSIC BY Daryl Waters, Zane Mark AND

Ann Duquesnay

———

April 25, 1996

Ambassador Theater

1,130 Performances

Savion Glover in *Bring in da Noise/Bring in da Funk*
SARA KRULWICH/THE NEW YORK TIMES

BRING IN DA NOISE, BRING IN DA FUNK. Book by Reg E. Gaines; music by Daryl Waters, Zane Mark and Ann Duquesnay; conceived and directed by George C. Wolfe; based on an idea by Savion Glover and Mr. Wolfe; choreography by Mr. Glover. Sets by Riccardo Hernandez; costumes by Paul Tazewell; lighting by Jules Fisher and Peggy Eisenhauer; sound by Dan Moses Schreier; projection by Batwin and Robin; musical supervision and orchestrations by Mr. Waters; musical director, Mr. Mark; vocal arrangements by Ms. Duquesnay; musical coordinator, Seymour Red Press. Presented by the Joseph Papp Public Theater/New York Shakespeare Festival, Mr. Wolfe, producer.
With Savion Glover, Baakari Wilder, Jimmy Tate, Vincent Bingham, Jeffrey Wright, Ann Duquesnay, Jared Crawford, Raymond King and Dule Hill.

It's a strange and mighty force that is connecting the audience and the performers at the Ambassador Theater. People watching the show there seem to find themselves yelping, whooping and sobbing without even being aware of it. And when the dancers onstage conclude a number with a jubilant roar, the audience roars right back.

This white-hot exchange of energy can sometimes be found at rock concerts, but rarely at a Broadway musical anymore. And that, improbably enough, is what is being described here.

Sing hallelujah! *Bring in da Noise, Bring in da Funk,* George C. Wolfe and Savion Glover's telling of black American history through tap dancing, is alive and flying higher than ever on Broadway.

There was speculation that *Noise,* first produced at the Joseph Papp Public Theater last November, would get lost in a cavernous midtown theater catering to mainstream audiences. But this show, with beautifully enhanced production values, has not only transferred gracefully; it now also seems clear that Broadway is its natural and inevitable home. And it is speaking to its audiences with an electricity and immediacy that evoke the great American musicals of decades past.

Sometimes you're not fully aware of a vacuum until it has been filled. For years now, the Broadway musical slate has been dominated by revivals and pastiche operettas. Attending them was like visiting a pop museum: a perfectly pleasant expe-

rience, but underlined with a sense of detachment. They usually had very little to do with the world outside the theater.

Yet the best American musicals, of both stage and screen, have seldom been just slices of chipper escapism; they have also persistently struck, both directly and subliminally, chords of concerns with which their audiences would be very familiar.

Consider a list as varied as *West Side Story,* the Busby Berkeley movies of the Great Depression and the sentimental Rodgers and Hammerstein musicals of the 1940s and '50s. These all, in their ways, addressed the fears and anxieties of their times—about urban tensions, poverty, the losses of war and the disorientation of the succeeding boom years—then recast them in forms that found sense and affirmation through the rhythms of music and dance.

Noise restores that link. Though the show's historic sweep goes back to the earliest days of slavery, every scene throbs with a visceral sense of the contemporary. The pulse of conflict and exasperation you sense walking to the theater through Times Square—with the aggressive pace of its crowds, the nerve-jangling noises of jackhammers and the attention-getting cries of street performers—is the pulse that informs *Noise.* And while it may be the story of one race, the ways in which Mr. Glover, the show's star and choreographer, and Mr. Wolfe, its director, turn exasperation and anger into art belong to all audiences.

There is, accordingly, a fertile spirit of generosity about *Noise.* It is evident from its very first moments, in which Mr. Glover and his fellow dancers conduct a dialogue in tap. They are tossing a rhythm among themselves, like children with a ball, and they seem to pass it on to the show's narrators, the singer Ann Duquesnay and the actor Jeffrey Wright. And when the dancers directly face the house, it's as if they're throwing the ball to the audience. You actually feel that you've somehow joined in the dance.

This is enriched by the feeling that we're being let in on the creative process, on the shaping of the dance itself. Almost all the numbers trace an arc from tentativeness to full-blown, assured performances. This is most evident in Mr. Glover's splendid second-act solo, in which he demonstrates the techniques of legendary tap artists of the past and then synthesizes them into an exultant style of his own.

The same pattern assumes an astonishing number of other forms: Mr. Glover, as a manacled man on a slave ship, moving from a rolling, fetal crouch into a circular sprint; the company as field hands, in the days when plantation holders had banned drums from the slave quarters, finding the beat in assorted menial chores; the superb sequence, set in early-twentieth-century Chicago, in which the dancers are transformed from cogs in a machine into forces of pure, frustrated energy, equally ready to strut and fight; the sad, funny scene showing four black men in search of a taxi.

All the dancers—Baakari Wilder, Jimmy Tate, Vincent Bingham and Dule Hill—maintain the distinct, loose-jointed styles they displayed last fall, but they also seem to have grown in presence. Their movements project through the larger theater like lightning. Jared Crawford and Raymond King, the drummers who find symphonic music in plastic buckets and pots and pans, match the dancers in their contagious exuberance. It's as if they're all blissfully drunk on their own talent.

As for Mr. Glover, he appears more than ever to be today's answer to Fred Astaire, with the same prodigious inventiveness and a nimble elegance all his own. Like Astaire, he wears perfection with a shrug; everything he does feels utterly spontaneous, yet not at all accidental. A natural star whose charisma lies not in a fixed persona but a fluid mutability, he seems to be always reinventing himself before our eyes.

The dancing, however, was excellent even in the earliest days of *Noise* at the Public Theater. It was the elements around it that didn't gel. The show's narration was spoken by its author, Reg E. Gaines, who lacked theatrical presence and diction. The songs, though performed winningly by Ms. Duquesnay, could feel tacked on. And the supertitles and slide projections by Batwin and Robin had the feeling of dangling footnotes.

But Mr. Wolfe, it should be remembered, is the director who brought us the dazzlingly slick Broadway productions of *Angels in America* and *Jelly's Last Jam.* He actually seems more at home with the richer, broader canvas that Broadway affords than in the workshop atmosphere of the Public, where he is the producer.

The Broadway *Noise* feels both more sumptuous and clearer than its predecessor, and it coheres in ways it just didn't before. The same sensibility is evident in Paul Tazewell's bright, slyly exaggerated costumes; Riccardo Hernandez's crisp, shorthand scenery; and, above all, in Jules Fisher and Peggy Eisenhauer's masterly lighting, which can all by itself evoke prison bars, a Hollywood premiere and a dreamland of a Harlem nightclub. And the score, by Daryl Waters, Zane Mark and Ms. Duquesnay, now seems to enhance, rather than compete with, the primary, multi-shaded music of the tapping.

Mr. Gaines's text is at least audible now, though its labored lyricism can make delivering it an uphill battle for Mr. Wright, an excellent actor. The greater bonus is the manner in which Mr. Wolfe has refined the show's satirical aspects, going beyond the savage wit of his *Colored Museum,* a survey of black cultural stereotypes.

Mr. Wright is wonderful as a drawling, white-jacketed guide (with a Bobby Short voice, no less) to the Harlem Renaissance. And the commanding Ms. Duquesnay, who can change voices like a mockingbird, wickedly speaks the part of a Shirley Temple-ish child star (danced by Mr. Glover, with Mr. Wilder devastatingly on target as a Bill Robinson type) and does a bold impersonation of a bleary Billie Holiday selling her pain.

What these scenes are taking on, of course, is the manner in which black talent has been appropriated, tamed and marketed for the mainstream. The same feeling is suggested in the Harlem Renaissance and Hollywood dance sequences.

But none of these vignettes are merely derisive. Mr. Wolfe and his company know that even when the beat that the show celebrates seems submerged, it is always waiting to erupt again. And when it does, in its purest, most ecstatic form, the foundations of the Ambassador seem to shake in happy response.

Ben Brantley ON

Chicago

BOOK BY Fred Ebb AND Bob Fosse

LYRICS BY Fred Ebb

MUSIC BY John Kander

November 14, 1996

Richard Rodgers Theater

1,981+ Performances

Bebe Neuwirth *(left)* and Ann Reinking in *Chicago,* a sardonic musical about celebrity worship

CHICAGO. Book by Fred Ebb and Bob Fosse; music by John Kander; lyrics by Mr. Ebb; based on the play by Maurine Dallas Watkins; original production directed and choreographed by Fosse. Based on the presentation by City Center's Encores! Directed by Walter Bobbie; choreography by Ann Reinking, in the style of Fosse. Music director, Rob Fisher; sets by John Lee Beatty; costumes by William Ivey Long; lighting by Ken Billington; sound by Scott Lehrer; original orchestration by Ralph Burns; dance music arrangements by Peter Howard; script adaptation by David Thompson; musical coordinator, Seymour Red Press; associate producer, Alecia Parker; presented in association with Pace Theatrical Group. Presented by Barry and Fran Weissler, in association with Kardana Productions.

Roxie Hart	Ann Reinking
Velma Kelly	Bebe Neuwirth
Billy Flynn	James Naughton
Amos Hart	Joel Grey
Matron "Mama" Morton	Marcia Lewis
Mary Sunshine	D. Sabella

Who would have thought there could be such bliss in being played for a patsy?

In the pulse-racing revival of the musical *Chicago,* which opened last night at the Richard Rodgers Theater, all the world's a con game, and show business is the biggest scam of all. It makes a difference, though, when the hustle involves a cast of top-flight artists perfectly mated to their parts and some of the sexiest, most sophisticated dancing seen on Broadway in years. By the time the priceless Bebe Neuwirth, playing a hoofer turned murderer, greets the audience at the beginning of the second act with the salutation "Hello, suckers!" it's a label we're all too happy to accept. The America portrayed onstage may be a vision of hell, but the way it's being presented flies us right into musical heaven.

This sharp-edged, self-defined tale of "murder, greed, corruption, violence, exploitation, adultery and treachery" received a healthy initial run in the mid-1970s but very ambivalent reviews. Even with such mesmerizing stars as Gwen Verdon and Chita Rivera, swell vaudeville-pastiche songs by John Kander and Fred Ebb and the acutely stylish direction and choreography of Bob Fosse, *Chicago* seemed too chilly, in those days, to be truly loved in the way *Oklahoma!* or *A Chorus Line,* its warm-hearted contemporary and rival, might be. Yet this new incarnation, directed by Walter Bobbie and choreographed by Ann Reinking (who also stars), makes an exhilarating case both for *Chicago* as a musical for the ages and for the essential legacy of Fosse, whose ghost has never been livelier than it is here.

There's been talk in the press that theatergoers, in the era of O. J. Simpson and Amy Fisher, are now more likely to accept the work's jaded take on pathological celebrity worship and a fractured justice system. But that's not what makes this *Chicago* so immensely appealing.

What this production makes clear is how much *Chicago* is about the joy of seducing an audience that goes to the theater, above all, to be seduced. Fosse, who had a fiercely conflicted relationship with his profession, may have regarded entertainers as applause-addicted grifters. (Take another look at his autobiographical movie, *All That Jazz,* if you want confirmation.) Yet he also reveled in the adrenaline rush that comes from singers and dancers doing what they do best, at their best. Every number in this *Chicago* (and most of them are show-stoppers) buzzes with an implicit, irresistibly arrogant declaration: "Watch me. What I'm about to do is going to be terrific, and you're going to love every second of it."

This sensibility was already evident when the show, which is set in the violence-drunken Chicago of the 1920s (and based on Maurine Dallas Watkins's play of that period), was staged last spring in a concert version as part of the Encores! series at City Center. Underscoring the conceit of this musical as a self-conscious series of vaudeville turns, the show (which had the same stars and much of the same production team) brought down the house, using only minimal scenery and costumes. Still, there were worries about how the production might transfer to Broadway. To dress it up more elaborately for a big house might dilute what was magic about it to begin with. On the other hand, would theatergoers paying top ticket prices of $70 feel cheated by the lack of the flashy scenery and special effects to which they had become accustomed?

Well, this is not a show to leave anyone feeling bilked. The revival's creators have indeed retained the spare visual essence of what was seen at City Center. The orchestra (still sublime under the direction of Rob Fisher) remains center stage in John Lee Beatty's witty evocation of a giant witness box in a courtroom. An elevator (for grand

entrances and exits) has been added, but most of the scenery is still nothing more than some chairs and ladders. And nearly everything, down to the last, flesh-framing inch of William Ivey Long's sleek costumes, is in shades of black and white, set off by Ken Billington's expert film-noir lighting.

And yet somehow everything feels richer, like an expensive, perfectly constructed sheath from a designer like Mainbocher. It creates the ideal environment for a tribute to the illusions that can be woven out of air by the right combination of music, actors, singers and dancers. And each of the performances has been polished like the Astors' silver.

Much of the credit, of course, goes to Mr. Bobbie, whose delightfully inventive direction sustains just the right tone of heady irony. Ms. Reinking, a former dancer for Fosse (and, for a time, his companion), has brought her own lighthanded sparkle in evoking the Fosse spirit, and the corps de ballet couldn't be better, physically capturing the wry, knowing pastiche of some of Kander and Ebb's best songs.

Dance for Fosse, a man who came of age backstage at Chicago's bump-and-grind houses, always had an air of the striptease. And the numbers, which usually begin with Mr. Kander's gripping, sustained vamps, are all built on the idea of tantalizing. They often start with Fosse's come-hither pelvic thrusts and finger snapping, segue into slow, silky routines (punctuated by eruptions of splits and leaps) and finally burst into orgasmic displays of energy that never spin out of control.

It's hard to know where to start in singling out cast members. Ms. Reinking's Roxie Hart, the over-the-hill chorine who becomes a star when she murders her straying lover, emerges as the most entertainingly erotic cartoon character since Jessica Rabbit. Every vocal inflection and gesture is writ large (watch how she keeps extending her arms as if to embrace an entire adoring throng) but also with precise, elegant calligraphy.

Ms. Reinking meets her match, though, in her co-star. As Velma Kelly, a vaudevillian in jail for a bloody crime of passion and Roxie's competitor in publicity seeking, Ms. Neuwirth has translated her deadpan comic persona and technical proficiency as a dancer into an ecstatic benchmark performance. The deliciously mechanical wriggle in her walk embodies the very soul of the show. And to see her turn her legs into a pair of air-slicing scissors, her face set in a bewitching expression of self-satisfaction, is like falling in love, against your better judgment, with a specialist in breaking hearts.

James Naughton, a superb musical leading man who in another age would have the status of a Robert Preston, brings flawless timing and a velvety crooner's voice to the role of the press-manipulating lawyer. Marcia Lewis, as a predatory prison matron, and D. Sabella, as a gooey gossip columnist who is not what she appears to be, have refined what were already superior performances.

And as Amos, Roxie's limp dupe of a husband, Joel Grey (best known as the decadent emcee in another Kander-Ebb musical, *Cabaret*) achieves the miracle of turning passivity into pure show-biz electricity, all the more arresting for being kept a low voltage. Amos's big number, "Mr. Cellophane," is a lament on the worst thing that can befall an actor: not to be noticed. "You can look right through me," he wails. *Chicago* is, of course, all about being noticed, with the characters' lust for attention mirrored by that of the performers playing them.

The show takes the bold extra step of breaking down the methodology of getting attention in a musical. When Roxie sings of the raptures of being famous, she summons a phalanx of chorus boys to "frame me better." Her lawyer lets us know in advance just how he's going to sing to win over reporters (and then does so using Roxie as a ventriloquist's dummy). And when Velma rehearses her appearance on the witness stand, it's a dancer's anatomy lesson.

See, the performers seem to be saying, what we're doing is all illusion, and you're falling for it. Or as a line from the song "Razzle Dazzle" has it, "Long as you keep 'em way off balance, how can they spot you got no talents?"

Nonsense. This production isn't smoke and mirrors. It's flesh and blood shaped by discipline and artistry into a parade of vital, pulsing talent. If there's any justice in the world (and *Chicago* insists that there isn't), audiences will be exulting in that parade for many, many performances to come.

Ben Brantley ON
A Doll's House
BY Henrik Ibsen

———

April 2, 1997
Belasco Theater
150 Performances

Janet McTeer as Nora and Owen Teale as her husband in *A Doll's House* SARA KRULWICH/THE NEW YORK TIMES

A DOLL'S HOUSE by Henrik Ibsen; a new version by Frank McGuinness; directed by Anthony Page; designed by Deirdre Clancy; lighting by Peter Mumford; music composed by Jason Carr; sound by Scott Myers and John Owens; production stage manager, Sally J. Jacobs; production supervisor, Gene O'Donovan; general manager, Stuart Thompson Productions. Presented by Bill Kenwright, in association with Thelma Holt.

Nora Helmer	Janet McTeer
Torvald Helmer	Owen Teale
Kristine Linde	Jan Maxwell
Nils Krogstad	Peter Gowen
Dr. Rank	John Carlisle
Anne-Marie	Robin Howard
Helene	Rose Stockton
The Messenger	John Ottavino
Bobby	Liam Aiken
Ivan	Paul Tiesler

It just doesn't happen that often, and when it does, you sit there, open-mouthed, grateful, admiring and shaken, and think, "This is why I love the theater."

It's the response that comes when a dramatic performance is so completely and richly realized that you find yourself truly living through the character portrayed onstage, even when you want to pull back to a comfortable spectator's distance. The pulse quickens, the eyes well. And there is somehow the sense that ordinary life has been heightened to the bursting point.

The occasion for this revelation is the new production of Ibsen's *Doll's House,* a London import that opened last night at the Belasco Theater. The name of the revelation is Janet McTeer, an actress, little known in America, whose apparition on Broadway suggests the theater's timely answer to the Hale-Bopp comet. What Ms. McTeer achieves, with the magnificent support of the director Anthony Page and a flawless supporting cast, is the sense that the landmark, century-old role of Ibsen's Nora Helmer, the childlike housewife who comes so painfully of age, was only just written, and written specifically for her. You may think you know *A Doll's House* inside out. This production is guaranteed to prove you wrong.

The 1879 classic, with its iconoclastic portrayal of a woman who leaves her marriage to find herself, assumed an instant, thundering social significance and that has clouded perceptions of the play. There was a theory, starting with George Bernard Shaw, that the drama's greatness was more historical than artistic, and that, like most things searingly topical, it was destined to become a fossil. Still, the play has never left the international repertory, with great actresses repeatedly drawn to Nora like the proverbial moths to the flame. Very often, they have indeed been burned, provoking criticism that Nora's conversion from domestic plaything to proto-feminist requires radical jumps in psychological continuity, accompanied by the creaking of a mechanical, agenda-driven plot.

Not a single creak is heard in Mr. Page's production, Ms. McTeer's performance or Frank McGuinness's wonderfully loose-limbed adaptation. They never impose on Ibsen's text but instead mine it for an emotional consistency and logic that is very definitely there. And marvel of marvels, the most stirring part of this interpretation comes in its last twenty minutes, when Nora speaks the lines that, out of context, have become feminist rallying cries.

Ms. McTeer's Nora, confronting her husband, Torvald (the masterly Owen Teale), with the failure of their marriage, is no coolly articulate visionary, for whom a light has suddenly been turned on after a lifetime of benightedness. She is still fumbling in the dark, still struggling to find words to match her growing belief that something is very, very wrong. She seems surprised, in fact, by her own perceptions, as if they were only just taking form in her consciousness. The entire evening builds carefully to this moment in ways you are aware of only after you've arrived there.

From the outset, Ms. McTeer's performance has suggested a struggle between willful self-delusion and a subterranean uneasiness that Nora reflexively works to suppress. She's a hardworking actress who doesn't even know she's playing a part or how tired she has grown of it. Ms. McTeer starts off with a mannered intensity some audience members may at first find grating. There's a glow of fever about Nora as she busily trims her comfortably appointed living room for Christmas. The laughter with which she punctuates her speech has a loonlike quality; she tries on different, silly voices like an eager-to-please comedian; she flaps her wrists in a way that dismisses what she's saying even as she calls attention to it.

It is a brave, risky conception that even comes

across as grotesque at moments, a feeling underscored by the fact that Ms. McTeer is no doll-size ingénue but a woman of towering height and erotic presence. (She compliantly bends her knees for her long, frequent kisses with Torvald.) She's a fluttery geisha in overdrive, on call to entertain and make merry whenever her husband chooses to appear from his invincible fortress of a study.

What cannot be doubted is that Nora behaves like this out of love for the man she married. It's the same impulse that drove her to commit the criminal act—the forging of her father's signature when she needed to borrow money to take her ailing husband to Italy—that provides the play with its plot. And this production ingeniously melds Nora's apprehension about being exposed by the embittered money lender Nils Krogstad (Peter Gowen) with the encroaching awareness that her love for Torvald, the center of her existence, is built on sand.

There are moments throughout, especially in Nora's scenes with her childhood friend Kristine Linde (Jan Maxwell) and her cynical admirer, Dr. Rank (John Carlisle), when shafts of light break into the doll's house, a sense of how hard and unfair the world can be and of the imbalance in the Helmers' marriage. The scene when, in conversation with Dr. Rank, Nora realizes that her relationship with her husband is like that she had with her doting father, is remarkable both for how the perception astonishes her and for how she seems to brush it away. So when the play reaches its climax, it feels less like an abrupt turn than the inevitable end of a single, well-paved road.

Mr. Page, best known here for his productions of *Heartbreak House* (with Rex Harrison and Rosemary Harris) and *Inadmissible Evidence* (with Nicol Williamson), reminds you of the virtues of pure naturalism in theater. There's a ripe physicality to the production, an awareness of the comforts of the warmth of home and clothing (deliciously embodied by Deirdre Clancy's set and costumes) and of the literal coldness outside. (This is the first production of *A Doll's House* I've seen in which, when Nora makes her famous final exit, I worried whether she was dressed warmly enough.)

There is a definite sensual heat as well. It's apparent in the coded, tantalizing body language between Nora and Helmer; in the hungry kisses stolen by Kristine and Nils after they declare their love for each other; in Nora's mischievously displaying her silk stockings to the terminally ill Dr. Rank, an act that registers as one of infinite, if misplaced, kindness to a dying man; and, above all, in Ms. McTeer's dancing the tarantella as a giddy, erotic collapse into nervous exhaustion.

It is also hard to imagine a more persuasively balanced ensemble. Mr. Carlisle's flinty, troubled doctor; Ms. Maxwell's sober, pragmatic Kristine (a perfect foil to Ms. McTeer's agitation); Mr. Gowen's all-too-human, self-preserving desperation: these performances remind you that Ibsen did indeed create complete characters who are always waiting to be rediscovered.

As Torvald, the handsome, imposingly centered Mr. Teale couldn't be better. For once, you understand the magnetic hold this husband has over his wife, as well as why he is destined to lose her. His blunt air of authority is so compelling that when it finally shatters, the effect is devastating.

Nora leaves this broken man less in anger than in sorrow, a fitting conclusion to an evening infused not with polemical rage but with a sad compassion for the mess people make of their lives. The "something glorious" that Nora so ravenously craves, a heroic act from her husband that would redeem their marriage, doesn't happen, of course. But thanks to Ms. McTeer and company, something glorious is very definitely occurring at the Belasco.

Ben Brantley ON

The Lion King

BOOK BY Roger Allers AND Irene Mecchi

MUSIC AND LYRICS BY

Elton John and Tim Rice

November 13, 1997

New Amsterdam Theater

1,603+ Performances

The cast from *The Lion King*   JOAN MARCUS

THE LION KING. Music and lyrics by Elton John and Tim Rice; additional music and lyrics by Lebo M, Mark Mancina, Jay Rifkin, Julie Taymor and Hans Zimmer. Book by Roger Allers and Irene Mecchi; adapted from the screenplay by Ms. Mecchi, Jonathan Roberts and Linda Woolverton. Directed by Ms. Taymor; choreography by Garth Fagan. Sets by Richard Hudson; costumes by Ms. Taymor; lighting by Donald Holder; mask and puppet design by Ms. Taymor and Michael Curry; music director, Joseph Church; music produced for the stage and additional score by Mr. Mancina; associate music producer, Robert Elhai; additional vocal score, vocal arrangements and choral director, Mr. M. Presented by Disney.

Scar	John Vickery
Mufasa	Samuel E. Wright
Simba	Jason Raize
Young Simba	Scott Irby-Ranniar
Zazu	Geoff Hoyle
Nala	Heather Headley
Young Nala	Kajuana Shuford
Timon	Max Casella
Pumbaa	Tom Alan Robbins
Shenzi	Tracy Nicole Chapman
Banzai	Stanley Wayne Mathis
Ed	Kevin Cahoon
Rafiki	Tsidii Le Loka

Suddenly, you're four years old again, and you've been taken to the circus for the first time. You can only marvel at the exotic procession of animals before you: the giraffes and the elephants and the hippopotamuses and all those birds in balletic flight. Moreover, these are not the weary-looking beasts in plumes and spangles that usually plod their way through urban circuses but what might be described as their Platonic equivalents, creatures of air and light and even a touch of divinity.

Where are you, really, anyway? The location is supposed to be a theater on Forty-second Street, a thoroughfare that has never been thought of as a gateway to Eden. Yet somehow you have fallen into what appears to be a primal paradise. And even the exquisitely restored New Amsterdam Theater, a former Ziegfeld palace, disappears before the spectacle within it.

Such is the transporting magic wrought by the opening ten minutes of *The Lion King*, the director Julie Taymor's staged version of the Midas-touch cartoon movie that has generated millions for the Walt Disney Company. And the ways in which Ms. Taymor translates the film's opening musical number, "Circle of Life," where an animal kingdom of the African plains gathers to pay homage to its leonine ruler and his newly born heir, is filled with astonishment and promise.

For one thing, it is immediately clear that this production, which opened last night, is not going to follow the path pursued by Disney's first Broadway venture, *Beauty and the Beast,* a literal-minded exercise in turning its cinematic model into three dimensions. Ms. Taymor, a maverick artist known for her bold multicultural experiments with puppetry and ritualized theater, has her own distinctive vision, one that is miles away from standard Disney fare.

And while this *Lion King* holds fast to much of the film's basic plot and dialogue (the book is by Roger Allers and Irene Mecchi), Ms. Taymor has abandoned none of the singular, and often haunting, visual flourishes she brought to such surreal works as *Juan Darien,* which was revived at Lincoln Center last season, and *The Green Bird.*

There has been much jokey speculation about the artistic marriage of the corporate giant and the bohemian iconoclast, which has been discussed as though Donald Trump and Karen Finley had decided to set up housekeeping. But that rich first number, in which those life-size animal figures assume a transcendent, pulsing existence, seems to suggest that these strange bedfellows might indeed live in blissful harmony.

Unfortunately, it turns out that these glorious opening moments are only the honeymoon part of this fable of the coming of age of a lion with a father fixation. Throughout the show's 2 hours and 40 minutes (as against the 75-minute movie), there will be plenty of instances of breathtaking beauty and scenic ingenuity, realized through techniques ranging from shadow puppetry to Bunraku. Certainly, nowhere before on Broadway has a stampede of wildebeests or a herd of veldt-skimming gazelles been rendered with such eye-popping conviction.

But in many ways, Ms. Taymor's vision, which is largely rooted in ritual forms of theater from Asia and Africa, collides with that of Disney, where visual spectacle is harnessed in the service of heartwarming storytelling. There were hopes that the Disney-Taymor collaboration might reflect what Katharine Hepburn reportedly said about Fred Astaire and Ginger Rogers: "He gives

her class, and she gives him sex" (if you think of Ms. Taymor as Astaire and you substitute sentiment for sex).

But Ms. Taymor's strengths have never been in strongly sustained narratives or fully developed characters. It is the cosmic picture that she's after, a sense of the cycles of life and death, of rebirth and metamorphosis. Accordingly, many of the strongest scenes in this *Lion King* are edged in mortal darkness, including a lovely vignette in which lionesses stalk their prey.

Since the movie version had a fashionably eco-friendly aspect, with pointed reference to the delicate balance of nature, Ms. Taymor's animistic viewpoint is not entirely out of place here. But although many of the actors have charm and freshness, they are hampered to some extent by the masks and puppet effigies that turn them into animals. You will gasp again and again at the inventive visual majesty of this show, realized through the masks and puppets of Ms. Taymor and Michael Curry, scenic design by Richard Hudson, and Donald Holder's wonderful elemental lighting. But you may be harder pressed to muster the feelings of suspense and poignancy that the film, for all its preachiness, really did evoke.

If you have young children, you probably know the plot. The lion cub Simba (Scott Irby-Ranniar), the heir to the throne of his heroic father, Mufasa (Samuel E. Wright), becomes the pawn of his father's evil brother and archrival, Scar (John Vickery). When Scar murders Mufasa, he convinces the vulnerable cub that it is he who is responsible for the death. And Simba, in the tradition of young fairy-tale heroes, goes into exile in a forest, where he finally comes to terms with his inner self and is ready to reclaim the throne.

The words and the jokes here are familiar from the movie. So are many of the mostly unexceptional songs, with music and lyrics by Elton John and Tim Rice, although this production includes additional music and lyrics (by Lebo M, Mark Mancina, Jay Rifkin, Hans Zimmer and Ms. Taymor) that incorporate a more authentic sense of tribal rhythms and call-and-response choruses.

There's an irresistible pull to this music, and

when the performers take to the aisles, their puppet appendages in tow, the show takes on a celebratory carnival feeling that almost matches its opening. It's when *The Lion King* decides to fulfill its obligations as a traditional Broadway book musical that it goes slack.

Garth Fagan's choreography is, for the most part, on the clumsy side. A romantic ballet in which the grown Simba (Jason Raize) and his lioness girlfriend (Heather Headley) discover their attraction while other pairs of lovers float in the air above them still seems like a concept waiting to be worked out. And the rendering of the show's best-known number, "Hakuna Matata," a paean to the easy life, surprisingly lacks effervescence.

The vaudeville-ish comedy from the movie has been imported more or less intact, and, on its own grade-school terms, it's still pretty funny. As Simba's pals Timon the meerkat and Pumbaa the wart hog, Max Casella and Tom Alan Robbins are a winning burlesque team. Mr. Casella and Geoff Hoyle, who plays an officious hornbill named Zazu, manipulate puppets that are attached to their bodies and yet somehow manage to make both parts of their divided selves into one character.

As the sinister Scar, in a part spoken to perfection by Jeremy Irons in the movie, Mr. Vickery is too campy to be very menacing, and he isn't helped by his silly costume, which looks more armadillo than lion. Tracy Nicole Chapman, Stanley Wayne Mathis and Kevin Cahoon, who play a trio of scavenging hyenas, are actually more satisfactory villains. And Tsidii Le Loka as Rafiki, the shaman baboon, is a delightful force of gibbering energy.

Mr. Wright, Mr. Raize and Ms. Headley are all attractive performers with melodious voices. But only Mr. Irby-Ranniar, in a most convincing portrait of impetuous, conflicted youth, strikes a spontaneous human chord that invites emotional engagement.

Still, *The Lion King* remains an important work in a way that *Beauty and the Beast* simply is not. Ms. Taymor has introduced a whole new vocabulary of images to the Broadway blockbuster, and you're unlikely to forget such sights as the face of Simba's dead father forming itself into an astral mask among the stars.

There will inevitably be longueurs for both adults and children who attend this show. But it offers a refreshing and more sophisticated alternative to the standard panoply of special effects that dominate most tourist-oriented shows today. Seen purely as a visual tapestry, there is simply nothing else like it.

Ben Brantley ON
The Beauty Queen of Leenane
BY Martin McDonagh

February 26, 1998
473 Performances

Anna Manahan *(left)* as Mag Folan, Brian F. O'Byrne as Pato Dooley, and Marie Mullen as Maureen Folan in *The Beauty Queen of Leenane*   SARA KRULWICH/THE NEW YORK TIMES

THE BEAUTY QUEEN OF LEENANE by Martin McDonagh; directed by Garry Hynes; sets and costumes by Francis O'Connor; lighting by Ben Ormerod; original music by Paddy Cunneen; production stage manager, Matthew Silver; general manager, Bardo S. Ramirez; production manager, Tor Ekeland for Crux. A Druid Theater Company/Royal Court Theater production presented by the Atlantic Theater Company, Neil Pepe, artistic director; Hilary Hinckle, managing director. At 336 West 20th Street, Chelsea.

Mag Folan...Anna Manahan
Maureen Folan..Marie Mullen

Ray Dooley ....Tom Murphy
Pato Dooley ....Brian F. O'Byrne

Sometimes you don't even know what you've been craving until the real thing comes along. Watching the Druid Theater Company's production of *The Beauty Queen of Leenane*, the stunning new play from the young Anglo-Irish dramatist Martin McDonagh, is like sitting down to a square meal after a long diet of salads and hors d'oeuvres. Before you know it, your appetite has come alive again, and you begin to feel nourished in ways you had forgotten were possible.

For what Mr. McDonagh has provided is something exotic in today's world of self-conscious, style-obsessed theater: a proper, perfectly plotted drama that sets out, above all, to tell a story as convincingly and disarmingly as possible.

The Beauty Queen of Leenane, which opened last night at the Atlantic Theater Company with the sterling team that first performed it two years ago in Galway, Ireland, is on many levels an old-fashioned, well-made play. Yet it feels more immediate and vital than any new drama in many seasons.

Simply saying what the play is about, at least on the surface, is to invite yawns. A plain middle-aged woman, trapped in a life as a caretaker to her infirm but iron-willed mother in rural Ireland, is offered a last chance at love. Haven't we all been this way before? Doesn't this sound like an eye-glazing variation on the themes so reliably manipulated in the revival of *The Heiress,* the stalwart stage adaptation of Henry James's *Washington Square,* several seasons ago?

But wait. If *Beauty Queen* is a bucolic cousin to *The Heiress,* it also has the more toxic elements found in Grand Guignol films like *Whatever Happened to Baby Jane?* And Mr. McDonagh, who is only twenty-seven years old, has a master's hand at building up and subverting expectations in a cat-and-mouse game with the audience, of seeming to follow a conventional formula and then standing it on its head. The play offers the satisfactions of a tautly drawn mystery, yet it is by no means airless. There's plenty of room for ambiguity and for the intricacy of character that actors live for.

Under the finely modulated direction of Garry Hynes, a founder of the Druid Theater Company, the splendid four-member ensemble gives full due to the play's cunning twists and reversals while creating the sense that character is indeed fate. It's the thorough integration of every element that astonishes here, the meshing of psychology and action. There's not a single hole in the play's structural or emotional logic, and yet it constantly surprises. Even as the plot grips and holds you, the performances engage you on a darker, deeper level.

Mr. McDonagh's reputation is already so firmly established in Britain that it has undergone a full cycle of star-making praise and skeptical backlash. Since the debut of *Beauty Queen* in London at the Royal Court Theater (a co-producer of the New York incarnation), the city has seen the two other plays in his *Leenane* trilogy, as well as the popular National Theater production of his *Cripple of Inishman,* to be staged here later this month with a largely American cast at the New York Shakespeare Festival.

The excitement is justified, at least on the basis of *Beauty Queen.* The work isn't revolutionary; it doesn't open a window onto new experimental vistas. It's intelligent but not intellectual. And while it uses language and wit and precision, it is not, as so many contemporary plays are, about language and its limitations.

Instead, *Beauty Queen* confirms the viability of the well-made play, reminding us at the same time of how difficult the genre is to execute. Compare it to such current examples of the form as *The Last Night of Ballyhoo* or even the compelling revival of Arthur Miller's *View from the Bridge.* There's always at least a slight feeling of something imposed from without, of plot as a pegboard for theme.

With *Beauty Queen,* on the other hand, nearly everything feels organic, an inevitable outgrowth of character and environment. The play never leaves its single setting, realized with merciless detail by Francis O'Connor, a shabby room in the hilltop country cottage inhabited by old Mag Folan (Anna Manahan) and her embittered daughter, Maureen (Marie Mullen). And though we are told the women do in fact step out of their house from time to time, you feel they never really leave it.

They come to seem as imprisoned as the characters in Sartre's *No Exit.* The evening's opening image finds Mag seated, stock-still, before a television set, and she looks as if she has been there for centuries. Ms. Manahan is a large woman, her girth enhanced by Mr. O'Connor's scruffy layers of clothing, and Mag seems to fill and anchor the room. It is obvious that if Maureen is ever to escape into a life of her own, she will have to dislodge a mother who appears as immovable as a mountain.

The symbiosis between Ms. Manahan and Ms. Mullen is extraordinary as Mag and Maureen swap insults, demands and recriminations in a circular game of one-upmanship. It is a game that has obviously been going on for many years, and while the resentment behind it is real, so is the devious pleasure each takes from it. Mr. McDonagh's spare, brutal dialogue is measured out by these actresses with a refined timing that is both comic and ineffably sinister.

For as the talk continues, spanning topics from Mag's peevish demands for tea and biscuits to local gossip to a murder in Dublin, the subtle shifts in power become dizzying. Who really has the upper hand? Why do references to banal subjects seem so menacing? Who is the victim of whom?

Mr. McDonagh is too smart to provide hard and fast answers. When two visitors from the outside world, the Dooley brothers, Ray (Tom Murphy) and Pato (Brian F. O'Byrne), are used as pawns by Mag and Maureen in their continuing war, the rules that govern the women's relationship become more and more complicated. With small flicks of the eyes and resettings of their mouths, both actresses transform, at different moments, from torturer to hostage and back again.

Ms. Mullen, a pale, red-haired woman who can look terminally worn out one instant and electrically vibrant the next, undergoes another metamorphosis. That's when Maureen brings Pato, a local man working in England, home from a party. In the awkward, exquisitely rendered courtship scene between them, Maureen acquires a melting gentleness and openness that is infinitely sad. Neither actress nor playwright, however, allows you to bathe for very long in the sentiments called forth here.

As performers, the men are a match for the women, which is high praise. Mr. O'Byrne's Pato is a delicate study in self-consciousness, a shy man pulling himself into postures of virile dignity before he makes sexual overtures or a pretty speech. When he gallantly calls Maureen by the epithet of the play's title, it jolts both lovers in unexpected ways. The silence that follows echoes with the sense that a perilous frontier has been crossed.

As Pato's much younger brother, who serves a plot function out of *Romeo and Juliet,* Mr. Murphy offers comic relief without ever presenting it as such. His, more than any other character, must embody the provincial society beyond the women's home, and Ray's irritable restlessness is eloquent on the subject.

In all of Mr. McDonagh's plays, there's a sense that life is cheap and a piquant awareness of the skull beneath the skin. (His second play in the *Leenane* trilogy is called *A Skull in Connemara* for literal reasons.) Ms. Hynes accordingly brings a haunting physical dimension to her production, an aura of mortal decay.

It's evident not only in the presentation of the sheer bulk of Mag, but also in the arresting moment when Maureen takes off her coat to reveal a sleeveless dress that is too young for her. Seen later in a pearlescent slip after her night with Pato, Ms. Mullen's Maureen brings to mind the anatomical portraits of Philip Pearlstein, with their sobering suggestions of the way of all flesh.

Correspondingly, seemingly prosaic objects acquire resonant weight in Mr. McDonagh's plays, much as they do in the movies of Alfred Hitchcock. Even in reading *Beauty Queen,* you can gather how carefully Mr. McDonagh sets up and develops the use of such things as a frying pan, a pair of rubber gloves and, most classically, an unopened letter.

It's all the more pleasurable to see how Ms. Hynes, with the invaluable assistance of the lighting designer, Ben Ormerod, summons those objects into our consciousness at different times, miraculously achieving on stage what Hitchcock did with cinematic close-ups. And you may find images from *Beauty Queen* creeping unbidden into your imagination long after you've seen it.

Toward the end of the play, Ray talks about his affection for foreign shows on television. "Who wants to see Ireland on telly?" he asks. "All you have to do is look out your window and see Ireland. And it's bored you'd be." He adds, pantomiming a slow, sweeping gaze, "There goes a calf."

In Mr. Murphy's interpretation, it's a pricelessly funny moment. Fortunately, though, Ray's creator understands that the most static picture is often teeming with hidden life, that frustration and boredom create dangerous diversions and that simple lives are often filled with contradiction.

Beauty Queen finds the tragic pattern in these things, while acknowledging that the forces beneath it can never be fully explained. In the telling, this play seems as clear as day. When you look back on it, it's the shadows that you can't stop thinking about.

Ben Brantley ON

The Emperor Jones

BY Eugene O'Neill

March 12, 1998

The Performing Garage

15 Performances

THE EMPEROR JONES by Eugene O'Neill; directed by Elizabeth LeCompte; music by David Linton; sound by James Johnson and John Collins; video by Christopher Kondek; designed by Jim Clayburgh; lighting by Georg Bugiel; lighting consultant, Jennifer Tipton; costumes and choreography by the Wooster Group; stage manager, Clay Hapaz. Presented by the Wooster Group.

Brutus Jones	Kate Valk
Smithers	Willem Dafoe
Stage assistants	Dave Shelley and Ari Fliakos

An uncommonly powerful and imaginative performance, in several respects unsurpassed this season," wrote Alexander Woollcott in the fall of 1920 in *The New York Times*. The object of praise was a then little-known actor named Charles S. Gilpin, who was appearing in a strange, bruising new play that had uptown cosmopolites swarming to a small theater in Greenwich Village.

After a series of marginal supporting roles, Gilpin finally had a star part: the title character of the black railroad porter turned West Indies monarch in Eugene O'Neill's *Emperor Jones*. Woollcott rounded off his tribute to the actor with a coda that you might have thought was unnecessary: "Mr. Gilpin is a Negro."

Seventy-eight years later, *The Emperor Jones* has been revived by the Wooster Group at the Performing Garage in SoHo, some blocks south of where the work was first seen at the Playwrights' Theater. The drama still seems strange and bruising, and it has again provided the occasion for an uncommonly powerful and imaginative performance in the title role. That part is played by Kate Valk. Ms. Valk is a Caucasian.

A tidy reversal, no? It was a source of pride for the Provincetown Players, the show's first producers, that they had cast a black man as a black man, after seriously considering the safer choice of a white actor in black face. Brutus Jones, later portrayed by the great Paul Robeson in a Broadway revival and the 1933 film, remained for years one of the few parts of any complexity available to black actors. So what are we to make of the current image of the emperor according to Ms. Valk, who wears shoe-polish-like makeup that evokes Al Jolson singing "Mammy"?

Don't call in the police of political correctness just yet. In casting, as in many things, timing is crucial. America has long passed the point where a straightforward production of *The Emperor Jones*, with a black man delivering O'Neill's dialectical speeches as written, could be other than embarrassing. Yet the drama remains fascinating, and it would be a shame to consign it to the shelves of unplayable plays.

It would also be a shame, however, to present *The Emperor Jones* as a camp relic, worthy of only a post-modern smirk. The particular triumph of Elizabeth LeCompte's interpretation, which also features Willem Dafoe (a member of the Wooster Group before he became a movie star), is its ability to relocate the play in a contemporary context while holding on to the shadowy, hypnotic qualities that first unsettled audiences of the 1920s. You should know that while doing so, this production uses such unlikely (but for this company, classic) devices as a set of television monitors, a wheelchair and Kabuki-flavored soft-shoe routines.

Since its inception two decades ago, the Wooster Group has made a specialty of dislocating theatrical classics, from *Our Town* to *The Three Sisters,* exploding traditional texts with tools ranging from simulcast video cameras and state-of-the-art synthesizers to fly swatters. Along the way, the troupe has consistently drawn the sort of knowing, exotic-looking audiences who seem destined to drift on to cool clubs with unlisted phone numbers after the show.

While it would be gratifying to report that the Wooster Group is merely chic and self-important, it is a company of exceptional discipline and intelligence. Even more uncommonly, it has created a distinctive artistic vocabulary. It may not always hit its targets, but it has refined and strengthened its craft over the years, working both in New York and on international tour. And under Ms. LeCompte's direction, the company has shown an especially persuasive affinity for O'Neill.

This conjunction actually makes sense. O'Neill is certainly the most ardent experimentalist of America's major playwrights. Moreover, his bleak sense of the consequences of a mechanized society is well matched, in a way, by a company that uses technology to scramble and fragment its productions.

O'Neill created characters who bury their most primal needs beneath layers of "science and materialism," leading to deeply divided selves. For the Wooster Group, dealing with another half-

century's worth of scientific and industrial innovations, any solid sense of self appears to have dissolved into atoms.

This theme was evident last season in the company's visually arresting but slightly off-kilter production of *The Hairy Ape,* with a compelling Mr. Dafoe in the title role. Like that work, *Jones* traces a descent down a historical ladder within its central character.

Brutus Jones, a former Pullman porter and convict from the United States, has set himself up as emperor on an island in the West Indies. Confronted with the imminence of revolution, he flees into the jungle, where his regal persona is steadily dismantled by his own terror. By the end, having taken an inward, backward journey through his life and on into an atavistic past, Jones is reduced to aboriginal horror.

The Wooster Group stays close to O'Neill's text, though not to his stage directions, which specify the apparitions of a slave auction and some characters identified (I swear) as Little Formless Fears. There are only two central performers here, Ms. Valk and Mr. Dafoe as Jones's sinister cockney henchman, Smithers. Two stage assistants, Dave Shelley and Ari Fliakos, are also visible presences, however.

The production consistently calls attention to its artificiality and its methods of disorientation. The microphones through which Ms. Valk and Mr. Dafoe speak become at moments jaunty props, like canes in a vaudeville skit, and at others seem like biological appendages. The dialogue is often addressed to cameras that register bizarrely distorted images of the performers, including one that turns the blackened Ms. Valk an ashen white.

There is no doubt that the actors, in costumes that suggest ceremonial Japanese drama, are only actors. But this only adds to the overall feeling of alienation. O'Neill saw personality as a construct, something he emphasized by using masks in other plays. Here, Jones's self-created identity as emperor is given yet another layer, that of the grotesque perception of blacks by whites in the early part of this century.

Her eyes rolling feverishly and her voice a

brazen evocation of the dumb but crafty black figures in minstrel shows and melodramas, Ms. Valk initially registers as an obscene cartoon. Yet as the performance continues, it acquires a searing depth, a compounded feeling of entrapment. It's a performance that sucks you in just when you're feeling safely distanced from it.

Mr. Dafoe's taunting, epicene Smithers, whose very body seems shaped into a sneer, offers superb support. And both actors, speaking in distorted amplified voices against a collage of precisely coded sound effects and stray melodies, find the music in O'Neill's dialectic speech. You're reminded that this playwright's reputation for having a tin ear was largely unearned; he wrote for the stage, not the page. Accordingly, the overall effect of this production is more like that of a concerto than a traditional theater piece.

Ms. LeCompte and her team have been working on *Jones* for at least five years. Even if you find the result pretentious or ponderous, you can't deny the meticulousness with which it has been executed.

Nor can you deny the sheer joy of craft that infuses every element. Watch the dances that the performers break into at unexpected moments: fusions of undulating hips, bouncy sidesteps and geisha-style gestures. The dances have an intellectual function, of course, rearranging our responses to the show once again. But they are also an exhilarating and touchingly old-fashioned tribute to the pure pleasures of performing. This company may practice its own theater of alienation, but it knows how to seduce while doing so.

Peter Marks ON
Wit
BY Margaret Edson

September 17, 1998
Manhattan Class Company Theater
620 Performances

Kathleen Chalfant as a dying professor in *Wit*
SARA KRULWICH/THE NEW YORK TIMES

WIT by Margaret Edson; directed by Derek Anson Jones; sets by Myung Hee Cho; costumes by Ilona Somogyi; lighting by Michael Chybowski; original music and sound by David Van Tieghem; wigs by Paul Huntley; production manager, Kai Brothers; production stage manager, Katherine Lee Boyer; associate producer, Robert G. Bartner. The Long Wharf Theater Production presented by MCC Theater and Long Wharf Theater.

Vivian Bearing, Ph.D...........................Kathleen Chalfant
Harvey Kelekian, M.D. ....Walter Charles
Dr. Jason Posner...Alec Phoenix
Susie Monahan ....Paula Pizzi

E. M. Ashford ....Helen Stenborg
Mr. Bearing...Walter Charles
Lab technicians ....Brian J. Carter, Daniel Sarnelli, Alli
Steinberg and Lisa Tharps

Wit is the chilling chronicle of a professor dying an agonizing death in a teaching hospital. The instructor is an expert on the seventeenth-century poet John Donne, which proves entirely apt, because the performance at the center of the play is pure poetry.

Kathleen Chalfant, the veteran stage actress best known for her work in *Angels in America,* draws around herself the brittle, unsparing aura of Vivian Bearing, the dying teacher, like a frost-encrusted cloak. Vivian is a vastly recognizable character out of academia: intimidatingly disciplined, accustomed to pushing herself to the maximum and expecting her students to do the same. A deep love of literature and a career devoted to analyzing Donne's poems down to their punctuation marks have both sharpened her mental prowess and limited her capacity for empathy; like a miler in tip-top condition, she runs so far ahead of the pack, she no longer thinks of herself as part of it.

That makes her a wonderfully compelling subject for Margaret Edson's brutally human and beautifully layered new play, which opened last night at the MCC Theater in Chelsea. Ms. Edson, an Atlanta elementary school teacher who once worked in a hospital oncology unit, is herself a lover of mind-expanding irony: she finds poetry in the reading of a sonogram and science in the deconstruction of a sonnet. It is no coincidence, either, that the poem Vivian made the subject of her doctoral thesis contains Donne's immortal valediction, "Death be not proud."

To be sure, *Wit,* directed with care and clarity by Derek Anson Jones, is an eggheady piece, continually drawing our attention to parallels in the worlds of words and wards. (One of the satisfactions is Ms. Edson's unabashed crush on language and her skillful demonstration of the ways in which words both humble and inspire.) But the play never totally leaves its senses. By the moment of the stunning, final fadeout—in this instance, actually, a flare-up, thanks to the gifted lighting designer Michael Chybowski—you feel both enlightened and, in a strange way, enormously comforted.

Wit was presented last season by the Long Wharf Theater in New Haven with the identical cast and creative team; it has only improved in its New York restaging. One advantage here is MCC's claustrophobic space on West 28th Street. In a larger theater in New Haven, Ms. Chalfant, dressed in a hospital gown and robe, and wearing a red baseball cap to hide the effects of her character's chemotherapy, seemed to discourse into a void. In the more compact theater, it's as if we are sitting in Vivian's hospital room, sharing her trials rather than merely witnessing them. Ms. Chalfant, too, is more at ease now; the proximity appears to invigorate her.

Set in a research hospital in an unnamed city— Ms. Edson smartly provides only as much biographical detail as is absolutely necessary—*Wit* is a turning of the tables, a case of a detached examiner who becomes an increasingly needy specimen. In the hospital, it's the doctors who are emotionally at a remove. Vivian's academic accomplishments mean zilch to them. What they care about is the viability of her innards, her ability to withstand the onslaught of the toxic chemicals they pump into her body to try to thwart her advanced ovarian cancer. Vivian, predictably, views her struggle as a graduate-level course in humility. "It's highly educational," she says of the degrading, painful rounds of medical procedures. "I am learning how to suffer."

Intriguingly, though, *Wit* is not so much concerned with coming to terms with death, as with love. Vivian reveals little about her history outside the classroom; no one, for instance, comes to see her in the hospital. She neither expects nor rejects the kindness of others; accepting or giving affection was extraneous to her life of the mind, muscles she never exercised. In this regard she meets her match in her ambitious young doctor, Jason Posner (the appealing Alec Phoenix), a brilliant if heartless cancer researcher who looks upon patients as little more than complex structures to be decoded—not unlike the way Vivian seizes on Donne's poems.

It's not, however, the intense cerebration, in her career or treatment, that ultimately consoles Vivian. *Wit* is an exploration of what transpires when words fail, as they always must, of how, in the end, art and science are equally useless, equally detached. No, Vivian at last wants only to be enfolded in the arms of another caring being, embodied in Ms. Edson's play by one representative of the medical world, her nurse Susie Monahan (Paula Pizzi), and one from the academic, her mentor, the professor E. M. Ashford (Helen Stenborg).

As played so warmly and affectingly by Ms. Pizzi and Ms. Stenborg, the nurse and the teacher are almost fantasy figures; you would want each of them at your own bedside. The nurse's defense of Vivian's dignity, in the face of Dr. Posner's excessive efforts to keep her alive, is both gentle and ferocious, an unvarnished expression of respect. Ms. Stenborg, too, is sublime in a heartbreaking, final scene—perhaps a delusion of Vivian's confabulating mind—as she kicks off her shoes, climbs into the hospital bed and reads to her dying acolyte from the tender children's classic *The Runaway Bunny.*

Ms. Chalfant's performance, as intelligent and uncompromising as you're likely to come across on a New York stage these days, is what matters here the most, of course. She hooks us with her openness to the closed corners in Vivian's life, her own pleasure in finding the sense of occasion in a woman's last, great struggle. Ms. Chalfant is as convinced of the urgency of Vivian's story as Vivian is in the vitality of Donne's poems. And she'll convince you, too.

Ben Brantley ON
The Play About the Baby
BY Edward Albee

February 1, 2001
Century Center for the Performing Arts
244+ Performances

From left: Marian Seldes, Kathleen Early, David Burtka and Brian Murray in *The Play About the Baby* SARA KRULWICH/THE NEW YORK TIMES

THE PLAY ABOUT THE BABY by Edward Albee; directed by David Esbjornson; set by John Arnone; costumes by Michael Krass; lighting by Kenneth Posner; sound by Donald DiNicola; production manager, Kai Brothers; production stage manager, Mark Wright; general manager, Roy Gabay; associate producer, Franci Neely Crane. Presented by Elizabeth Ireland McCann, Daryl Roth, Terry Allen Kramer, Fifty-Second Street Productions, Robert Bartner, Stanley Kaufelt, in association with the Alley Theater.

Man ....Brian Murray
Woman ....Marian Seldes
Girl...Kathleen Early
Boy ....David Burtka

Sorry, Mayor Giuliani. Recent developments have conclusively shown that you are not the most powerful man in New York City. That distinction belongs to a fellow known only as—wouldn't you know it?—the Man.

In a twinkling, this guy can tarnish innocence,

push hopeful youth into guarded maturity and forever destroy any dreams that the world might be a kind and nurturing place. He is, in short, a strutting, smirking embodiment of what life does to everyone. And he can be found, represented by the actor Brian Murray in a gray double-breasted suit, complacently governing the stage of the Century Center, where Edward Albee's delightful and disturbing *Play About the Baby* opened last night.

This funny, harrowing dramatic fable, which features a four-member ensemble led with spectacular style by Mr. Murray and Marian Seldes, is as explicit and concise a statement of what Mr. Albee believes as he is ever likely to deliver. It is presented in the form of what might be called a cosmic vaudeville, in which two old pros in this old world teach a pair of untried tyros just how bleak and dangerous the universe can be.

Not, you might think, a subject for steady laughter, except of the dry and rueful variety. But while *The Play About the Baby,* which has been directed with sharpness and agility by David Esbjornson, offers nothing at all reassuring about human destiny, it has a marvelous time being negative. It also radiates a cocky confidence that the theater is the only place that could deliver such dour home truths so entertainingly.

The Play About the Baby, first produced in London in 1998, is an invaluable self-portrait of sorts from one of the few genuinely great living American dramatists: a pointed summing up of what he's been saying in plays ranging from the succinct *Zoo Story* to the recently revived (and prolix) *Tiny Alice.*

Not that *Baby* is literally autobiographical in the way that Mr. Albee's popular *Three Tall Women,* inspired by his adoptive mother, sometimes seemed to be. This latest offering is far more abstract, and its characters have the one-size-fits-everyman shapes of commedia dell'arte figures.

They may describe events that belong to specific pasts. But as always in Mr. Albee's plays, nothing that is remembered can be relied upon as accurate. The past is not only a different country; it is also one that can never be successfully mapped.

That's one of the many lessons taught in *Baby* by Man (Mr. Murray) and Woman (Ms. Seldes), whose unwitting and unwilling pupils are of course called Boy (David Burtka) and Girl (Kathleen Early). Now you may be thinking of another play by Mr. Albee in which an older couple initiates a younger one into the unseemly games people play. That's *Who's Afraid of Virginia Woolf?,* which is also about a baby whose very existence becomes a matter of debate.

It is in fact possible to read the relationships between the two couples in the later work as a sort of theoretical distillation of those in the earlier one. And the plays are firmly agreed that "truth and illusion"—as Martha was wont to mutter irritably throughout *Woolf*—are mutable and interchangeable. As the Man says, speaking sharply to the audience as if it were an especially sleepy high school class: "Pay attention to this. What's true and what isn't is a tricky business, no?"

But while the older couple in *Woolf* worked hard at convincing their young guests of the existence of a fictional child, the Man and Woman in *Baby* spirit away the title infant and then try to persuade Boy and Girl that there never was such a thing.

In terms of plot, that's it. *Baby* takes place in an allegorical ether in which innocence collides with experience, and irrevocable damage is done.

If this sounds like something better suited to a lectern, you have underestimated Mr. Albee's thorough command of the tricks of his trade, both subtle and shamelessly flashy. And who but Mr. Murray and Ms. Seldes, two of the most theatrical presences in theater, could so deliciously translate those tricks into performances that belong equally to the music hall and an academic drawing room?

Actually, John Arnone's fine set is more a nursery of the mind, all wistful pastels and oversize baby toys and accouterments, including giant alphabet blocks (that spell out, a bit too pointedly, AGES) and an immense benippled pacifier. Under Kenneth Posner's ominously serene lighting, these grotesquely enlarged objects change sweetness into absurdity. If this is a young parents' paradise, it is clearly one on the verge of explosion.

The characters who inhabit this world are similarly exaggerated. For Boy and Girl, as we first see them, nothing much exists except: (a) their strong physical attraction to each other and (b) the baby to which the girl noisily but efficiently gives birth in the first minutes of the show.

The only cloud in their shared sunniness is the boy's memory of the pain of a violently broken arm. Enter Man and Woman, blithely bearing the promise of much more pain to come. As the Man says to the Boy, "If you have no wounds, how can you know you're alive?"

Boy and Girl are tough roles to play, and not just because they have to romp about buck naked in their Edenic bliss. In their opening scenes, the characters must be improbably and earnestly naïve and able to wield that semantically fancy Albee-speak. Ms. Early and especially Mr. Burtka grow appealingly into their characters once danger looms. But they have yet to find a comfortable, convincing style for the play's opening scenes.

Once Mr. Murray and Ms. Seldes take charge, however, *Baby* rockets into that special corner of theater heaven where words shoot off like fireworks into dazzling patterns and hues. As an actress, Ms. Seldes has spent years refining ham into something as rich as foie gras. As the Woman, she is appropriately dressed in purple, a color that matches both prose and performance.

Just watch this streamlined, sharp-featured creature turn herself into the femme fatale of her highly improbable past, when polo players and painters swooned at her feet. "Really, sir, you go too far," the Woman remembers saying, quickly adding, "Phrases like that just came to me then."

In her glorious, gothic self-dramatizing, Ms. Seldes, a veteran of Albee productions, gives irresistibly watchable life to the contention that we always reinvent our own pasts. Her style is equally serviceable in underlining the play's wry, celebratory self-consciousness about being a play. And there is nothing, but nothing, funnier on a New York stage just now than Ms. Seldes's interpreting Mr. Murray's speeches in her own, very personal sign language.

Mr. Murray is equally adept at communicating directly with the audience, most notably in a postintermission speech that channels Mr. Albee's famous disgust with theatergoers' lazy attention spans and intellects. This actor, who has been known to match Ms. Seldes for flamboyance, is more measured here, giving one of his most potent performances.

His Man turns what might have registered as facile cynicism into something scarier and more compelling. With his quick, switched-on smiles and tauntingly authoritative carriage, Mr. Murray suggests a cross between the weary title character of John Osborne's *Entertainer* (a role he has played) and a satanic quiz-show host. (His catalog of what people want out of life is priceless.)

That the voice of experience, as Mr. Murray delivers it, is arch and slippery does not mean it is shallow. Beneath the bravura is an appalled acceptance of life as it is. And while the Man is great fun in his high (and low) wit and posturing, he can instantly shift into thundering minor keys of anger, contempt, menace and a sadness beyond tears.

Well, mostly beyond tears. The Man admits to crying at movies in which "good things happen to good people." This comes, he says, from "a troubling sense of what should be rather than what is." Later he observes, "We can't take glory because it shows us the abyss."

Mr. Albee's gaze has always focused on the abyss. *Baby* is about nothing less than being forced to acknowledge its existence. The Boy, in speeches rendered with heartbreaking openness and incomprehension by Mr. Burtka, repeatedly asks that he be allowed to dwell in innocence for just a bit longer, to let the "pain and loss" come later. "Give us some time," he begs. The Man's summary answer: "Time's up."

Tragic theater, from Oedipus onward, has always centered on that moment when time is up. Mr. Albee, who has cited both Sophocles and Noël Coward as significant influences, accepts this harsh given of existence unconditionally. But he refuses to sob and whine about it. Cursing the darkness is easy; lighting candles of defiant, fiery wit, like those that illuminate *The Play About the Baby,* is heroic.

Ben Brantley ON
The Producers
BOOK BY Mel Brooks AND Thomas Meehan
MUSIC AND LYRICS BY Mel Brooks

April 19, 2001

St. James Theater

138+ Performances*

Nathan Lane as Max Bialystock and Matthew Broderick as Leo Bloom in *The Producers*   SARA KRULWICH/ THE NEW YORK TIMES

THE PRODUCERS. Book by Mel Brooks and Thomas Meehan; music and lyrics by Mr. Brooks and by special arrangement with StudioCanal. Direction and choreography by Susan Stroman. Musical arrangements and supervision by Glen Kelly. Sets by Robin Wagner; costumes by William Ivey Long; lighting by Peter Kaczorowski; sound by Steve C. Kennedy; associate director, Steven Zweigbaum; associate choreographer, Warren Carlyle; wigs and hair designed by Paul Huntley; music direction and vocal arrangements by Patrick S. Brady; orchestrations by Doug Besterman; music coordinator, John Miller; general management, Richard Frankel Productions, Laura Green; technical supervisor, Juniper Street Productions; associate producers, Frederic H. and Rhoda Mayerson and Lynn Landis. Presented by Rocco Landesman; SFX Theatrical Group; the Frankel, Baruch, Viertel, Routh Group; Bob and Harvey Weinstein; Rick Steiner; Robert F. X. Sillerman and Mr. Brooks, in association with James D. Stern/Douglas Meyer.

* For plays still running as this book went to press, the number of performances indicates the play's run as of August 16, 2001.

Max Bialystock	Nathan Lane
Leo Bloom	Matthew Broderick
Franz Liebkind	Brad Oscar
Carmen Ghia	Roger Bart
Roger De Bris	Gary Beach
Ulla	Cady Huffman

How do you single out highlights in a bonfire? Everybody who sees *The Producers*—and that should be as close to everybody as the St. James Theater allows—is going to be hard-pressed to choose one favorite bit from the sublimely ridiculous spectacle that opened last night.

There is, for starters, that swanning song-and-dance man Adolf Hitler having his Judy Garland moment, lovingly seated in a spotlight at the edge of the stage. And of course there are those Nazi storm troopers making like the June Taylor Dancers, and all those sweet, oversexed little old ladies using their aluminum walkers to tap-dance.

But how about those glittering, Swastika-wearing pigeons in cages that coo a fluttery backup to a demented Nazi on a roof in Greenwich Village? And what about Matthew Broderick bringing out the Fred Astaire in his nerdlike character and reminding us in the process that Fred Astaire really was kind of a nerd? And how about—yeah, how about—Nathan Lane, in his most delicious performance ever, re-enacting the entire show in a song that lasts about five minutes and feels like thirty seconds?

Oh, let's stop for breath, step back a second and admit that *The Producers,* the comic veteran Mel Brooks's stage adaptation of his own cult movie from 1968, is as full of gags, gadgets and gimmicks as an old vaudevillian's trunk. But the show, which has a book by Mr. Brooks and Thomas Meehan with songs by Mr. Brooks (you heard me), is much more than the sum of its gorgeously silly parts.

It is, to put it simply, the real thing: a big Broadway book musical that is so ecstatically drunk on its powers to entertain that it leaves you delirious, too. Mr. Brooks, a Brooklyn boy who grew up in the age of Cole Porter and Busby Berkeley, is totally, giddily in love with the show-biz mythology he is sending up here.

With the inspired assistance of Susan Stroman, his director and choreographer, and the happiest cast in town, Mr. Brooks has put on a show that is a valentine to every show there is, good and bad, about putting on a show. And the expert production team—Robin Wagner (sets), William Ivey Long (costumes) and Peter Kaczorowski (lighting)—turns the stage into a bright, endlessly evocative dreamscape that skewers and celebrates the looks of great musicals from *Gypsy* to *Follies.*

Whether as an actor, film director or writer, Mr. Brooks has always worked from a manic imagination, in which jokes breed jokes that keep morphing into ever-more absurd mutant forms. Here, he channels the hyper-charged, free-associating style of the stand-up improviser into a remarkably polished riff on the kinds of entertainment he grew up with. The whole evening operates on a self-perpetuating, can-you-top-this energy, generating enough electricity to light up California for the next century.

For a production that makes a point of being tasteless, *The Producers* exudes a refreshing air of innocence. In fact, ardent fans of the film, which starred Zero Mostel and Gene Wilder, may feel it has been defanged. As a movie, *The Producers* was harsher and cruder in its satire, though you could also detect the sentimental streak that emerges more fully here. For the musical adaptation, Mr. Brooks is still biting the hand that feeds him, but at the same time he is kissing it quite sincerely.

If you grew up in the 1960s, you probably know the plot. Max Bialystock (Mr. Lane), an operatically desperate impresario of Broadway flops, meets Leopold Bloom (Mr. Broderick), a public accountant who is as repressed as Max is flamboyant. This unlikely couple cooks up what would seem to be a sure-fire scam, given Max's history: produce a play that is guaranteed to fail, selling more than 1,000 percent in investments, and then abscond with the backers' money.

Their choice as the worst of all possible plays? A paean to the Third Reich by one Franz Liebkind (Brad Oscar), a pigeon-keeping Nazi, called "Springtime for Hitler." And for the worst of all

possible directors? A theater queen to end all theater queens, the lavender-voiced Roger De Bris (Gary Beach), first seen in a ballgown and headdress that he worries makes him look like the Chrysler Building. (He's right.)

This is all more or less straight from the movie, as is Max's systematic trading of sexual favors for checks (made out to "Cash," which is remarked upon as an unusual title for a play) with scores of rich, lonely geriatric women. But Mr. Brooks, whose knack for musical pastiche was evident in the screwball production numbers in the movies *Blazing Saddles* and *High Anxiety,* here turns practically everything into an occasion for song and dance.

The show comes at you like a supersonic train from its first scene, which represents an opening night of yet another Bialystock fiasco, and it never lets up. Mr. Lane's opening number, in which Max gets down (way down) with the winos on the street as he laments his lost glory, sets the tone for everything that follows.

It's fast, fierce, shameless, vulgar and altogether blissful. The song features blunt but perfectly cadenced lyrics, a simple tune that joyfully recalls every Gypsy violin–Russian cossack specialty number ever performed and matching choreography from Ms. Stroman that accelerates to the point that you expect friction fires.

When Mr. Lane's Max, suggesting a cozy version of David Merrick (if such a phenomenon were possible), flings his opera cape around himself, we're goners. He is so clearly enamored of that self-dramatizing gesture, so absolutely thrilled to be strutting in a way that only Broadway musicals permit.

Tirelessly agile (great extensions, Mr. Lane), droll and exhibitionistic, with a clarinet speaking voice that segues naturally into song, this Max is the perfect agent for seducing timid little Leo into the unholy pleasures of showbiz. For that, finally, is what *The Producers* is about.

And what a pleasure it is to watch Mr. Broderick being seduced. This popular movie actor puts aside the boyish charm, for once, creating a slumped, adenoidal figure that suggests a male version of Peggy Cass's Agnes Gooch in *Auntie Mame*. It's a cartoon, you think at first; he won't be able to sustain it. But he does, somehow managing to make hunched introversion into an extroverted style. Leo remains a deadpan hysteric, even as he picks up a top hat and cane to lead a bevy of Amazonian chorines through a fantasy routine in which he sees his name in lights.

That scene is a homage to "Rose's Turn" in *Gypsy*. (Ethel Merman's name is invoked in the show, though hardly in vain.) In fact, *The Producers* is more packed with steals and references than a deconstructionist's college term paper. For Max's marathon courting of rich old ladies, Mr. Wagner has come up with a doily of a set that spoofs the Loveland fantasy sequence in *Follies*.

There's even a dancer-reflecting mirror à la *Chorus Line*, for the big Nazi numbers, which then turns into a crucial visual aid in Ms. Stroman's answer to Busby Berkeley-style formation dancing. And you can find gleefully over-the-top reworkings of the classic Ziegfeld beauty parades and the office as prison routines of *How to Succeed in Business Without Really Trying*.

In like manner, Mr. Brooks's bouncy, endearingly generic melodies (given robust flesh by Glen Kelly's arrangements) keep recalling songs you know you've heard before but can't quite place. The lyrics are charmingly straightforward, joke-laden and often obscene, although they never feel remotely offensive.

There should, in fact, be plenty in *The Producers* to offend all sorts of people. You could start with the characterization of the effete Roger De Bris and the Village People–like artistic crew overseen by his sinuously swishy assistant (Roger Bart), who of course becomes a victim of the old "walk this way" gag. And then there's Ulla (Cady Huffman), the ultimate sex machine of a Swedish secretary with the requisite unpronounceable name.

But in this production, shrill stereotypes are transformed into outsize comic archetypes, recalling the prelapsarian days of ethnic and sexual humor before political correctness. And that the jokes are often so hoary (an African-American policeman is, of course, "black Irish") only adds to the feeling of a buoyant comic free-for-all, an American answer to commedia dell'arte.

Mr. Bart, Ms. Huffman and Mr. Oscar (who does a German beer-garden number that crosses the Führer with Al Jolson) are all wonderfully enjoyable company. And Mr. Beach's Roger, who winds up filling in for the original Adolf (he breaks a leg, natch) on the opening night of "Springtime," becomes every aging crooner who played the Palace rolled into one brilliantly mismatched package.

It seems inevitable that a show that keeps trying to top itself is eventually going to hit the ceiling. And after the "Springtime for Hitler" musical-within-the-musical sequence, which fulfills one's wildest expectations, *The Producers* can't really get any bigger, though it works hard at attempting it. But there are always the diverting presences of Mr. Lane and Mr. Broderick, who have the most dynamic stage chemistry since Natasha Richardson met Liam Neeson in *Anna Christie*.

Really, the only thing to lament about the arrival of *The Producers*, aside from the impossibility of getting tickets, is the extent to which it outdoes its competition. You want vaudeville-style fantasy sequences à la *Follies*? You want a 1950s-style musical courtship à la *Bells Are Ringing*? Or predatory transvestites à la *The Rocky Horror Show*?

The Producers has all of these things in forms that for pure spiritedness and polish trump every one of these current revivals. Mr. Brooks has taken what could have been overblown camp into a far warmer realm in which affection always outweighs irony. Who wants coolness, anyway, when you can have such blood-quickening heat?

The Pulitzer Prizes in Drama

No award was made for the years not listed here.

1918 *Why Marry?* by Jesse Lynch Williams

1920 *Beyond the Horizon* by Eugene O'Neill

1921 *Miss Lulu Bett* by Zona Gale

1922 *Anna Christie* by Eugene O'Neill

1923 *Icebound* by Owen Davis

1924 *Hell-Bent fer Heaven* by Hatcher Hughes

1925 *They Knew What They Wanted* by Sidney Howard

1926 *Craig's Wife* by George Kelly

1927 *In Abraham's Bosom* by Paul Green

1928 *Strange Interlude* by Eugene O'Neill

1929 *Street Scene* by Elmer L. Rice

1930 *The Green Pastures* by Marc Connelly

1931 *Alison's House* by Susan Glaspell

1932 *Of Thee I Sing* by George S. Kaufman, Morrie Ryskind, and Ira Gershwin

1933 *Both Your Houses* by Maxwell Anderson

1934 *Men in White* by Sidney Kingsley

1935 *The Old Maid* by Zöe Akins

1936 *Idiot's Delight* by Robert E. Sherwood

1937 *You Can't Take It with You* by Moss Hart and George S. Kaufman

1938 *Our Town* by Thornton Wilder

1939 *Abe Lincoln in Illinois* by Robert E. Sherwood

1940 *The Time of Your Life* by William Saroyan

1941 *There Shall Be No Night* by Robert E. Sherwood

1943 *The Skin of Our Teeth* by Thornton Wilder

1945 *Harvey* by Mary Chase

1946 *State of the Union* by Russel Crouse and Howard Lindsay

1948 *A Streetcar Named Desire* by Tennessee Williams

1949 *Death of a Salesman* by Arthur Miller

1950 *South Pacific* by Richard Rodgers, Oscar Hammerstein 2d, and Joshua Logan

1952 *The Shrike* by Joseph Kramm

1953 *Picnic* by William Inge

1954 *The Teahouse of the August Moon* by John Patrick

1955 *Cat on a Hot Tin Roof* by Tennessee Williams

1956 *The Diary of Anne Frank* by Frances Goodrich and Albert Hackett

1957 *Long Day's Journey into Night* by Eugene O'Neill

1958 *Look Homeward, Angel* by Ketti Frings

1959 *J.B.* by Archibald MacLeish

1960 *Fiorello!* by George Abbott, Jerome Weidman, Jerry Bock, and Sheldon Harnick

1961 *All the Way Home* by Tad Mosel

1962 *How to Succeed in Business Without Really Trying* by Frank Loesser and Abe Burrows

1965 *The Subject Was Roses* by Frank D. Gilroy

1967 *A Delicate Balance* by Edward Albee

1969 *The Great White Hope* by Howard Sackler

1970 *No Place to Be Somebody* by Charles Gordone

1971 *The Effect of Gamma Rays on Man-in-the-Moon Marigolds* by Paul Zindel

1973 *That Championship Season* by Jason Miller

1975 *Seascape* by Edward Albee

1976 *A Chorus Line* by Michael Bennett, James Kirkwood, Nicholas Dante, Marvin Hamlisch, and Edward Kleban

1977 *The Shadow Box* by Michael Cristofer

1978 *The Gin Game* by Donald L. Coburn

1979 *Buried Child* by Sam Shepard

1980 *Talley's Folly* by Lanford Wilson

1981 *Crimes of the Heart* by Beth Henley

1982 *A Soldier's Play* by Charles Fuller

1983 *'Night, Mother* by Marsha Norman

1984 *Glengarry Glen Ross* by David Mamet

1985 *Sunday in the Park with George* by Stephen Sondheim and James Lapine

1987 *Fences* by August Wilson

1988 *Driving Miss Daisy* by Alfred Uhry

1989 *The Heidi Chronicles* by Wendy Wasserstein

1990 *The Piano Lesson* by August Wilson

1991 *Lost in Yonkers* by Neil Simon

1992 *The Kentucky Cycle* by Robert Schenkkan

1993 *Angels in America: Millennium Approaches* by Tony Kushner

1994 *Three Tall Women* by Edward Albee

1995 *The Young Man from Atlanta* by Horton Foote

1996 *Rent* by Jonathan Larson

1998 *How I Learned to Drive* by Paula Vogel

1999 *Wit* by Margaret Edson

2000 *Dinner with Friends* by Donald Margulies

2001 *Proof* by David Auburn

The Tony (Antoinette Perry) Awards
for Best Play and Best Musical

1947
BEST AUTHOR Arthur Miller (*All My Sons*)
BEST COMPOSER Kurt Weill (*Street Scene*)

1948
BEST PLAY *Mister Roberts* by Thomas Heggen and Joshua Logan

1949
BEST PLAY *Death of a Salesman* by Arthur Miller
BEST MUSICAL *Kiss Me, Kate:* book by Bella and Samuel Spewack; music and lyrics by Cole Porter

1950
BEST PLAY *The Cocktail Party* by T. S. Eliot
BEST MUSICAL *South Pacific:* book by Oscar Hammerstein II and Joshua Logan; music by Richard Rodgers and lyrics by Oscar Hammerstein II

1951
BEST PLAY *The Rose Tattoo* by Tennessee Williams
BEST MUSICAL *Guys and Dolls:* book by Jo Swerling and Abe Burrows; music and lyrics by Frank Loesser

1952
BEST PLAY *The Fourposter* by Jan de Hartog
BEST MUSICAL *The King and I:* book and lyrics by Oscar Hammerstein II; music by Richard Rodgers

1953
BEST PLAY *The Crucible* by Arthur Miller
BEST MUSICAL *Wonderful Town:* book by Joseph Fields and Jerome Chodorov; music by Leonard Bernstein and lyrics by Betty Comden and Adolph Green

1954
BEST PLAY *The Teahouse of the August Moon* by John Patrick
BEST MUSICAL *Kismet:* book by Charles Lederer and Luther Davis; music by Alexander Borodin, adapted and with lyrics by Robert Wright and George Forrest

1955

BEST PLAY *The Desperate Hours* by Joseph Hayes

BEST MUSICAL *The Pajama Game:* book by George Abbott and Richard Bissell; music and lyrics by Richard Adler and Jerry Ross

1956

BEST PLAY *The Diary of Anne Frank* by Frances Goodrich and Albert Hackett

BEST MUSICAL *Damn Yankees:* book by George Abbott and Douglass Wallop; music and lyrics by Richard Adler and Jerry Ross

1957

BEST PLAY *Long Day's Journey into Night* by Eugene O'Neill

BEST MUSICAL *My Fair Lady:* book and lyrics by Alan Jay Lerner; music by Frederick Loewe

1958

BEST PLAY *Sunrise at Campobello* by Dore Schary

BEST MUSICAL *The Music Man:* book by Meredith Willson and Franklin Lacey; music and lyrics by Meredith Willson

1959

BEST PLAY *J.B.* by Archibald MacLeish

BEST MUSICAL *Redhead:* book by Herbert and Dorothy Fields, Sidney Sheldon and David Shaw; music by Albert Hague and lyrics by Dorothy Fields

1960

BEST PLAY *The Miracle Worker* by William Gibson

BEST MUSICAL (tie) *Fiorello!:* book by Jerome Weidman and George Abbott; music by Jerry Bock and lyrics by Sheldon Harnick; AND *The Sound of Music:* book by Howard Lindsay and Russel Crouse; music by Richard Rodgers and lyrics by Oscar Hammerstein 2d

1961

BEST PLAY *Becket* by Jean Anouilh

BEST MUSICAL *Bye, Bye Birdie:* book by Michael Stewart; music by Charles Strouse and lyrics by Lee Adams

1962

BEST PLAY *A Man for All Seasons* by Robert Bolt

BEST MUSICAL *How to Succeed in Business Without Really Trying:* book by Abe Burrows, Jack Weinstock and Willie Gilbert; music and lyrics by Frank Loesser

1963

BEST PLAY *Who's Afraid of Virginia Woolf?* by Edward Albee

BEST MUSICAL *A Funny Thing Happened on the Way to the Forum:* book by Burt Shevelove and Larry Gelbart; music and lyrics by Stephen Sondheim

1964

BEST PLAY *Luther* by John Osborne

BEST MUSICAL *Hello, Dolly!:* book by Michael Stewart; music and lyrics by Jerry Herman

1965

BEST PLAY *The Subject Was Roses* by Frank Gilroy

BEST MUSICAL *Fiddler on the Roof:* book by Joseph Stein; music by Jerry Bock and lyrics by
Sheldon Harnick

1966

BEST PLAY *Marat/Sade* by Peter Weiss

BEST MUSICAL *Man of La Mancha:* book by Dale Wasserman; music by Mitch Leigh and lyrics by
Joe Darion

1967

BEST PLAY *The Homecoming* by Harold Pinter

BEST MUSICAL *Cabaret:* book by Joe Masteroff; music by John Kander and lyrics by Frank Ebb

1968

BEST PLAY *Rosencrantz and Guildenstern Are Dead* by Tom Stoppard

BEST MUSICAL *Hallelujah, Baby!:* book by Arthur Laurents; music by Jule Styne and lyrics by
Betty Comden and Adolph Green

1969

BEST PLAY *The Great White Hope* by Howard Sackler

BEST MUSICAL *1776:* book by Peter Stone; music and lyrics by Sherman Edwards

1970

BEST PLAY *Borstal Boy* by Frank McMahon

BEST MUSICAL *Applause:* book by Betty Comden and Adolph Green; music by Charles Strouse and
lyrics by Lee Adams

1971

BEST PLAY *Sleuth* by Anthony Shaffer

BEST MUSICAL *Company:* book by George Furth; music and lyrics by Stephen Sondheim

1972

BEST PLAY *Sticks and Bones* by David Rabe

BEST MUSICAL *Two Gentlemen of Verona:* book by John Guare and Mel Shapiro; music by
Galt MacDermot and lyrics by John Guare

1973

BEST PLAY *That Championship Season* by Jason Miller

BEST MUSICAL *A Little Night Music:* book by Hugh Wheeler; music and lyrics by Stephen Sondheim

1974

BEST PLAY *The River Niger* by Joseph A. Walker

BEST MUSICAL *Raisin:* book by Robert Nemiroff and Charlotte Zaltzberg; music by Judd Woldin and lyrics by Robert Brittan

1975

BEST PLAY *Equus* by Peter Shaffer

BEST MUSICAL *The Wiz:* book by William F. Brown; music and lyrics by Charlie Smalls

1976

BEST PLAY *Travesties* by Tom Stoppard

BEST MUSICAL *A Chorus Line:* book by James Kirkwood and Nicholas Dante; music by Marvin Hamlisch and lyrics by Edward Kleban

1977

BEST PLAY *The Shadow Box* by Michael Cristofer

BEST MUSICAL *Annie:* book by Thomas Meehan; music by Charles Strouse and lyrics by Martin Charnin

1978

BEST PLAY *Da* by Hugh Leonard

BEST MUSICAL *Ain't Misbehavin':* based on an idea by Murray Horwitz and Richard Maltby Jr.; a celebration of the music of Fats Waller

1979

BEST PLAY *The Elephant Man* by Bernard Pomerance

BEST MUSICAL *Sweeney Todd:* book by Hugh Wheeler; music and lyrics by Stephen Sondheim

1980

BEST PLAY *Children of a Lesser God* by Mark Medoff

BEST MUSICAL *Evita:* book by Tim Rice; music by Andrew Lloyd Webber and lyrics by Tim Rice

1981

BEST PLAY *Amadeus* by Peter Shaffer

BEST MUSICAL *42nd Street:* book by Michael Stewart and Mark Bramble; music and lyrics by Al Dubin and Harry Warren

1982

BEST PLAY *The Life and Adventures of Nicholas Nickleby* by David Edgar

BEST MUSICAL *Nine:* book by Arthur Kopit; music and lyrics by Maury Yeston

1983

BEST PLAY *Torch Song Trilogy* by Harvey Fierstein

BEST MUSICAL *Cats:* book by T. S. Eliot; music by Andrew Lloyd Webber and lyrics by T. S. Eliot

1984

BEST PLAY *The Real Thing* by Tom Stoppard

BEST MUSICAL *La Cage aux Folles:* book by Harvey Fierstein; music and lyrics by Jerry Herman

1985

BEST PLAY *Biloxi Blues* by Neil Simon

BEST MUSICAL *Big River:* book by William Hauptman; music and lyrics by Roger Miller

1986

BEST PLAY *I'm Not Rappaport* by Herb Gardner

BEST MUSICAL *The Mystery of Edwin Drood:* book, music and lyrics by Rupert Holmes

1987

BEST PLAY *Fences* by August Wilson

BEST MUSICAL *Les Misérables:* book by Alain Boublil and Claude-Michel Schönberg; music by Claude-Michel Schönberg and lyrics by Herbert Kretzmer and Alain Boublil

1988

BEST PLAY *M. Butterfly* by David Henry Hwang

BEST MUSICAL *The Phantom of the Opera:* book by Richard Stilgoe and Andrew Lloyd Webber; music by Andrew Lloyd Webber and lyrics by Charles Hart

1989

BEST PLAY *The Heidi Chronicles* by Wendy Wasserstein

BEST MUSICAL *Jerome Robbins' Broadway:* an anthology of the choreography of Jerome Robbins

1990

BEST PLAY *The Grapes of Wrath* by Frank Galati

BEST MUSICAL *City of Angels:* book by Larry Gelbart; music by Cy Coleman and lyrics by David Zippel

1991

BEST PLAY *Lost in Yonkers* by Neil Simon

BEST MUSICAL *The Will Rogers Follies:* book by Peter Stone; music by Cy Coleman and lyrics by Betty Comden and Adolph Green

1992

BEST PLAY *Dancing at Lughnasa* by Brian Friel

BEST MUSICAL *Crazy for You:* book by Ken Ludwig; music by George Gershwin and lyrics by Ira Gershwin

1993

BEST PLAY *Angels in America: Millennium Approaches* by Tony Kushner

BEST MUSICAL *Kiss of the Spider Woman:* book by Terrence McNally; music by John Kander and lyrics by Fred Ebb

1994

BEST PLAY *Angels in America: Perestroika* by Tony Kushner

BEST MUSICAL *Passion:* book by James Lapine; music and lyrics by Stephen Sondheim

1995

BEST PLAY *Love! Valour! Compassion!* by Terrence McNally

BEST MUSICAL *Sunset Boulevard:* book by Christopher Hampton and Don Black; music by Andrew Lloyd Webber and lyrics by Christopher Hampton and Don Black

1996

BEST PLAY *Master Class* by Terrence McNally

BEST MUSICAL *Rent:* book, music and lyrics by Jonathan Larson

1997

BEST PLAY *The Last Night at Ballyhoo* by Alfred Uhry

BEST MUSICAL *Titanic:* book by Peter Stone; music and lyrics by Maury Yeston

1998

BEST PLAY *Art* by Yasmina Reza

BEST MUSICAL *The Lion King:* book by Roger Allers and Irene Mecchi; music and lyrics by Elton John, Tim Rice, Lebo M, Mark Mancina, Jay Rifkin, Julie Taymor, and Hans Zimmer

1999

BEST PLAY *Side Man* by Warren Leight

BEST MUSICAL *Fosse:* an anthology of the choreography of Bob Fosse

2000

BEST PLAY *Copenhagen* by Michael Frayn

BEST MUSICAL *Contact:* book by Susan Stroman and John Weidman; music and lyrics from an assortment of recorded music

2001

BEST PLAY *Proof* by David Auburn

BEST MUSICAL *The Producers:* book by Mel Brooks and Thomas Meehan; music and lyrics by Mel Brooks